Encyclopedia
of Weird Detectives

ALSO BY PAUL GREEN
AND FROM McFARLAND

*Encyclopedia of Weird War Stories: Supernatural
and Science Fiction Elements in Novels, Pulps, Comics, Film,
Television, Games and Other Media* (2017)

*Encyclopedia of Weird Westerns: Supernatural
and Science Fiction Elements in Novels, Pulps, Comics, Films,
Television and Games,* 2d ed. (2016)

Pete Duel: A Biography, 2d ed. (2015)

Roy Huggins: Creator of Maverick, 77 Sunset Strip,
The Fugitive *and* The Rockford Files (2014)

*Jeffrey Hunter: The Film, Television, Radio
and Stage Performances* (2014)

Jennifer Jones: The Life and Films (2011)

A History of Television's The Virginian, *1962–1971*
(2006; paperback 2010)

Encyclopedia of Weird Detectives

Supernatural and Paranormal Elements in Novels, Pulps, Comics, Film, Television, Games and Other Media

PAUL GREEN
Foreword by Frank Price

McFarland & Company, Inc., Publishers
Jefferson, North Carolina

LIBRARY OF CONGRESS CATALOGUING-IN-PUBLICATION DATA

Names: Green, Paul, 1955– author. | Price, Frank, 1930– writer of foreword.
Title: Encyclopedia of weird detectives : supernatural and paranormal elements in novels, pulps, comics, film, television, games and other media / Paul Green ; foreword by Frank Price.
Description: Jefferson, North Carolina : McFarland & Company, Inc., Publishers, 2019 | Includes bibliographical references and index.
Identifiers: LCCN 2019032470 | ISBN 9781476678009 (paperback : acid free paper) ♾ | ISBN 9781476638379 (ebook)
Subjects: LCSH: Detectives in literature—Encyclopedias. | Detectives in mass media—Encyclopedias. | Fictitious characters—Encyclopedias.
Classification: LCC PN3448.D4 G73 2019 | DDC 809.3/87203—dc23
LC record available at https://lccn.loc.gov/2019032470

BRITISH LIBRARY CATALOGUING DATA ARE AVAILABLE

ISBN (print) 978-1-4766-7800-9
ISBN (ebook) 978-1-4766-3837-9

© 2019 Paul Green. All rights reserved

No part of this book may be reproduced or transmitted in any form or by any means, electronic or mechanical, including photocopying or recording, or by any information storage and retrieval system, without permission in writing from the publisher.

On the cover: shown from left: Jude Law, and Robert Downey Jr., in *Sherlock Holmes*, 2009, Warner Bros./Photofest

Printed in the United States of America

*McFarland & Company, Inc., Publishers
Box 611, Jefferson, North Carolina 28640
www.mcfarlandpub.com*

To Bev and Simba

Table of Contents

Foreword by Frank Price   1
Preface   3
Introduction   5

The Encyclopedia   11

Appendix: Listing by Medium   187
Bibliography   193
Index   195

Foreword
by Frank Price

"The oldest and strongest emotion of mankind is fear, and the oldest and strongest kind of fear is fear of the unknown."—H.P. Lovecraft

In 1972–73, the ABC Television Network had aired two highly rated 90-minute made-for-television movies starring Darren McGavin. They were titled *The Night Stalker* and *The Night Strangler*. They decided to order a series based on these movies, but because of the anticipated risks in production costs, they wanted the series not based at an independent producer but at a major studio, which would have the financial resources to cope with any deficits. I was the head of Universal Television and we were the largest and most successful production company. ABC approached us, and I responded with immediate interest. Universal was the studio that saved itself in the 1930s Great Depression by mining the horror genre with profitable hits like *Frankenstein*, *Dracula* and the *Wolfman*. In difficult financial straits in the 1950s, once again Universal turned to horror with the *Creature from the Black Lagoon* and *It Came from Outer Space*. Universal was the natural home for horror pictures. Horror was in the studio's DNA. When I first worked on the Universal lot, as a very young writer-producer, I had great fun visiting Stage 17, nicknamed the Phantom Stage, where the elaborate interior of the Opera House for the 1925 *Phantom of the Opera* had been built as a set, with stage and balconies included.

But what also stimulated my interest was that in my own teenage years I had discovered the chilling stories of H.P. Lovecraft and read them all. "The Rats in the Walls," "The Dunwich Horror," "Pickman's Model" were favorites. So *Kolchak the Night Stalker* was a natural for Universal Television.

Since the original Night Stalker writer-producer Dan Curtis did not wish to produce a weekly series, I interested Cy Chermak in taking the reins as executive producer. Cy had been with me as a producer on several series, including *The Virginian* and *Ironside*. Dealing with Darren McGavin was like a trip to the past. He had been the star of a 1952 CBS television show called *Casey, Crime Photographer*. The first story I ever sold was to that show.

Some very good episodes were created for

Frank Price

Kolchak but our ratings were held down because of the hit NBC show airing opposite Kolchak. It was Jim Garner's *Rockford Files*, another of our Universal TV series. That competition meant Kolchak unfortunately played only one season.

Kolchak was an investigative reporter whose job crossed paths with detective work. Whereas Jim Rockford investigated traditional cases with his own unique personality, Carl Kolchak investigated the paranormal and downright weird. Two detectives with their own spin on life. Jim Rockford won out in the ratings, but Kolchak has survived to become a cult favorite among devoted fans. So much so that producer-writer Chris Carter cites Kolchak as the inspiration behind *The X-Files*. Some series last one season but their influence extends through generations.

In contrast, some years later, when I had changed studios and moved from television and become head of motion pictures at Columbia Pictures, I had the authority and desire to green light a controversial motion picture tentatively titled *Ghostbusters*. It was controversial because there had never been a comedy produced with a sky-high budget of $27 million. It was expensive because it required comedy stars like Bill Murray, Dan Ackroyd and Harold Ramos, plus it needed expensive special effects. The combination made for a big budget. Columbia's corporate officers tried to talk me out of going ahead, but I was firm in my intention to make it. My worst-case calculation was that we wouldn't lose money on it.

When it opened, audiences enthusiastically adopted our "paranormal investigation and elimination" heroes. "Who ya gonna call?" blared from every radio and Walkman. I had never been part of such a huge hit before and I felt like a character in Boomtown where they struck oil and black gold gushed into the air and rained down on them. The mixture of comedy with fearsome monsters drawn from the unknown was instant box office magic. H.P Lovecraft would have loved our movie.

I am a fan of Paul Green's books. He deals with subjects that he likes and uniquely appreciates. Every sentence of his is backed with thorough and painstaking research. Combine that with the sensitivity he has for each subject or the subject matter, and each of his books becomes the definitive statement in that field.

Frank Price is the former president of Universal Television, chairman, president and CEO of Columbia Pictures, chairman of MCA Motion Picture Group and president of Universal Pictures.

Preface

This book covers the history of the weird detective in literature, film, television, radio, pulps, comic books and video games.

The Oxford English Dictionary defines the origin of the word "weird" as follows:

> Old English wyrd "destiny," of Germanic origin. The adjective (late Middle English) originally meant "having the power to control destiny," and was used especially in the Weird Sisters, originally referring to the Fates, later the witches in Shakespeare's Macbeth; the latter use gave rise to the sense "unearthly" (early 19th century).

Many weird detectives investigate the "unearthly." Sometimes by choice, sometimes by chance. Others have unearthly qualities that give them an advantage in their investigations. They can be divided into various categories that often cross over.

Psychic Detective: One who has psychic powers. The detective employs his or her psychic gifts during his or her investigations.

Occult Detective: A specialist detective who primarily investigates occult activity such as hauntings, demons, poltergeists, and so on.

Medical Detective: A person who investigates supernatural activity as a bi-product of his or her profession. In Victorian fiction the medical profession was a prime source.

Amateur Detective: In the early years of weird detective fiction almost all detectives were amateur sleuths. They often have genius-level detective skills and clash with the police due to their eccentric investigative techniques.

Professional Detective: These detectives work for a police department, are highly trained special agents employed by a government or a private agency or are hired by the public as private detectives. They normally experience paranormal events during routine investigations and are often skeptics. Police detectives usually investigate crimes within a specific area whereas special agents, including the FBI, can be assigned anywhere in the country.

Investigative Reporter Detective: Newspaper reporters and news correspondents who investigate the paranormal on assignment.

Unearthly Detective: A detective with weird physical qualities, ranging from the ability to metamorphose to achieving invisibility.

Magical Detective: A person who uses sorcery in his or her investigations.

Accidental Detective: The person ends up investigating the paranormal due to events that have impacted him or her personally. Sometimes he or she focuses on hunting supernatural entities that threaten his or her safety.

I have concentrated on supernatural and paranormal detectives. Science fiction detectives in general are outside the scope of this book, although the supernatural and science fiction genres do occasionally cross paths. Individual entries are listed in alphabetical order in the main body of the encyclopedia. Cross-referenced subjects are featured in bold type. Entries represent a cross-section of a flexible hybrid genre.

Introduction

To gain a greater appreciation of weird detective fiction we need to understand the cultural context that helped form the hybrid genre. Belief in mischievous spirits can be traced back to ancient history. Roman author Pliny the Younger (C.E. 61–c. 115) wrote one of the first accounts of a haunted house. Philosopher Athenodorus is the reluctant ghost-hunter. This abridged version of Pliny the Younger's "Letter to Sura" was translated by William Melmoth in 1760.

> There was in Athens a house, spacious and open, but with an infamous reputation, as if filled with pestilence. For in the dead of night, a noise like the clashing of iron could be heard. And if one listened carefully, it sounded like the rattling of chains. At first the noise seemed to be at a distance, but then it would approach, nearer, nearer, nearer. Suddenly a phantom would appear, an old man, pale and emaciated, with a long beard, and hair that appeared driven by the wind. The fetters on his feet and hands rattled as he moved them.
>
> Any dwellers in the house passed sleepless nights under the most dismal terrors imaginable. The nights without rest led them to a kind of madness, and as the horrors in their minds increased, onto a path toward death. Even in the daytime—when the phantom did not appear—the memory of the nightmare was so strong that it still passed before their eyes. The terror remained when the cause of it was gone.
>
> Damned as uninhabitable, the house was at last deserted, left to the spectral monster. But in hope that some tenant might be found who was unaware of the malevolence within it, the house was posted for rent or sale.
>
> It happened that a philosopher named Athenodorus came to Athens at that time. Reading the posted bill, he discovered the dwelling's price. The extraordinary cheapness raised his suspicion, yet when he heard the whole story, he was not in the least put off. Indeed, he was eager to take the place. And did so immediately.
>
> As evening drew near, Athenodorus had a couch prepared for him in the front section of the house. He asked for a light and his writing materials, then dismissed his retainers. To keep his mind from being distracted by vain terrors of imaginary noises and apparitions, he directed all his energy toward his writing.
>
> For a time, the night was silent. Then came the rattling of fetters. Athenodorus neither lifted up his eyes, nor laid down his pen. Instead he closed his ears by concentrating on his work. But the noise increased and advanced closer till it seemed to be at the door, and at last in the very chamber. Athenodorus looked round and saw the apparition exactly as it had been described to him. It stood before him, beckoning with one finger.
>
> Athenodorus made a sign with his hand that the visitor should wait a little and bent over his work. The ghost, however, shook the chains over the philosopher's head, beckoning as before. Athenodorus now took up his lamp and followed. The ghost moved slowly, as if held back by his chains. Once it reached the courtyard, it suddenly vanished.
>
> Athenodorus, now deserted, carefully marked the spot with a handful of grass and leaves. The next day he asked the magistrate to have the spot dug up. There they found—intertwined with chains—the bones that were all that remained of a body that had long lain in the ground. Carefully, the skeletal relics were collected and given proper burial, at public expense. The tortured ancient was at rest. And the house in Athens was haunted no more.

The belief in a tortured soul seeking rest was popular with the Roman Catholic church and its doctrine of Purgatory. The Protestant reformation across Europe in the 16th century rejected Catholic doctrine. No longer could ghosts be lost souls atoning for their sins. Instead the Protestants, inspired by Bible-based teaching, viewed ghosts as demons, roaming the earth through possessed witches.

Although influenced by the witchcraft dominated culture of his time the Reverend Joseph Glanvill, chaplain to King Charles II, paved the way for modern psychical research.

The Reverend Joseph Glanvill, chaplain to King Charles II, was the first person to record and appraise paranormal experiences in an organized manner using basic detective techniques. Glanvill opposed rationalism and skepticism and preferred what he viewed as new "scientific" approaches to the exploration of ghosts and poltergeists. Using argument and counter-argument he documented twenty case histories in an early account of poltergeist activity, *A Blow at Modern Sadducism. In Some Philosophical Considerations about Witchcraft*, published in 1668, and the later *Saducismus Triumphatus* in 1681.

Joseph Glanvill's account of *The Drummer of Tidworth* documents the tale of the haunted home of magistrate John Mompesson of Tidworth, England. Following Mompesson's arrest of roaming musician William Drury in March 1661 for extortion using false documentation, Drury's drum was placed in care of Mompesson at his home. Poltergeist activity including the sound of a beating drum on the roof of the house and in the room where the drum was stored and moving furniture and bedclothes occurred at Mompesson's home. The hauntings were treated with skepticism and derision by many at the time but Mompesson and Glanvill remained convinced of their supernatural origin. William Drury, claiming he had been responsible for the activity, was found guilty of witchcraft. When he was deported the drumming stopped but upon his return to England some years later it resumed.

Arguably the greatest influence on Victorian authors of weird detective fiction was the popular Spiritualism movement in Britain and America. Swedish philosopher Emanuel Swedenborg (1688–1772) is regarded by many as the first Spiritualist. In 1744 he wrote: "Of the Lord's Divine Mercy, it has been granted me now for several years, to be constantly and uninterruptedly in company with spirits and angels, hearing them converse with each other, and conversing with them." His experience with the spirit world would make him cautious, however. "Spirits narrate things wholly false and lie. When spirits begin to speak to man, care should be taken not to believe them."

In 1847, Andrew Jackson Davis (1826–1910) published *The Principles of Nature, Her Divine Revelations, and a Voice to Mankind* where he claimed to be in spirit communication with Emanuel Swedenborg. On March 31, 1848, Andrew Jackson Davis recorded the following in his diary: "About daylight this morning a warm breathing passed over my face and I heard a voice, tender and strong, saying, 'Brother, the good work has begun—behold, a living demonstration is born.' I was left wondering what could be meant by such a message."

Davis' diary entry would take on a special significance when, in late March 1848, the young Fox sisters, Maggie and Kate, claimed to be in contact with a murdered peddler in their Hydesville, New York, farmhouse. Claiming the ability to act as mediums between the living and the dead, the sisters began performing in public. Interest in the sisters transferred to an influx of mediums all claiming contact with the dead. Séances became increasingly popular as distraught family members sought to contact their departed loved ones.

The Society for Psychical Research founded in England in 1882 was the first official society to investigate and study paranormal activity. In 1886, founder members Edmund Gurney, Frederic Myers and Frank Podmore published a two-volume report titled *Phantasms of the Living*. Based on firsthand accounts, the massive 1,400-page collection included

701 ghost encounters. Gurney and Myers believed ghosts were hallucinations caused by a form of telepathy involving the person receiving impressions of his or her loved ones from the living.

The public's renewed interest in the supernatural transferred to fictional exploits of ghost hunters and detectives in popular magazines of the day. It was a fascination that began many years earlier with the birth of Gothic literature and Horace Walpole's *The Castle of Otranto* (1764). The Age of Reason was being countered with flights of the imagination where reason took a back seat to Romanticism and a supernatural narrative. The medieval haunted castle and its environs became the stock setting for many Gothic novels of this period. Authors M.G. "Monk" Lewis, C.R. Maturin and E.T.A. Hoffmann all looked to the gloomy and mysterious past for their inspiration. Heavy, creaking doors leading to secret rooms and passages were reflections of the subconscious mind in the days before Freud or Jung explored the inner workings of the psyche.

Edgar Allan Poe continued the Gothic tradition into the 19th century and is generally attributed as the creator of the modern detective story with "The Murders in the Rue Morgue" (1841), followed by "The Mystery of Marie Rogêt" (1842), "The Gold-Bug" (1843) and "The Purloined Letter" (1844). In "The Murders in the Rue Morgue" amateur detective C. Auguste Dupin acknowledges Vidocq as a flawed detective who "erred continually by the very intensity of his investigations."

Eugène François Vidocq (1775–1857) was a former criminal and informer for Napoleon who founded the first known detective agency in 1832. This real-life character was an inspiration for Poe's fictional creation along with Voltaire's *Zadig* (1748). Poe acknowledged Dupin was not a new creation. "All novel conceptions are merely unusual combinations. The mind of man can imagine nothing which has not already existed."

Despite Poe being a master craftsman of the macabre, his detective fiction didn't involve the supernatural but was highly influential in defining the tropes of the new genre. C. Auguste Dupin is an eccentric intellectual who views the investigative methods of the police as inferior. "There is no method in their proceedings, beyond the method of the moment." The first-person narrator telling the story of his friend's detective work would become a common stylistic device.

In 1868 British author Wilkie Collins published what is generally regarded as the first detective novel. *The Moonstone* featured amateur detective Franklin Blake and Scotland Yard policeman Sergeant Cruff investigating a stolen Moonstone diamond. But Collin's novel was pre-dated by *Three Times Dead* (1860), a.k.a. *The Trail of the Serpent*. Author Mary Elizabeth Braddon's novel introduced police detective Mr. Jinks and mute detective Joseph Peters. Charles Dickens' *Bleak House* (1853) pre-dated both Collins and Braddon and includes Inspector Bucket, arguably the first detective in British fiction.

One of the first weird detectives in fiction from this period was Harry Escott, the creation of Fitz-James O'Brien. In the *Harper's* short story "A Pot of Tulips" (November 1855) Escott investigates a ghost in his country home. "I had devoted much time to the investigation of, what are popularly called, supernatural matters ... to discover that none of these apparent miracles are supernatural, but all, however singular, directly dependent on certain natural laws."

In the following decades numerous weird sleuths made their debut. These ranged from ghost hunters, to physicians, to psychic psychologists, to clairvoyant detectives. The haunted house, dating back to Pliny the Younger, was one of the most popular forms of the hybrid genre. The home is supposed to be a sanctuary, so it isn't surprising that this format became the most popular in early supernatural literature. The psychic invasion of the house represented an attack on personal territory. The role of the detective was to resolve conflict and uncover the truth behind the hauntings. Sometimes the ghost would be sympathetic, as in a trapped soul. But the haunting could also be destructive and demonic in nature. Resolution would come from enabling the spirit to move forward to the next life or disabling the demon through religious ritual or exorcism.

Many of the weird detectives were amateurs who had psychic abilities, believed in the supernatural and searched for proof of its existence. Others investigated the paranormal as regular detectives with the intention of debunking supernatural phenomena using scientific methods. A common plot device, which has survived to the present day, involved a person or family buying or renting a new home. The ghost is either a remnant of previous owners or tenants or is attached to a person in the family. The detective must unravel the clues of the past to reveal the truth of the present.

The rise of science in popular consciousness during the Victorian and Edwardian era was at odds with the supernatural mindset of Spiritualism. This conflict between rationalism and what many considered to be superstition gave the weird detective genre added life. But with fraudulent mediums all too willing to exploit the bereaved, Spiritualism came under increased scrutiny and the line between fact and fiction became increasingly blurred. Reality was in many cases a fiction created by frauds who insisted spirit photography and slate writing was real.

One of Spiritualism's most ardent supporters was Sir Arthur Conan Doyle. In his detective fiction Sherlock Holmes used logic and scientific deduction to solve his cases, but Conan Doyle's real-life detective skills were lacking. He had led a revolt against the Society for Psychical Research, insisting the society was opposed to Spiritualism. His gullibility placed a strain on his relationship with stage magician Harry Houdini, who exposed mediums as frauds. Despite Houdini's detective work the public remained fascinated with the supernatural.

Another Victorian movement of note was the Hermetic Order of the Golden Dawn. Founded in 1887 by three British Freemasons the organization was devoted to the study and practice of magic, divination, alchemy and philosophy. Members Algernon Blackwood and Arthur Machen would become famous for their weird fiction work and the creation of occult detectives John Silence and Dyson.

Readers followed the psychic detective tales of Flaxman Low, Mr. John Bell, Sheila Crerar, Moris Klaw and Aylmer Vance in periodicals such as *Cassell's Family Magazine, London Magazine, The Weekly Tale-Teller, Pearson's Magazine, Edinburgh Magazine, Detective Story Magazine* and *The Blue Magazine*.

Pulp fiction was considered low-brow sensationalistic fodder for the masses, with its low-quality printing on pulp paper and its lurid cover art. *Weird Tales* was one of the most popular titles of the 1930s, whose sensational covers often featured near naked females. But within its pages were many authors of note, including H.P. Lovecraft, Robert E. Howard, Clark Ashton Smith and Seabury Quinn. In October 1925 Quinn introduced French physician and amateur detective Jules de Grandin in "Horror on the Links." Grandin's assistant Dr. Trowbridge narrated his supernatural cases that often centered on the haunted town of Harrisonville, New Jersey.

H.P. Lovecraft's *Weird Tales* (January 1927) story "The Horror at Red Hook" featured New York police detective Thomas F. Malone investigating a sinister cult practicing sorcery in the Red Hook district of Brooklyn. Lovecraft described the Irish-born Malone as having "the Celt's far vision of weird and hidden things, but the logician's quick eye for the outwardly unconvincing." He followed this in 1927 with "The Call of Cthulhu" and Inspector John Raymond Legrasse's encounter with a cult practicing human sacrifice.

Occult detective Ascott Keane, aided by his secretary Betty Dale, first encountered the evil Doctor Satan in the August 1935 issue of *Weird Tales*. Author Paul Ernst was also the creator of the pulp fiction weird detective *The Avenger* in 1936.

Comic books, which evolved out of the pulps, were aimed at a younger reader but were equally lambasted as junk by adults. Weird detectives were often populated with doctors and psychologists such as Dr. Drew Murdoch, Dr. Whisper Drew, Dr. Desmond Drew, Dr. Thirteen and Dr. Occult. Weird comic book detectives weren't confined to humans. Detective Chimp and Rex the Wonder Dog both solved crimes using their paranormal skills.

DC Comics' *The Spectre* originally appeared in *More Fun Comics* #52 (February 1940). Hard-boiled cop Jim Corrigan is murdered but is refused entry into the after-life. He must return to earth to fight evil. He resumes his life as Jim Corrigan but fights crime as the hooded Spectre.

Dr. Fredric Wertham's book *Seduction of the Innocent* (1954) was the culmination of his crusade against what he perceived as the harmful effects of comic books. His efforts resulted in greater public awareness of the more violent aspects of the horror and crime genres. The creation of the Comics Code Authority in 1954 included guidelines that stated:

> No comic magazine shall use the words "horror" or "terror" in its title.
> Inclusion of stories dealing with evil shall be used or shall be published only where the intent is to illustrate a moral issue and in no case shall evil be presented alluringly, nor so as to injure the sensibilities of the reader.
> Scenes dealing with, or instruments associated with walking dead, torture, vampires and vampirism, ghouls, cannibalism, and werewolfism are prohibited.
> These guidelines were enforced until the relaxation of the code in the 1970s when weird detective titles such as *The Tomb of Dracula*, *The Occult Files of Dr. Spektor* and *Weird Mystery Tales* surfaced.

The hybrid genre peaked again in the late 20th century in literature, film and television, from investigative reporter Carl Kolchak and his encounters with the supernatural in *Kolchak: The Night Stalker* (1974) to Mulder and Scully in *The X-Files* (1993). The dawn of the 21st century continued the trend with *Medium* (2005). Allison DuBois (Patricia Arquette) used her psychic gifts to help solve crimes. *Supernatural* (2005) featured the brothers Sam and Dean Winchester hunting down various paranormal and occult manifestations. The public's fascination with weird detectives will continue in the decades ahead, because the public loves tales of the supernatural. The hidden, suddenly manifesting before returning to its shadowy abode elicits childhood fears. And as adults we never completely shake off those fears. They remain buried in our subconscious, connecting us to our ancestral roots when the spirit world was closer to the surface. Weird detective fiction opens a portal to that shrouded world once again.

The Encyclopedia

Abby Cooper, Psychic Eye (Psychic Eye Mystery #1) [Novel]

Author: Victoria Laurie; First publication: New York, NY: Signet, 2004.

Abby Cooper earns her living as a psychic intuitive. When her client Allison Pierce is murdered Abby comes under suspicion from the police. Now she must investigate the murder to clear her reputation but in doing so she places her own life in danger.

Later in the series of fifteen books Abby teams up with her business partner and best friend Candice Fusco and becomes a Civilian Profiler for the F.B.I.

Titles in the series: *Abby Cooper, Psychic Eye* (2004); *Better Read Than Dead* (2005); *A Vision of Murder* (2005); *Killer Insight* (2006); *Crime Seen* (2007); *Death Perception* (2008); *Doom with a View* (2009); *A Glimpse of Evil* (2010); *Vision Impossible* (2012); *Lethal Outlook* (2013); *Deadly Forecast* (2014); *Fatal Fortune* (2015); *Sense of Deception* (2016); *A Grave Prediction* (2017); *A Panicked Premonition* (2018).

Adam Wolfe [Video game]

Release date: October 7, 2016; Developer: Mad Head Games; Platforms: Macintosh, Windows; Perspective: 1st-Person; Publisher: Mad Head Games.

Paranormal investigator Adam Wolfe is searching for his missing sister in the dark streets of San Francisco. As his search continues, he delves deeper into dangerous paranormal territory when he is assigned to investigate fires that may have a supernatural cause. The player is Adam Wolfe searching for clues among hidden objects in order to make progress. Along the way he engages in shootouts with supernatural enemies.

Followed by *Adam Wolfe: Flames of Eternity* (2016) and *Adam Wolfe: Blood of Eternity* (2017) where Wolfe finally finds his sister but must confront the leader of the cult who abducted her.

The Adept (Book #1) [Novel]

Authors: Katherine Kurtz, Deborah Turner Harris; First Publication: New York, NY: Ace Books, 1991.

In the first book of the series psychiatrist and occult expert Sir Adam Sinclair teams up with psychic portrait artist Peregrine Lovat and policeman and medium Noel Macleod to discover who stole a wizard's sword from a Scottish museum. Sinclair is the latest incarnation of the immortal Adept whose mission is to defeat the dark forces that have been unleashed in Scotland through the unholy cult known as the Lodge of the Lynx. Sinclair is commander-in-chief of the Huntsmen, a secret organization fighting Darkness with the Light.

Titles in the series: *The Adept* (1991); *The Lodge of the Lynx* (1992); *The Templar Treasure* (1993); *Dagger Magic* (1995); *Death of an Adept* (1996).

"The Adventure of the Sussex Vampire" [Short story]

Author: Arthur Conan Doyle; Illustrators: Howard K. Elcock (UK); W. T. Benda (U.S.); First publication: London: The Strand Magazine (January 1924); New York: Hearst's International (January 1924).

Sherlock Holmes' latest client presents a macabre tale. Communicating by letter Mr. Robert Ferguson tells Holmes he thinks his Peruvian wife has been sucking the blood of their baby boy in the manner of a vampire. Ferguson's fifteen-year-old son Jack by his first wife who lost the use of his legs in an accident has also been the target of Mrs. Ferguson's anger. Holmes travels to their Sussex home to uncover a possible link between the bloodsucking wife and Jack Ferguson.

See: *The Case-Book of Sherlock Holmes*

Again a.k.a. *Again: FBI Parapsychological Investigator* [Video game: Japan]

Release date: December 10, 2009; Scenario: Yuki Tsuruta, Hidetake Itoh; Director: Shigeru Komine; Developer: CING Inc.; Original platform: Nintendo DS; Perspective: First-person; Publisher: Tecmo.

FBI Special Agent Jonathan Weaver, who goes by the nickname of "J" is the only survivor of a serial killer who terrorized Clockford, Pennsylvania, 19 years ago. Now the killer known as the "Eye of Providence" is at work again. "J" investigates the murders with the psychic gift that allows him to see into the past, thus reliving the scene of the crimes.

The game player must use J's psychic powers, displayed on the psychic gauge sparingly while investigating, otherwise the game is lost when his power is drained.

All-Consuming Fire (Virgin New Adventures #27) [Novel; Audio drama]

Author: Andy Lane; First publication: London: Virgin Books, 2014.

The seventh doctor comes to the aid of Sherlock Holmes and Dr. Watson after forbidden mystical books are stolen from the Library of St. Jon the Beheaded in 1887.

A mix of the universes of Arthur Conan Doyle, Doctor Who and H.P. Lovecraft

[Audio drama] Premiere: December 9, 2015; Voice Cast: Sylvester McCoy as The Doctor, Sophie Aldred as Ace, Lisa Bowerman as Bernice Summerfield, Nicholas Briggs as Sherlock Holmes, Richard Earl as Dr. John Watson, Hugh Fraser as Sherringford Holmes, Anthony May as Baron Maupertuis, Aaron Neil as Tir Ram, Samantha Beart as Mrs. Prendersly/Azazoth, Michael Griffiths as Ambrose, Guy Adams as K'Tcar'ch; Story Andy Lane; Adapted by Guy Adams; Director: Scott Handcock; Big Finish Productions.

This adaptation of the novel by Andy Lane omits the appearances of James Moriarty and Mrs. Hudson and the framing narrative of an Arthur Conan Doyle story within a story.

Alone in the Dark [Video game; Film]

Release date: 1992; Original developer: Infogrames; Publishers: Infogrames, Interplay Entertainment, Atari Inc., THQ Nordic; Original platform: MS-DOS.

Paranormal private investigator Edward Carnby is hired to locate a piano for antique dealer Emily Hartwood. The piano is connected to the suicide of artist Jeremy Hartwood at the Derceto mansion in Louisiana. But when Carnby and Hartwood enter the mansion they quickly learn it is haunted by various supernatural beings including the spirit of occultist Ezechiel Pregzt.

Set in the year 1924 the player assumes the character of Edward Carnby or Emily Hartwood as they encounter spirits, zombies and monsters.

The original video game has spawned six sequels.

[Film] Premiere: January 28, 2005; Voice Cast: Christian Slater as Edward Carnby, Tara Reid as Aline Cedrac, Stephen Dorff as Commander Richard Burke, Frank C. Turner as Sam Fischer, Matthew Walker as Professor Lionel Hudgens, Will Sanderson as Agent Miles, Mark Atcheson as Captain Chernick, Darren Shahlavi as John Dillon, Karin Konoval as Sister Clara; Story: Elan Mastai, Michael Roesch, Peter Scheerer; Producer: Shawn Williamson; Director: Uwe Boll; 96 min.; AITD Productions; Lions Gate Films; Color.

Paranormal detective Edward Carnby is joined by anthropologist and former girlfriend Aline Cedrac in deciphering an ancient artifact believed to have belonged to the vanished Indian tribe the Abkani. Demons summoned 10,000 years ago by the Abkani have been inadvertently released by Abkani obsessed Professor Hudgens who experimented on Carnby and nineteen other children at the Our Lady of the Perpetual Light orphanage. Carnby has no recollection of the experiments but can sense paranormal activity.

Loosely based on the video game *Alone in the Dark: The New Nightmare* the film was a box office and critical failure.

[Video game; France] Release date: June 24, 2008 [U.S.]; Voice cast: James McCaffrey as Edward Carnby, John Cunningham as Theopile Paddington, Alexandra Williamson as Sarah Flores, Chris Phillips as Crowley, Jason Griffith as Hammet/Jack the Watchman; Producer: Nour Polloni; Screenplay: Lorenzo Carcaterra; Director: David Nadal; Eden Studios; Developers: Eden Games. Hydravision Entertainment; Platforms: PlayStation 3, Xbox 360; Publisher: Atari.

Central Park, New York City is experiencing strange and sinister happenings. Enter Edward Carnby, paranormal investigator. The story is divided into 30–40-minute episodes with a video teaser of the next episode.

Alone in the Dark: Illumination [Video game]

Release date: June 11, 2015; Developer: Pure FPS; Original platform: Microsoft Windows; Perspective: Third-person shooter; Publisher: Atari.

Lorwich, Virginia, is under a curse. The Darkness envelops the mining ghost town. Four individuals have come to Lorwich on their own mission and must work together to defeat the supernatural creatures that roam through the Darkness.

The game characters are Theodore "Ted" Carnby, an alleged descendant of Edward Carnby, although many believe Edward may still be alive and posing as 'Ted.' Celeste Hartwood, the great granddaughter of Emily Hartwood is a witch who is searching for lost witches from her coven. Gabriella Saunders a.k.a. The Engineer in Lorwich searching for her missing father, who was a miner before disaster struck the mine and the town. Father Henry Giger is a Roman Catholic priest investigating mysterious events in Lorwich under orders from the Vatican.

Each character is armed with various weapons to fight the supernatural creatures emerging from the Darkness.

Alone in the Dark: The New Nightmare [Video game]

Release date: May 18, 2001; Scenario: Antoine Villette; Director: Bruno Bonnell; Original developer: Darkworks S.A.; Original platforms: Microsoft Windows, PlayStation, Dreamcast, Game Boy Color; Perspective: Third-person; Publisher: Infogrames Inc.

Edward Carnby sets out to find the killer of his partner Charles Friske. Frederick Johnson tells Carnby that Friske was searching for three ancient tablets on Shadow Island, off the coast of Maine, at the time of his death. Carnby is joined by university professor Aline Cedrac in the search for the killer and the missing tablets that are said to contain the key to unlocking alarming power. But they must survive the creatures of darkness and horror that await them on the island.

Alone in the Dark 2 [Video game]

Release date: 1993; Producer: Bruno Bonnell; Director: Franck De Girolami; Developer: Infogrames Europe SA; Original platform: MS-DOS; Perspective: Third-person; Publisher: Infogrames.

Edward Carnby is called to Hell's Kitchen to discover what happened to young Grace Saunders after Carnby's partner Ted Stryker is murdered while searching for her. He discovers One-Eyed Jack and his gangsters are immortal 15th century pirates thanks to a Voodoo witch. But to remain immortal they must kidnap human victims for sacrifice.

Alone in the Dark 3 [Video game]

Release date: 1994; Scenario: Hubert Chardot, Christian Nabais; Director: Bruno Bonnell; Developer: Infogrames Europe SA; Original platform: MS-DOS; Perspective: Third-person; Publisher: Infogrames.

When a film crew disappears in the Wild West ghost town of Slaughter Gulch, "Supernatural Private Eye" Edward Carnby arrives to save his friend Emily Hartwood from the evil spirit of Jebediah Stone and his gang of zombie cowboy outlaws.

Alphas (2011) [TV series]

Premiere: July 11, 2011; Main Cast: David Strathairn as Dr. Lee Rosen, Ryan Cartwright as Gary Bell, Warren Christie as Cameron Hicks, Azita Ghanizada as Rachel Pirzad, Laura Mennell as Nina Theroux, Malik Yoba as Bill Harken, Mahershala Ali as Nathan Clay, John Pyper-Ferguson as Stanton Parish, Erin Way as Kat; Executive Producers: Gene Stein, Gail Berman, Lloyd Braun, Bruce Miller, Zak Penn, Ira Steven Behr, Jack Bender; Creators: Michael Karnow, Zak Penn; 24 × 44 min.; BermanBraun; Universal Cable Productions; Syfy; Space; Color.

Five Alphas possessing unique paranormal powers work within the U.S. Department of Defense led by their mentor Dr. Lee Rosen. As members of the Defense Criminal Investigation Service the team investigate other Alphas who resort to crime and terrorism under the influence of the "Red Flag" group. Autistic Alpha team member Gary Bell can see and read electromagnetic wavelengths while former Marine Cameron Hicks has the paranormal power of hyperkinesis, granting him perfect body coordination. Rachel Pirzad can heighten her senses one at a time and Bill Harken increases his strength and speed by enhancing his fight or flight response. Nina Theroux uses Hyper Induction to mentally influence people into following her directions against their will. But their powers aren't limitless and are accompanied by mental and physical problems and anxieties.

SEASON ONE

Pilot (1:01); *Cause and Effect* (1:02); *Anger Management* (1:03); *Rosetta* (1:04); *Never Let Me Go* (1:05); *Bill and Gary's Excellent Adventure* (1:06); *Catch and Release* (1:07); *A Short Time in Paradise* (1:08); *Blind Spot* (1:09); *The Unusual Suspects* (1:10); *Original Sin* (1:11).

SEASON TWO

Wake Up Call (2:01); *The Quick and the Dead* (2:02); *Alpha Dogs* (2:03); *When Push Comes to Shove* (2:04); *Gaslight* (2:05); *Alphaville* (2:06); *Gods and Monsters* (2:07); *Falling* (2:08); *The Devil Will Drag You Under* (2:09); *Life After Death* (2:10); *If Memory Serves* (2:11); *Need to Know* (2:12); *God's Eye* (2:13).

The Amazing Ghost Detectives [Juvenile book]

Author: Daniel San Souci; First publication: Berkeley, CA: Tricycle Press 2006.

When a mischievous ghost appears to be creating havoc in the neighborhood clubhouse the Amazing Ghost Detectives get to work. Enlisting the aid of local ghost expert Alison and Molly the dog they track the ghost through the neighborhood.

The Amazing Screw-On Head [Comic book]

First publication: May 2002; Story & Art: Mike Mignola; Publisher: Dark Horse Comics.

Emperor Zombie, formerly known as H.G. Manifold master of ancient languages, has stolen the Kalakistan Fragment that details the life of Gung the Magnificent who conquered the ancient world using supernatural powers. Only Emperor Zombie can translate the document and unleash its secret powers.

President Abraham Lincoln turns to the mechanical Screw-On Head to track Emperor Zombie and recover the fragment. Screw-On Head has a removable head that can be attached to various mechanical bodies. Joining him on his quest to find Emperor Zombie is his butler Mr. Groin and undead dog Mister Dog.

Ambrose Bierce [Comic book character]

First appearance: *Stanley and His Monster* (Vol. 2) #2 (March 1993); Writer-Artist: Phil Foglio; Publisher: DC Comics.

Young Stanley Dover's companion is a big, furry demon cast out from Hell for being too good. But now the female demon Nyx wants him back in Hell. Enter magician, demon hunter and occult detective Ambrose Bierce who must conjure an amulet to protect the monster from Nyx.

Ambrose Bierce, based on the noted author, is also a humorous parody of **John Constantine**.

Ampney Crucis [Comic book character; UK]

First appearance: *2000 A.D.* #1611 (2008); Story: Ian Edginton; Art: Simon Davis; Publisher: Oxford: Rebellion Developments.

Lord Ampney Crucis has been able to

sense supernatural beings since an encounter with an entity during World War I drove him temporarily insane. Ampney now dedicates his life to investigating the paranormal aided by his butler Eddie Cromwell.

The comic strip *Ampney Crucis Investigates* has appeared sporadically in *2000 A.D.* and his early adventures collected by Solaris in the graphic novel *Vile Bodies* (2012).

An American Weredeer in Michigan
(*Bright Falls Mysteries* Book 2) [Novel]
Authors: C.T. Phipps, Michael Suttkus; First publication: Hertford, NC: Mystique Press–Crossroad Press 2017.

Jane Doe, Shaman of Bright Falls, Michigan and weredeer detective discovers a gruesome and upsetting sight when she comes across a mass grave of newborn babies in the local forest. She teams up with her best friend Emma, FBI Special Agent Alex Timmons and local crime lord Lucien Lyons to put a stop to the century old tradition. But a religious cult leader new to Bright Falls has his own reasons for finding those responsible for the discarding babies in the forest.

See: *I Was a Teenage Weredeer*

Andrew Latter [Short story character]
Author: Harold Begbie; First appearance: *The London Magazine* (June 1904); Publisher: London: Amalgamated Press.

Andrew Latter travels through his dream world to view and solve crimes which he later reports to Scotland Yard. In his first case "Murder in an Omnibus" Latter investigates the murder of his friend Colonel Lawrence Stake of Scotland Yard. An Hampstead omnibus conductor attempts to wake the Colonel at the terminus but instead and to his horror finds "his clothes saturated with blood, and a powerful dagger wedged tightly between his shoulder blades."

With the thought of the murder in his mind Latter falls into a deep sleep. In the early morning he awakes. "I have just come out of the vividest and most extraordinary dream that ever I had in all my life…. I dare not let a moment pass without writing down the story of my dream. I am trembling with excitement and can scarcely hold the pen … in a few hours' time I will go down and see Beaton at Scotland Yard. I believe in my dream. It can't have been delusion."

Latter's detailed lucid dream leads to the unraveling of an assassination plot by a secret society of foreigners in London. The Colonel had heard of their plan and was silenced before he could talk.

Harold Begbie wrote six stories featuring Andrew Latter for *The London Times*.

The Murder in the Omnibus (June 1904); *The Affair of the Duke of Nottingham* (July 1904); *The Eye at the Drawn Blind* (August 1904); *The Charge Against Lord William Grace* (September 1904); *The Missing Heir* (October 1904); *The Flying Blindness* (November 1904).

Angel (1999) [TV series]
First broadcast: October 5, 1999; Main Cast: David Boreanaz as Angel, Alexis Denisof as Wesley Wyndham-Pryce, J. August Richards as Charles Gunn, Charisma Carpenter as Cordelia Chase, Andy Hallett as Lorne, Amy Acker as Winifred "Fred" Burkle, Stephanie Romanov as Lilah Morgan, Vincent Kartheiser as Connor, James Marsters as Spike, Christian Kane as Lindsey McDonald, Julie Benz as Darla, Mercedes McNab as Harmony Kendall, Elizabeth Rohm as Detective Kate Lockley, Glenn Quinn as Allen Doyle; Executive Producers: Joss Whedon, David Greenwalt, Kaz Kuzui, Gail Berman, Sandy Gallin, Fran Rubel Kuzui; 110 × 42 min.; Mutant Enemy; Kuzui Enterprises; Greenwolf; Sandollar Television; 20th Century–Fox Television; WB Television Network; Color.

Born in Ireland in the 18th century Angelus becomes a notorious vampire. But when his actions lead to him being cursed with a soul, he changes his name to Angel seeking redemption for the evil deeds of his past. Angel's detective agency "Angel Investigations" a.k.a. "Team Angel" based in modern day Los Angeles specializes in supernatural cases helping to save lost souls and banish demons. The founding members of the investigative team are Angel, wannabe actress Cordelia Chase and half-human, half-Brachen demon Allen Francis Doyle.

As the series progresses the team adds new members and loses Allen Francis Doyle. He sacrifices his life to save half-breed demons from the deadly effects of the Beacon, created by pure-blood demons known as the Scourge. Angel forms a friendly relationship with LAPD detective Kate Lockley. Following her initial mistrust of Angel, she becomes fascinated with the supernatural. Unfortunately, this leads her down a dark path and her being fired from the LAPD. Angel must save her life after she attempts suicide. The agency eventually ceases as a business and the Angel Investigations team is referred to as Team Angel during the final season.

Angel began life as a recurring character on *Buffy the Vampire Slayer* (1996) before graduating to his own series.

Season One

City Of (1:01); *Lonely Heart* (1:02); *In the Dark* (1:03); *I Fall to Pieces* (1:04); *Rm w/a Vu* (1:05); *Sense and Sensitivity* (1:06); *Bachelor Party* (1:07); *I Will Remember You* (1:08); *Hero* (1:09); *Parting Gifts* (1:10); *Somnambulist* (1:11); *Expecting* (1:12); *She* (1:13); *I've Got You Under My Skin* (1:14); *The Prodigal* (1:15); *The Ring* (1:16); *Eternity* (1:17); *Five by Five* (1:18); *Sanctuary* (1:19); *War Zone* (1:20); *Blind Date* (1:21); *To Shanshu in L.A.* (1:22).

Season Two

Judgment (2:01); *Are You Now or Have You Ever Been* (2:02); *First Impressions* (2:03); *Untouched* (2:04); *Dear Boy* (2:05); *Guise Will Be Guise* (2:06); *Darla* (2:07); *The Shroud of Rahmon* (2:08); *The Trial* (2:09); *Reunion* (2:10); *Redefinition* (2:11); *Blood Money* (2:12); *Happy Anniversary* (2:13); *The Thin Dead Line* (2:14); *Reprise* (2:15); *Epiphany* (2:16); *Disharmony* (2:17); *Dead End* (2:18); *Belonging* (2:19); *Over the Rainbow* (2:20); *Through the Looking Glass* (2:21); *There's No Place Like Plrtz Girb* (2:22).

Season Three

Heartthrob (3:01); *That Vision Thing* (3:02); *That Old Gang of Mine* (3:03); *Cape Noctem* (3:04); *Fredless* (3:05); *Billy* (3:06); *Offspring* (3:07); *Quickening* (3:08); *Lullaby* (3:09); *Dad* (3:10); *Birthday* (3:11); *Provider* (3:12); *Waiting in the Wings* (3:13); *Couplet* (3:14); *Loyalty* (3:15); *Sleep Tight* (3:16); *Forgiving* (3:17); *Double or Nothing* (3:18); *The Price* (3:19); *A New World* (3:20); *Benediction* (3:21); *Tomorrow* (3:22).

Season Four

Deep Down (4:01); *Ground State* (4:02); *The House Always Wins* (4:03); *Slouching Toward Bethlehem* (4:04); *Supersymmetry* (4:05); *Spin the Bottle* (4:06); *Apocalypse Nowish* (4:07); *Habeas Corpses* (4:08); *Long Day's Journey* (4:09); *Awakening* (4:10); *Soulless* (4:11); *Calvary* (4:12); *Salvage* (4:13); *Release* (4:14); *Orpheus* (4:15); *Players* (4:16); *Inside Out* (4:17); *Shiny Happy People* (4:18); *The Magic Bullet* (4:19); *Sacrifice* (4:20); *Peace Out* (4:21); *Home* (4:22).

Season Five

Conviction (5:01); *Just Rewards* (5:02); *Unleashed* (5:03); *Hell Bound* (5:04); *Life of the Party* (5:05); *The Cautionary Tale of Numero Cinco* (5:06); *Lineage* (5:07); *Destiny* (5:08); *Harm's Way* (5:09); *Soul Purpose* (5:10); *Damage* (5:11); *You're Welcome* (5:12); *Why We Fight* (5:13); *Smile Time* (5:14); *A Hole in the World* (5:15); *Shells* (5:16); *Underneath* (5:17); *Origin* (5:18); *Time Bomb* (5:19); *The Girl in Question* (5:20); *Power Play* (5:21); *Not Fade Away* (5:22).

Angel Cop a.k.a. **Enzeru Koppu** (1989) [OVA; Manga; Japan]

[OVA] Premiere: September 1, 1989; Voice Cast: Mika Doi as Angel Mikawa, Masashi Ebara as Sakada Raiden, Kumiko Hironaka as Lucifer, Yuuko Mizutani as Freya, Kouichi Kitamura as Ichihara, Toshihiko Seki as Tachihara, Osamu Saka as Maisaka, Nozomu Sasaki as Asura, Tessyo Genda as Togawa. Massaki Yajima as Narrator; Producer: Yasushi Nomura; Story: Hiroyuki Kitakubo, Hideki Takayama, Ichiro Itano, Shou Aikawa; Director: Ichiro Itano; 6 × 30 min.; D.A.S.T.; Geneon Universal Entertainment; Soeishinsha Company Inc.; Color.

In the mid–1990s the Japanese government establishes a House Committee for Terrorist Affairs. It's function to investigate and stop terrorist activity. Angel and Raiden are members of the elite Special Security Force. A group of psychics known as Hunters are bringing the bad guys to justice, but one of them prefers to brutally kill members of the Communist terrorist group Red May—and Angel and Raiden are the next targets of the rogue psychic.

EPISODES

Special Security Force (1:01); *The Disfigured City* (1:02); *The Death Warrant* (1:03); *Pain* (1:04); *Wrath of the Empire* (1:05); *Doomsday* (1:06).

[Manga] First publication: *Newtype* (June 1989); Story & Art: Taku Kitazaki; Publisher: Kadokawa Shoten.

Manga adaptation of the Original Video Animation OVA.

Angel Heart (1987) [Film]

Premiere: March 6, 1987; Main Cast: Mickey Rourke as Harry Angel, Robert De Niro as Louis Cyphre, Lisa Bonet as Epiphany Proudfoot, Charlotte Rampling as Margaret Krusemark; Executive Producer: Andrew Vajna; Screenplay: Alan Parker; Based on the novel by William Hjortsberg; Director: Alan Parker; 113 min.; TriStar Pictures; Color.

Private investigator Harry Angel is hired by Louis Cyphre to locate popular singer Johnny Favorite. Angel soon finds himself immersed in Voodoo, the occult and the Devil himself.

The film is an adaptation of William Hjortsberg's novel **Falling Angel**.

Anita Blake: Vampire Hunter [Book series; Comic book character]

Author: Laurell K. Hamilton; First appearance: *Guilty Pleasures*; Publisher: New York: Ace Books, 1993.

In a universe where the supernatural is a part of everyday life St. Louis, Missouri based Anita Blake re-animates the dead, hunts and executes criminal vampires and works with the police. Headed by Sergeant Rudolph "Dolph" Storr the Regional Preternatural Investigation Taskforce, also referred to as the "Spook Squad" investigates supernatural crimes. Anita Blake acts as Federal Marshal and consultant.

Blake's detective training is put to good use in early novels in the series. Later novels concentrate on her personal and sexual relationships. Marvel Comics have adapted the first three books in the series.

Books in series: *Guilty Pleasures* (1993); *The Laughing Corpse* (1994); *Circus of the Damned* (1995); *The Lunatic Café* (1996); *Bloody Bones* (1996); *The Killing Dance* (1997); *Burnt Offerings* (1998); *Blue Moon* (1998); *Obsidian Butterfly* (2000); *Narcissus in Chains* (2001); *Cerulean Sins* (2003); *Incubus Dreams* (2004); *Micah* (2006); *Danse Macabre* (2006); *The Harlequin* (2007); *Blood Noir* (2008); *Skin Trade* (2009); *Flirt* (2010); *Bullet* (2010); *Hit List* (2011); *Kiss the Dead* (2012); *Affliction* (2013); *Jason* (2014); *Dead Ice* (2015); *Crimson Death* (2016); *Serpentine* (2018).

Anno Dracula [Novel]

Author: Kim Newman; First publication: New York: Simon & Schuster, 1992.

Set in an alternate reality where the widowed Queen Victoria marries Wallachian Prince Vlad Tepes alias Count Dracula. Vampire Genevieve Dieudonne and Diogenes Club agent Charles Beauregard investigate the Jack the Ripper Whitechapel murders of vampire prostitutes.

Anno Dracula series: *Anno Dracula* (1992); *The Bloody Red Baron* (1995); *Judgment of Tears* (1998); *Johnny Alucard* (2013); *One Thousand Monsters* (2017).

Anonymous Rex: A Detective Story [Novel]

Author: Eric Garcia; First publication: New York: Villard Books, 1999.

Los Angeles private eye Vincent Rubio is hiding a secret. Posing as a human behind a latex costume Rubio is a Velociraptor dinosaur. In this alternate history dinosaurs never became extinct and have secretly co-existed with humans for thousands of years. Arson at a dino nightclub leads Rubio to New York where he investigates illegal interspecies breeding between dinosaurs and humans and clues to the murder of his partner.

Arcana a.k.a. **Arukana** (2013) [Film; Japan]
Premiere: October 19, 2013; Main Cast: Masataka Nakagauchi as Detective Kensho Murakami, Tao Tsuchiya as Maki/Satsuki Nagase, Masahiro Noguchi as Kobayashi Munemitsu, Masashi Taniguchi as Taguchi, Mitsuki Tanimura as Mieko Tomochika, Goro Kishitani as Yutaka Hashi, Kaito as Michiru; Executive Producer: Keizo Yuri; Screenplay; Shotaro Oikawa, Yoshitaka Yamaguchi; Based on the novel and manga by Yua Kotegawa; Director: Yoshitaka Yamaguchi; 89 min.; Django Film; Nikkatsu; SKY PerfecTV!; Color.

During an investigation Detective Murakami meets amnesiac patient Maki. She can communicate with the dead who give her information on solving crimes. When Murakami and Maki team up to stop a mass murderer they fall in love. But Maki has a secret that's connected to doppelgangers and a lookalike named Satsuki.

Archibald the Koala (1998) [Animated TV series; France-UK]
First broadcast: September 4, 1998; Voice cast [UK]: Richard Griffiths as Archibald, Adrienne Posta as Agatha/Miss Julie/Jozette, Dan Russell as Sullivan/Soufflé, Kate Robbins as Iris Dory/Gazette/Marie, Bob Saker as Giovanni/John Dory, Keith Wickham as Archduke/Edison; Executive Producers: Kate Fawkes, Peter Orton, Roch Lener, Jonathan Peel, Victor Sleptsov; Based on the children's book series "The Adventures of Archibald the Koala on Rastepappe Island" by Paul Cox; Director: Claude Allix; 47 × 13 min.; Hit Entertainment PLC/ Millimages S.A.; Canal J; CITV; France 3; Color.

On the island of Rastepappe is Koalaville, home to Archibald the koala detective. The varied residents on the island consisting of koalas and badgers keep Archibald busy as he investigates all manner of strange happenings with the help of his magnifying glass. These include clouds that keep disappearing, an alleged haunted house, a destructive dragon, a sea monster and a giant mole.

SEASON ONE
The Heatwave (1:01); *Archduke's Amnesia* (1:02); *The Brass Band* (1:03); *The Haunted House* (1:04); *A Hazardous Fishing Contest* (1:05); *The Meteorite* (1:06); *Archduke's Statue* (1:07); *The Missing Boat* (1:08).

SEASON TWO
The Rugby-Basket Mystery (2:01); *The Dragon* (2:02); *Strange Vibrations* (2:03); *Read About Tomorrow, Today* (2:04); *A Star is Born* (2:05); (2:06); *The New Restaurant* (2:07); *The Flower and the Magician* (2:08).

SEASON THREE
The Fire Fighters (3:01); *The Snow Cannon* (3:02); *The Invasion* (3:03); *The Mystery of the Floating Island* (3:04); *The Flower Thief* (3:05); *The Very Greedy Sleepwalker* (3:06); *Ho Ho Ho Happy Merry Christmas* (3:07).

SEASON FOUR
Stop That Train (4:01); *The Messenger* (4:02); *The Dynamic Dynamo* (4:03); *The Misunderstanding* (4:04); *The Big Twister* (4:05); *Fake Necklace* (4:06); *Pizza Gazette* (4:07); *A Detective Goes Camping* (4:08).

SEASON FIVE
A Mysterious Rescuer (5:01); *The World of Giants* (5:02); *The Lucky Charm* (5:03); *Edison's Clock* (5:04); *Whale Song* (5:05); *The Treasure Hunt* (5:06); *Edison's Trophy* (5:07); *The Umbrellas of Rastepappe* (5:08).

SEASON SIX
The Sea Monster (6:01); *The Giant Mole* (6:02); *The Big Show* (6:03); *Ultra-Modern Town Hall* (6:04); *Lighthouse of Rastepappe* (6:05); *The Machine from the Sky* (6:06); *Archduke's Cockatoo* (6:07); *The Waxworks of Rastepappe* (6:08).

Ascott Keane [Pulp fiction character]
First appearance: *Weird Tales* (August 1935); Creator-Author: Paul Ernst; Illustrator Vincent Napoli; Publisher: Chicago, Ill: Popular Publications.

In his opening case titled "Doctor Satan" Ascott Keane introduces himself from the comfort of his Park Avenue penthouse. "I'm a dilettante. I inherited a fortune, and I loaf through life playing with first editions, polo ponies and big game hunting."

But Keane's client Ballard Walstead knows this description is just the public persona of the man he states is "one of the greatest criminal investigators that ever lived—a man whose achievements have something almost of black magic in them."

Walstead informs Keane that a sinister figure calling himself Doctor Satan is demanding one million dollars or he will suffer a macabre death. Doctor Satan is a bored playboy who enjoys using his occult powers to extort money from his victims. Assisting Satan is "monkey-man" Girse and the muscular legless giant Bostiff.

Title page for Ascott Keane's debut story "Doctor Satan" published in *Weird Tales* (August 1935). Illustrated by Vincent Napoli (author's personal collection).

Occult detective Ascott Keane and his secretary and assistant Beatrice Dale acted as supporting characters to Doctor Satan, the main character of the *Weird Tales* novelettes by Paul Ernst. Eight tales were published between 1935 and 1936.

Short stories: "Doctor Satan" (August 1935); "The Man Who Chained the Lightning" (September 1935); "Hollywood Horror" (October 1935); "The Consuming Flame" (November 1935); "Horror Insured" (January 1936); "Beyond Death's Gateway" (March 1936); The Death's Double (May 1936); Mask of Death (August/September 1936).

Aunt Dimity's Death (Aunt Dimity Mystery #1)

Author: Nancy Atherton; First publication: New York: Viking Penguin, 1992.

Struggling Lori Shepherd is informed by Boston law firm Willis & Willis of the death of Miss Dimity Westwood. Until now Lori has been convinced Aunt Dimity was a fictional creation of her recently deceased mother. The lawyers tell Lori that she must locate her aunt's cottage and prepare her writings for publication. But when Lori travels to England with Bill Willis and finds the cottage she has inherited in the Cotswolds she discovers it is haunted by Aunt Dimity's ghost.

Aunt Dimity communicates with Lori through her blue leather-bound writing journal. When Lori opens the journal Aunt Dimity's handwriting magically appears guiding her to a new mystery she must solve. Aunt Dimity literally becomes a paranormal detective.

The successful debut novel has spawned twenty-four books.

Book series: *Aunt Dimity's Death* (1992); *Aunt Dimity and the Duke* (1994); *Aunt Dimity's Good Deed* (1996); *Aunt Dimity Digs In* (1998); *Aunt Dimity's Christmas* (1999); *Aunt Dimity Beats the Devil* (2000); *Aunt Dimity: Detective* (2001); *Aunt Dimity Takes a*

Holiday (2003); *Aunt Dimity: Snowbound* (2004); *Aunt Dimity and the Next of Kin* (2005); *Aunt Dimity and the Deep Blue Sea* (2006); *Aunt Dimity Goes West* (2007); *Aunt Dimity: Vampire Hunter* (2008); *Aunt Dimity Slays the Dragon* (2009); *Aunt Dimity Down Under* (2010); *Aunt Dimity and the Family Tree* (2011); *Aunt Dimity and the Village Witch* (2012); *Aunt Dimity and the Lost Prince* (2013); *Aunt Dimity and the Wishing Well* (2014); *Aunt Dimity and the Summer King* (2015); *Aunt Dimity and the Buried Treasure* (2016); *Aunt Dimity and the Widow's Curse* (2017); *Aunt Dimity and the King's Ransom* (2018); *Aunt Dimity and the Heart of Gold* (2019).

The Avenger [Pulp fiction character; Radio show]

First appearance: *The Avenger* #1 (September 1936); Creator-Author: Paul Ernst (Kenneth Robeson); Publisher: Street & Smith.

Millionaire adventurer Dick Benson alias **The Avenger** loses his wife Alicia and small daughter Alice to an underworld crime ring.

"The tragedy had turned his coal-black hair dead white. Also, the nerve shock had paralyzed his facial muscles in some curious way which made the dead flesh like wax; it could not move at the command of his nerves, but when his fingers moved it, it stayed in whatever place it was prodded. Thus, he became a man of a thousand faces, for he could mold the obedient plastic of his countenance into the shape of the faces of others and pass as them."

With the help of sandy-haired Scotsman, Fergus "Mac" McMurdie and the gigantic Algernon Heathcote "Smitty" Smith he forms "*Justice Inc.*" dedicated to bringing criminals to justice. Assisting Benson in his crime-fighting adventures is martial arts expert Nellie Gray, Josh and Rosabel Newton, a negro husband and wife team posing as Benson's servants. In "Murder on Wheels" (November 1941) Benson is joined by former enemy Cole Wilson and undergoes a transformation when radiation returns his face, skin and hair to normal.

Cover for *The Avenger* #1 (September–December 1939). Illustrated by H. W. Scott. Published by Street & Smith (author's personal collection).

The original twelve stories by Paul Ernst are the only ones that qualify as weird detective fiction.

"Justice, Inc." (September 1939); "The Yellow Hoard" (October 1939); "The Sky Walker" (November 1939); "The Devil's Horns" (December 1939); "The Frosted Death" (January 1940); "The Blood Ring" (February 1940); "Stockholders in Death" (March 1940); "The Glass Mountain" (April 1940); "Tuned for Murder" (May 1940); "The Smiling Dogs" (June 1940); "River of Ice" (July 1940); "The Flame Breathers" (September 1940).

2. A series of 26 thirty-minute radio shows based on the pulp fiction character premiered on WHN, New York on July 18, 1941. Dick Benson introduced each episode with a warning to all criminals.

"You who operate beyond the Law, you who seek to wreck the peace of America. Beware! I shall crush your power, destroy the vultures who prey upon the innocent and the unsuspecting. I am the Avenger!"

The Avenger (Radio show)

First broadcast: September 1945; Main Cast: James Monk as Jim Brandon; Script: Walter Gibson (Maxwell Grant); 26 × 30 min.; Syndicated.

Each episode opened with the menacing narration, "The road to crime ends in a trap that justice sets. Crime does not pay."

Biochemist Jim Brandon, "sworn enemy of evil" fights crime with his telepathic indicator which enables him to read thoughts and his secret diffusion capsule which "cloaks him in the black light of invisibility." Only his glamorous assistant Fern Collier knows his secrets.

The character, created by Walter Gibson, creator of **The Shadow**, clearly displayed its influence but failed to make the same impact.

Aversion (2009) [Film]

Premiere: March 30, 2009; Main Cast: Andrew Roth as Alex Stokes, Melantha Blackthorne as Claire, David Wenzel as Private Investigator, Claire Dominguez as Lieutenant Bowne, Mary Amy as Burling, Josh Berresford as Cyril, George Walsh as Sarge, Christopher Illing as Max, Audrey St. James as Marie, Marc Raco as Neil; Producers: Sabrina Simone, Gaius Roberts, Karen Farinelli; Screenplay Jeffrey Roberts [Gaius Roberts], Ted Spencer; Director: Gaius Roberts; 99 min.; HYD Films; Color.

Investigator Alex Stokes is hired to follow the wife of his client. When his interest in her turns to romance he discovers she is possessed by a demon. But the demonic activity soon expands to the entire town.

"Aylmer Vance and the Vampire" [Short story]

Authors: Alice and Claude Askew; First publication: *The Weekly Tale-Teller* #274 (August 1, 1914).

Dexter, close friend of psychic investigator Aylmer Vance determines the time has come to lodge in Vance's home in Dover Street, Piccadilly. "I had decided to follow in his footsteps and to accept him as my instructor in matters psychic … he showed me how to develop that faculty of clairvoyance which I had possessed without being aware of it."

Now Dexter acts as the "recorder of his many strange adventures."

It isn't long before Vance receives a visitor named Paul Davenant, known for his athletic prowess, wealth and beautiful young wife. Dexter notes Davenant's recent dramatic change in appearance from a handsome young man to a sickly pale visage. Davenant is desperate to know who caused his loss of blood over time for he has no recollection of such an occurrence. Vance and Dexter examine the throat of Davenant and discover "two red marks, about an inch apart, each of which was inclined to be crescent in shape."

Davenant recalls how his wife Jessica MacThane initially rejected his marriage proposal stating she "had been born under a curse" dating back to the earliest time in her family history. "The walls of Blackwick Castle are impregnated with evil…" That reputation was initiated when Robert MacThane married a foreigner outside his clan. A woman "with glowing masses of red hair and a complexion of ivory whiteness." One day his wife Zaida disappeared and Robert, blaming his tenants for her death murdered them in cold blood. Now Zaida, who everyone thought to be a witch, haunted the cottages at night causing sickness and death. The MacThane clan thinned out over the years until Jessica was the last in line. Despite her warnings Davenant married Jessica and moved into Blackwick Castle.

But now she refuses to leave the castle and pleads with her husband to depart and escape the family curse. Vance and Dexter accompany Davenant to the castle to see if vampirism is at work. Upon meeting Jessica, the psychic investigator and his clairvoyant partner become convinced that despite her charming manner there is "evil within her." Zaida the witch possesses her, sucking the life blood out of Davenant.

Aylmer Vance breaks the spell of the vampire while Davenant sleeps. "When his eyes were opened … he saw her as she was—a hideous phantom of the corruption of the ages." Now there is one step left to remove Jessica's curse—the destruction of Blackwick Castle.

Aylmer Vance short stories by Alice and Claude Askew: "The Invader" (July 4, 1914); "The Stranger" (July 11, 1914); "Lady Greensleeves" (July 18, 1914); "The Unquenchable Fire" (July 25, 1914); "The Boy from Blackstock" (August 8, 1914); "The Insoluble Bond" (August 15, 1914); "The Fear" (August 22, 1914).

Baffled (1973) [Telefilm]

Premiere: January 30, 1973; Main Cast: Leonard Nimoy as Tom Kovack, Susan Hampshire as Michele Brent, Rachel Roberts as Mrs. Farrady, Vera Miles as Andrea Glenn, Jewel Branch as Jennifer Glenn, Valerie Taylor as Louise Sanford, Ray Brooks as George Tracewell, Angharad Rees as Peggy Tracewell; Executive Producer: Norman Felton; Teleplay: Theodore Apstein; Director: Philip Leacock; 98 min.; Arena Productions-ITC; Color.

U.S. race car driver Tom Kovack teams up with occult expert Michele Brent to investigate his menacing visions of Wyndham Manor in Devon, England.

Baffled (1973), **starring Leonard Nimoy as Tom Kovack and Susan Hampshire as Michele Brent (ITC).**

The Baker Street Peculiars [Comic book]

Story: Roger Langridge; Art: Andy Hirsch; 4-issue mini-series; First publication: March 2016; Publisher: Boom! Studios.

1933. London Town. A giant statue of a lion comes to life in Trafalgar Square creating havoc. Young rookie detectives Molly, Rajani, Humphry and Wellington the dog are recruited by Sherlock Holmes to solve the mystery of the Cockney Golem.

Batman: Damned [Comic book]

First publication: November 2018: Story: Brian Azzarello; Art: Lee Bermejo; Publisher: DC Comics.

Occult detective **John Constantine** helps Batman uncover the truth of who murdered The Joker in this supernatural mystery also featuring Deadman.

Created by writer Bob Kane and artist Bill Finger for *Detective Comics* #27 (May 1939) Batman is a master detective who often operates outside of the law as a vigilante. While most of his adventures involve inmates from Arkham Asylum or demented villains he does encounter occult adversaries including Ra's al Ghul who has prolonged his life by centuries thanks to the life restoring Lazarus Pits. Another foe named Deacon Blackfire has undergone various incarnations including crazed cult leader, reanimated corpse, evangelist who controls a demonic army, and an avenging ghost. Batman and alter-ego Bruce Wayne's home base of operations Gotham City has an occult heritage originating with the Founding Fathers and a trapped bat-demon. The warlock Doctor Gotham who was entombed for centuries under the land that is now Gotham City embodies the cursed nature of the city today.

See: **Gotham**

Baylor's Guide to Dreadful Dreams
[Beyond Baylor Book #2] [Juvenile book]

Author: Robert Imfeld; First publication: New York: Aladdin, 2017.

Thirteen-year-old boy medium Baylor Bosco can enter his own dreams and those of other people thanks to a magical amulet.

Entering the dream world through the portal known as Loved One's Lane Baylor comes across two teenagers lost at sea. But where are they located in the waking world? Baylor must solve the puzzle while avoiding the demonic Lost Souls spirits.

Baylor's Guide to the Other Side [Beyond Baylor Book #1] [Juvenile book]

Author: Robert Imfeld; First publication: New York: Aladdin, 2017.

Baylor Bosco is a thirteen-year-old medium with a gift for conversing with ghosts. That gift comes in handy when his twin sister Kristina happens to be a ghost. Together they connect the departed with their loved ones. But on Halloween Kristina goes missing and a man covered in a sheet with brown buckle shoes peeking out seems to hold the link to her disappearance.

The Beetle: A Mystery [Novel]

Author: Richard Marsh; Publisher: London: Skeffington, 1897.

On a trip to Egypt, Paul Lessingham comes under the influence of a beautiful 'woman of the songs' and is taken prisoner in a cult that worships the god Isis. In the cult he experiences all manner of ghastly events including torture, human sacrifice and a strange shape-shifting creature. "I found myself confronting a monstrous beetle,–a huge writhing creation of some wild nightmare. At first the creature stood as high as I did. But, as I stared at it in stupefied amazement,–as you may easily imagine,–the thing dwindled while I gazed … a stark raving madman for the nonce, I fled as if all the fiends in hell were at my heels."

The strange creature follows Lessingham to London on a reign of terror and revenge. Lessingham, now a successful politician, hires private detective Augustus Champnell to find Marjorie Lindon—a woman both Lessingham and inventor Sydney Atherton loves. Lindon has been abducted by the so-called Beetle who Lessingham concludes is "a creature born neither of God nor man."

Bishaash (2010) [TV series; Bangladesh-UK]

Premiere: October 16, 2010; Main Cast: Babu Md. Shaidul Islam Molla as Abir Zaman, Arabi Rahman as Laboni Zaman, Rahmat Ali as Ferdous. Shama Rahman as Zara Rahman, Ahmed Rubel as Abdul Ali, Shatabdi Wadud as Alien; Executive Producer: David Prosser; 24 × 25 min.; BBC World Service Trust; Bangladesh Television (Btv); Zee TV; Color.

Following the death of her grandfather a young British-Bangladeshi woman based in London discovers she has inherited co-ownership of an antique store in Dhaka and an ancient pendant. Observing her grandfather's final wish Zara Rahman relocates to Old Dhaka to claim her inheritance and meets co-owner Abir Zaman. Her life takes a magical turn when she is introduced to Abir's cousin Laboni and Uncle Ferdous who run a supernatural detective agency. Now she joins a quest to find treasure while being pursued by supernatural entities.

SEASON ONE

Treasure: Part 1 (1:01); *Treasure: Part 2* (1:02); *Treasure: Part 3* (1:03); *Heartland: Part 1* (1:04); *Heartland: Part 2* (1:05); *Love Never Dies: Part 1* (1:06); *Love Never Dies: Part 2* (1:07); *Twilight: Part 1* (1:08); *Twilight: Part 2* (1:09); *In/Compatible: Part 1* (1:10); *In/Compatible: Part 2* (1:11); *Antique Shop* (1:12); *London Calling: Part 1* (1:13); *London Calling: Part 2* (1:14); *Janmo Janmantor: Part 1* (1:15); *Janmo Janmantor: Part 2* (1:16); *Over and Over Again: Part 1* (1:17); *Over and Over Again: Part 2* (1:18); *Out of Control* (1:19); *Lies I Need to Believe* (1:20); *Revelations* (1:21); *The Choice* (1:22); *Family: Part 1* (1:23); *Family: Part 2* (1:24).

Bix Barton [Comic book character; UK]

First appearance: *2000 AD* (#663–668), 1990; Creators: Peter Milligan, Jim McCarthy; Publisher: Fleetway; Rebellion Developments.

In this tongue-in-cheek comic strip Bix Barton is the only employee of Her Majesty's Government's Department of the Irrational. Using his Sherlock Holmes like skills he solves cases of the "rum and uncanny" and weird and supernatural. A nutrient solution suspends his aging process. His assistant is the talking walking stick Michael Cane.

Black Alibi [Novel]

Author: Cornell Woolrich; First publication: New York: Simon & Schuster, 1942.

Kiki Walker, a "run-of-the-mill roadhouse entertainer from Detroit" is enjoying the most successful period of her career at the Casino Excelsior. Her vivid red hair is an attraction in the South American town of Ciudad Real. Plus, the antics of her press agent Jerry Manning have attracted the public's attention. Now Manning is planning his most outlandish stunt to date for Walker. Parading "along the Alemada" with a jaguar on a leash.

But when Walker stops at a café the animal is spooked by photographer's flashbulbs and escapes. Soon after the jaguar's escape young women are found mauled to death. But who is responsible? The police point to the obvious, but Manning is convinced the deaths are caused by human hands. But what kind of human could mimic the mauling of a jaguar?

See: ***The Leopard Man***

Black Butler a.k.a. ***Kuroshitsuji*** (2008) [Anime; Manga; Japan]

Premiere: October 2, 2008; Voice Cast: Daisuke Ono as Sebastian Michaelis, Maaya Sakamoto as Ciel Phantomhive, Jun Fukuyama as Grell Sutcliff, Romi Park as Madam Red, Akiko Yajima as Angela, Emiri Kato as Meirin, Hiroki Touchi as Bard, Yuuki Kaji as Finny, Shuni Fujimura as Tanaka, Koji Yusa as Lau, Junichi Suwabe as Undertaker, Hisayoshi Suganuma as Fred Abberline, Yukari Tamura as Elizabeth Ethel Cordelia Midford, Ayako Kawasumi as Queen Victoria; Executive Producers: Hideo Katsumata, Masuo Ueda; Story: Mari Okada, Hiroyuki Yoshino, Yuka Yamada; Directors: Toshiya Shinohara, Hirofumi Ogura; 36 × 24 min.; A-1 Pictures; Aniplex; MOVIC; Hakuhodo DY Partners; Square Enix; MBS; Yomiko Advertising Inc.; Color.

12-year-old orphan Lord Ciel Phantomhive has made a Faustian pact with Sebastian Michaelis to avenge the murder of his parents in return for his soul. While searching for the murderers Ciel is also employed by Queen Victoria as one of the "Queen's Watchdogs" solving crime in London with his demon butler Sebastian. One such case involves Jack the Ripper who is revealed to be two people. The supernatural grim reaper Grell Sutcliff and Madam Red.

SEASON ONE

His Butler, Able (1:01); *His Butler, Strongest* (1:02); *His Butler, Omnipotent* (1:03); *His Butler, Capricious* (1:04); *His Butler, Chance Encounter* (1:05); *His Butler, At the Funeral* (1:06); *His Butler, Merrymaking* (1:07); *His Butler, Training* (1:08); *His Butler, a Phantasm* (1:09); *His Butler, On Ice* (1:10); *His Butler, However You Please* (1:11); *His Butler, Lonely* (1:12); *His Butler, Dependent* (1:13); *His Butler, Unusually talented* (1:14); *His Butler, Competes* (1:15); *His Butler, Alone* (1:16); *His Butler, Dedicates* (1:17); *His Butler, Transfer* (1:18); *His Butler, Imprisonment* (1:19); *His Butler, Escape* (1:20); *His Butler, Servants* (1:21); *His Butler, Cancel* (1:22); *His Butler, On Fire* (1:23); *His Butler, Surging* (1:24).

SEASON TWO

Clawed Butler (1:01); *Solo Butler* (1:02); *Wench Butler* (1:03); *Terrorist Butler* (1:04); *Beacon Butler* (1:05); *Bedewed Butler* (1:06); *Deathly Butler* (1:07); *Divulging Butler* (1:08); *Hollow Butler* (1:09); *Zero Butler* (1:10); *Crossroads Butler* (1:11); *Black Butler* (1:12).

[Manga] First publication: *Monthly GFantasy* (September 16, 2006); Story: Yana Toboso; Publisher: Square Enix.

The manga that inspired the anime TV series has run to 27-volumes.

Black Butler: Book of the Atlantic [Anime; Japan]

Premiere: January 21, 2017; Voice Cast: Daisuke Ono as Sebastian Michaelis, Maaya Sakamoto as Ciel Phantomhive, Jun Fukuyama as Grell Sutcliff, Junichi Suwabe as Undertaker, Takuma Terashima as Snake, Emiri Kato as Mey-Rin, Yukari Tamura as Elizabeth Midford, Romi Park as Angelina Durless, Yuki Kaji as Finnian, Noriaki Sugiyama as William T. Spears; Producer: Christopher Sabat; Screenplay: Hiroyuki Yoshino; Director: Noriyuki Abe; 110 min.; A-1 Pictures; Aniplex; Square Enix; Color.

This feature-length animated film features Earl Ciel Phantomhive and his demon butler Sebastian Michaelis boarding a luxury liner to investigate reports of resurrected bodies.

Black Butler: Book of Circus (2014) [Anime; Japan]

Premiere: July 10, 2014; Voice Cast: Daisuke Ono as Sebastian Michaelis, Maaya Sakamoto as Ciel Phantomhive, Ayahi Takagaki as Doll, Mamoru Miyano as Joker, Nobuhiko Okamoto as Dagger, Takuma Terashima as Snake, Yuko Kaida as Beast, Jun Fukuyama as Grell Sutcliff, Junichi Suwabe as Undertaker, Hisayoshi Suganuma as Fred Abberline, Hiromi Seta as Queen Victoria; Animation Producer: Kenshiro Yamada; Story: Hiroyuki Yoshino, Ichiro Okouchi, Yana Toboso, Yuka Miyata; Director: Noriyuki Abe; 10 × 24 min.; A-1 Pictures; Aniplex; Asmik Ace Entertainment Inc.; MOVIC; Hakuhodo DY Partners; Kuroshitsuji Project; Square Enix; DeNa; MBS; Color.

In a letter to Lord Ciel Phantomhive, Queen Victoria informs him of missing children taken at the dead of night from various towns visited by Noah's Ark Circus. Ciel and his demon butler Sebastian Michaelis join the circus to uncover the mystery and encounter familiar figures from the past.

Season One

His Butler, Presenting (1:01); *His Butler, Taking the Stage* (1:02); *His Butler, Employed* (1:03); *His Butler, Co-worker* (1:04); *His Butler, Takes Flight* (1:05); *His Butler, Liaison* (1:06); *His Butler, Careful Trending* (1:07); *His Butler, Sneering* (1:08); *His Butler, Serene* (1:09); *His Butler, Fulfilling His Duty* (1:10).

Black Butler: Book of Murder (2014) [OAV; Japan]

Premiere: October 25, 2014; Voice Cast: Daisuke Ono as Sebastian Michaelis, Maaya Sakamoto as Ciel Phantomhive, Takuma Terashima as Snake, Junichi Suwabe as Undertaker, Shintaro Asanuma as Sir Arthur Conan Doyle, Emiri Kato as Mey-Rin, Hiroki Touchi as Baldroy, Hiroki Yasumoto as Agni, Koji Yusa as Lau, Ryohei Kimura as Charles Grey, Yukari Tamura as Elizabeth Midford, Sayuri Yahagi as Ran-Mao; Creator: Yana Toboso; Story: Hiroyuki Yoshino; Animation Directors: Chisato Kawaguchi, Minako Shiba; Director: Noriyuki Abe; 2 × 58 min.; A-1 Pictures; Aniplex; Asmik Ace Entertainment Inc.; MOVIC; Hakuhodo DY Partners; Kuroshitsuji Project; Square Enix; DeNa; MBS; Color.

During an extravagant dinner party held at the request of Queen Victoria one of the high-profile guests is murdered. Earl Ciel Phantomhive is chief suspect as more murders follow and even demon butler Sebastian Michaelis isn't safe from danger.

Episodes

Book of Murder Part 1; *Book of Murder Part 2*.

Black House [Novel]

Authors: Stephen King, Peter Straub; First publication: New York: Random House, 2001.

Retired Los Angeles homicide detective Jack Sawyer is coerced out of retirement to help the local Coulee County, Wisconsin police chief investigate a brutal child killer and cannibal dubbed "The Fisherman." Three children are dead and a fourth abducted but still alive in the Black House. The child must be rescued in a house of supernatural entities from a killer playing host to an evil unearthly force. Sawyer's time as a child spent in a world known as "The Territories" described in King and Straub's novel *The Talisman*, provides a link to the killer.

Black Magic (1944) [Film]

Premiere: August 19, 1944: Main Cast: Sidney Toler as Charlie Chan, Mantan Moreland as Birmingham Brown, Jacqueline deWit as Justine Bonner, Helen Beverley as Norma Duncan/Nancy Wood, Richard Gordon as William Bonner; Frances Chan as Frances Chan, Joseph Crehan as Police Sgt. Matthews, Ralph Peters as Officer Rafferty, Helen Beverley as Norma Duncan/Nancy Wood, Geraldine Wall as Harriet Green, Harry Depp as Charles Edwards, Frank Jaquet as Hamlin; Charles Jordan as Tom Starkey, Claudia Dell as Vera Starkey; Producers: Philip N. Krasne, James S. Burkett; Screenplay: George Callahan; based on characters created by Earl Derr Biggers; Director: Phil Rosen; 67 min.; Monogram Pictures Corp.; B/W.

Charlie Chan's planned vacation to Honolulu is placed on hold as he investigates the murder of medium William Bonner during a séance. The problem facing Chan is no gun can be found at the scene of the murder and no bullet can be found in Bonner's body. Matters are further complicated when Justine Bonner jumps to her death from a skyscraper while under a trance. An automobile accident in London on the night of October 5, 1935, is key to the motive for the murders.

Black Magic Woman (A Morris and Chastain Investigation #1)

Author: Justin Gustainis; First publication: Oxford UK: Solaris, 2008.

Occult investigators Quincey Morris and white witch Libby Chastain must put an end to an inherited family curse dating back to the killing of a witch in Salem over 400 years ago.

Book series: *Black Magic Woman* (2008); *Evil Ways* (2009); *Sympathy for the Devil* (2011); *Play with Fire and Midnight at the Oasis* (2012); *Strange Magic* (2015).

Bless the Child (2000) [Film; U.S./Germany]

Premiere: August 11, 2000; Main Cast: Kim Basinger as Maggie O'Connor, Jimmy Smits as Agent John Travis, Holliston Coleman as Cody O'Connor, Rufus Sewell as Eric Stark, Angela Bettis as Jenna O'Connor, Christina Ricci as Cheri Post, Michael Gaston as Detective Frank Bugatti, Lumi Cavazos as Sister Rosa, Dimitraaa Arlys as Dahyna, Eugene Lipinski as Stuart, Anne Betancourt as Maria, Ian Holm as the Reverend Grissom, Helen Stenborg as Sister Joseph; Executive Producers: Bruce Davey, Lis Kern, Robert Rehme; Screenplay: Tom Rickman, Clifford Green, Ellen Green; Based on the novel by Cathy Cash Spellman; Director: Chuck Russell; 107 min.; Paramount Pictures. Icon Productions; Munich Film Partners & Company (MFP) BTC Productions; Color.

Autistic six-year-old Cody O'Connor is no normal girl. She can restore life to a dead bird. When she is kidnapped by the mother who abandoned her as a baby and her husband Eric Stark, FBI agent John Travis, a specialist in occult crime is drawn to the case. Cody is the latest in a series of child abductions who all share the same birth-date. Together with Cody's guardian Maggie O'Connor they must find the girl before the Satanic cult that now holds Cody gains control of her supernatural powers.

Blood Alone [Manga; Japan]

First publication: April 21, 2004; Story & Art: Masayuki Takano; Publisher: Mediaworks, Kodansha.

Kuroe Kurose is a private investigator, author and former vampire hunter, whose investigative work often results in confrontations with vampires and the undead. He lives with a young girl named Misaki Minato, who recently became a vampire. Misaki has feelings for Kuroe and believes the only way to protect him from the creatures he encounters during his investigations is to turn him into a vampire.

Blood Rites (The Dresden Files Book #6)

Author: Jim Butcher; Publisher: New York: Roc, 2004.

Chicago wizard Harry Dresden goes undercover on the set of an adult film to investigate a producer's alleged curse and the untimely deaths of the females around him.

See: **Dead Beat**

Blood Ties (2007) [TV series; Canada]

Premiere: March 11, 2007; Main Cast: Christina Cox as Victoria "Vicki" Nelson, Kyle Schmid as Henry Fitzroy, Dylan Neal as Mike Celluci, Gina Holden as Coreen Fennel, Francoise Yip as Kate Lam, Nimet Kanji as Dr. Rajan Mohadevan, Keith Dallas as Dave Graham, Eileen Peddle as Crowley; Executive Producers: Marshall Kesten, Peter Mohan, Kirk Shaw, Randall H. Zalken, Stanton W. Kamens; 22 × 45 min.; Insight Film Studios; Chum Television; Lifetime Television; Color.

With her eyesight failing Vicki Nelson leaves the Toronto Police to become a private investigator. But she soon finds herself with a problem. She's still in love with a cop and has an unnatural desire for her new partner Henry Fitzroy. The illegitimate son of Henry VIII who has survived and kept his handsome looks for 470-years as a vampire. Promoted as "a supernatural crime series that pits demons against lovers with a little help from the undead."

Season One

Blood Price: Part One (1:01); *Blood Price: Part Two* (1:02); *Bad JuJu* (1:03); *Gifted* (1:04); *Deadly Departed* (1:05); *Love Hurts* (1:06); *Heart of Ice* (1:07); *Heart of Fire* (1:08); *Stone Cold* (1:09); *Necrodrome* (1:10); *Post-Partum* (1:11); *Norman* (1:12).

Season Two

D.O.A. (2:01); *Wild Blood* (2:02); *5:55* (2:03); *Bugged* (2:04); *The Devil You Know* (2:05); *Drawn and Quartered* (2:06); *Wrapped* (2:07); *The Good, the Bad and the Ugly* (2:08); *We'll Meet Again* (2:09); *Deep Dark* (2:10).

Bookburners [Novel; Serial]

Authors: Max Gladstone, Margaret Dunlap, Mur Lafferty, Brian Francis Slattery, Andrea Phillips, Amal El-Mohtar; First publication: Serial Box, 2015.

Detective Sal Brooks travels the world working for Team Three of the Societas Librorum Occultorum—a Vatican-backed black-ops magic hunting team tracking dangerous magic books and artifacts.

Originally published online by Serial Box as weekly written episodes, divided into seasons, that take approximately 42-minutes each to read. A team of writers collaborate to create an entire story including plot lines and character arcs. Various authors then write individual episodes overseen by lead writers and editors.

Season One

Badge, Book ad Candle (1:01); *Anywhere But Here* (1:02); *Fair Weather* (1:03); *A Sorcerer's Apprentice* (1:04); *The Market Arcanum* (1:05); *Big Sky* (1:06); *Now and Then* (1:07); *Under My Skin* (1:08); *Ancient Wonders* (1:09); *Shore Leave* (1:10); *Codex Umbra* (1:11); *Puppets* (1:12); *Keeping Friends Close* (1:13); *An Excellent Day for an Exorcism* (1:14); *Things Lost* (1:15); *Siege* (1:16).

Season Two

Creepy Town (2:01); *Webs* (2:02); *Mistakes Were Made* (2:03); *Ghosts* (2:04); *Debtor's Prison* (2:05); *Incognita* (2:06); *Fire and Ice* (2:07); *Present Infinity* (2:08); *The Village* (2:09); *One With the World* (2:10); *Shock and Awe* (2:11); *Coming Home* (2:12); *The End of the Day* (2:13).

Season Three

Bubbles of Earth (3:01); *Faces of the Beast* (3:02); *Hard Bargain* (3:03); *All in a Day's Work* (3:04); *Time Capsule* (3:05); (3:06); *Oracle Bones* (3:07); *Making Amends* (3:08); *Homecoming* (3:09); *Into the Woods* (3:10); *Crossing Over* (3:11); *Broken Vessels* (3:12); *Live in London* (3:13).

Season Four

Body Problems (4:01); *The Blood-Dimmed Tide* (4:02); *Alexander Norse* (4:03); *Man about Town* (4:04); *Hell Gate Bridge* (4:05); *O'er the Deep Blue Sea* (4:06); *Wax* (4:07); *A Message Across Worlds* (4:08); *Eating Words* (4:09); *Alexandria Leaving* (4:10).

Border Patrol (2000) [Telefilm]

Premiere: March 24, 2000; Main Cast: Michael DeLorenzo as Detective Freddie Chavez, Clayton Rohner as Cal Newman, Anthony Wong as Captain Takeyama, Lewis Fitz-Gerald as Dr. Roderick Helms, Mary Elkins as Janet Helms, Bianca Nacson as Maureen Ryder. Jacqueline Graham as Emily Wells, Tony Harvey as Hieronymous, Michael Scott as Martin Eldridge, Don Batte as Detective Copeland; Executive Producer: Ian Valentine; Story: Miguel Tejada-Flores; Director: Mark Haber; 89 min; Wilshire Court Productions; United Paramount Network (UPN); Color.

The Border Patrol applies the rule of law between the living and the dead. Supernatural law enforcer Cal Newman finds himself in Purgatory where he attempts to stop a serial killer from returning to the land of the living with the help of mortal detective Freddie Chavez.

The Borderlands a.k.a. Final Prayer (2013) [Film; UK]

Premiere: June 24, 2013; Main Cast: Gordon Kennedy as Deacon, Robin Hill as Gray, Patrick Godfrey as Father Calvino, Aidan McArdle as Mark, Marcus Cunningham as Mr. Proudley, Sarah Amis as Mrs. Proudley, Kevin Johnson as Jim, Luke Neal as Father Crellick; Producers: Jennifer Handorf, Jezz Vernon; Screenplay-Director: Elliot Goldner; 89 min.; Metrodome Distribution; Color.

In the 13th century a Catholic church was built in a remote English village. Strange happenings occurred that nobody could explain. Now the Vatican has sent investigators to the church to disprove the centuries old paranormal activity. But the team uncover a terrible secret. Evil lies underneath the church and has returned.

Bright (2017) [Film]

Premiere: December 22, 2017; Main Cast: Will Smith as Detective Daryl Ward, Joel Edgerton as Nick Jakoby, Noomi Rapace as Leilah, Edgar Ramirez as Kandomere, Lucy Fry as Tikka, Veronica Ngo as Tien, Alex Meraz as Serafin, Happy Anderson as Montehugh, Margaret Cho as Sergeant Ching, Ike Barinholtz as Pollard, Jay Hernandez as Rodriguez, Brad William Henke as Dorghu; Executive Producers: Sarah Bowen, Pauline Fischer, Max Landis, Adam Merims, Sarah Bremner; Story: Max Landis; Director: David Ayer; 117 min.; Clubhouse Pictures (II); Overbrook Entertainment; Netflix; Color.

In an alternate Los Angeles mystical orcs, elves and fairies live alongside humans. LAPD officer Daryl Ward finds himself working with Nick Jacoby, the first Orc cop. Together they must find a magical wand that grants wishes, and protect a female elf from those who want the wand for evil purposes.

Brimstone (1998) [TV series]

Premiere: October 23, 1998; Main Cast: Peter Horton as Ezekiel Stone, John Glover as The Devil, Lori Petty as Max, Teri Polo as Ashur Badaktu, Maria Costa as Teresita, Albert Hall as Father Horn, Scott Lawrence as Detective Fraker; Executive Producers: Charles Grant Craig, Ethan Reiff, Cyrus Voris; Creators: Ethan Reiff, Cyrus Voris; 13 × 45 min.; BEI Brimstone; Warner Bros. Television; Fox Network; Color.

Former cop Ezekiel Stone tracked down the man who raped his wife and killed him in cold blood. Two months later Stone was killed by a petty thief and sentenced to Hell. Now he is back on Earth on a mission from the Devil. 113 of the vilest creatures to have roamed the Earth have escaped from Hell. Stone must find them and send them back. To do this he must destroy the windows to their souls—their eyes. But the Devil warns Stone that what he should fear most is losing his second chance at redemption. But can anyone trust the Devil?

Season One

Pilot (1:01); *Heat* (1:02); *Encore* (1:03); *Repentance* (1:04); *Poem* (1:05); *Executioner* (1:06); *Slayer* (1:07); *Ashes* (1:08); *Lovers* (1:09); *Carrier* (1:10); *Faces*(1:11); *It's a Helluva Life* (1:12); *Mourning After* (1:13).

B.R.P.D.: 1946 [Comic book]

First publication: January 2008; Five-issue mini-series; Story: Mike Mignola, Joshua Dysart; Art: Paul Azaceta; Publisher: Dark Horse Comics.

Amid the ruins of post–World War II Berlin, occult investigator Professor Trevor Bruttenholm, and his demon guardian **Hellboy**, form the Bureau for Paranormal Research and Defense. It's first mission to investigate the Nazi Occult Bureau's, Project Vampir Sturm.

Followed by *B.R.P.D.: 1947* (November 2009) and *B.R.P.D.: 1948* (October 2012).

Buffy the Vampire Slayer [Film; TV series]

[Film] Premiere: July 31, 1992; Main Cast: Kristy Swanson as Buffy Summers, Luke Perry as Oliver Pike, Donald Sutherland as Merrick Jamison-Smythe, Paul Reubens as Amilyn/Lefty, Rutger Hauer as Lothos, Michele Abrams as Jennifer, Hilary Swank as Kimberly Hannah, David Arquette as Benny Jacks, Stephen Root as Gary Murray, Randall Batinkoff as Jeffrey, Natasha Gregson Wagner as Cassandra, Paris Vaughn as Nicole "Niki," Candy Clark as Buffy's Mom; Executive Producers: Carol Baum, Sandy Gallin, Franz Rubel Kuzui; Story:

Joss Whedon; Director: Franz Rubel Kuzui; 86 min.; Twentieth Century–Fox; Sandollar; Kuzui Enterprises; Color.

When Merrick the Watcher informs cheerleader Buffy Summers, she is the Chosen One she ignores him until he describes her recurring dream. It takes a romantic friendship with Oliver Pike to spark Buffy's interest in slaying vampires.

[TV series] Premiere: March 10, 1997; Main Cast: Sarah Michelle Gellar as Buffy Summers/Faith, Nicholas Brendon as Xander Harris, Alyson Hannigan as Willow Rosenberg, Anthony Head as Rupert Giles, James Marsters as Spike, Emma Caulfield Ford as Anya, Michelle Trachtenberg as Dawn Summers, David Boreanaz as Angel, Charisma Carpenter as Cordelia Chase, Kristine Sutherland as Joyce Summers; Executive Producers: Fran Rubel Kuzui, Kaz Kuzui, Joss Whedon, Gail Berman, Sandy Gallin, Marti Noxon; Creator: Joss Whedon; 144 × 44 min.; Mutant Enemy; Kuzui Enterprises; Sandollar Television; 20th Century–Fox Television; WB Television Network; United Paramount Network (UPN); Color.

Buffy Summers has reluctantly inherited the title of "The Chosen One" destined to slay vampires, demons and the forces of darkness. Helping her in her calling are "The Scooby Gang" or "Scoobies" initially comprising of her friends from Sunningdale High School, Xander Harris and Willow Rosenberg and her Watcher Rupert Giles. Although they take part in detective work, they work in secret and don't encourage clients. Their work consists of patrolling the streets or consulting with occult expert Rupert Giles who also trains Buffy Summers to fight demons and vampires.

Season One

Welcome to the Hellmouth (1:01); *The Harvest* (1:02); *Witch* (1:03); *Teacher's Pet* (1:04); *Never Kill a Boy on the First Date* (1:05); *The Pack* (1:06); *Angel* (1:07); *I, Robot…. You, Jane* (1:08); *The Puppet Show* (1:09); *Nightmares* (1:10); *Out of Mind, Out of Sight* (1:11); *Prophecy Girl* (1:12).

Season Two

When She Was Bad (2:01); *Some Assembly Required* (2:02); *School Hard* (2:03); *Inca Mummy Girl* (2:04); *Reptile Boy* (2:05); *Halloween* (2:06); *Lie to Me* (2:07); *The Dark Age* (2:08); *What's My Line?: Part 1* (2:09); *What's My Line?: Part 2* (2:10); *Ted* (2:11); *Bad Eggs* (2:12); *Surprise* (2:13); *Innocence* (2:14); *Phases* (2:15); *Bewitched, Bothered, Bewildered* (2:16); *Passion* (2:17); *Killed by Death* (2:18); *I Only Have Eyes for You* (2:19); *Go Fish* (2:20); *Becoming: Part 1* (2:21); *Becoming: Part 2* (2:22).

Season Three

Anne (3:01); *Dead Man's Party* (3:02); *Faith, Hope & Trick* (3:03); *Beauty and the Beasts* (3:04); *Homecoming* (3:05); *Band Candy* (3:06); *Revelations* (3:07); *Lovers Walk* (3:08); *The Wish* (3:09); *Amends* (3:10); *Gingerbread* (3:11); *Helpless* (3:12); *The Zeppo* (3:13); *Bad Girls* (3:14); *Consequences* (3:15); *Doppelgangland* (3:16); *Enemies* (3:17); *Earshot* (3:18); *Choices* (3:19); *The Prom* (3:20); *Graduation Day: Part 1* (3:21); *Graduation Day: Part 2* (3:22).

Season Four

The Freshman (4:01); *Living Conditions* (4:02); *The Harsh Light of Day* (4:03); *Fear Itself* (4:04); *Beer Bad* (4:05); *Wild at Heart* (4:06); *The Initiative* (4:07); *Pangs* (4:08); *Something Blue* (4:09); *Hush* (4:10); *Doomed* (4:11); *A New Man* (4:12); *The I in Team* (4:13); *Goodbye Iowa* (4:14); *This Year's Girl* (4:15); *Who Are You?* (4:16); *Superstar* (4:17); *where the Wild Things Are* (4:18); *New Moon Rising* (4:19); *The Yoko Factor* (4:20); *The Primeval* (4:21); *Restless* (4:22).

Season Five

Buffy vs. Dracula (5:01); *Real Me* (5:02); *The Replacement* (5:03); *Out of My Mind* (5:04); *No Place Like Home* (5:05); *Family* (5:06); *Fool for Love* (5:07); *Shadow* (5:08); *Listening to Fear* (5:09); *Into the Woods* (5:10); *Triangle* (5:11); *Checkpoint* (5:12); *Blood Ties* (5:13); *Crush* (5:14); *I Was Made to Love You* (5:15); *The Body* (5:16); *Forever* (5:17); *Intervention* (5:18); *Tough Love* (5:19); *Spiral* (5:20); *The Weight of the World* (5:21); *The Gift* (5:22).

Season Six

Bargaining: Part 1 (6:01); *Bargaining: Part 2* (6:02); *After Life* (6:03); *Flooded* (6:04); *Life*

Serial (6:05); *All the Way* (6:06); *Once More, with Feeling* (6:07); *Tabula Rasa* (6:08); *Smashed* (6:09); *Wrecked* (6:10); *Gone* (6:11); *Doublemeat Palace* (6:12); *Dead Things* (6:13); *Older and Far Away* (6:14); *As You Were* (6:15); *Hell's Bells* (6:16); *Normal Again* (6:17); *Entropy* (6:18); *Seeing Red* (6:19); *Villains* (6:20); *Two to Go* (6:21); *Grave* (6:22).

Season Seven

Lessons (7:01); *Beneath You* (7:02); *Same Time, Same Place* (7:03); *Help* (7:04); *Selfless* (7:05); *Him* (7:06); *Conversations with Dead People* (7:07); *Sleeper* (7:08); *Never Leave Me* (7:09); *Bring on the Night* (7:10); *Showtime* (7:11); *Potential* (7:12); *The Killer in Me* (7:13); *First Date* (7:14); *Get It Done* (7:15); *Storyteller* (7:16); *Lies My Parents Told Me* (7:17); *Dirty Girls* (7:18); *Empty Places* (7:19); *Touched* (7:20); *End of Days* (7:21); *Chosen* (7:22).

See: ***Angel***

Buffy the Vampire Slayer (1996), which starred David Boreanaz as Angel and Sarah Michelle Gellar as Buffy Summers (20th Century–Fox-WB-UPN).

Bureau 13: Stalking the Night Fantastic
[Role-playing game]

Release date: 1983; Designers: Richard Tucholka, Chris Beiting, Robert Sadler; System: Custom/d20; Publisher: Tri Tac Games.

Under cover of the Civil War the U.S. government created a secret agency dealing with ancient magic and supernatural threats. In the present-day Bureau 13 remains top secret in a society that dismisses the supernatural as superstition. Agents of Bureau 13, in the manner of a detective agency, investigate the paranormal across America.

The player is an agent for the elite Bureau 13, tracking the supernatural menace in all its forms, choosing to preserve or destroy it with the best weapons and technology available.

A *Bureau 13* video game based on the RPG was released in 1995 by GameTek.

The Burrowers Beneath [Novel]

Author: Brian Lumley; First publication: New York: Daw Books, 1974.

Paranormal investigator Titus Crow and his Dr. Watson influenced companion Henri-Laurent de Marigny explore a series of underground disturbances that have their roots in a primordial evil dating back to the time before mankind existed.

An alien race known as the Elder Gods trapped the evil monstrosities known as the Great Old Ones in various locales on Earth. Now millennia later they await their chance for revenge. Shudde-M'ell and its evil minions have escaped and only Titus Crow can stop them.

The Titus Crow series of books lean heavily on the Cthulhu Mythos created by H.P. Lovecraft.

Book series: *The Burrowers Beneath* (1974); *The Transition of Titus Crow* (1975); *The Clock of Dreams* (1978); *Spawn of the Winds* (1978); *In the Moons of Borea* (1979); *Elysia* (1989).

Short story collection: *The Compleat Crow* (1987).

Caballistics Inc. [Comic strip; UK]

First appearance: *2000 A.D.* #1322

(January 2003); Story: Gordon Rennie; Art: Dom Reardon; Publisher: Rebellion Developments.

During World War II the British Ministry of Defense forms Department Q to counter Nazi Germany's occult warfare division, Sonderkommando Thule. Department Q is disbanded after the war and reformed by millionaire rock star Ethan Kostabi as the private agency Caballistics Inc. Its members investigate paranormal threats, and at times are forced to break the agreement between the British Crown and Hell known as The Accord.

The *2000 A.D.* strip has been collected in the graphic novels *Caballistics Inc. #1: Hell on Earth* (2006), *Caballistics Inc. #2: Better the Devil* (2009), *Caballistics Inc.: Creepshow* (2014) and *The Complete Cabbalistic Inc.* (2019).

See: **Harry Absalom**

"The Call of Cthulhu" [Short story; Film]
Author: H.P. Lovecraft; First publication: *Weird Tales* (February 1928).

Francis Wayland Thurston recounts the notes of his late great uncle Professor George Gammell Argyll. Inspector of Police John Raymond Legrasse, "a commonplace-looking middle-aged man" has traveled from New Orleans to St. Louis with "a grotesque, repulsive, and apparently very ancient stone statuette" whose origins he cannot determine. It had been captured some months earlier in the wooded swamps of New Orleans during a raid on an apparent voodoo meeting.

Inspector Legrasse seeks clarification on the fetish from members of the American Archaeological Society. Professor William Channing Webb links the fetish to a devil worshipping cult he encountered in West Greenland. The rituals of the Louisiana swamp priests and the Greenland cultists both contain the words, "In this house at R'lyeh dead Cthulhu waits dreaming."

The carved idol is the great priest Cthulhu who is waiting to rise again "from his dark house in the mighty city of R'lyeh under the water … and bring the earth again under its sway."

2. [Film] Premiere: October 7, 2005; Main Cast: Ralph Lucas as Professor Angell, David Mersault as Inspector Legrasse, Matt Foyer as The Man, John Bolen as The Listener, Chad Fifer as Henry Wilcox, John Klemantaski as Prof. Bell, Jason Owens as Prof. Quintana, D. Grigsby Poland as Prof. Tutchton, Barry Lynch as Prof. Webb, Dan Novy as Shaman/Cultist; Producers: Sean Branney, Andrew Leman; Adapted from the H.P. Lovecraft short story by Sean Branney; Director: Andrew Leman; 47 min.; H.P. Lovecraft Historical Society (HPLH); Silent; b/w.

Adaptation of the H.P. Lovecraft story in the style of a silent movie.

Call of Cthulhu: Dark Corners of the Earth [Video game]
Release date: March 15, 2005; Voice Cast: Milton Lawrence as Jack Walters; Writer/Producer: Chris Gray; Director: Lani Minella; Developer: Headfirst Productions; Platforms: Microsoft Windows, Xbox; Perspective: 1st-Person; Publisher: 2K Games, Inc., Bethesda Softworks LLC.

Based on the H.P. Lovecraft short story "The Shadow Over Innsmouth" the player is unstable private investigator Jack Walters who years earlier was committed to Arkham Asylum after coming face-to-face with alien beings. Now it is 1922 and Walters is on a missing person case at the coastal town of Innsmouth. His investigations lead him to co-operating with the FBI as they discover a shrine to the cosmic entity Cthulhu and the Esoteric Order of Dagon cult. Wizards, fish-men known as Deep Ones, extraterrestrial flying polyps and the Great Race of Yith are all encountered by Walters who possesses Yithian psychic powers which give him warning of dangers ahead. On the downside he suffers from acrophobia, blurred vision and voices in his head when his stress levels rise.

Carry On Screaming! (1966) [Film; UK]
Premiere: August 16, 1966; Main Cast: Harry H. Corbett as Detective Sergeant Sidney Bung, Peter Butterworth as Detective Constable Slobotham, Kenneth Williams as Doctor Orlando West, Fenella Fielding as Valeria Watt, Jim Dale as Albert Potter, Joan Sims as Emily Bung, Angela Douglas as Doris Mann, Bernard

Carry on Screaming (1966), starring (left to right) Fenella Fielding as Valeria Watt, Angela Douglas as Doris Mann, Harry H. Corbett as Detective Sergeant Sidney Bung, and Kenneth Williams as Dr. Orlando Watt (Anglo-Amalgamated).

Bresslaw as Sockett, Charles Hawtrey as Dan Dann, Jon Pertwee as Doctor Fettle; Producer: Peter Rogers; Screenplay: Talbot Rothwell; Director: Gerald Thomas; 97 min.; Peter Rogers Productions; Anglo-Amalgamated Film Distributors; Color.

In this parody of horror films Detective Sergeant Bung and his assistant Detective Constable Slobotham investigate the kidnapping of Albert Potter's girlfriend Doris Mann. The voluptuous Valeria Watt throws Bung off the trail when she seduces him. Meanwhile the Valeria's brother the undead Dr. Watt has been kidnapping girls and transforming them into mannequins.

The Case of the Man Who Died Laughing: From the Files of Vish Puri, India's Most Private Investigator [Novel]

Author: Tarquin Hall; First publication: London: Hutchinson, 2009.

The Rajpath Laughing Club gathers in Delhi Park. Suddenly Khali, the four-armed Hindu goddess of destruction rises out of the mist, draws a sword and kills renowned scientist Dr. Suresh Jha before disappearing.

Private investigator Vish Puri is skeptical of any supernatural connection and together with his team Facecream, Tubelight and Flush he aims to uncover the truth. Puri faces many obstacles in his investigations including Maharaji Swami and India's community of hereditary magicians.

The Case of the Whitechapel Vampire (2002)

Premiere: October 27, 2002; Main Cast: Matt Frewer as Sherlock Holmes, Kenneth Welsh as Dr. Watson, Shawn Lawrence as Brother Marstoke, Neville Edwards as Dr. Chagas, Cary Lawrence as Sister Helen, Jane Gilchrist as Sister Mardaret, Michel Perron as

Inspector Attley Jones, Isabel Dos Santos as Signora de la Rosa, Danny Blanco Hall as Hector de la Rosa; Executive Producers: Steven Hewitt, Michael Prupas; Story: Rodney Gibbons; Based on characters created by Arthur Conan Doyle; Director: Rodney Gibbons; 90 min.; Muse Entertainment Enterprises; Color.

A vampire is suspected to be at work in a Whitechapel monastery. One of the monks has a different explanation. He believes the murders to be the work of a demon he is familiar with named Desmondo. Sherlock Holmes approaches the supernatural theories with a grain of salt and is convinced deduction based on logic will get to the truth.

The Case-Book of Sherlock Holmes (1991) [TV series; UK]

"THE LAST VAMPYRE" (3:01)

First broadcast: January 27, 1993 [UK]; Main Cast: Jeremy Brett as Sherlock Holmes, Edward Hardwicke as Doctor Watson, Roy Marsden as John Stockton, Keith Barron as Rob Ferguson, Yolanda Vasquey as Carlotta, Maurice Denham as the Reverend Merridew, Richard Dempsey as Jack, Freddie Jones as Pedlar; Executive Producers: Sally Head, Rebecca Eaton; Teleplay: Jeremy Paul; Based on "The Adventures of the Sussex Vampire" by Arthur Conan Doyle; Director: Tim Sullivan; 102 min.; Granada Television; WGBH; Color.

Sherlock Holmes investigates the death of a baby and an apparent link to John Stockton who is alleged to be descended from a family of vampires. Is the murderer really a vampire or something more mundane?

See: **"The Adventure of the Sussex Vampire"**

Cast a Deadly Spell (1991) [Telefilm]

Premiere: September 7, 1991; Main Cast: Fred Ward as Detective Harry Philip Lovecraft, David Warner as Amos Hackshaw, Julianne Moore as Connie Stone, Clancy Brown as Harry Borden; Producer: Gale Anne Hurd; Story: Joseph Dougherty; Director: Martin Campbell; 96 min.: Home Box Office (HBO); Pacific Western; Color.

Los Angeles, 1948. Hard-boiled private detective Harry Philip Lovecraft lives in a world of black magic but refuses to use magic himself. Amos Hackshaw hires Lovecraft to find the stolen "Necronomicon" book. Lovecraft soon discovers the book holds the key to occult powers aimed at taking over the world.

The character of H. Philip Lovecraft was revisited in ***Witch Hunt*** (1994) with Dennis Hopper in the title role.

The Cat Creeps (1946) [Film]

Premiere: May 17, 1946; Main Cast: Lois Collier as Gay Elliot, Noah Beery, Jr., as Pidge Lorry, Paul Kelly as Ken Grady, Fred Brady as Terry Nichols, Douglass Dumbrille as Tom McGalvey, Rose Hobart as Connie Palmer; Executive Producer: Howard Welsch; Screenplay: Edward Dein, Jerry Warner; Story: Gerald Geraghty; Director: Erle C. Kenton; 58 min.; Universal Pictures; B/W.

In this low budget weird menace "B" feature from Universal *Morning Chronicle* reporter Terry Nichols investigates a fifteen-year-old suicide on a small island. Resident Cora Williams claims Eric Goran was murdered over $200,000 in hidden money. The case attracts a group of interested people who all have their own motives for being on the island. Soon after they arrive Cora is murdered. Her pet black cat who witnessed the murder is said to have supernatural powers by Kyra, the daughter of Eric Goran. More murders follow as the cat leads them to a child's dollhouse.

The Cat Who Talked to Ghosts [Novel]

Author: Lilian Jackson Braun; First publication: New York: Jove Books, 1990.

Former crime-beat reporter Jim Qwilleran retired at the relatively early age of fifty when he became heir to a fortune. Now he lives in Pickax City, Moose County sharing his apartment with his Siamese cats—the psychic Koko and Yum Yum. One evening he receives a telephone call from his former housekeeper Iris Cobb in a state of panic. She's been hearing strange, unearthly noises in her farmhouse. But it is only later when Iris Cobb dies of apparent fright that Jim Qwilleran and his two cats move into her farmhouse to investigate the cause of her death.

Celestial Dogs [Novel]

Author: Jay Russell; First publication: Robinson Publishing, 1996.

Former teen sitcom star Marty Burns is down on his luck. Now he's a private investigator looking for Jenny Leo, the stripper girlfriend of pimp Long John Silver. His investigations take him into the underbelly of Los Angeles' snuff film industry. Worse still a Japanese demon is now attached to him.

Followed by *Burning Bright* (1997) centered on voodoo rituals in Liverpool and Druidic rituals in Cornwall.

The Champions (1968) [TV series; UK]

Premiere: September 25, 1968; Main Cast: Stuart Damon as Craig Stirling, Alexander Bastedo as Sharron Macready, William Gaunt as Richard Barrett, Anthony Nicholls as Commander W.L. Tremayne; Producer: Monty Berman; Creators: Monty Berman, Dennis Spooner; 30 × 50 min.; Incorporated Television Company (ITC); Independent Television (ITV); Color.

Three Nemesis law enforcement operatives working on assignment in China to collect deadly bacteria crash land in the Himalayas. When they recover, they discover they have paranormal powers of heightened intuition, telepathy, super-human strength and amplified hearing. A lost civilization has transformed their bodies and senses with heightened powers. Now they tackle crime from their Geneva headquarters as Champions of law, order and justice.

The Champions (1968), starring Alexander Bastedo as Nemesis agent Sharron Macready (ITC).

SEASON ONE

The Beginning (1:01); *The Invisible Man* (1:02); *Reply Box No. 666* (1:03); *The Experiment* (1:04); *Happening* (1:05); *Operation Deep-Freeze* (1:06); *The Survivors* (1:07); *To Trap a Rat* (1:08); *The Iron Man* (1:09); *The Ghost Plane* (1:10); *The Dark Island* (1:11); *The Fanatics* (1:12); *Twelve Hours* (1:13); *The Search* (1:14); *The Gilded Cage* (1:15); *Shadow of the Panther* (1:16); *A Case of Lemmings* (1:17); *The Mission* (1:18); *The Interrogation* (1:19); *The Silent Enemy* (1:20); *The Body Snatchers* (1:21); *Get Me Out of Here!* (1:22); *The Night People* (1:23); *Project Zero* (1:24); *Desert Journey* (1:25); *Full Circle* (1:26); *Nutcracker* (1:27); *The Final Countdown* (1:28); *The Gun-Runners* (1:29); *Autokill* (1:30).

Chandu the Magician [Radio drama; Film]

Premiere: 1932; Main Cast: Gayne Whitman as Frank Chandler/Chandu, Margaret MacDonald as Dorothy, Bob Bixby as Bob Regent, Betty Webb as Betty Regent; Creators: Raymond R. Morgan, Harry A. Earnshaw; Writer: Vera Oldham; Director: Cyril Armbrister; KHJ Los Angeles; Don Lee Network/Mutual.

American born Frank Chandler adopts his occult powers to solve cases worldwide. Learning his mystic powers from a yogi in India Chandler goes under the guise of Chandu. Helping him is his sister Dorothy and her children Betty and Bob Regent. Chandu's arch-nemesis is master criminal Roxor who exploits the weakness that makes Chandu's magic ineffective—fear.

The original radio show ceased production in 1936 but was revived on June 28, 1948, with Tom Collins portraying Frank Chandler/

Chandu. Scriptwriter Vera Oldham revamped her original scripts for the new production which had a relatively short run. Its final season was broadcast in 1949.

2. Premiere: August 4, 1932; Main Cast: Edmund Lowe as Frank Chandler/Chandu, Bela Lugosi as Roxor, Henry B. Walthall as Robert Regent, Michael Stuart as Bobby Regent, June Vlasek as Betty Lou Regent, Virginia Hammond as Dorothy Regent, Irene Ware as Princess Nadji, Herbert Mundin as Albert Miggles, Weldon Heyburn as Abdulah; Screenplay: Barry Conners, Philip Klein; Based on the radio drama by Harry A. Earnshaw, Vera M. Oldham, R. R. Morgan; Directors: Marcel Varnel, William C. Menzies; 71 min.; Fox Film Corp.; B/W.

After many years of study with the Yogi of the East, Frank Chandler, under his new identity as Chandu, has developed supernatural powers including the ability to astral project and control minds with powerful illusions.

Chandu's brother-in-law Robert Regent has invented a death ray that can destroy life across continents. In Egypt, the evil Roxor sees his chance for world domination and kidnaps Regent and the death ray. But only Regent possesses the knowledge to use the device and kidnaps Regent's wife and two children to get him to share his expertise. Chandu must rescue them and stop Roxor from using the death ray with the aid of his magical powers of detection.

See: *The Return of Chandu*.

Changes (The Dresden Files Book #12)
Author: Jim Butcher; Publisher: New York: Roc, 2010.

Arianna Ortega, Duchess of the Red Court has a secret weapon she intends to use against paranormal investigator Harry Dresden. His former girlfriend, half-vampire Susan Rodriguez has disappeared in South America, with her own secret—an eight-year-old daughter. Dresden is the father and now he must rescue her from the Red Court vampires.

See: *Ghost Story*

Charlie Chan at Treasure Island (1939) [Film]

Premiere: September 9, 1939; Main Cast: Sidney Toler as Charlie Chan, Cesar Romero as Rhadini, June Gale as Myra Rhadini, Pauline Moore as Eve Cairo, Sen Yung as Jimmy Chan, Douglas Fowley as Pete Essex, Sally Blane as Stella Essex, Douglas Dumbrille as Thomas Gregory, Billie Seward as Bessie Sibley, Wally Vernon as Elmer Kelner, Donald MacBride as Chief J.J. Kilvaine, Charles Halton as Redley, Trevor Bardette as Abdul, Louis Jean Heydt as Paul Essex; Story/Screenplay: John Larkin; Based on the character Charlie Chan created by Earl Derr Biggers; Director: Norman Foster; 74 min.; 20th Century–Fox; b/w.

Author Paul Essex dies on a flight from Honolulu to San Francisco and his manuscript goes missing after receiving a radiogram warning him that he "cannot escape Zodiac." Charlie Chan who is onboard the flight learns that three recent suicides have been clients of the psychic Dr. Zodiac. "In humble opinion suicide induced by blackmail is murder."

Magician Rhadini offers $1,000 to any psychic whose stunts Rhadini cannot duplicate in his stage act in "The Temple of Magic" on San Francisco's Treasure Island. Zodiac fails to

Chandu the Magician (1932), **starring Bela Lugosi as the evil Roxor (Fox Film).**

accept the challenge and Chan receives a typewritten warning. "Do not challenge the supernatural unless you are prepared to meet your ancestors."

Charlie Chan visits Dr. Zodiac who claims to contact Paul Essex through an Egyptian Princess. He is not impressed and states, "To destroy false prophet must first unmask him in eyes of believers." Chan uncovers a "psychic" network of organized blackmail and finally the true psychic mind-reading powers of Eve Cairo unravels the unexpected truth behind the identity of Dr. Zodiac.

Charlie Chan's Secret (1936) [Film]

Premiere: January 10, 1936; Main Cast: Warner Oland as Charlie Chan, Rosina Lawrence as Alice Lowell, Henrietta Crosman as Henrietta Lowell, Charles Quigley as Dick Williams, Gloria Roy as Carlotta, Edward Trevor as Fred Gage, Astrid Allwyn as Janice Gage, Herbert Mundin as Baxter, Jonathan Hale as Warren T. Phelps, Egon Brecher as Ulrich, Arthur Edmund Carew as Professor Bowen, Jerry Miley as Allen Colby; Original story: Robert Ellis, Helen Logan, Joseph Hoffman; Screenplay: Robert Ellis, Helen Logan; Director: Gordon Wiles; 72 min.; Twentieth Century–Fox; b/w.

Allen Colby, heir to a family fortune, is presumed dead in the sunken wreckage of an ocean liner. Charlie Chan's investigations lead him to a different conclusion. Chan travels to San Francisco and the Colby family estate where he attends a séance. Colby's spirit is apparently summoned by Carlotta the medium. But when the séance is concluded Chan discovers Colby's slain body. Chan attempts to find those responsible for cheating Colby out of his inheritance as their lives in turn come under attack.

Cheo Yong: The Paranormal Detective (2014) [TV series; South Korea]

Premiere: February 9, 2014: Main Cast: Ji-Ho Oh as Yoon Cheo-yong, Jun Hyo-Seong as Han Na-young, Seung-mok Yoo as Byeon Kook-jin, Je-wook Yeon as Lee Jong-hyun, Ji-eun Oh as ha Sun-woo, Yoo Min-Kyu as Park Min-jae; Writer: Hong Seung-hyeon; Director: Lim Chan-ik; 20 × 23 min.; CMG Chorok Stars; Darin Media; Orion Cinema Network; Color.

Detective Cheo-yong was born with the ability to communicate with ghosts. The spirit of former high school student Han Na-young and female detective Ha Sun-woo help Cheo-yong in his investigations.

SEASON ONE

Ghost-Seeing Detective Part 1 (1:01); *Ghost-Seeing Detective Part 2* (1:02); *Message of the Soul* (1:03); *Memories* (1:04); *City of Silence* (1:05); *Irreversible* (1:06); *Evil Lethargy* (1:07); *Some Justice* (1:08); *Man Abandoned by God Part 1* (1:09); *Man Abandoned by God Part 2* (1:10).

SEASON TWO

Venus Part 1 (2:01); *Venus Part 2* (2:02); *Kiss of Death* (2:03); *Rebirth* (2:04); *Weathercock* (2:05); *2 Memories* (2:06); *Signal*

Charlie Chan's Secret (1936), starring Warner Oland as Charlie Chan (Twentieth Century–Fox).

Truth (2:07); *Memories of Murder* (2:08); *The Definition of the Devil Part 1* (2:09); *The Definition of the Devil Part 2* (2:10).

Chrono Crusade (2003) [Anime; Manga; Japan]

Premiere: November 24, 2003; Voice Cast: Tomoko Kawakami as Rosette Christopher, Akira Ishida as Chrono, Saeko Chiba as Azmaria Hendric, Shou Hayama as Ewan Remington, Yoshiko Sakakibara as Kate Valentine, Junko Minagawa as Joshua Christopher, Natsuko Kuwatani as Florette "Fiore" Harvenheit, Michiko Nieya as Satella Harvenheit, Kazuhiko Inoue as Aion, Norio Wakamoto as Duke Duffau, Tomomichi Nishimura as Edward "Elder" Hamilton; Writers: Atsuhiro Tomioka, Natsuko Takahashi, Kiyoko Yoshimura; Art Director: Toshiro Nozaki; Director: Yuu Kou; 24 × 25 min.; Studio Hoo Bow; Fuji Television Network; Gospel Bullet; Kadokawa Shoten; The Klockworx Co. Ltd.; Color.

New York, 1928. The Catholic Magdalene Order has a mission to protect the seven "Apostles" from the demonic Sinners. Rosette Christopher, armed with a Colt .45 and holy bullets, and her demonic renegade assistant, Chrono are exorcists within the order with a mission to defeat the Sinners. Helping them is Stella Harvenheit and her demon fighting crystals. Rosette is also on another mission to find her brother Joshua who went missing after turning everyone at his orphanage to stone.

Season One

Sister Rosetta (1:01); *The Covenant/Contractor* (1:02); *Apostles/The Angel* (1:03); *Sinners* (1:04); *Militia* (1:05); *Jewel Summer* (1:06); *The Devil* (1:07); *Falling Down/The Puppet* (1:08); *Joshua* (1:09); *Horn* (1:10); *Gabriel Hound/Beast* (1:11); *Holy Night* (1:12); *Marionette Train/Older Sister* (1:13); *Invocation/Prayer* (1:14); *The Pursuers* (1:15); *Believer* (1:16); *Accomplices* (1:17); *Photograph/Four People* (1:18); *Atonement/Neck* (1:19); *Temptation/Poison* (1:20); *Mary Magdalene* (1:21); *Farewell* (1:22); *The Noise* (1:23); *Chrono* (1:24).

[Manga] First publication: *Monthly Dragon Magazine* (December 1999); Writer-Artist: Daisuke Moriyama; Publisher: Kadokawa Shoten.

This manga, later adapted into the anime series, ran to 14 chapters.

The Clockwork Scarab (Stoker & Holmes Book #1) [Juvenile book]

Author: Colleen Gleason; First publication: San Francisco: Chronicle Books, 2014.

Evaline, the sister of Bram Stoker and Mina, the niece of Sherlock Holmes reluctantly agree to work together when they are summoned to the British Museum where Irene Adler requests their help. Young society women have been found murdered or have gone missing. The girls go undercover and join a cult under the leadership of the mysterious Ankh. They learn the cult's mission is to restore the Egyptian goddess Sekhmet to power.

See: ***The Spiritglass Charade***

Clue Club (1976) [Animated TV series]

Premiere: August 14, 1976; Voice Cast: Robert Hastings as D.D., David Jolliffe as Larry, Jim MacGeorge as Wimper, Patricia Stitch as Pepper, Tara Talboy as Dotty, Paul Winchell as Woofer, John Stephenson as Sheriff Bagley; Executive Producers: William Hanna, Joseph Barbera; 16 × 25 min.; Hanna-Barbera Productions; CBS; Color.

D.D., Larry, Pepper and Dotty, with the help of talking dog detectives Wimper and Woofer solve weird mysteries as the Clue Club. From sea monsters to werewolves to dinosaurs, the show was heavily influenced by ***Scooby-Doo, Where Are You?*** which it replaced at CBS.

The Paper Shaper Caper (1:01); *The Case of the Lighthouse Mouse* (1:02); *The Real Gone Gondola* (1:03); *Who's to Blame for the Empty Frame?* (1:04); *The Weird Seaweed Caper* (1:05); *The Green Thumb Caper* (1:06); *The Disappearing Airport Caper* (1:07); *The Walking House Caper* (1:08); *The Solar Energy Caper* (1:09); *The Vanishing Train Caper* (1:10); *The Dissolving Statue Caper* (1:11); *The Missing Pig Caper* (1:12); *One of Our Elephant's Is Missing* (1:13); *The Amazing Heist* (1:14); *The Circus Caper* (1:15); *The Prehistoric Monster Caper* (1:16).

The Cobra [Pulp fiction character]
Author: Richard B. Sale; First appearance: *Ten Detective Aces* (January 1934); Publisher: Ace Publications.

American Deen Bradley was raised by a Hindu priest following the massacre of his parents in an Indian uprising. Educated at Oxford University he returned to India working for British Intelligence in Bombay. Thanks to mystical teachings of his adopted parent Bradley can create illusions in people's minds and is capable of suspended animation allowing him to survive being buried alive.

Bradley is a striking figure with a dark complexion that could pass him off as an Indian. But his most striking feature is his dual identity as the crime fighting Cobra who strikes terror into criminals with his poison darts dipped in cobra venom.

Despite his colorful backstory the Cobra only appeared in three issues of *Ten Detective Aces*.

"Terror Towers" (January 1934); "The House of Kaa" (February 1934); The Grinning Ghoul" (March 1934).

Cognition: An Erica Reed Thriller [Video game]
Release date: October 30, 2012; Voice Cast: Raleigh Holmes as Erica Reed, Michael Fortunato as Scott Reed, Ed Crane as John McCoy, Daniel Humbarger as Officer Jonathan Duffner, Cordelia Smith as Amy K. Browne, Arabella Grayson as Rose Duvalier, Stephanie Harris as Madison Davies, Reid Martin Basso as Terence Bowlby/The Wise Monkey/Stelios; Executive Producers: Richard Flores, Vitek Goyel; Developer; Phoenix Online Studios LLC; Platforms: Microsoft Windows, Macintosh OS X, iOS; Perspective: 3rd-Person; Publisher: Reverb Publishing.

Boston-based FBI agent Erica Reed has postcognition, the ability to see certain images of past events through touch. Episode One begins with a flashback to the murder of her brother Scott by the Cain Killer. In the present-day Reed is investigating a midnight hanging of an unknown man. But Reed's over-riding obsession is to find the Cain Killer. Each of the four episodes centers on a serial killer with the final episode providing answers to the Cain Killer in a final encounter.

Episode One: *The Hangman* (2012); Episode Two: *The Wise Monkey* (2013); Episode Three: *The Oracle* (2013); Episode Four: *The Cain Killer* (2013).

Cold Days (The Dresden Files Book #14)
Author: Jim Butcher; Publisher: New York: Roc, 2012.

Harry Dresden the professional wizard is no more. Now he is under the control of Mab, the Queen of Air and Darkness as her Winter Knight. And her latest command is the death of an immortal. Dresden must find a way to escape Mab's control to save his soul.

See: **Skin Game**

The Conjuring (2013) [Film]
Premiere: July 19, 2013; Main Cast: Vera Farmiga as Lorraine Warren, Patrick Wilson as Ed Warren, Lili Taylor as Carolyn Perron, Ron Livingston as Roger Perron, Shanley Casswell as Andrea Perron, Hayley McFarland as Nancy Perron, Joey King as Christine Perron, Mackenzie Foy as Cindy Perron, Kyla Deaver as April Perron, Shannon Kook as Drew Thomas, John Brotherton as Brad Hamilton, Sterling Jerins as Judy Warren, Marion Guyot as Georgina Moran, Steve Coulter as Father Gordon, Joseph Bishara as Bathsheba Sherman, Morganna May as Debbie, Amy Tipton as Camilla, Zach Pappas as Rick, Christof Veillon as Maurice Theriault; Executive Producers: Walter Hamada, Dave Neustadter; Story: Chad Hayes, Carey W. Hayes; Director: James Wan; 112 min.; New Line Cinema; The Safran Company; Evergreen Media Group; Color.

Paranormal investigators and demonologists Ed and Lorraine Warren are called upon to investigate strange occurrences plaguing the Perron family in their Rhode Island home. This film loosely based on real-life events takes the predictable route of over-the-top effects and shocks that turn any reality into pure fiction.

Followed by *The Conjuring 2* (2016) starring the same lead actors portraying Ed and Lorraine Warren in a story featuring a spirit terrorizing a London mother and her young daughter.

Constantine [Film; TV series]

[Film] Premiere: February 18, 2005; Main Cast: Keanu Reeves as John Constantine, Rachel Weisz as Detective Angela Dodson/Isabel Dodson, Shia LaBeouf as Chas Kramer, Djimon Hounsou as Midnite, Max Baker as Beeman, Gavin Rossdale as Balthazar, Tilda Swinton as Gabriel, Pruitt Taylor Vince as Father Hennessy, Peter Stormare as Satan, Jose Zuniga as Detective Weiss, Francis Guinan as Father Garret, April Grace as Dr. Leslie Archer; Executive Producers: Gilbert Adler, Michael Aguilar; Story: Kevin Brodbin; Screenplay: Frank Cappello, Kevin Brodbin; Director: Francis Lawrence; 121 min.; Warner Bros.; Village Roadshow Pictures; DC Comics Vertigo; 3 Arts Entertainment; Donners' Company; Batfilm Productions; Weed Road Pictures; Color.

Police detective Angela Dodson seeks the expertise of occult detective **John Constantine** in uncovering the truth behind her twin sister's suicide. Angela is convinced demons played a part in Isabel's death. Her instincts prove to be true as mankind is in imminent danger from the son of Satan and his minions.

The nationality of Constantine was changed from English to American and his hair color changed from blond to dark brown for the movie. The opening weekend box-office fell far below the original budget but eventually went into profit worldwide.

[TV series] Premiere: October 24, 2014; Main Cast: Matt Ryan as John Constantine, Harold Perrineau as Manny, Angelica Celaya as Zed Martin, Charles Halford as Chas Chandler, Michael James Shaw as Papa Midnite, Jeremy Davies as Ritchie Simpson, Mark Margolis as Felix Faust; 13 × 43 min.; Executive Producers: Daniel Cerone, Mark Verheiden, David S. Goyer; Warner Bros. Television; DC Comics; National Broadcasting Company (NBC); Color.

Occult detective **John Constantine**, master sorcerer and major con artist, tries to save his soul by sending demons back to Hell. The NBC adaptation of the DC-Vertigo comic book character failed to gain an audience and was cancelled after one season.

Season One

Non Est Asylum (1:01); *The Darkness Beneath* (1:02); *The Devil's Vinyl* (1:03); *Feast of Friends* (1:04); *Dance Vaudou* (1:05); *The Rage of Caliban* (1:06); *Blessed are the Damned* (1:07); *The Saint of Last Resorts: Part One* (1:08); *The Saint of Last Resorts: Part Two* (1:09); *Quid Pro Quo* (1:10); *A Whole World Out There* (1:11); *Angels and Ministers of Grace* (1:12); *Waiting for the Man* (1:13).

Constantine: City of Demons (2018) [Animated web series]

Premiere: March 24, 2018; Voice cast: Matt Ryan as John Constantine, Damien O'Hare as Chas Chandler, Emily O'Brien as Renee Chandler, Laura Bailey as Asa the Healer/Nightmare Nurse/Trish, Robin Atkin Downes as Butler, Jim Meskimen as Beroul, Kevin Michael Richardson as Mahonin, Rick D. Wasserman as Mictlantecuhtli, Rachel Kimsey as Announcer; Executive Producers: Sam Register, Sarah Schechter, Greg Berlanti, Marc Guggenheim; Story: J.M. DeMatteis; Director: Doug Murphy; 90 min.; Warner Bros. Animation; DC Comics; DC Entertainment; CW Seed; Color.

Chas Chandler's daughter Trish is in a coma with the safety of her soul in mortal danger. Chandler's friend **John Constantine** enlists the aid of the Nightmare Nurse a.k.a. Asa the Healer who cannot locate Trish's soul. Constantine soon learns that Trish is being used as a pawn in a greater plan. The demon Beroul wants Constantine to pave the way for him to reign in his own vision of Hell by destroying his demon rivals.

Based on the Vertigo graphic novel *Hellblazer: All His Engines* (2005) by author Mike Carey and artist Leonardo Manco.

Continuum (2012) [TV series; Canada]

Premiere: May 27, 2012; Main Cast: Rachel Nichols as Detective Kiera Cameron, Victor Webster as Detective Carlos Fonnegra, Eric Knudsen as Alec Sadler, Stephen Lobo as Matthew Kellog, Omari Newton as Lucas Ingram, Roger Cross as Travis Verta, Luvia Petersen as Jasmine Garza, Brian Markinson as Inspector Dillon, Lexa Doig as Sonya Valentine, Jennifer Spence as Betty Robertson, Richard Harmon as Julian Randol, Ryan Robbins as Brad Tonkin; Executive Producers: Simon Barry, Pat Williams, Tom Rowe, Matthew O'Connor, Lisa Richardson, Jeff King; Creator: Simon Barry; 42 × 45 min.; Reunion Pictures; Boy Meets Girl Film Company, Shaw Media; Showcase (Canada); Syfy (USA); Color.

Detective Kiera Cameron finds herself transported from 2077 to 2012 along with a group of terrorists escaping execution. In 2012 she joins forces with Detective Carlos Fonnegra of the Vancouver Police Department who eventually learns his partner is a time traveler. With the help of computer whizz-kid Alec Sadler she hopes to track and capture the members of Liber8 before they can change history.

SEASON ONE

A Stitch in Time (1:01); *Fast Times* (1:02); *Wasting Time* (1:03); *A Matter of Time* (1:04); *A Test of Time* (1:05); *Time's Up* (1:06); *The Politics of Time* (1:07); *Playtime* (1:08); *Family Time* (1:09); *Endtime* (1:10).

SEASON TWO

Second Chances (2:01); *Split Second* (2:02); *Second Thoughts* (2:03); *Second Skin* (2:04); *Second Opinion* (2:05); *Second Truths* (2:06); *Second Degree* (2:07); *Second Listen* (2:08); *Seconds* (2:09); *Second Wave* (2:10); *Second Guessed* (2:11); *Second Last* (2:12); *Second Time* (2:13).

SEASON THREE

Minute by Minute (3:01); *Minute Man* (3:02); *Minute to Win It* (3:03); *A Minute Changes Everything* (3:04); *30 Minutes to Air* (3:05); *Wasted Minute* (3:06); *Waning Minutes* (3:07); *So Do Our Minutes Hasten* (3:08); *Minute of Silence* (3:09); *Revolutions Per Minute* (3:10); *3 Minutes to Midnight* (3:11); *The Dying Minutes* (3:12); *Last Minute* (3:13).

SEASON FOUR

Lost Hours (4:01); *Rush Hour* (4:02); *Power Hour* (4:03); *Zero Hour* (4:04); *The Desperate Hours* (4:05); *Final Hour* (4:06).

Cosmopath [*Bengal Station* Trilogy #3] [Novel]

Author: Eric Brown; First publication: Nottingham, UK: Solaris, 2009.

Billionaire tycoon Rabindranath Chandrasakar asks telepath detective Jeff Vaughn to read the mind of a dead spacer on the unexplored world of Delta Cephei VII. Vaughn discovers a secret that could change the course of human exploration of the galaxy.

See: ***Necropath***

Creature Cops Special Varmint Unit [Comic book]

First appearance: January 2015; Story: Rob Anderson; Art: Fernando Melek, Novo Malgapo; 3-issue limited series; Publisher: Comics Experience-IDW Publishing.

"Duo-spliced" hybrid animals, both legal and illegal have transformed society. Animal control officers are on the front-line trying to maintain order. Novelist and cult founder James Addison believes he can open the gates from another dimension for the Outer Gods. Veteran officer Kaminski sees a link to a ten-year-old case involving a ritual and a "monster" that tore off his partner's arm.

Criminal Macabre [Comic book]

First publication: May 2003; Five-issue mini-series; Creator-Story: Steve Niles; Art: Ben Templesmith; Publishers: Dark Horse Comics.

Set amid a backdrop of a dark and gritty Los Angeles, hard-boiled private detective Cal McDonald is addicted to drugs, alcohol and the paranormal. When Los Angeles is over-run with vampires, werewolves and other creatures McDonald must track down the cause and those responsible.

Cal McDonald first appears in "Big Head" included in an anthology of stories in *Daughters of Fly in My Eye*, published by Arcane Comix in 1990. McDonald also features in two novels published by IDW between 2002 and 2004 and a series of comic books published by Dark Horse between 2003 and 2014.

Novels: *Savage Membrane: A Cal McDonald Mystery* (2002); *Guns, Drugs & Monsters* (2004).

Short story collections: *Dial M for Monster* (2003); *Criminal Macabre: The Complete Cal McDonald Stories* (2007).

Curandero (2005) [Film; Mexico]
Premiere: October 18, 2005 [U.S.A.]; Main Cast: Carlos Gallardo as Carlos, Gizeht Galatea as Magdalena, Gabriel Pingarron as Castaneda, Jose Carlos Ruiz as Don Carlos, Jorge Zepeda as Comandante, Sergio Acosta as Oscar, Ernesto Yanez as Don Chi Chi, Javier Escobar as Alex, Eligio Melendez as Gomez, Rene Campero as Blascoe, Antonio Monroi as Roberto; Executive Producers: Elizabeth Avellan, Robert Rodriguez, Bob Weinstein, Harvey Weinstein; Screenplay: Robert Rodriguez; Adaptation: Luz Maria Rojas, Eduardo Andrés Rodriguez González; Director: Eduardo Andrés Rodriguez González; 92 min.; R.I.P. Rodriguez International Pictures; Dimension Films; Miramax; Color.

A federal agent enlists the help of a local curandero to track a Satanic drug-trafficking cult responsible for brutal black magic murders in Mexico City.

Curse of the Black Widow a.k.a. **Love Trap** (1977) [Film]
Premiere: September 16, 1977; Main Cast: Tony Franciosa as Mark Higbie, Donna Mills as Leigh Lockridge, Patty Duke Astin as Laura Lockridge, June Lockhart as Mrs. Lockridge; June Allyson as Olga, Jeff Corey as Aspa Soldado, Sid Caesar as Lazlo Cozart, Vic Morrow as Lt. Gully Conti; Executive Producer: Dan Curtis; Teleplay: Robert Blees, Earl Wallace; Director: Dan Curtis; 100 min.; Dan Curtis Productions; ABC Circle Films; Color.

Private eye Mark Higbie and Lieutenant Gully Conti seek to find the truth behind a series of gruesome murders involving male victims of human black widow spiders.

Curse of the Demon a.k.a. **Night of the Demon** (1957) [Film]
Premiere: November 9, 1957; Main Cast: Dana Andrews as Dr. John Holden, Peggy Cummins as Joanna Harrington, Niall MacGinnis as Doctor Julian Karswell, Maurice Denham as Professor Harrington; Executive Producer: Hal E. Chester; Screenplay: Charles Bennett, Hal E. Chester; Based on the short story by Montague R. James; Director: Jacques Tourneur; 95 min. (UK release); Columbia Pictures Corporation; Sabre Films, Ltd.; B/W.

Skeptical American scientist Dr. John Holden finds his beliefs turned inside out when he accepts an invitation to the country estate of occult practitioner Dr. Julian Karswell. Holden becomes the object of a curse linked to a parchment that Karswell placed in his possession during their initial meeting at the British Museum.

Director Jacques Tourneur was frustrated by interference from producer Hal. E. Chester, who included lingering shots of the "demon in the woods" at the beginning and conclusion of the film.

"The only monster I did—and this is how I wanted to do the whole thing—was the scene in the woods where Dana Andrews is chased by a cloud. Then I wanted, at the very end, when the train goes by, to include only four frames of the monster coming up with the guy and throwing him down. Boom, boom—did I

Curse of the Demon (1957), staring Dana Andrews as John Holden (Columbia Pictures).

see it or not? People would have to sit through it a second time to be sure of what they saw."

Tourneur was impressed with the demon's appearance which was based on a 3,400-year-old print. But he was less impressed with the "man in a mask" application, saying it belonged in a teenage horror film. Tourneur had envisioned it as a drawn animation whose exact form is suggested rather than delineated.

The film was originally released in the UK as *Night of the Demon* at a running length of 95 minutes. In the U.S. it was released as part of a double bill with Hammer Film's *The Revenge of Frankenstein* (1958) with almost fourteen minutes of original footage cut from the print.

The Dain Curse [Novel; TV series]

[Novel] Author: Dashiell Hammett; Publisher: New York: Alfred A. Knopf, 1929.

The nameless detective known as the Continental Op investigates a case of stolen diamonds from the Leggett family. Edgar Leggett's daughter Gabrielle is convinced her connection to the Dain family on her mother's side is placing her life in danger. The Dain Curse has seen numerous gruesome deaths associated with friends and family. The Continental Op discovers Gabrielle is a member of a strange religious cult based in San Francisco known as The Temple of the Holy Grail. As he delves deeper into the workings of the cult the detective encounters an apparent paranormal presence.

"Not more than three feet away, there in the black room, a pale bright thing like a body, but not flesh, stood writhing before me ... hovered with its feet a foot or more above the floor.... I didn't believe in the supernatural—but what of that?"

The Continental Op must help Gabrielle escape both the destructive cult and her morphine addiction and finally put an end to the Dain Curse.

Originally serialized in *Black Mask* pulp magazine between November 1928 and February 1929.

[TV series] Premiere: May 22, 1978; Main Cast: James Coburn as Hamilton Nash, Nancy Addison as Gabrielle Leggett, Jean Simmons as Aaronia Haldorn, Hector Elizondo as Ben Feeney, Jason Miller as Owen Fitzstephans, Beatrice Straight as Alice Dain Leggett, Paul Stewart as Old Man; Executive Producer: Bob Markell; Developed for television by Robert W. Lenski; Based on the novel by Dashiell Hammett; Director: E.W. Swackhamer; 3 × 120 min.; Martin Poll Productions; CBS; Color.

This 3-part mini-series based on Dashiell Hammett's novel sees the Continental Op going under the name of Hamilton Nash. It was later adapted for a feature-length home video release.

Dark Intruder (1965) [Telefilm]

Premiere: July 21, 1965; Main Cast: Leslie Nielsen as Brett Kingsford, Mark Richman as Robert Vandenburg, Gilbert Green as Harvey Misbach, Judi Meredith as Evelyn Lang, Charles

Dark Intruder (1965), starring Leslie Nielsen as Brett Kingsford (Universal).

Bolender as Nikola, Werner Klemperer as Professor Malaki; Producer: Jack Laird; Story: Barre Lyndon; Director: Harvey Hart; 59 min.; Universal Pictures; Shamley Productions; B/W.

San Francisco 1890. Brett Kingsford, "chronic dabbler in the occult" investigates a beast-like serial killer who claws his victims to death and leaves idols of a Sumerian demon at the scene of the gruesome murders. Kingsford's friend, Robert Vandenburg, fears he may be the killer as he knew two of the female victims as a child and has been suffering sleepwalking trances that suck him into a "horrible darkness." A visit to the mysterious, all-seeing Professor Malaki soon brings events to a tragic conclusion.

A pilot from Alfred Hitchcock's Shamley Productions for a proposed TV series titled "The Black Cloak." When the networks showed no interest in the pilot it was released in theaters.

Dark Parables [Video game]

Release date: March 11, 2010; Developers: Blue Tea Games, Elpix Entertainment; Platforms: Microsoft Windows, Mac OS X, iOS, Android; Publisher: Big Fish Games.

A classic fairytale becomes a hidden object adventure as the "Fairytale Detective" searches for clues. Fifteen titles have been released up to and including November 2018. In the first installment the Detective investigates Sleeping Beauty and the evil sorceress who is now focused on Princess Briar Rose. Subsequent games include the Fairytale Detective investigating missing children connected to the Snow Queen, rescuing Cinderella from the evil Godmother and a mysterious deadly pollen with a link to Rapunzel.

Game 1: *Dark Parables: Curse of the Briar Rose*; 2. *Dark Parables: The Exiled Princess* 3. *Dark Parables: Rise of the Snow Queen* 4. *Dark Parables: The Red Riding Hood Sisters* 5. *Dark Parables: The Final Cinderella* 6. *Dark Parables: Jack and the Sky Kingdom* 7. *Dark Parables: The Ballad of Rapunzel*; 8. *Dark Parables: The Little Mermaid and the Purple Tide*; 9. *Dark Parables: Queen of Sands* 10. *Dark Parables: Goldilocks and the Fallen Star* 11. *Dark Parables: Swan Princess and the Dire Tree* 12. *Dark Parables: The Thief and the Tinderbox* 13. *Dark Parables: Requiem for the Forgotten Shadow* 14. *Dark Parables: Return of the Salt Princess* 15. *Dark Parables: The Match Girl's Lost Paradise*

The Dark Side of the Cross [Novel]

Author: James S. Parker; First publication: New York: Post Hill Press, 2016.

James MacBridan is an investigator for the Hawthorn Insurance Group. When religious artifacts are stolen from Catholic churches and held to ransom MacBridan is called upon by the church to handle the exchange. But when he meets the thief another dark force is present. The thief is murdered and the most prized artifact, the Cross of St. Patrick stolen. MacBridan tracks the killer and the Cross to the coast of New England and encounters supernatural forces that threaten his life.

Dark Tales: Edgar Allan Poe's [Video game]

Release date: March 2015; Developers; ERS Game Studios, AMAX Interactive; Platforms: Windows, Mac OS X, iOS; Perspective: 1st-Person; Publisher: Big Fish Games Inc.

Based on the stories and poems by Edgar Allan Poe, the player assists Detective Dupin in his investigations. The hidden object games series features four installments with a supernatural theme.

Game 7. *The Mystery of Marie Roget*; 9. *Metzengerstein*; 12. *Morella*; 14. *The Oval Portrait*

Dark Tower (1989) [Film; U.S./UK/Spain]

Premiere: March 29, 1989; Main Cast: Michael Moriarty as Dennis Randall, Jenny Agutter as Carolyn Page, Carol Lynley as Tilly, Theodore Bikel as Dr. Max Gold, Kevin McCarthy as Sergie, Anne Lockhart as Elaine, Patch Mackenzie as Maria, Radmiro Oliveros as Joseph, Rick Azulay as Charlie; Executive Producers: Tom Fox, Ken Wiederhorn; Writers: Robert J. Avrech, Ken Blackwell, Ken Wiederhorn; Story: Robert J. Avrech; Directors: Freddie Francis, Ken Wiederhorn (both credited as Ken Barnett); Sandy Howard Productions; Fries Distribution Company (U.S.); Color.

Security officer Dennis Randall investigates the death of a window-washer from a Barcelona skyscraper only to discover supernatural forces are at work. After seeking the help of paranormal investigator and exorcist Dr. Max Gold they discover Carolyn Page, the architect of the building, is the target of the vengeful spirit of her murdered husband.

Darker Than Black (2007) [Anime; Japan]
Premiere: April 5, 2007; Voice Cast: Hidenobu Kiuchi as Hei, Ikuya Sawaki as Mao, Masaru Ikeda as Huang, Misato Fukuen as Yin, Nana Mizuki as Misaki Kirihara, Sanae Kobayashi as Kanami Ishizaki, Shinichiro Miki as Eric Nishijima, Tomoko Kawakami as Amber, Tomoyuki Shimura as Yuusuke Saitou, Yuuna Inamura as Mayu Ootsuka; Producers: Ryo Oyama, Yoshihiro Oyabu; Art Director: Takashi Aoi; Director: Tensai Okamura; 26 × 24 min.; Aniplex; DTB; Hakuhodo; BONES; Color.

Ten years ago, the Hell's Gate appeared in Tokyo followed days later by Contractors with superhuman powers and passive mediums known as Dolls. Civilians who encounter Contractors have their memories erased, while psychic agent Hei and his blind partner Yin compete with various agencies to investigate the secret of Hell's Gate.

SEASON ONE

The Fallen Star of a Contract: Part 1 (1:01); *The Fallen Star of a Contract: Part 2* (1:02); *A New Star Shines in the Dawn Sky: Part 1* (1:03); *A New Star Shines in the Dawn Sky: Part 2* (1:04); *Red Giant Over Eastern Europe: Part 1* (1:05); *Red Giant Over Eastern Europe: Part 2* (1:06); *The Scent of Gardenias Lingers in the Summer Rain: Part 1* (1:07); *The Scent of Gardenias Lingers in the Summer Rain: Part 2* (1:08); *The White Dress, Stained with the Girl's Dreams and Blood: Part 1* (1:09); *The White Dress, Stained with the Girl's Dreams and Blood: Part 2* (1:10); *When One Takes Back What Was Lost Within the Wall: Part 1* (1:11); *When One Takes Back What Was Lost Within the Wall: Part 2* (1:12); *On a Silvery Night, the Heart Shakes on the Water's Surface: Part 1* (1:13); *On a Silvery Night, the Heart Shakes on the Water's Surface: Part 2* (1:14); *Memories of Betrayal in an Amber Smile: Part 1* (1:15); *Memories of Betrayal in an Amber Smile: Part 2* (1:16); *A Love Song is Sung in a Trash Heap: Part 1* (1:17); *A Love Song is Sung in a Trash Heap: Part 2* (1:18); *Renouncing Superficial Dreams, and Falling Drunk: Part 1* (1:19); *Renouncing Superficial Dreams, and Falling Drunk: Part 2* (1:20); *The Enforced City is Moistened by Tears: Part 1* (1:21); *The Enforced City is Moistened by Tears: Part 2* (1:22); *God is in His Heaven* (1:23); *Meteor Shower* (1:24); *Does the Reaper Dream of Darkness Darker Than Black?* (1:25); *Beneath Cherry Blossoms in Full Bloom* (1:26).

Followed by *Darker Than Black: Gemini of the Meteor* (2009) and *Darker Than Black: Contractor Side Story* (2010).

Darkness Visible (Comic book)
First publication: February 2017; Writers; Mike Carey, Arvind Ethan David; Art: Brendan Cahill; Publisher: IDW.

For the past eighty years humanity has reluctantly co-existed with demons. London based Detective Daniel Aston maintains the peace between the homeless, criminal class of demon known as the Shaitan and humans. But when Aston's daughter Maggie finds her life in danger he joins forces with the Shaitan who, alone can save her.

Darkness Within: In Pursuit of Loath Nolder [Video game]
Release date: November 6, 2007; Developer: Zoetrope Interactive; Platforms: Windows; Cloud; Perspective: 1st-Person; Publishers: Lighthouse Interactive; Iceberg Interactive.

The player is police detective Howard E. Loreid working out of the small town of Wellsmoth. He must locate private investigator Loath Nolder, the prime suspect in the murder of wealthy occultist Clark Field. Nolder has recently reappeared after an absence of five years. But Detective Loreid must also fight his own inner demons as he pursues Nolder.

Inspired by the writings of H.P. Lovecraft the investigations of Detective Loreid continues in *Darkness Within 2: The Dark Lineage* (2010).

Darkside Detective [Video game]
Release date: July 27, 2017; Developer: Spooky Doorway; Platforms: PC, Mac OS, Nintendo Switch; Perspective: First-person; Publisher: Spooky Doorway.

Detective Francis McQueen is the lead investigator of the Darkside Division of the Twin Lakes police department. Twin Lakes is a city inhabited by all manner of spooky creatures. McQueen is joined by the bumbling Officer Patrick Dooley as they investigate strange happenings with more than a touch of humor. This single-player point and click game features six cases to solve.

Dead Beat (The Dresden Files Book #7)
Author: Jim Butcher; Publisher: New York: Roc, 2005.

Paranormal detective Harry Dresden is summoned by his vampire foe Marva to locate the Word of Kemmler or his Chicago PD friend Karrin Murphy will be framed for murder. The only problem is Dresden has no idea what the Word of Kemmler is.

See: **Proven Guilty**

The Dead Boy Detectives [Comic book characters]
First appearance: *The Sandman* #25 (April 1991); Creators: Neil Gaiman, Matt Wagner; Publisher; DC-Vertigo.

St. Hilarion's School for Boys. Charles Rowland is unhappy at the boarding school and confused. He is surrounded by the ghosts of boys who all died at the school and are now tormented by a dead headmaster from 1916. When three ghosts decide to bully Rowland, they go too far, and he ends up dead. Now he is joined by the ghost of murdered Edward Paine who describes his journey through Hell. The two dead boys decide to leave the school behind them and join forces as dead detectives investigating the paranormal.

The Dead Case [Video game]
Release date: 2004; Developer: Zachary C. Shaffer; Platform: Flash; Perspective: First-person.

In this point-and-click online game the player is a ghost suffering from amnesia investigating his own murder from beyond the grave. He soon learns he isn't the only ghost with problems.

The Dead Detective [Novel]
Author: William Hefferman; Publisher: New York, NY: Akashic Books, 2010.

When his fanatical crazed mother murdered 10-year-old Harry Doyle and his brother Jimmy, Harry was resuscitated by two Tampa cops even though he was technically dead. Now detective Harry Doyle works for the Pinellas County Sheriff's Department and can hear the voices of murder victims after their death. The latest victim is a disgraced schoolteacher who slept with a teenage student. With her throat cut and the word "Evil" carved on her forehead Doyle and his latest partner Vicky Stanopolis are set the task of investigating the murder.

The Dead Don't Die (1975) [Telefilm]
Premiere: January 14, 1975; Main Cast: George Hamilton as Don Drake, Ray Milland as Jim Moss, Linda Cristal as Vera LaValle, Ralph Meeker as Lieutenant Reardon, James McEachin as Frankie Specht, Joan Blondell as Levenia; Executive Producers: Douglas S. Cramer, Wilford Lloyd Baumes; Teleplay: Robert Bloch; Director: Curtis Harrington; 75 min.; Douglas S. Cramer Co.; Color.

A sailor attempts to prove his brother was executed for a murder he didn't commit. But his investigations lead him into the world of voodoo and zombies.

"The Dead Hand" [Short story]
Authors: L.T. Meade and Robert Eustace; First publication: *Pearson's Magazine* (February 1902). Publisher: New York, NY: J.J. Little.

Diana Marburg is a palmist by profession with a keen interest in occult phenomena, spiritualism, clairvoyance and general mysteries of the unseen world. She works out of Maddox Street where her palmistry has brought her great fame. "My prophecies turned out correct, my intuition led me to the right conclusions." Now she is sought out by high society. Lady

Fortescue has invited Marburg to a reception in Curzon Street where she meets her latest client—a tall, dark man named Philip Harman. After reading his palm Marburg delivers a disturbing message to the man. "You are about to commit murder, and you will suffer a shameful death on the scaffold." The man gives a harsh laugh and leaves the room. Miss Marburg notes his face "was white as death."

Miss Marburg then reads the palm of Harman's aunt, Mrs. Kenyon. "You are about to undergo a severe shock, a very great grief.... You will need all your strength to withstand it." The woman takes the news in her stride as she has no faith in Miss Marburg's predictions.

Upon returning home Miss Marburg's brother Rupert informs her of gossip concerning Philip Harman. He has run through the Harman estate but cannot touch the property of his uncle Walter Kenyon because Kenyon has left it to his thirteen-year-old grandson. Now Harman plans to marry the beautiful heiress Lady Maude Greville. Miss Marburg tells her brother the marriage cannot proceed.

One month later after the London season has come to an end Mrs. Kenyon pleads with Miss Marburg to visit Philip Harman's place in Godalming. Marburg agrees to Mrs. Kenyon's request despite having no idea whose hand she must read. Upon arrival she is led into a large luxuriously furnished room with the blinds down.

"I found myself gazing down at the beautiful dead face of a child, a boy of about thirteen years of age." Mrs. Kenyon declares, "Dead! My only son! He was drowned this morning. Here is his hand; yesterday it was warm and full of life, now it is cold as marble.... I want you to tell me if he met his death by accident or by design."

Miss Marburg takes the child's hand and concludes he died a violent death by design. "I see something in his hand more than mere drowning, something that baffles me, yet it is plain—Lightning." Miss Marburg promises to bring the murderer to justice. She learns that Philip Harman's marriage proposal to the heiress has been rejected and the dead boy is the only means to inheriting the Kenyon family estate. An artificial pool situated in a stream beyond the garden is the likely place the boy met his death.

"I must sift through the apparent facts of the case the awful truth which lies beneath. The sixth sense which has helped me up to the present shall help me to the end. Beyond doubt foul play has taken place."

The official cause of death is drowning due to cramp. But why would a healthy boy suffer cramps so severe they would cause him to drown? Miss Marburg inspects the pool and finds fine wire netting which goes to its bottom. Dragging the pool with a net and sinkers Mrs. Kenyon notes a dark body lashing the surface of the water "breaking to and fro against the net." Rupert leans over the water and fires his gun. "In the meshes of the net "struggling in its death agony" is a six-foot long electric eel. Not native to the area it was placed there by Harman to kill the boy.

"The crime was brought home to the murderer, who suffered the full penalty of the law."

Other Diana Marburg short stories by L.T. Meade and Robert Eustace: "Finger Tips" (August 1902); "Sir Penn Caryll's Engagement (December 1902).

The Dead Kid Detective Agency [Juvenile book]

Author: Evan Munday; First publication; Toronto, Ontario; ECW Press, 2011.

Lonely thirteen-year-old October Schwartz is new to Sticksville and spends much of her time in the local cemetery where she befriends the ghosts of five dead teenagers from different periods in time. Together they form the Dead Kid Detective Agency dedicated to solving mysteries. Their first case involves the suspicious death of the high school French teacher.

Books in series: *The Dead Kid Detective Agency* (2011); *Dial M for Morna* (2013); *Loyalist to a Fault* (2015); *Connect the Scotts* (2018).

The Dead Letter [Novel]

Author: Seeley Register (Metta Victoria Fuller Victor); First publication: *Beadle's Monthly* (January 1866).

Henry Moreland is found murdered with

a stab wound to his back close to the home of his fiancée Eleanor Argyll. Richard Redfield who works for the girl's father as a law student comes under suspicion from the Argyll family because of his affection for Eleanor. Renowned New York City detective Mr. Burton comes to Redfield's defense as they seek the true killer. Helping Burton is his clairvoyant daughter and his own talent for feeling the presence of criminals.

Originally serialized in *Beadle's Monthly* the story was published in its entirety in 1867 as the first full-length detective novel by an American author.

Dead Men Tell (1941) [Film]

Premiere: March 28, 1941; Main Cast: Stanley Toler as Charlie Chan, Sen Young as Jimmy Chan, Sheila Ryan as Kate Ransome, Robert Weldon as Steve Daniels, Don Douglas as Jed Thomasson, Katherine Aldridge as Laura Thursday, Ethel Griffies as Miss Patience Nodbury, Paul McGrath as Mr. Parks, George Reeves as Bill Lydig, Truman Bradley as Captain Kane, Lenita Lane as Dr. Anne Bonney, Milton Parsons as Gene LaFarge; Producers: Ralph Dietrich, Walter Morosco; Screenplay: John Francis Larkin; Based on the character created by Earl Derr Biggers; Director: Harry Lachman; 61 min; Twentieth Century–Fox; b/w.

"Buried Treasure—Dig for $60,000,000 on Cocos Island. Join the Treasure Hunt Cruise aboard the Suva Star."

Miss Nodbury who owns the pirate map that leads to the treasure has divided it into four parts and given three of the parts to passengers departing on the cruise. Once they arrive at Cocos Island it will be reassembled. Before the treasure hunt begins somebody has attempted to steal Miss Nodbury's map.

Meanwhile Honolulu police detective Charlie Chan has been searching for his number two son on board the ship. Miss Nodbury tells Chan of a family legend that each time a Nodbury dies Black Hook, the Nodbury ancestral pirate escorts them into the other world. That evening Miss Nodbury hears the noise of a wooden peg leg approaching followed by the scratching of a hook on her door. Soon she is face-to-face with the ghost pirate and drops dead on the spot as he takes her part of the map. Charlie Chan doesn't believe in ghosts. Somebody on board has scared the old lady to death. After the discovery of a pirate face mask, wooden leg and hook the passengers become the main suspects.

Dead of the Nite (2013) [Film; UK]

Premiere: April 4, 2013; Main Cast: Tony Todd as Ruber, Joseph Millson as Detective Anderson, Gary Mavers as Detective Jenkins, Cicely Tennant as Amanda, Paul fox as Paul, Simon Bamford as Gary, Suzi Lorraine as Crystal, Simone Kaye as Ann-Marie, Stuart Boother as Jason, Rachel Littlemac as Sheila, Anna Carteret as Mrs. Matthews, Sousila Pillay as Newsreader, Jonathon Farrell as Police Officer; Executive Producer: Joseph Millson; Story/Director: S.J. Evans; 86 min.; Dark Art Films; Pillay-Evans Productions; Ascort International; Color.

Police Detectives Jenkins and Anderson investigate the brutal death of a group of ghost hunters at Jericho Manor. The caretaker claims it was the ghost of Jeffery Heath, a notorious killer, to blame for their deaths. But who is responsible for the slaughter at the haunted Manor?

Deadly Premonition [Video game]

Release date: October 29, 2010; Voice Cast: Jeff Kramer as Special Agent Francis York Morgan/Zach Morgan; Melissa Hutchison as Anna Graham/Sallie Graham; Amy Provenzano as Becky Ames/'Freckly' Fiona; Amy Rubinate as Carol MacLaine/Lilly Ingram; Christiana Crawford as Diane Ames/Polly Oxford; Casey Robertson as The Raincoat Killer/Sheriff George Woodman; Doug Boyd as Forest Kaysen; Rebecca Wink as Deputy Sheriff Emily Watt/Valentine Morgan; Gary Martinez as Harry Stewart/Jim Green; Writers: Kenji Goda, Swery; Director: Swery (Hidetaka "Swery" Suehiro); Developer: Access Games Inc.; Platforms: Xbox 360, PlayStation3, Microsoft Windows; Perspective: 3rd-Person; Publishers: Ignition Entertainment Inc., Marvelous Entertainment, Rising Star Games, Mastertronic.

FBI agent Francis York Morgan assists the law in Greenvale, Washington to solve the murder of Anna Graham and her connection to strange red seeds and a man in a red raincoat. The player controls the dual-personality of York as he explores Greenvale for clues and evidence. He soon discovers Greenvale is a town with hostile supernatural creatures and a shape-shifting killer.

Death Masks (The Dresden Files Book #5)
Author: Jim Butcher; Publisher: New York: Roc, 2003.

Harry Dresden, paranormal investigator and Chicago's only practicing wizard, is hired by a priest to find the missing Shroud of Turin. But he also has the imminent threat of the Red Court of Vampires to contend with. Dresden's life is in danger from their champion who plans to kill him to end the war between vampires and wizards. And Dresden's half-vampire girlfriend Susan Rodriguez has returned with another man. Plus, the Chicago police need Dresden's help in identifying a mutilated corpse. Just another week in the life of Harry Dresden.

See: **Blood Rites**

Death Note [Manga; Anime; TV series; Japan]

[Manga] First publication: *Weekly Shonen Jump* (April 2004); Story: Tsugumi Ohba; Art: Takeshi Obata; Publisher: Shueisha.

The popular manga *Death Note* was published over 108 chapters and adapted into the anime and live-action TV series and video games.

[Anime] Premiere: October 4, 2006; Voice Cast: Mamoru Miyano as Light Yagami, Shidou Nakamura as Ryuk, Kappei Yamaguchi as L, Norika Hidaka as Nate River, Aya Hirano as Misa Amane, Kimoko Saita as Rem; Producers: Masao Maruyama, Manabu Tamura; Story: Toshiki Inove; Director: Tetsuro Araki; 37 × 23 min.; Madhouse; D.N. Dream Partners; Konami; Ashi Production; Nippon Television Network (NTV); VAP; Shueisha; Color.

This highly successful, but controversial anime TV series centers on high school student Light Yagami who discovers a mystical notebook, known as the Death Note. Belonging to a Shinigami death god named Ryuk, the Death Note has the power to kill. Instructions in the Death Note must be followed precisely. "The human whose name is written in this notebook shall die." The person writing the name must also visualize the face of that person in their mind. The Death Note becomes the bond between Ryuku, the god of death and Light.

Light adopts the person of "Kira" to confuse the police, but the mysterious genius detective known simply as "L" vows to find the person responsible for over 100 deaths and dares Kira to kill him.

In April 2015 *Death Note* was banned in China in a crackdown against anime and manga titles that "include scenes of violence, pornography, terrorism and crimes against public morality."

In 2007, dismembered body parts were discovered by the police in the forest of Belgium's Duden Park. Two notes were left next to the body parts saying, "I am Kira" in a reference to the character in *Death Note*.

SEASON ONE

Rebirth (1:01); *Confrontation* (1:02); *Transaction* (1:03); *Pursuit* (1:04); *Bargaining* (1:05); *Open Seam* (1:06); *Clouded Sky* (1:07); *Gaze* (1:08); *Contact* (1:09); *Suspicion* (1:10); *Entrance* (1:11); *Love* (1:12); *Confession* (1:13); *Friend* (1:14); *Gamble* (1:15); *Decision* (1:16); *Execution* (1:17); *Companion* (1:18); *Matsuda* (1:19); *Makeshift* (1:20); *Activity* (1:21); *Guidance* (1:22); *Mania* (1:23); *Revival* (1:24); *Silence* (1:25); *Reincarnation* (1:26); *Abduction* (1:27); *Impatience* (1:28); *Father* (1:29); *Justice* (1:30); *Transfer* (1:31); *Selection* (1:32); *Ridicule* (1:33); *Glare* (1:34); *Murderous Intent* (1:35); *1:28* (1:36); *New World* (1:37).

Anime TV Specials: Director's Cut Conclusion Rewrite: *The Visualizing God*; Director's Cut Conclusion Rewrite 2: *L's Successor's*.

[TV series] Premiere: July 5, 2015; Main Cast: Masataka Kubota as Light Yagami, Kento Yamazaki as L, Mio Yuki as Near/Mello, Hinako Sano as Misa Amane, Jun Fukushima as Ryuk, Ayumi Tsunematsu as Rem, Yutuka Matsushige as Soichiro Yagami, Reiko Fujiwara as Sayu

Yagami; Executive Producer: Katsu Kamikura; Story: Yoshihiro Izumi; Based on the manga by Tsugumi Ohba and Takeshi Obata; Directors: Ryuichi Inomata, Ryo Nishimura, Marie Iwasaki; 11 × 55–85 min.; Nippon Television Network (NTV); AXON; Color.

This live-action TV mini-series based on the manga and anime spanned eleven untitled episodes.

Death Valley (2011) [TV series]

Premiere: August 29, 2011; Main Cast: Texas Battle as Officer John Johnson, Bryce Johnson as Officer Billy Pierce, Tania Raymonde as Officer Carla Rinaldi, Charlie Sanders as Officer Joe Stubeck, Bryan Callen as Officer Dashell, Caity Lotz as Officer Kirsten Landray, Toby Meuli as Jamie, Vene L. Arcoraci as Detective Dunwalt; Executive Producers: Tony DiBari, Tim Healy, Austin Reading, Julie Reading, Eric Weinberg; Creator: Curtis Gwinn; 12 × 22 min.; Liquid Theory; Music Television (MTV); Color.

A mockumentary following the Undead Task Force (UTF) and the camera crew who film their encounters with zombies, werewolves and vampires in the San Fernando Valley.

Season One

Pilot (1:01); *Help Us Help You* (1:02); *Blood Vessels* (1:03); *Two Girls, One Cop* (1:04); *Zombie Fights* (1:05); *The Hottest Day of the Year* (1:06); *Who, What, When, Werewolf.... Why?* (1:07); *Undead Hookers* (1:08); *Tick.... Tick.... BOOM!* (1:09); *Assault on Precinct UTF* (1:10); *Partners* (1:11); *Peace in the Valley* (1:12).

Death Warmed Over: Dan Shamble, Zombie P.I. (Volume 1)

Author: Kevin J. Anderson; First publication: New York: Kensington Publishing, 2012.

A decade ago the Big Uneasy allowed zombies, werewolves, vampires, ghouls, succubi and ghosts to return. Dan Chambeaux was murdered and rose from the grave as a zombie. Now, private undead investigator Dan Chambeaux and compassionate human lawyer Robin Deyer working as "Chambeaux and Deyer Investigations" specialize in cases in the Unnatural Quarter. Helping him is Sheyenne, his dead girlfriend's ghost and Best Human Friend (BHF) Officer Toby McGoohan.

Book series: *Death Warmed Over* (2012); *Unnatural Acts* (2013); *Hair Raising* (2013); *Slimy Underbelly* (2014); *Working Stiff* (2014); *Tastes Like Chicken* (2017); *Services Rendered* (2018).

Deliver Us from Evil (2014) [Film]

Premiere: July 2, 2014; Main Cast: Eric Bana as Ralph Sarchie, Edgar Ramirez as Father Mendoza, Olivia Munn as Jen Sarchie, Lulu Wilson as Christina Sarchie, Chris Coy as Jimmy Tratner, Sean Harris as Mick Santino, Joel McHale as Butler, Dorian Missick as Gordon, Mike Houston as Nadler, Olivia Horton as Jane Crenna, Valentina Rendon as Claudia, Rhona Fox as Zookeeper; Executive Producers: Paul Harris Boardman, Glenn S. Gainor, Chad Oman, Mike Stenson, Ben Waisbren; Screenplay: Scott Derrickson, Paul Harris Boardman: Adapted from the book based on real-life events by Ralph Sarchie and Lisa Collier Cool; Director: Scott Derrickson; 88 min.; Screen Gems; Jerry Bruckheimer Films; LStar Capital; Color.

New York police sergeant Ralph Sarchie and his partner Butler investigate a series of strange murders and crimes in the Bronx. Sarchie is a lapsed Catholic who no longer believes in demonic activity until a Jesuit priest's warning that his investigations place him and his family in danger prove to be true.

Descendants of Darkness (2000) [Anime; Manga; Japan]

Premiere: October 2, 2000; Voice Cast: Shinichiro Miki as Asato Tsuzuki, Mayumo Asano as Hisoka Kurosaki, Sho Hayami as Kazutaka Muraki, Tomomichi Nishimura as Chief Konoe, Toshiyuku Morikawa as Seiichiro Tatsumi; Producers: Atsushi Moriyama, Toshimichi Ootsuki, Yuji Matsukura; Story: Akiko Horii, Masaharu Amiya; Director: Hiroko Tokita; 13 × 25 min.; J.C. Staff; WOWOW; Hakusensha; MOVIC; Starchild Records; Color.

Tsuzuki Asato is a young Shinigami (god of death) who is sent to Earth by his boss Chief Kenoe to track a serial killer with the profile of a vampire, on the loose in Nagazaki. Helping Asato in his investigations is Hisoka Kurosaki.

Season One

The Nagasaki File: Part 1 (1:01); *The Nagasaki File: Part 2* (1:02); *The Nagasaki File: Part 3* (1:03); *The Devil's Trill: Part 1* (1:04); *The Devil's Trill: Part 2* (1:05); *The Devil's Trill: Part 3* (1:06); *The King of Swords: Part 1* (1:07); *The King of Swords: Part 2* (1:08); *The King of Swords: Part 3* (1:09); *The Kyoto File: Part 1* (1:10); *The Kyoto File: Part 2* (1:11); *The Kyoto File: Part 3* (1:12); *The Kyoto File: Part 4* (1:13).

[Manga] First publication: *Hana to Yume* (1996); Story & Art: Yoko Matsushita; Publisher: Hakusensha.

The original inspiration for the anime TV series. Currently in its 13th volume.

Detective Anna (2016) [TV series; Russia]

Premiere: November 7, 2016; Main Cast: Aleksandra Nikiforova as Anna Mironova, Dimitry Frid as Iakov Shtolman, Sergey Druzyak as Anton Korobejnikov, Inna Sidorova as Maria Mironova, Andrey Ryklin as Victor Mironov, Audrey Lukyanov as Doctor Milts, Boris Khvoshnyanskiy as Pyotr Mironov, Elena Polyakova as Nina Neginskaya, Algis Arlauskas as Prince Razumovsky; Producers: Vitaliy Bordachev; Daria Legoni-Fialko; Ekaterina Andrienko; Vlad Ryashin; 56 × 45 min.; Star Media; Color.

The year is 1888. In the Russian town of Zatonsk lives nineteen-year-old Anna Mironova. The spirits of the dead ask for her help in solving their murders. Together with thirty-seven-year-old detective Iakov Shtolman they solve crimes together as love blossoms.

Detective Chimp (Comic book character)

First appearance: *Adventures of Rex the Wonder Dog* #4 (July–August 1952); Creators: John Broome, Carmine Infantino; Publisher: DC Comics.

Bobo T. Chimpanzee began life in the African continent. On a visit to Africa Fred Thorpe was looking for a chimpanzee to train for his carnival act, "Bobo the Detective Chimp." The captured chimpanzee was treated humanely by Thorpe and taught to answer simple questions for his act. But a trip to Florida where he encountered **Rex the Wonder Dog** changed the course of Bobo's life forever. Rex took Bobo to the Fountain of Youth where he not only gained eternal youth but the ability to speak to both humans and animals.

Bobo could now be independent, forming his own detective agency and was briefly employed by the **Bureau of Amplified Animals**. As a member of Mensa, Bobo is highly intelligent and has worked with **Batman** and Commissioner Gordon in Gotham City.

Detective Conan a.k.a. ***Case Closed*** (1996) [Anime; Manga; Japan]

Premiere: January 8, 1996; Voice Cast: Minami Takayama as Conan Edogawa, Megumi Hayashibara as Ai Haibara, Wakana Yamazaki as Ran Mouri, Rikiya Koyama as Kogorou Mouri, Yukiko Iwai as Ayumi Yoshida, Ikue Ootani as Mitsuhiko Tsuburaya, Kenichi Ogata as Hiroshi Agasa, Wataru Takagi as Genta Kojima; Creator: Gosho Aoyama; Producers: Michihiko Suwa, Masahito Yoshioka; Directors: Kenji Kodama, Masato Sato, Kojin Ochi; 911 × 25 min.; Yomuri Telecasting; Animax; YTV; Shogakukan; TMS-Kyokuchi; Color.

High school student Shinichi Kudou is a highly skilled detective, solving cases for the Japanese Police Department. One fateful day Shinichi's life changes when he is apprehended by members of the Black Organization and forced to drink a deadly poison. But instead of killing him the poison transforms Shinichi into a seven-year-old child. With his intelligence still intact Shinichi assumes a new identity to hide the fact he is still alive. As Conan Edogawa he seeks to restore his body to normal size while continuing his secret detective work for private detective Kongorou Mouri.

While Detective Conan can be defined as a weird detective due to his origin story his cases contain no supernatural elements. The anime has reached 16 seasons and over 900 episodes, with numerous spin-offs. These include twenty-two animated feature-length films, two original video animated series (OVA), video games and a live-action TV series.

[Manga] First publication: *Shonen Sunday* (January 19, 1994); Story & Art: Gosho Aoyama; Publisher: Shogakukan.

The manga that inspired the long-running anime TV series has been published in 95-volumes.

Detective Dee: The Four Heavenly Kings a.k.a. ***Di Renjie zhi Sidatianwang*** (2018) [Film; China; Hong Kong]

Premiere: July 27, 2018; Main Cast: Mark Chao as Dee, Gengxin Lin as Shatou Zhong, Shaefeng Feng as Yuchi Zhenjin, Carina Lau as Empress Wu Zetian, Sichun Ma as Shui Yue, Ethan Juan as Master Yuan Ce, Sandra Ma as Moon Water; Producers: Kuo-Fu Chen, Nansun Shi, Hark Tsui; Story: Chia-Lu Cheng; Director: Hark Tsui; 132 min.; Huayi Brothers; Color.

Detective Dee, head of the Department of Justice, comes to the attention of Empress Wu Zetian who desires his powerful "Dragon Taming Mace" for herself. But waiting in the background are wizards intent on overthrowing the Tang Dynasty.

Detective Dee: Mystery of the Phantom Flame a.k.a. ***Di renjie: Tong tian di guo*** (2010) [Film; China; Hong Kong]

Premiere: September 30, 2010; Main Cast: Andy Lau as Detective Dee, Tony Ka Fai Leung as Shatou Zhong, Chao Deng as Pei Donglai, Carina Lau as Empress Wu Zetian, Li Bing Bing as Shangguan Jing'er; Producers: Peggy Lee, Nansun Shi, Hark Tsui; Story: Kuo-Fu Chen; From an original story by Qianyu Lin; Screenplay: Chia-Lu Chang; Director: Hark Tsui; 123 min.; China Film Co-Production Corporation; Film Workshop; Huayi Brothers Media; Xian Longrui Film and TV Culture Media Co.; Indomina Releasing; Color.

On the eve of her inauguration Empress Wu Zetian's courtiers have spontaneously combusted. Now the ancient world's greatest detective is freed from prison to solve the mystery.

Followed by the prequel ***Young Detective Dee: Rise of the Sea Dragon*** (2013) and its sequel ***Detective Dee: The Four Heavenly Kings*** (2018).

Detective Pikachu [Video game; Japan]

Release date: March 23, 2018; Voice cast: Kaiji Tang as Detective Pakachu, Khoi Dao as Tim Goodman, Kira Buckland as Emilia Christie, David Lodge as Mike Baker, Erica Mendez as Amanda Blackstone, Taylor Henry as Frank Holiday, Bill Rogers as Brad McMaster, Cherami Leigh as Meiko Okamoto, Paul Stewart as Ethan Graham, Xander Mobus as Roger Clifford, Chris Smith as Mewtwo; Story: Tomokazu Ohara, Haruka Utsui; Art: Masataka Hata; Director: Naoki Miyashita; Developer: Creatures Inc.; Platform: Nintendo 3DS; Publisher: Nintendo.

Tim Goodman teams up with gruff talking Detective Pikachu to find Tim's missing father. Their investigation uncovers strange happenings over Ryme City which they must solve. The player takes the role of Tim Goodman looking for clues and collecting testimonies and items from crime scenes to include in his Case File.

The video game is an expansion of *Great Detective Pikachu: Birth of a New Duo* that was released exclusively in Japan on February 3, 2016. A live-action/animated film version ***Pokemon Detective Pikachu*** premiered in May 2019.

"The Detective's Album: The Phantom Hearse" [Short story]

Author: W.W. (Mary Fortune); First publication: *The Australian Journal* (September 1889).

Constable Lumsden "was an especially raw recruit and as full of an idea of his own importance as raw police recruits generally are." Lumsden listens with skepticism to the local gossip of a phantom hearse. The corner shop owner Old Jones tells the tale of the "Phantom Funeral." "It's getting on for twelve years ago now since that hearse was first seen. Sam Brown was murdered or committed suicide—and from that day to this the hearse haunts the place as a sort of revenge on the neighbors that they didn't pay more respect to his remains."

Lumsden doesn't believe a word of the story but continues to listen to Jones. "It's the scoffers as see it, and it's not lucky to see it...."

There has never been a man foolhardy enough to watch it, but he died within the year."

Lumsden laughs out loud, but later comes to believe in the Dead Hearse when he sees it for himself. "I put out my hand twice to try and touch it, but I only had air in my grip." But for now, Constable Lumsden has a murder to solve. Old Jones has been found dead of a stab wound to the stomach.

Devil (2010) [Film]

Premiere: September 17, 2010; Main Cast: Chris Messina as Detective Bowden, Logan Marshall-Green as Mechanic, Jenny O'Hara as Old Woman, Bojana Novakovic as Young Woman, Bokeem Woodbine as Guard, Geoffrey Arend as Salesman, Jacob Vargas as Ramirez, Matt C raven as Lustig, Josh Peace as Detective Markowitz, Caroline Dhavernas as Elsa Nahai, Joe Cobden as Dwight, Zoie Palmer as Cheryl, Vincent Laresca as Henry; Executive Producers: Drew Dowdle, Trish Hofmann; Story: M. Night Shyamalan; Screenplay: Brian Nelson; Director: John Erik Dowdle; 80 min.; Media Rights Capital (MRC); Night Chronicles; Universal Pictures; Color.

In a Philadelphia skyscraper five strangers are trapped on an elevator. Meanwhile Detective Bowden is investigating a possible murder-suicide from the same building. Now he must find a way to rescue the people in the elevator. But tensions increase among the five and talk of the Devil hiding among the living circulates. When people in the elevator start dying Detective Bowden realizes there is a link between the deaths and the death of his wife and son in a hit-and-run accident years ago.

Devil May Cry (2007) [Anime; Japan]

Premiere: June 14, 2007; Voice Cast: Toshiyuki Morikawas as Dante, Misato Fukuen as Patty, Akio Ohtsuka as Morrison, Atsuko Tanaka as Trish, Fumiko Orikasa as Lady; Story: Shotaro Suga, Bingo Morihashi, Toshiki Inoue, Ichiro Sakaki; Animation Director: Hisashi Abe; Director: Shin Itagaki; 12 × 24 min.; Madhouse; CAPCOM; Media Factory; Toshiba Entertainment; WOWOW; Color.

Half demon, half human Dante is the son of a human mother and the legendary dark knight, Sparda. Dante promotes himself as a demon hunter for hire through his investigation agency "Devil May Cry." Investigations include a possessed motorcycle, a wish fulfilling demonic mask and a demonic gambler.

The animated series is loosely based on the 2001 action-adventure video game by Capcom.

SEASON ONE

Devil May Cry (1:01); *Highway Star* (1:02); *Not Love* (1:03); *Rolling Thunder* (1:04); *In Private* (1:05); *Rock Queen* (1:06); *Wishes Come True* (1:07); *Once Upon a Time* (1:08); *Death Poker* (1:09); *The Last Promise* (1:10); *Showtime!* (1:11); *Stylish!* (1:12).

The Devil Rides Out [Novel; Film; UK]

Author: Dennis Wheatley; First publication: London: Hutchinson, 1934).

Occultist, adventurer and French exile the Duke de Richleau, wealthy young American Rex van Ryn and Richard Eaton rescue their friend Simon Aron from a Satanic cult led by Damien Mocata, but in doing so place their lives and souls in danger.

Author Dennis Wheatley featured "Those Modern Musketeers" in two more occult novels. In *Strange Conflict* (1941) the Duke must stop Nazi occultists targeting the secret routes of Atlantic Convoys during World War II. *Gateway to Hell* (1970) also centers around a Satanic cult. When Rex van Ryn steals over a million dollars from his family bank in Buenos Aires the Duke and his friends know he is under some dark force and must come to his aid.

[Film] Premiere: July 20, 1968; Main Cast: Christopher Lee as Duc de Richleau, Charles Gray as Mocata, Leon Greene as Rex Van Ryn, Patrick Mower as Simon Aron, Nike Arrighi as Tanith Carlisle, Gwen Ffrangcon Davies as Countess, Sarah Lawson as Marie Eaton, Paul Eddington as Richard Eaton, Rosalyn Landor as Peggy Eaton, Russell Waters as Malin; Producer: Anthony Nelson Keys; Screenplay: Richard Matheson; Based on the novel by Dennis Wheatley; Director: Terence Fisher; 95

min.; Associated British Pathe; Hammer Film Production; Seven Arts Productions; Warner-Pathe Distributors; Color.

Simon Aron and his friend Tanith Carlisle become entangled in a Satanic cult led by the evil Mocata. Before they are baptized at the Grand Sabbat the Duke and Van Ryn rescue them only to face greater danger in the form of the Angel of Death.

D4: Dark Dreams Don't Die [Video game]
Release date: September 18, 2014; Voice Cast: Ben Pronsky as David Young, Elizabeth Thomas as Peggy Young, David Lodge as Forrest Kaysen, Erika Harlacher as Olivia Jones, Liam O'Brien as Phillip Cheney, Amanda Rollins as Deborah Anderson, Ben Giroux as Antonio "Rabbit" Zapatero, Chris Tergliafera as Roland Walken, Michael Sorich as Derek Buchanan, Ray Chase as Duncan, Richard Epcar as August Oldmann; Writers: Hidetaka Suehiro, Hiroyuki Saegusa, Kenji Goda; Director: Hidetaka Suehiro; Developer: Access Games; Platforms: Xbox One, Microsoft Windows; Perspective: 3rd-Person; Publishers: Microsoft Studios, Playism.

Private detective David Young can travel through time by touching "mementos." Now he has the chance to change the fate of his wife who was murdered two years ago by an unknown killer. A memento holds the key to taking Young back to the day his wife died. Together with his wife's final words "Look for D" Young finally hopes to bring her killer to justice.

Dirk Gently's Holistic Detective Agency (2016) [TV series]
Premiere: October 22, 2016; Main Cast: Samuel Barnett as Dirk Gently, Elijah Wood as Todd Brotzman, Hannah Marks as Amanda Brotzman, Jade Eshete as Farah Black, Mpho Koaho as Ken, Dustin Milligan as Sgt. Hugo Friedkin, Fiona Dourif as Bart Curlish, Osric Chau as Vogel, Michael Eklund as Martin, Bentley as Rapunzel the Corgi, Zak Santiago as Cross, Viv Leacock as Gripps; Executive Producers: Arvin Ethan David, Rick Jacobs, Ted Adams, David Ozer, David Alpert, Zainir Aminullah, Robert C. Cooper, Max Landis; Creator: Max Landis; Based on the novels by Douglas Adams; 18 × 44 min.; AMC Studios; BBC America; Circle of Confusion; IDW Entertainment; Ideate Media; Netflix; Color.

Dirk Gently is a self-proclaimed holistic detective who approaches his cases in the belief all things are inter-connected. He is attracted to the supernatural with his first case involving a soul-swapping machine.

SEASON ONE

Horizons (1:01); *Lost & Found* (1:02); *Rogue Wall Enthusiasts* (1:03); *Watkin* (1:04); *Very Erectus* (1:05); *Fix Everything* (1:06); *Weaponized Soul* (1:07); *Two Sane Guys Doing Normal Things* (1:08).

SEASON TWO

Space Rabbit (2:01); *Fans of Wet Circles* (2:02); *Two Broken Fingers* (2:03); *The House Within a House* (2:04); *Shapes and Colors* (2:05); *Girl Power* (2:06); *This Is Not Miami* (2:07); *Little Guy, Black Hair* (2:08); *Trouble Is Bad* (2:09); *Nice Jacket* (2:10).

Discworld Noir [Video game]
Release date: 1999; Voice Cast: Rob Brydon as Lewton, Kate Robbins as Carlotta von Uberwald, Robert Llewellyn as Jasper Horst, Nigel Planer as Count Henning von Uberwald; Writer: Chris Bateman; Director: Greg Barnett; Developer: Perfect Entertainment; Platforms: PlayStation, Microsoft Windows; Perspective: 3rd-Person; Publisher: GT Interactive Software Europe Ltd.

Private investigator Lewton is hired to find a man named Mundy by the mysterious Carlotta only to find himself the prime suspect in Mundy's murder. And to add to his woes Lewton becomes a werewolf who can communicate with a talking dog. Set in the Discworld city of Ankh-Morpork where trolls and dwarves seek possession of the "Golden Sword" the player controls Lewton as both a human detective and a werewolf.

The Diviners [Juvenile book]
Author: Libba Bray: First publication: New York: Little, Brown Books for Young Readers, 2012.

1920s New York City. Evangeline O'Neil lives with her Uncle Will, curator of the Museum of American Folklore, Superstition, and the Occult. Unknown to her uncle Evie has a supernatural gift as a diviner who can read people's secrets. A gift she uses to track the killer of a girl branded with a cryptic symbol. Soon she will be a celebrity known as "America's Sweetheart Seer"—but other Diviners are not so enamored.

Books in series: *The Diviners* (2012); *Lair of Dreams* (2015); *Before the Devil Breaks You* (2017).

Doctor Dale [Pulp fiction character]

Author-Creator: Hugh Davidson (Edmond Hamilton); First appearance: "The Master Vampire" *Weird Tales* (October 1933).

Introduced to readers of *Weird Tales* as a "specialist in combating forces of evil whose manifestations lie beyond ordinary medical science." In the serialized story "The Vampire Master" (October 1933–January 1934), Doctor Dale and his assistant Harley Owen come to the aid of Dr. Henderson who is concerned about his patient Olivia. Each night she is under attack from a vampire that has returned after lying dormant for 200 years.

In "The House of the Evil Eye" (June 1936), Dr. Henry Carlin asks Doctor Dale for help when he fears his son is slowly being killed by the evil eye.

Dr. Desmond Drew (Comic book character)

First appearance: *Rangers Comics* #47 (June 1949); Creators: Marilyn Mercer; Jerry Grandenetti; Publisher: Fiction House.

In the castle mansion atop isolated Bone Hill lives Dr. Drew, investigator of the unknown. From his gloomy retreat the pipe smoking detective recalls his "experiences in the eerie world that lies somewhere between reality and infinity."

In his first adventure, "The Strange Case of the Absent Floor" Dr. Drew is approached by an elevator operator at the Wainwright building. He tells Dr. Drew that the man he let off at the mysterious 13th floor was the deceased murderer Joseph Wainwright. Dr. Drew investigates the 13th floor and is witness to events that happened twenty years earlier when Lucy and Adam Wainwright were murdered.

The Secret Files of Dr. Drew ran to fourteen issues before he retired in August 1951.

Dr. Edward Carstairs M.D. [Short story character]

Author-Creator: Agatha Christie; First appearance: *The Hound of Death and Other Stories*; Publisher: London: Odhams, 1933.

Dr. Edward Carstairs makes his one and only appearance in Agatha Christie's short story "The Strange Case of Dr. Arthur Carmichael." As a doctor-detective Carstairs along with Dr. Settle investigate young Arthur Carmichael who has lost the ability to speak and act human. To add to the mystery Carstairs is the only person

The cover for *Weird Tales* (October 1933) featuring "The Vampire Master." Cover art by Margaret Brundage (Popular Fiction).

The first appearance of occult detective Dr. Desmond Drew in "The Strange Case of the Absent Floor," *Rangers Comics* #47 (June 1949), page 15. Story by Marilyn Mercer. Art by Jerry Grandenetti. Published by Fiction House.

who can see a grey Persian cat on the property in Wolden, Hertfordshire. And Lady Carmichael appears to be the target of the cat's anger.

Dr. Ivan Brodsky [Short story character]

Author-Creator: H. M. Egbert (Victor Rousseau Emanuel); First appearance: "The Woman with the Crooked Nose" *Goshen Daily Democrat* (October 7, 1910).

"Remarkable achievements of Ivan Brodsky, physician, whose investigations into psychic phenomena enabled him to cure spiritual diseases and exorcise evil spirits from the bodies of their victims"

Dr. Ivan Brodsky, formerly a professor in nervous diseases at a London hospital is now in private practice. Described as "an undersized man with a great head disproportionate to his body" Dr. Brodsky is also a part-time occult detective and master hypnotist.

Eleven of the twelve stories were reprinted in *Weird Tales* between September 1926 and July 1927.

Short stories: "The Woman with the Crooked Nose" (October 7, 1910); "The Case of the Jailer's Daughter" (October 14, 1910); "The Legacy of Hate" (October 28, 1910); "The Tenth Commandment" (November 19, 1910); "The Major's Menagerie" (December 9, 1910); "The Fetish of the Waxworks" (December 23, 1910); "The Seventh Symphony" (January 6, 1911); "The Man Who Lost His Luck" (January 14, 1911); "The Chairs of Stuyvensant Baron" (February 3, 1911); "Homo Homunculus" (February 17, 1911); "The Dream That Came True" (March 3, 1911); "The Ultimate Problem" (March 17, 1911).

Dr. John Richard Taverner [Short story character]

Author-Creator: Dion Fortune (Violet Mary Firth); First appearance: *Royal Magazine* (1922).

From his mysterious nursing home at Hindhead and his Harley Street consulting room Dr. Taverner helps those in psychic distress. Assisting him is medical doctor Rhodes who narrates his cases.

"…Taverner, by his peculiar methods of work, laid bare causes operating both within the soul and in the shadowy realm where the soul has its dwelling, that threw an entirely new light upon the problem, and often enabled him to rescue a man from the dark influences that were closing in upon him."

Author Dion Fortune based the character on the real-life person Thomas Moriarty. Fortune founded the Society of the Inner Light, professed a working knowledge of the occult and stated her stories "are all founded on fact."

In "Blood Lust" the hungry ghost of a German soldier killed in World War I possesses the body of Captain Donald Craigie who then develops a "blood hunger" for fresh blood from the veins of his victims.

"The Man Who Sought" sees Arnold Black seeking help from Dr. Taverner for a peculiar problem. "Can't sit still. Can't do a thing except tear all over the country in my car as hard as ever I can lick…. I drive and drive and drive until I'm clean tuckered out…" His trouble began with an accident that left him unconscious for three days and now he feels he's "in love with a woman who doesn't exist…. That's why I drive so much, because I feel that round the next bend, I'll find her." When Black is involved in another car crash Taverner and Rhodes see Black's etheric double leave his body attracted to the reborn soul of the woman he loved in a past life. Her love for him allows Black to re-enter his body. Two souls have found each other again.

"The Death Hound" begins with Mr. Martin telling Dr. Taverner of a ferocious black spectral dog who seeks repeated opportunities to spring at his throat. Taverner sees a link to the occult Black Lodges and "mental assassination" by means of thought transference.

Other short stories originally published in *Royal Magazine* were collected into one volume *The Secrets of Dr. Taverner* (1926). These include: "The Return of the Ritual"; "The Soul That Would Not Be Born"; "The Scented Poppies"; "A Daughter of Pan"; "The Subletting of the Mansion"; "Recalled"; "The Sea Lure"; "The Power House"; "A Son of the Night."

Dr. Martin Hesselius [Short story character]

Author-Creator: Joseph Sheridan Le Fanu; First appearance: "Green Tea" *All the Year Round* (October 23, 1869).

In the serialized story "Green Tea" Dr. Martin Hesselius, an expert in Metaphysical Medicine listens to the Reverend Robert Jennings' accounts of his encounters with a demonic monkey that "…is always urging me to crimes, to injure others or myself." The Reverend, thinking his drinking of green tea to be a factor abandons his favorite pastime. But the spectral monkey continues to haunt him with tragic results.

Dr. Hesselius, one of the first paranormal doctor-detectives features in other works by Le Fanu but is not central to the stories.

Short stories: "Green Tea" (four-part story October 23, 1869–November 13, 1869); "Carmilla" (December 1871–March 1872)

Short story collection: *In a Glass Darkly* (1872).

Doctor Martinus [Pulp fiction character]
Author-Creator: Victor Rousseau (Avigdor Rousseau Emanuel); First appearance: "Child or Demon—Which?" *Ghost Stories* (October 1926); Publisher: Constructive Publishing Corp.

In his first recorded case Dr. Martinus and his personal assistant Eugene Branscombe are asked to come to the aid of baby Robert who is possessed by the spirit of resentful old maid Emma Wishart. Emma is jealous of her sister Thyra who married Richard Adrian, the man she loved. Now the baby is feeding off his parent's blood.

Short stories: "Child or Demon -Which?" (October 1926); "The Doll That Came to Life" (January 1927); "The Ghost of the Red Cavalier" (March 1927); "Fire-Water-and What?" (June 1927); "The Souls That Lost Its Way" (August 1927); "The House of the Living Dead" (Six-part story: December 1927–May 1928).

Dr. Miles Pennoyer [Short story character]
Author-Creator: Margery Lawrence; First appearance: *Number Seven, Queer Street*; Publisher: London: Robert Hale, 1945.

Psychic doctor Miles Pennoyer lives with his housekeeper and dog Hans at No. 7, Queer Street. Abstaining from alcohol and meat is said to heighten his intuitive powers. Dr. Pennoyer is a physician of the occult who takes on cases that ultimately lead to psychical healing. Jerome Latimer acts as his chronicler.

His initial seven cases are collected in *Number Seven, Queer Street*. In "The Case of the Bronze Door" a man is haunted by a demon lover. "The Case of the Haunted Cathedral" involves two ghosts and an exorcism. "The Case of Ella McLeod" details the relationship between a dog and a Scottish maid with a knowledge of Ancient Greek that points to a reincarnated soul. "The Case of the White Snake" sees a ghostly snake haunt a girl's orphanage that hints at a psychic umbilical cord connecting young Collette to somebody in the orphanage. "The Case of the Moonchild" features occultist Father Aloysius, an ancient cult and Dr. Pennoyer's "bogey-bag" which contains all the tools required to tackle the "forces of the Outer Dark." "The Case of the Young Man with the Scar" involves a psychic connection between a random scar resembling a dull red snake on a man's arm and a ghost. The final story "The Case of the Leannabh Sidhe" centers on troubled Patrick Flaherty, a boy who has turned sour following the death of his father in an automobile accident. Now anyone who annoys or chastises him suffers an accident. Dr. Pennoyer becomes the boy's tutor to solve the mystery behind his strange personality disorder. A mystery that ends in an ancient ritual in Ireland on Halloween.

A second collection of Dr. Miles Pennoyer stories titled *Master of Shadows* was published by Robert Hale in 1959.

Dr. Occult (Comic book character)
First appearance: *New Fun* #6 (October 1935); Creators: Jerry Siegel, Joe Shuster; Publisher: National Allied Publication (DC Comics).

Introduced in a one-page continuing strip "Dr. Occult, the Ghost Detective has sworn to combat supernatural evil in this world." In his debut case he uses his lovely assistant Rose Psychic as bait for a vampire but discovers his "magic symbol has no effect upon the vampire!" As the story continues, we learn that Dr. Occult is up against "The Vampire Master."

Occult possesses paranormal powers including the ability to cast illusions, move within the astral plane, observe events in his astral body to avoid detection, telekinesis and teleportation. Starting life as a trenchcoat detective Dr. Occult becomes "Dr. Mystic, the Occult Detective" for one issue in Centaur Publications' *The Comics Magazine* #1 (May 1936). The story continues in *New Fun Comics* #14 under the original moniker as Dr. Occult joins forces with "The Seven" and acquires a cape, magical belt and sword to battle the evil Koth.

After an absence of 47 years Dr. Occult returns as a member of World War II's *All-Star Squadron* and later as part of the **Trenchcoat Brigade** guiding young Tim Hunter through otherworlds as part of his training as a master magician.

Doctor Thirteen (Comic book character)

First appearance: *Star-Spangled Comics* #122 (November 1951); Co-creator: Leonard Starr; Publisher: DC Comics.

Dr. Terrence Thirteen doesn't believe in curses, despite a tragic family history through the centuries, said to be the work of witches and warlocks. Influenced by his late father, who died in a car crash, "Terry" Thirteen sets out to debunk all paranormal phenomena. With the official title of "Ghost-Breaker" Dr. Thirteen successfully explains all manner of supernatural events until he encounters the Phantom Stranger.

2. First appearance: *All-Star Western* #11 (September 2012); Creators: Justin Gray, Jimmy Palmiotti, Scott Kolins; Publisher: DC Comics.

Doctor Terrence Thirteen, an inventor and man of science and reason, is a debunker of the occult and supernatural in 1880s Gotham City.

Don't Knock Twice (2016) [Film; UK]

Premiere: September 22, 2016; Main Cast: Katee Sackhoff as Jess, Lucy Boynton as Chloe, Richard Mylan as Ben, Nick Moran as Detective Boardman, Javier Botet as Ginger Special, Jordan Bolger as Danny, Pooneh Hajimohammadi as Tira, Ania Marson as Mary Aminov; Executive Producers: Jamie Carmichael, Alan Martin, Robert Norris, Adam Partridge, Ali Pour; Story: Mark Huckerby, Nick Ostler; Director: Caradog James; 93 min.; Red & Black Films; Seymour Films; Color.

Detective Boardman investigates the disappearance of Chloe's boyfriend Danny. Chloe is convinced she is haunted by an evil spirit after knocking twice on the door of a legendary witch. But Boardman believes Chloe's estranged mother Jess in trying to regain custody of her daughter is manipulating her emotions.

Double Vision a.k.a. **Shuang tong** (2002) [Film; Taiwan/Hong Kong]

Premiere: October 25, 2002; Main Cast: Tony Leung Ka-fai as Huang Huo-tu, David Morse as Kevin Richter, Rene Liu as Ching-fang, Leon Dai as Li Feng-bo, Yang Kuei-Mei as Coroner, Sihung Lung as Dr. Sheng, Brett Climo as Serial Killer, Huang wei-han as Mei-Mie; Executive Producers: Chen Kuo-fu, Roger Huang; Writers: Chen Kuo-fu, Su Chao-pin; Director: Chen Kuo-fu; 113 min.; Columbia Pictures Film Productions Asia; Nan Fang Film Productions; Color.

Taiwan police detective Huang Huo-tu has been ostracized by his fellow police officers for exposing corruption in the force. Now he is acting as liaison to FBI agent Kevin Richter who is investigating a series of weird deaths. Huang senses a supernatural link to a Taoist immortality cult. All the victims have one thing in common—a hallucinatory fungus found in their brains resulting in their suicides.

Dracula [Novel; Stage play; Film]

Author: Bram Stoker; First publication: London: Archibald Constable and Company, 1897.

The first appearance of vampire hunter and occult detective Professor Abraham Van Helsing. Lucy Westenra begins to act strangely and is spotted at night in Whitby cemetery by her friend Mina Murray. Soon after Lucy becomes seriously ill and his former student Dr. John Seward asks Van Helsing for help. After examining puncture marks on her neck Van Helsing fears she may have been the victim of a vampire and orders garlic to protect her. But when her mother removes the garlic Lucy's health declines and multiple blood transfusions fail to revive her. An attack by a wolf entering the home finally kills Lucy.

Arthur Holmwood, Quincey Morris and Dr. Seward join Van Helsing as they open Lucy's tomb and plunge a stake through her heart to save her soul. Then they decapitate her and place garlic in her mouth. Now the source of the vampirism must be destroyed. Count Dracula must be tracked to his lair with the aid of Jonathan Harker's journals from his encounter with Count Dracula in his castle in Transylvania.

2. [Stage play] Premiere: Grand Theatre, Derby, England; August 5, 1924; Main Cast: Edward Blake as Count Dracula, Hamilton Deane as Abraham Van Helsing, Stuart Lomath as Doctor Seward, Bernard Guest as Jonathan Harker, Dora Mary Patrick as Mina Harker, Frieda Hearn as Quincey P. Morris, Peter Jackson as Lord Godalming, G. Malcolm Russell as R. M. Renfield; Playwrights: Hamilton Deane (1924), John L. Balderston (1927).

Bela Lugosi and Edward Van Sloan made their initial appearances as Count Dracula and Abraham Van Helsing on Broadway at the Fulton Theatre in October 1927.

3. [Film] Premiere: February 12, 1931; Main Cast: Bela Lugosi as Count Dracula, Edward Van Sloan as Dr. Abraham Van Helsing, David Manners as John Harker, Helen Chandler as Mina Seward, Dwight Frye as Renfield, Herbert Bunston as Doctor Seward, Joan Standing as Nurse Briggs, Frances Dade as Lucy Weston, Charles K. Gerrard as Martin; Producers: Tod Browning, Carl Laemmle, Jr.; Based on the novel by Bram Stoker; Adapted from the stage play by Hamilton Deane and

Dracula (1931), starring Edward Van Sloan as Van Helsing (left) and Bela Lugosi as Count Dracula (Universal).

John L. Balderston; Director: Tod Browning; 85 min.; Universal Pictures; b/w.

This successful and highly influential adaptation of Bram Stoker's novel changes names, locations and events. Whitby, Yorkshire is replaced by Carfax Abbey, London and Van Helsing is called upon to help Mina Seward and not Lucy who has already become a vampire.

Edward Van Sloan would reprise his role as Abraham Van Helsing in *Dracula's Daughter* (1936). Peter Cushing assumed the role in Hammer's *Dracula* (1958), *The Brides of Dracula* (1960) and *The Legend of the 7 Golden Vampires* (1974). Other notable actors who have portrayed Van Helsing in film and television include Laurence Olivier, Anthony Hopkins and Christopher Plummer among others.

See: **Van Helsing**

The Dresden Files (2007) [TV series]
Premiere: January 21, 2007: Main Cast Paul Blackthorne as Harry Dresden, Valerie Cruz as Lt. Connie Murphy, Terrence Mann as Bob, Hrothbert of Bainbridge, Raoul Bhaneja as Detective Sid Kirmani, Conrad Coates as Morgan, Jonathan Higgins as Malcolm Dresden, Matthew Knight as Young Harry Dresden; Executive Producers: Nicolas Cage, Norman Golightly, Robert Hewitt Wolfe, Morgan Gendel, David Simkins, Hans Beimer; Developed by Hans Beimer, Robert Hewitt Wolfe from the novels by Jim Butcher; 12 × 45 min.; Dresden Files Productions, Lions Gate Entertainment, NBC Universal Television, Saturn Films; Sci-Fi Channel; Color.

Harry Dresden the only wizard in an alternate Chicago where magic is real, works as a private investigator specializing in the paranormal. Loosely based on the best-selling book series by Jim Butcher.

SEASON ONE

Birds of a Feather (1:01); *The Boone Identity* (1:02); *Hair of the Dog* (1:03); *Rules of Engagement* (1:04); *Bad Blood* (1:05); *Soul Beneficiary* (1:06); *Walls* (1:07); *Storm Front* (1:08); *The Other Dick* (1:09); *What About Bob?* (1:10); (*Things That Go Bump* 1:11); *Second City* (1:12).

The Dresden Files Roleplaying Game [RPG]
Release date: 2010; System: Fate 3.0; Setting: Dresdenverse; Designer: Leonard Balsera; Publisher: Evil Hat Productions.

The game uses a customized version of the FATE (Fantastic Adventures in Tabletop Entertainment) system as the engine to run RPG's in the Dresdenverse. This alternate world where magic is real is populated with wizards, werewolves, vampires, demons, zombies, sprites and faeries. Only those in the know are aware magic exists. The other half of the population have no idea they are surrounded by magic.

The game comprises of two core books. *Volume One: Your Story* details the game rules required to build characters and tell stories. *Volume Two: Our World* is a setting guide that features details of over 200 creatures and characters that can be brought into the game. Major factions include The High Council of Wizards who are policed to ensure nobody breaks the rules. Wizards, including Harry Dresden, disrupt technology and must avoid certain environments to maintain their safety.

Volume Three: The Paranet Papers was published in 2015. The organization of the forces of good known as the Paranet fights evil in the form of the Red Court and the Denarians. The RPG Sourcebook details rules and settings for the Nevernever spirit world and information on Dresdenverse Las Vegas, South America, Novgorod during the Russian Revolution and the Florida Everglades. The second half of the book is an addendum to Our World containing updates and new characters from Harry Dresden's case files.

Drew Murdoch [Comic book character]
First appearance: *Jumbo Comics* #42 (August 1942); Art: Bob Hebberd; Publisher: Fiction House.

Drew Murdoch is introduced in the supernatural anthology strip "The Ghost Gallery" where he works out of his office in the mist-wrapped tower of the Triborough building.

"Weird, fantastic, yet undeniably true, are the strange cases of ghost lore unearthed by Drew Murdoch. His professional services are

"The Ghost Gallery" featuring "Ghost Specialist" Drew Murdoch in *Jumbo Comics* #44 (October 1942), page 13. Art by Bob Hebberd. Published by Fiction House.

sought whenever spirits of the dead emerge from troubled graves to haunt the living. For Murdoch knows the method and madness of ghosts, and the evil that ofttimes follows in their footsteps."

Drew Murdoch's "Ghost Gallery" was a regular feature in *Jumbo Comics* until the final issue #167 (March 1953).

Dusk Maiden of Amnesia (2012) [Anime; Manga; Japan]

Premiere: April 8, 2012; Voice Cast: Tsubasa Yonaga as Teiichi Niiya, Yumi Hara as Yuko Kanoe, Eri Kitamura as Kirie kanoe, Misato Fukuen as Momoe Okonogi; Story: Katsuhiko Takayama, Ayumi Sekine; Directors: Shin Oonuma, Takashi Sakamoto; 13 × 24 min.; Silver Link; Media Factory; Square Enix; TO Entertainment; Color.

Student Teiichi Niiya meets the ghost of Yuko Kanoe who died in the derelict, abandoned wing of Seikyo Academy sixty years ago. Intrigued by her story he forms a paranormal club with Yuko to investigate the circumstances surrounding her untimely death.

SEASON ONE

Ghost Maiden (1:01); *Maiden of a Chance Meeting* (1:02); *Maiden of Dusk* (1:03); *Maiden of Dawn* (1:04); *Maiden of Longing* (1:05); *Maiden of Vengeance* (1:06); *Maiden of Oblivion* (1:07); *Maiden of Recollection* (1:08); *Maiden of Hatred* (1:09); *Maiden of Defeat* (1:10); *Maiden of Bitter Tears* (1:11); *The Dusk Maiden* (1:12); *Maiden of Exorcism* (1:13).

[Manga] First publication: Gangan Joker (April 22, 2009); Story & Art: Maybe; Publisher: Square Enix.

The inspiration for the animated TV series was published over ten volumes.

Dylan Dog [Comic book]

First publication: October 1986; Creator: Tiziano Sclavi; Art; Angelo Stano, Claudio Villa; Publisher: Sergio Bonnelli Editore.

Working out of a house with a screaming doorbell at 7 Craven Road, London, Dylan Dog describes himself as a "nightmare investigator." Assisting Dylan is Groucho, a Groucho Marx look-alike and wisecracking impersonator. Scotland Yard Inspector Bloch has a father-son relationship with Dylan, to the detriment of Bloch's real son who became a drug addict and was killed during a robbery. Bloch and his hapless assistant Jenkins often work with Dylan on cases.

In the first issue of the long-running Italian comic book Sybil Browning seeks the help of Dylan Dog to find the truth behind her husband's murder. Sybil's claims that her husband was already dead before she supposedly killed him are backed up by Dylan's investigation into his death. Doctor Xabaras has created a virus in his laboratory that turns his victims into the living dead.

Dylan Dog: Dead of Night (2010) [Film]

Premiere: November 2010; Main Cast: Brandon Routh as Dylan Dog, Anita Briem as Elizabeth, Sam Huntingdon as Marcus, Taye Diggs as Vargas, Kurt Angle as Wolfgang, Peter Stormare as Gabriel; Producers: Gilbert Adler, Scott Mitchell Rosenberg; Writers: Thomas Dean Donnelly, Joshua Oppenheimer; Based on the comic book series by Tiziano Sclavi; Director: Kevin Munroe; 109 min.; Hyde Park Films; Long Distance Films; Platinum Studios; Prana Studios; Color.

Retired "nightmare investigator" Dylan Dog initially refuses to handle the case of an attractive young woman named Elizabeth, whose father has been murdered. But when his partner Marcus is also found murdered events take a strange turn. His assistant has been resurrected as a zombie and the streets of New Orleans are infested with the undead.

The film bears little relationship to the comic book series, with Dylan's assistant Groucho and Inspector Bloch both absent and the London backdrop moved to New Orleans.

The film was a major box-office failure in the U.S. with an opening weekend of only $754, 779 falling well below the estimated $20,000,000 budget

Dylan Dog: Il trillo del diavolo (2012) [Film; Italy]

Premiere: June 24, 2012; Main Cast: Roberto D'Antona as Dylan Dog, Francesco

Emulo as Groucho, Ciro De Angelis as Inspector Bloch, Michele Friuli as Xabaras, Barbara De Florio as Spring, Angelo Boccuni as Padre Dylan, Francesco Santagada as Blitz, Giovanni Navolio as Lucifero, Federica Gomma as Sandra, Biago Sampietro as Gnut, Valentia Pignatale as Beatrix, Stefania Attanasio as Madre Dylan; Producers: Roberto D'Antona, Francesco Emulo, Michele Friuli; Story/Director: Roberto D'Antona; 50 min.; Grage Pictures; Color; b/w.

This low budget independent production has Dylan Dog venturing through a nightmare landscape populated by people who want to kill him.

Ectoplasm (2000) [Radio drama; UK]

First broadcast: July 11, 2000; Main Cast: Nick Romero as Lord Zimbabwe, Dan Freedman as Doctor Lilac, Peter Donaldson as Theremin, Sophie Aldred, Owen Oakeshott, Colin Guthrie; Producer: Helen Williams; Story: Dan Freedman, Nick Romero; 4 × 30 min.; BBC Radio 4.

This BBC radio sitcom features famous occult investigator Lord Zimbabwe, madcap psychotic German scientist Doctor Lilac, Zimbabwe's unfaithful butler Theremin and a quantum cat named Schrodinger. Sherlock Holmes turns up with the occasional garbled telephone call asking for advice from Lord Zimbabwe and Hercule Poirot is rescued from Hades. Stories involve a pharaoh's curse, Contessa Del Monte who must win back her soul or suffer the fate of being a Barry Manilow fan for eternity, a time traveling journey to Tombstone in the Old West and a voyage to the moon to rescue hillbillies from aliens.

EPISODES

The Curse of Tutancommon (1:01); *The Case of the Missing Lost Soul* (1:02); *The Affair of the Baddie's Niece* (1:03); *The Adventure of the Stupid, Ignorant Americans* (1:04).

18 Seconds (Sherry Moore book #1) [Novel]

Author: George D. Shuman; First publication: New York: Simon & Schuster, 2006.

Following a childhood injury blind Sherry Moore can see the last eighteen seconds of memory of a dead person by touching their corpse. Her gift is used to comfort grieving families and help the police solve cases. With a serial killer on the loose and Police Lieutenant Kelly Lynch-O'Shaughnessy in his sights Sherry Moore offers her help in finding the killer but in doing so places her own life in danger.

Sherry Moore series: *18 Seconds* (2006); *Last Breath* (2007); *Lost Girls* (2008); *Second Sight* (2009).

Elongated Man [Comic book character]

First appearance: *The Flash* #112 (May 1960); Creators: John Broome, Carmine Infantino; Publisher: DC Comics.

Fascinated as a child by the India Rubber Man sideshow act Ralph Dibny continued his fascination into adulthood. Seeking the secret of the act Dibny is met with silence by the various Rubber Men. Then he realizes they all have one thing in common. They all drink the soda Gringold. As a skilled amateur chemist Dibny extracts the concentrate of the tropical Gingo fruit and to his amazement discovers he can stretch to any size and shape.

Dibny the professional detective solves all manner of strange mysteries with the help of his wife Sue. He can smell trouble with a nose twitch and mold his face into any disguise.

The character has undergone many transformations in DC Comics' various rebooted timelines including his mental decline and death following the murder of his pregnant wife. Reunited in the afterlife they work together as ghost detectives. He has also transferred to the live-action TV show *The Flash* (2014) where he is portrayed by Hartley Sawyer.

Eureka (2006) [TV series]

Premiere: July 18, 2006; Main Cast: Colin Ferguson as Jack Carter, Salli Richardson-Whitfield as Allison Blake, Erica Cerra as Jo Lupo, Neil Grayston as Douglas Fargo/S.A.R.A.H., Joe Morton as Henry Deacon, Chris Gauthier as Vincent/Virtual Vincent, Jordan Hinson as Zoe Carter, Niall Matter as Zane Donovan, Ed Quinn as Nathan Stark, Deborah Farentino as Beverly Barlowe, Tembi Locke as Grace Monroe, Christopher Jacot as

Larry Haberman, Kavan Smith as Deputy Andy/Deputy Andy 2.0; Executive Producers: Jaime Paglia, Bruce Miller, Charles Grant Craig, Thania St. John, Andrew Cosby; Creators: Andrew Cosby, Jaime Paglia; 77 × 44 min.; NBC Universal Television; Universal Cable Productions; Sci-Fi Channel/Syfy; Color.

The Pacific Northwest town of Eureka cannot be found on any maps, for it is home to genius scientists working on government projects for the top-secret Global Dynamics. Keeping law and order in this eccentric community is Sheriff Jack Carter. During the five-season run of the series Sheriff Carter encounters clones, crop circles, miraculous artifacts, androids, spontaneous human combustion, shared dreams, time travel, time loops, time lapses, interdimensional travel, Eureka and its residents turning into an animated cartoon, a Matrix Eureka and wormholes.

Season One

Pilot (1:01); *Many Happy Returns* (1:02); *Before I Forget* (1:03); *Alienated* (1:04); *Invincible* (1:05); *Dr. Nobel* (1:06); *Blink* (1:07); *Right as Raynes* (1:08); *Primal* (1:09); *Purple Haze* (1:10); *H.O.U.S.E. Rules* (1:11); *Once in a Lifetime* (1:12).

Season Two

Phoenix Rising (2:01); *Try, Try Again* (2:02); *Unpredictable* (2:03); *Games People Play* (2:04); *Duck, Duck Goose* (2:05); *Noche de suenos* (2:06); *Family Reunion* (2:07); *E=MC...?* (2:08); *Sight Unseen* (2:09); *God is in the Details* (2:10); *Maneater* (2:11); *All That Glitters* (2:12); *A Night in Global Dynamics* (2:13).

Season Three

Bad to the Drone (3:01); *What About Bob?* (3:02); *Best in Faux* (3:03); *I Do Over* (3:04); *Show Me the Mummy* (3:05); *Phased and Confused* (3:06); *Here Come the Suns* (3:07); *From Fear to Eternity* (3:08); *Welcome Back, Carter* (3:09); *Your Face or Mine* (3:10); *Insane in the P-Brane* (3:11); *It's Not Easy Being Green* (3:12); *If You Build It ...* (3:13); *Ship Happens* (3:14); *Shower the People* (3:15); *You Don't Know Jack* (3:16); *Have an Ice Day* (3:17); *What Goes Around, Comes Around* (3:18).

Season Four

Founder's Day (4:01); *A New World* (4:02); *All the Rage* (4:03); *The Story of O2* (4:04); *Crossing Over* (4:05); *Momstrosity* (4:06); *Stoned* (4:07); *The Ex-Files* (4:08); *I'll Be Seeing You* (4:09); *O Little Town ...* (4:10); *Liftoff* (4:11); *Reprise* (4:12); *Glimpse* (4:13); *Up in the Air* (4:14); *Omega Girls* (4:15); *Of Mites and Men* (4:16); *Clash of the Titans* (4:17); *This One Time at Space Camp ...* (4:18); *One Small Step ...* (4:19); *One Giant Leap ...* (4:20); *Do You See What I See* (4:21).

Season Five

Lost (5:01); *The Real Thing* (5:02); *Force Quit* (5:03); *Friendly Fire* (5:04); *Jack of All Trades* (5:05); *Worst Case Scenario* (5:06); *Ex Machina* (5:07); *In Too Deep* (5:08); *Smarter Carter* (5:09); *The Honeymooners* (5:10); *Mirror, Mirror* (5:11); *Double Take* (5:12); *Just Another Day* (1:13).

European Travel for the Monstrous Gentlewoman [Novel]

Author: Theodora Goss; First publication: New York: Saga Press, 2017.

The Athena Club comprising of Mary Jekyll, her half-sister Diane Hyde, Beatrice Rappaccini, Catherine Moreau and Justine Frankenstein travel through the Austro-Hungarian Empire. Their mission to rescue Lucinda Helsing from the vile experimentations of her father. On their journey they meet Count Dracula and finally confront the secretive Alchemical Society.

The Exorcist III (1990) [Film]

Premiere: August 17, 1990; Main Cast: George C. Scott as Lt. William F. Kinderman, Ed Flanders as Father Dyer, Jason Miller as Patient X; Brad Dourif as The Gemini Killer, Nicol Williamson as Father Morning, Scott Wilson as Dr. Temple, Nancy Fish as Nurse Allerton, George Dicenzo as Stedman, Don Gordon as Ryan, Grand L. Bush as Sergeant Atkins, Viveca Lindfors as Nurse X; Executive Producers: James G. Robinson, Joe Roth; Screenplay/Director: William Peter Blatty; 110

min.; Morgan Creek Entertainment; Twentieth Century–Fox; Color.

Police Lieutenant William F. Kinderman investigates a series of brutal murders in Georgetown that resemble a serial killer who was executed seventeen years ago. Kinderman uncovers a case of possession at a psychiatric hospital.

Eye of the Daemon (Daemons Inc. #1) [Novel]

Author: Camille Bacon-Smith; First publication: New York: DAW Books, 1996.

Daemon/human half-breed Evan Davis, his daemon father Kevin Bradley and distant daemon cousin Lily Ryan run a detective agency out of Philadelphia specializing in the occult. Brad and Lily are daemons of the House of Ariton, while Davis is merely tolerated for being a half-breed in a world where daemons and humans co-exist. When Marnie Simpson contacts the agency to find her kidnapped half-brother the kidnapper demands a ransom for the Eye of Omage.

Followed by: *Eyes of the Empress* (1998); *A Legacy of Daemons* (2010).

The Eyes of Charles Sand (1972) [Telefilm]

Premiere: February 29, 1972; Main Cast: Peter Haskell as Charles Sand; Joan Bennett as Aunt Alexandra; Barbara Rush as Katherine Winslow; Sharon Farrell as Emily Parkhurst; Bradford Dillman as Jeffrey Winslow; Adam West as Dr. Paul Scott; Gary Clarke as Raymond; Producer: Hugh Benson; Teleplay: Henry Farrell and Stanford Whitmore; Director: Reza Badiyi; 75 min.; Warner Bros. Television; Color.

Charles Sands inherits "the sight" from his uncle following his sudden death. He uses his new psychic powers to help Emily Pankhurst discover if her brother has been murdered or is still alive.

This ABC Movie of the Week was a failed pilot for a proposed series.

Eyes of Laura Mars (1978) [Film]

Premiere: August 2, 1978; Main Cast: Faye Dunaway as Laura Mars, Tommy Lee Jones as Police Lieutenant John Neville, Brad Dourif as Tommy Ludlow, Rene Auberjonois as Donald Phelps, R.J. (Raul Julia) as Michael Reisler, Frank Adonis as Sal Volpe, Lisa Taylor as Michelle, Darlene Fluegel as Lulu, Rose Gregorio as Elaine Cassel, Bill Boggs as Himself, Steve Marachuk as Robert, Meg Mundy as Doris Spenser, Marilyn Meyers as Sheila Weissman, John Sahag as Hairdresser; Executive Producer: Jack H. Harris; Story: John Carpenter; Screenplay: John Carpenter, David Zelag Goodman; Director: Irvin Kershner; 104 min. Columbia Pictures; Color.

Renowned fashion photographer Laura Mars seeks the help of police lieutenant John Neville when she begins to see visions of murders through the killer's eyes and believes she is the next victim.

> "When I arrived at Columbia, Laura Mars was being audience tested. It tested poorly. There were some McKinsey & Company smart MBA executives, hired by Alan Hirschfield, who knew nothing about entertainment but had lots of ideas. They were making a short documentary film to run before the picture to explain to the audience what they didn't understand about the film. Bad idea, which didn't help. I ultimately terminated all those aspiring MBA filmmakers. The picture was released and performed poorly."— Frank Price (former Chairman, President and CEO, Columbia Pictures).

The Eyre Affair (Thursday Next #1)

Author: Jasper Fforde; First publication: London: Hodder and Stoughton, 2001.

1985 in an alternate reality where the Crimean War is still raging, and time travel and cloning are everyday realities. Thursday Next is Special Operative for the literary branch of the special police. In a world where kidnapping famous characters from books is a reality Thursday must find Jane Eyre, the latest character abduction by Acheron Hades.

Book series: *The Eyre Affair* (2001); *Lost in a Good Book* (2002); *The Well of Lost Plots* (2003); *Something Rotten* (2004); *First Among Sequels* (2007); *One of Our Thursdays Is Missing* (2011); *The Woman Who Died a Lot* (2012).

The Facts in the Case of Mister Hollow (2008)

[Animated short; Canada]

Premiere: July 17, 2008; Main Cast: Julian

Richings as Kneeling Man, Alan Alderton as Waving Man, Lea Lawrynowicz, Tony Morrone as Thin Man, Darryl Dougherty as Young Priest, Rogelio Gudino as Old Priest, Behnaz Siahpustan as Ker; Executive Producers: Rodrigo Gudino, Marco Pecota; Writer: Rodrigo Gudino; Animation: Tomasz Dysinski; Directors: Rodrigo Gudino, Vincent Marcone; 6 min.; Rue Morgue Cinema; Someone at the Door Productions; My Pet Skeleton Productions; Veni Vidi Vici Motion Pictures; Color.

The viewer takes on the role of detective as they are guided through an old sepia photograph from the 1930s depicting clues to child disappearances and murder. Allusions to a cult of female death spirits are implied. In Greek mythology the Keres were malevolent spirits who flew over areas of conflict searching for dying people.

Fallen (1998) [Film]

Premiere: January 16, 1998; Main Cast: Denzel Washington as Detective John Hobbes, John Goodman as Detective Jonesy, Donald Sutherland as Lt. Stanton, Embeth Davidtz as Gretta Milano, James Gandolfini as Lou, Elias Koteas as Edgar Reese, Gabriel Casseus as Art Hobbes, Michael J. Pagan as Sam Hobbes, Robert Joy as Charles Olom; Executive Producers: Robert Cavallo, Elon Dershowitz, Patricia Graf, Nicholas Kazan, Ted Kurdyla; Story: Nicholas Kazan; Director: Gregory Hoblit; 124 min.; Turner Pictures; Atlas Entertainment; Warner Bros.; Color.

Detective John Hobbes investigates a series of murders resembling those by executed killer Edgar Reese. Far from being a copycat killer the murders are linked to demonic possession by fallen angel Azazel who can possess his victims by touch. The demon taunts Hobbes by announcing his presence and continually changing bodies to possess as the murders continue.

Falling Angel [Novel; Opera]

First publication: 1978; Author: William Hjortsberg; Publisher: New York: Harcourt Brace Jovanovich.

New York State, 1959. Private investigator Harry Angel is hired to track down famous '40s singer Johnny Favorite, last seen as a patient in a Poughkeepsie clinic more than fifteen years ago. His investigations take him down a dark path that leads to Black Magic and Voodoo and ultimately fear of losing his own soul.

Mickey Rourke starred as Harry Angel in the 1987 film adaptation *Angel Heart*.

[Opera]: First performance: June 30, 2016; Main Cast: Matthew Queen as Harry Angel, Steele Fitzwater as Louis Cyphre, Myles Garver as Johnny Favorite, Evelyn Saavedra as Epiphany Proudfoot, Melanie Burbules as Margaret Krusemak; Orin Strunk as Dr. Fowler, Brandon Bell as Toots Sweet, August Bair as Detective Deimos, Frederick Schlick as Ethan Krusemark, Adam Wells as Young Soldier; Janiec Opera Company of the Brevard Music Center; Conductor: Jerome Shannon; Adaptation: J. Mark Scearce; Libretto: Lucy Thurber.

The opera was staged at the Brevard Music Center Summer Institute located in the Blue Ridge Mountains of western North Carolina. Heidi Waleson of *The Wall Street Journal* (July 5, 2016) stated:

Librettist Lucy Thurber and Mr. Scearce skillfully distilled the complicated detective story, which is laced with voodoo, Satanism and murder, and went one step further: their operatic treatment makes Harry Angel a tragic figure…. Mr. Scearce's engaging, tonal score borrows imaginatively from numerous genres, including musical theater, blues and African drumming.

Father Dowling Mysteries (1989) [TV series]

Main Cast: Tom Bosley as Father Frank Dowling, Tracy Nelson as Sister Stephanie "Steve" Oskowski, Mary Wickes as Marie Murkin, James Stephens as Father Philip Prestwick; Developed for television by Dean Hargrove, Joel Steiger; Executive Producers: Dean Hargrove, Fred Silverman; Based on the characters from the "Father Dowling Mystery" book series by Ralph McInerny; 42 × 48 min.; Fred Silverman Company; Dean Hargrove Productions; Viacom Productions; NBC; ABC; Color.

Catholic priest Father Frank Dowling is

also a part-time detective. Together with streetwise and worldly nun Sister Stephanie Oskowski a.k.a. Steve they investigate crime on the streets of Chicago.

"The Ghost of a Chance Mystery" (2:06)

Air date: February 8, 1990; Guest Cast: Lisa Langlois as Carol Van Horn, Michael Durrell as Dr. Latimer, David Spielberg as Douglas Hopkins, Nan Martin as Mrs. Dansky, Richard Minchenberg as Mr. Simpson, Regina Krueger as Sgt. Clancy; Story: Robert Schlitt; Director: Charles S. Dubin.

Father Dowling and Sister Steve investigate when parishioner Carol Van Horn claims she is haunted by her dead father who communicates with her.

"The Falling Angel Mystery" (2:08)

Air date: February 22, 1990; Guest Cast: James McEachin as Michael, Timothy Gibbs as Rick McMasters, Lisa Waltz as Sarah McMasters, Victor Argo as Tony Lakka, Regina Krueger as Sgt. Clancy; Story: Dean Hargrove, Joyce Burditt; Director: James Frawley.

Michael is an angel assigned to Father Dowling to help him protect Rick McMasters from crime boss Tony Lakka who has just been released from prison.

"The Devil in the Deep Blue Sea Mystery" (3:03)

Air date: October 4, 1990; Guest Cast: Michael Champion as Harry Deal, Michelle Little as Janie Oskowski, Joe Dorsey as Dr. Pryor, Anne T. Haney as Mrs. Blanchard; Regina Krueger as Sgt. Clancy; Story: Dean Hargrove, Joyce Burditt; Director: Christopher Hibbler.

To the public Harry Deal is an infamous underworld crime boss, but to Father Dowling he is literally the Devil in human form. Now he must save Sister Steve's soul from his demonic grasp.

"The Mummy's Curse Mystery" (3:17)

Air date: February 21, 1991; Guest Cast: David Hemmings as Kenneth Brubaker, Frances Lee McCain as Helen Austin, Aharon Ipale as Amnon Bey, Peter Donat as Thomas Douglas, Duke Stroud as Carson, Deryl Caitlyn as Wolfe, Grant Heslov as Omar the Waiter, Regina Kreuger as Sgt. Clancy; Story: Michael Reaves; Director: James Frawley.

Father Dowling and Sister Steve chance upon an Egyptian curse while visiting the Pharaoh's burial chamber at the Chicago Museum. And Father Prestwick could become the next victim of the curse.

"The Consulting Detective Mystery" (3:21)

Air date: April 25, 1991: Guest Cast: Rupert Frazier as Sherlock Holmes, Kurt Fuller as Lloyd Eastland, Susan Krebs as Mrs. Maggie Eastland, Richard Roat as Martin Kruicki, Kevin Scannell as Larry Gable, Patrick Kilpatrick as The Killer, Timothy Stack as Stu, Richie Allan as Werner; Story: Dean Hargrove, Gerry Conway; Teleplay: Gerry Conway; Director: Sharron Miller.

The ghost of Sherlock Holmes helps Father Dowling in a murder investigation. But only Father Dowling can see him.

Fear No Evil (1969) [Telefilm]

Premiere: March 3, 1969; Main Cast: Louis Jordan as Dr. David Sorell; Carroll O'Connor as Myles Donovan; Bradford Dillman as Paul Varney; Wilfred Hyde-White as Harry Snowden; Lynda Day as Barbara Anholt; Marsha Hunt as Mrs. Varney; Katherine Woodville as Ingrid Dorne; Harry Davis as Mr. Wyant; Producers: Richard Alan Simmons, David Levinson; Teleplay: Richard Alan Simmons; Director: Paul Wendkos; 98 min., Universal; Color.

"Hidden in mystery and superstition is the promise of love beyond infinity."

Psychiatrist David Sorell specializes in the occult. When a young woman's boyfriend is killed in an auto accident her grief turns to joy when she discovers an antique mirror can return him to life. Dr. Sorell investigates the truth behind her claim and comes to believe, "there is something in the mirror."

This NBC Movie of the Week spawned a sequel ***Ritual of Evil*** (1970) with Louis Jordan and Wilfred Hyde-White reprising their roles.

Fiction Squad (Comic book)

First publication: October 2014; Story: Paul Jenkins; Art: Ramon Bachs; Publisher: BOOM! Studios.

In the enchanted forest of Fablewood lies the realm of children's stories and the golden city of Rimes. The sudden great fall of Humpty Dumpty is a crime scene. Mystery Realm refugee Detective Frankie Mack and his partner Simple Simon are looking for clues. But soon Humpty Dumpty goes from victim to murderer and the nations of Oz and Wonderland become embroiled in a turf war.

Firewalk [Novel]

Author: Chris Roberson; First publication: Jersey City, NJ: Night Shade Books, 2016.

Five years ago, FBI agent Izzie Lefevre and homicide detective Patrick Tevake tracked down and killed a vicious serial killer in the coastal town of Recondito. Five years later Lefevre and Tevake have uncovered a link to a new lethal street drug and serial killings dating back one-hundred years. Demons are at large in Recondito and Lefevre and Tevake are in their line of fire.

The story is continued in *Firewalkers* (2018).

The First Power (1990) [Film]

Premiere: April 6, 1990; Main Cast: Lou Diamond Phillips as Detective Russell Logan, Tracy Griffith as Tess Seaton, Jeff Kober as Patrick Channing, Mykel T. Williamson as Detective Oliver Franklin, Elizabeth Arlen as Sister Marguerite, Dennis Lipscomb as Commander Perkins, Carmen Argenziano as Lieutenant Al Grimes, Sue Giosa as Carmen; Executive Producers: Robert W. Cort, Ted Field, Melinda Jason; Story/Director: Robert Resnikoff; 98 min.; Interscope Communications; Nelson Entertainment; Orion Pictures; Color.

Detective Russell Logan teams up with psychic Tess Seaton to track a resurrected Satanic serial killer who can disappear into thin air and possess his victims.

Flaxman Low (Short story character)

First appearance: *Pearson's Magazine* (January 1898); Authors: E. and H. Heron; Publisher: Cyril Arthur Pearson.

Psychic detective Flaxman Low was the creation of mother and son team Kate O'Brien Ryall Prichard and Hesketh Prichard. Low is a renowned psychologist, working under an alias, who delights in investigating and debunking the paranormal. "The Story of Konnor Old House" (1899) displays his mental approach.

"I hold." Mr. Flaxman Low, the eminent psychologist, was saying, "that there are no other laws in what we term the realm of the supernatural but those which are the projections or extensions of natural laws."

Flaxman Low featured in twelve stories between January 1898 and June 1899.

"The Story of the Spaniards, Hammersmith" (January 1898); "The Story of Medhans Lea" (February 1989); "The Story of the Moor Road" (March 1898); "The Story of Baelbrow" (April 1898); "The Story of the Grey House" (May 1898); "The Story of Yand Manor House," (June 1898); "The Story of Sevens Hall" (January 1899); "The Story of Saddler's Croft" (February 1899); "The Story of No. 1 Karma Crescent" (March 1899); "The Story of Konner Old House" (April 1899); "The Story of Crowsedge," (May 1899); "The Story of Mr. Flaxman Low," (June 1899).

Fool Moon (The Dresden Files Book #2)

Author: Jim Butcher; Publisher: New York: Roc, 2001.

Harry Dresden is having a hard time finding work until a brutally mutilated corpse turns up. Just another murder except for strange paw prints under a full moon. Now his supernatural expertise is required to unravel the truth behind the murder and track the creature responsible.

See: ***Grave Peril***

Foreign Devils (*Doctor Who Novellas* #5) [Novella; UK]

Author: Andrew Cartmel; First Publication: 2003; Publisher: Tolworth, Surrey: Telos Publishing Ltd.

Doctor Who joins forces with occult detective Thomas Carnacki in 1900 to solve a series of peculiar murders in a house that has been disconnected from space and time. The story features the second Doctor.

Forever Knight (1992) [TV series; Canada-West Germany]

Premiere: May 5, 1992; Main Cast: Geraint Wyn Davies as Detective Nick Knight, Catherine Disher as Dr. Natalie Lambert, Nigel Bennett as Lucien LaCroix, Deborah Duchene as Janette, John Kapelos as Detective John Schanke, Natsuko Ohama as Captain Amanda Cohen, Lisa Ryder as Detective Tracy Vetter, Gary Farmer as Captain Joe Stonetree, Ben Bass as Javier Vachon, Blu Mankuma as Captain Joe Reese; Executive Producers: James D. Parriott, Jon Slan; Creators: James D. Parriott, Barney Cohen; 70 × 45 min.; Glen Warren Productions; Paragon Entertainment Corp.; TMG; TriStar Television; USA Network; CBS; Color.

Nick Knight has preyed on humans for their blood since the 13th century. Now he wants to repay society for his past sins. Working as a homicide cop in Toronto he seeks to emerge from the darkness and become human again.

The opening episodes are a reworking of the telefilm *Nick Knight* which featured Rick Springfield as the vampire turned cop and Michael Nader as his nemesis LaCroix.

SEASON ONE

Dark Knight (1:01); *Dark Knight: The Second Chapter* (1:02); *For I Have Sinned* (1:03); *Last Act* (1:04); *Dance by the Light of the Moon* (1:05); *Dying to Know You* (1:06); *False Witness* (1:07); *Cherry Blossoms* (1:08); *I Will Repay* (1:09); *Dead Air* (1:10); *Hunters* (1:11); *Dead Issue* (1:12); *Father Figure* (1:13); *Spin Doctor* (1:14); *Dying for Fame* (1:15); *Only the Lonely* (1:16); *Unreality TV* (1:17); *Feeling the Beast* (1:18); *If Looks Could Kill* (1:19); *Fatal Mistake* (1:20); *1966* (1:21); *Love You to Death* (1:22).

SEASON TWO

Killer Instinct (2:01); *A Fate Worse Than Death* (2:02); *Stranger Than Fiction* (2:03); *Bad Blood* (2:04); *Forward into the Past* (2:05); *Capital Offense* (2:06); *Hunted* (2:07); *Faithful Followers* (2:08); *Undue Process* (2:09); *Father's Day* (2:10); *Can't Run, Can't Hide* (2:11); *Amateur Night* (2:12); *Beyond the Law* (2:13); *The Fix* (2:14); *Be My Valentine* (2:15); *The Fire Inside* (2:16); *Blood Money* (2:17); *Partners of the Month* (2:18); *Queen of Harps* (2:19); *A More Permanent Hell* (2:20); *The Code* (2:21); *Curiouser and Curiouser* (2:22); *Near Death* (2:23); *Baby Baby* (2:24); *Close Call* (2:25); *Crazy Love* (2:26).

SEASON THREE

Black Buddha: Part 1 (3:01); *Black Buddha: Part 2* (3:02); *Outside the Lines* (3:03); *Blackwing* (3:04); *Blind Faith* (3:05); *My Boyfriend is a Vampire* (3:06); *Hearts of Darkness* (3:07); *Trophy Girl* (3:08); *Let No Man Tear Asunder* (3:09); *Night in Question* (3:10); *Sons of Belial* (3:11); *Strings* (3:12); *Fever* (3:13); *Dead of Night* (3:14); *The Games Vampires Play* (3:15); *The Human Factor* (3:16); *Avenging Angel* (3:17); *Fallen Idol* (3:18); *Jane Doe* (3:19); *Francesca* (3:20); *Ashes to Ashes* (3:21); *Last Knight* (3:22).

1408 (2007) [Film]

Premiere: June 22, 2007; Main Cast: John Cusack as Mike Enslin, Samuel L. Jackson as Gerald Olin, Mary McCormack as Lily Enslin, Tony Shalhoub as Sam Farrell, Len Cariou as Mike's father, Jasmine Jessica Anthony as Katie Enslin, Isiah Whitlock, Jr., as Hotel Engineer, Kim Thomson as Hotel Desk Clerk, Andrew Lee Potts as Mailbox Guy, Kevin Dobson as Priest; Executive Producers: Jake Myers, Richard Saperstein, Bob Weinstein, Harvey Weinstein; Screenplay: Matt Greenberg, Scott Alexander, Larry Karaszewsi; Based on the short story by Stephen King; Director: Mikael Hafstrom; 104 min.; Dimension Films; Metro-Goldwyn Mayer (MGM); Color.

Author Mike Enslin debunks the supernatural for a living. For his latest book he travels to the Dolphin Hotel in New York City, insisting he stay overnight at the 'haunted' room 1408. Despite warnings from the hotel manager Gerald Olin informing Enslin of the guests who have died in that room, Enslin persists in his demands. As the night progresses the cynical Enslin slowly finds himself face-to-face with his worst fears and a psychological meltdown.

Francis Chard [Short story character]
   Author-Creator: A.M. Burrage; First appearance: "The Affair at Penbillo" *The Blue Magazine* (February 1927).

   Paranormal investigator Francis Chard also writes articles on the supernatural. His companion Torrance joins him in his investigations and narrates his adventures.

   Short stories: "The Affair at Penbillo" (February 1927); "The Pit in the Garden" (March 1927); "The Woman with Three Eyes" (April 1927); "The Third Visitation" (May 1927); "The Girl in Blue" (June 1927); "The Bungalow at Shammerton" (July 1927); "The Protector" (August 1927); "The Soldier" (September 1927); "The Hiding Hole" (October 1927); "The Tryst" (November 1927).

Fringe (2008) [TV series]
   Premiere: September 9, 2008; Main Cast: Anna Torv as Olivia Dunham, Joshua Jackson as Peter Bishop, Jasika Nicole as Astrid Farnsworth, John Noble as Dr. Walter Bishop, Lance Reddick as Phillip Broyles, Blair Brown as Nina Sharp, Michael Cerveris as The Observer, Kirk Acevedo as Charlie Francis, Seth Gabel as Lincoln Lee, Ryan McDonald as Brandon Fayette, Mark Valley as John Scott, Leonard Nimoy as Dr. William Bell; Executive Producers: J.J. Abrams, Bryan Burk, Jeff Pinker, J.H. Wyman, Joe Chappelle; Creators; J.J. Abrams, Alex Kurtzman, Roberto Orci; 100 × 46 min.; Bad Robot; Warner Bros. Television; FB2 Films; Fringe Element Films; Fox Network; Color.

   F.B.I. Agent Olivia Dunham joins forces with scientist Dr. Walter Bishop, recently released from a mental institution, and his estranged son Peter. As the Fringe Division of the F.B.I. they investigate paranormal events on the fringe of science. Each character has a counterpart in an alternate universe.

SEASON ONE

Pilot (1:01); *The Same Old Story* (1:02); *The Ghost Network* (1:03); *The Arrival* (1:04); *Power Hungry* (1:05); *The Cure* (1:06); *In Which We Meet Mr. Jones* (1:07); *The Equation* (1:08); *The Dreamscape* (1:09); *Safe* (1:10); *Bound* (1:11); *The No-Brainer* (1:12); *The Transformation* (1:13); *Ability* (1:14); *Inner Child* (1:15); *Unleashed* (1:16); *Bad Dreams* (1:17); *Midnight* (1:18); *The Road Not Taken* (1:19); *There's More Than One of Everything* (1:20).

SEASON TWO

A New Day in the Old Town (2:01); *Night of Desirable Objects* (2:02); *Fracture* (2:03); *Momentum Deferred* (2:04); *Dream Logic* (2:05); *Earthling* (2:06); *Of Human Action* (2:07); *August* (2:08); *Snakehead* (2:09); *Grey Matters* (2:10); *Unearthed* (2:11); *Johari Window* (2:12); *What Lies Below* (2:13); *The Bishop Revival* (2:14); *Jacksonville* (2:15); *Peter* (2:16); *Olivia. In the Lab. With the Revolver* (2:17); *White Tulip* (2:18); *The Man from the Other Side* (2:19); *Brown Betty* (2:20); *Northwest Passage* (2:21); *Over There: Part 1* (2:22); *Over There: Part 2* (2:23).

SEASON THREE

Olivia (3:01); *The Box* (3:02); *The Plateau* (3:03); *Do Shapeshifters Dream of Electric Sheep?* (3:04); *Amber 31422* (3:05); *6955 kHz* (3:06); *The Abducted* (3:07); *Entrada* (3:08); *Marionette* (3:09); *The Firefly* (3:10); *Reciprocity* (3:11); *Concentrate and Ask Again* (3:12); *Immortality* (3:13); *6B* (3:14); *Subject 13* (3:15); *Os* (3:16); *Stowaway* (3:17); *Bloodline* (3:18); *Lysergic Acid Diethylamide* (3:19); *6:02 AM EST* (3:20); *The Last Sam Weiss* (3:21); *The Day We Died* (3:22).

SEASON FOUR

Neither Here Nor There (4:01); *One Night in October* (4:02); *Alone in the World* (4:03); *Subject 9* (4:04); *Novation* (4:05); *And Those We Left Behind* (4:06); *Wallflower* (4:07); *Back to Where You've Never Been* (4:08); *Enemy of My Enemy* (4:09); *Forced Perspective* (4:10); *Making Angels* (4:11); *Welcome to Westfield* (4:12); *A Better Human Being* (4:13); *The End of All Things* (4:14); *A Short Story About Love* (4:15); *Nothing As It Seems* (4:16); *Everything in Its Right Place* (4:17); *The Consultant* (4:18); *Letters of Transit* (4:19); *Worlds Apart* (4:20); *Brave New World: Part 1* (4:21); *Brave New World: Part 2* (4:22).

SEASON FIVE

Transilience Thought Unifier Model-11 (5:01); *In Absentia* (5:02); *The Recordist* (5:03);

The Bullet That Saved the World (5:04); *An Origin Story* (5:05); *Through the Looking Glass and What Walter Found There* (5:06); *Five-Twenty-Ten* (5:07); *The Human Kind* (5:08); *Black Blotter* (5:09); *Anomaly XB-6783746* (5:10); *The Boy Must Live* (5:11); *Liberty* (5:12); *An Enemy of Fate* (5:13).

From Dusk till Dawn: The Series (2014) [TV series]

Premiere: March 11, 2014; Main Cast: D. J. Coltrona as Seth Gecko, Zane Holtz as Richie Gecko, Jesse Garcia as Ranger Ferdinand Gonzalez, Eiza Gonzalez as Santanico Pandemonium/Kisa, Madison Davenport as Kate Fuller/Amaru, Brandon Soo Hoo as Scott Fuller, Robert Patrick as Jacob Fuller, Wilmer Valderama as Carlos Madrigal, Jamie Tisdale as Margaret Gonzalez; Jake Busey as Professor Aidan Tanner, Esai Morales as Lord Amancio Malvado, Danny Trejo as The Regulator, Don Johnson as Ranger Earl McGraw; Executive Producers: Juan Carlos Coto, Robert Rodriguez, Christina Patwa, John Fogelman, Zanne Devine, Daniel Pipski; Developed for television by Robert Rodriguez; 30 × 45 min.; FactoryMade Ventures; Miramax; Rodriguez International Pictures; El Rey Network; Color.

Texas Ranger Freddie Gonzalez pursues bank robbers Seth and Richie Gecko cross country to the Mexican border and the Titty Twister bar, where vampires and an ancient evil await. Based on the original movie of the same name.

Season One

Pilot (1:01); *Blood Runs Thick* (1:02); *Mistress* (1:03); *Let's Get Ramblin'* (1:04); *Self-Contained* (1:05); *Place of Dead Roads* (1:06); *Pandemonium* (1:07); *La Conquista* (1:08); *Boxman* (1:09); *The Take* (1:10).

Season Two

Opening Night (2:01); *In a Dark Time* (2:02); *Attack of the 50-ft. Sex Machine* (2:03); *The Best Little Horror House in Texas* (2:04); *Bondage* (2:05); *Bizarre Tales* (2:06); *Bring Me the Head of Santanico Pandemonium* (2:07); *The Last Temptation of Richard Gecko* (2:08); *There Will Be Blood* (2:09); *Santa Sangre* (2:10).

Season Three

Head Games (3:01); *La Reina* (3:02); *Protect and Serve* (3:03); *Fanglorious* (3:04); *Shady Glen* (3:05); *Straitjacket* (3:06); *La Llorona* (3:07); *Rio Sangre* (3:08); *Matanzas* (3:09); *Dark Side of the Sun* (3:10).

From Hell (2001) [Film]

Premiere: October 19, 2001; Main Cast: Johnny Depp as Inspector Frederick Abberline, Heather Graham as Mary Kelly, Ian Holm as Sir William Gull, Robbie Coltrane as Sergeant Peter Godley, Ian Richardson as Sir Charles Warren, Jason Flemyng as Netley, Katrin Cartlidge as Dark Annie Chapman, Terence Harvey as Benjamin Kidney, Susan Lynch as Liz Stride, Paul Rhys as Dr. Ferral, Lesley Sharp as Kate Eddowes, Annabelle Apsion as Polly Nichols; Executive Producers: Thomas M. Hammel, Albert Hughes, Allen Hughes, Amy Robinson; Screenplay: Terry Hayes, Rafael Yglesias; Based on the graphic novel by Alan Moore and Eddie Campbell; Directors: The Hughes Brothers; 122min.; Twentieth Century–Fox; Underworld Pictures; Color.

Whitechapel, London 1888. A group of prostitutes are being murdered in horrific circumstances. Inspector Frederick Abberline is assigned to the case. But he is no ordinary police inspector. He is clairvoyant, receiving visions of the murders fueled by his opium addiction. The case takes on added significance for Abberline when he falls in love with one of the prostitutes named Mary Kelly. All clues lead to the Freemasons playing a role in the brutal killings.

The Funky Phantom (1971) [Animated TV series]

Premiere: September 11, 1971; Voice Cast: Daws Butler as Jonathan Wellington "Mudsy" Muddlemore, Kristina Holland as April Stewart, Micky Dolenz as Skip Gilroy, Tommy Cook as Augie Anderson, Jerry Dexter as Elmo, Don Messick as Boo; Executive Producers: William Hanna, Joe Barbera; 17 × 25 min.; Hanna-Barbera Productions; Air Programs International (API); American Broadcasting Company (ABC); Color.

Teenagers April Stewart, Skip Gilroy and Augie Anderson stumble across the ghost of Jonathan "Mudsy" Middlemore and his cat Boo one stormy night. Correcting the time of a grandfather clock to midnight has set the cowardly ghost of Colonial Patriot "Mudsy" and his cat free. Now they help the teenagers solve spooky mysteries in their "Looney Duney" buggy.

SEASON ONE

Don't Fool With a Phantom (1:01); *Heir Scare* (1:02); *I'll Haunt You Later* (1:03); *Who's Chicken* (1:04); *The Headless Horseman* (1:05); *Spirit Spooked* (1:06); *Ghost Town Ghost* (1:07); *We Saw a Sea Serpent* (1:08); *Haunt in Inn* (1:09); *Mudsy Joins the Circus* (1:10); *Pigskin Predicament* (1:11); *The Liberty Bell Caper* (1:12); *April Foolish Day* (1:13); *The Forest's Prime-Evil* (1:14); *The Hairy Scary Houndman* (1:15); *Mudsy and Muddlemore Manor* (1:16); *Ghost Grabbers* (1:17).

Gargoyles (1972) [Telefilm]

Premiere: November 21, 1972; Main Cast: Cornel Wilde as Mercer Boley, Jennifer Salt as Diana Boley, Grayson Hall as Mrs. Parks, Bernie Casey as Head Gargoyle, Scott Glenn as James Reeger, William Stevens as Police Chief, Woodrow Chambliss as Uncle Willie, John Gruber as Jesse; Executive Producer: Roger Gimbel; Teleplay: Stephen Karpf, Elinor Karpf; Director: B. W. L. Norton;

75 min.; Tomorrow Entertainment Inc.; Color.

Anthropologist Mercer Boley's investigations into the truth behind a grotesque winged skeleton and the death of the old man who discovered it, bring him and his daughter face-to-face with centuries old Gargoyles.

Ga-Rei [Manga; Japan]

First publication: *Shonen Ace* (October 26, 2005); Creator-Story: Hajime Segawa; Publisher: Kadokawa Shonen.

High school student Kensuke Nimura joins forces with Kagura Tsuchimiya at the Supernatural Disaster Countermeasure Division (SDCD). Their first mission is Kagura's former partner and friend Yomi Isayama who has been possessed by an evil spirit.

This 12-volume series was followed by *Ga-rei: Tsuina no Sho* in 2008.

Ga-Rei-Zero (2008) [Anime; Japan]

Premiere: October 6, 2008; Voice Cast: Kaoru Mizuhara as Yomi Isayama, Minori Chihara as Kagura Tsuchimaya, Minoru Shiraishias as Kensuke Nimura, Shinya Takahashi as Noriyuki Izuna, Eri Kitamuri as Natsuki Kasuaga; Story: Katsuhiko Takayama; Director: Ei Aoki; 12 × 23 min.; AIC Spirits; Asread; Landis; Kadokawa Shoten; Rakuonsha; KlockWorx; Color.

When the Ministry of Defense's Paranormal Disaster Countermeasure Headquarters (PCDH) falls short in its missions, the Ministry of Environment's Supernatural Disaster Countermeasure Division (SDCD) takes over.

Working for the SDCD are teenage girl operatives Yomi Isayama and Kagura Tsuchimaya, who as exorcists protect the public from supernatural creatures. But the girls take different paths when the supernatural menace takes a darker turn and possesses Yomi.

This animated TV series serves as a prequel to the manga **Ga-Rei**.

SEASON ONE

Above Aoi (1:01); *Expression of Hatred* (1:02); *The Times of the Chance Encounter* (1:03); *The Cause of the Duty* (1:04); *Obstinate Feelings* (1:05); *Beautiful Enemy* (1:06); *Chains of Blame* (1:07); *Whereabouts of Revenge* (1:08); *Spiral of Sin* (1:09); *The Other Side of the Tragedy* (1:10); *Turmoil of Fates* (1:11); *Yearning Prayer* (1:12).

The Gates (2010) [TV series]

Premiere: June 20, 2010; Main Cast: Rhona Mitra as Clair Radcliff, Frank Grillo as Nick Monohan, Marisol Nichols as Sarah Monohan, Luke Maby as Dylan Radcliff, Travis Caldwell as Charlie Monohan, Skyler Samuels as Andie Bates, Chandra West as Devon, Colton Hayes as Brett Crezski, Janina Gavankar as Leigh Turner, Justin Miles as Marcus Jordan, Victoria Gabrielle Platt as Peg Meuller, James

Preston as Lukas Ford; Executive Producers: Richard Hatem, Gina Matthews, Grant Scharbo; Creators: Grant Scharbo, Richard Hatem; 13 × 45 min.; Little Engine Entertainment; Summerland Entertainment; Fox Television Studios; American Broadcasting Company (ABC); Color.

Nick Monohan is the new Chief of Police for an upmarket community called "The Gates." But adapting to his new job is more difficult than Monohan could imagine as he and his family find themselves surrounded by werewolves, vampires and witches.

SEASON ONE

Pilot (1:01); *What Lies Beneath* (1:02); *Breach* (1:03); *The Monster Within* (1:04); *Repercussions* (1:05); *Jurisdiction* (1:06); *Digging the Dirt* (1:07); *Dog Eat Dog* (1:08); *Identity Crisis* (1:09); *Little Girl Lost* (1:10); *Surfacing* (1:11); *Bad Moon Rising* (1:12); *Moving Day* (1:13).

The Ghost Busters (1975) [TV series]

Premiere: September 6, 1975: Main Cast: Forrest Tucker as Kong, Larry Storch as Spencer, Bob Burns as Tracy the Gorilla, Lou Scheimer as Voice of Zero; Executive Producers: Norm Prescott, Richard M. Rosenbloom. Lou Scheimer; Creator: Marc Richards; Directors: Norman Abbott, Larry Peerce; 15 × 22 min.; Filmation Associates; CBS; Color.

In this short-lived sitcom aimed at children detectives Kong, Spencer and their assistant and driver Tracy the Gorilla are given weekly paranormal assignments at a general store by Zero via recorded messages hidden in inanimate objects that self- destruct "Mission Impossible" style. Episodes are often resolved with Kong zapping the ghosts back to their spectral abode with the "Ghost De-Materializer."

Due to the success of the unrelated **Ghostbusters** movie in 1984 the producers decided to relaunch *Ghost Busters* as a weekly animated series in 1986.

SEASON ONE

The Maltese Monkey (1:01); *Dr. Whatshisname* (1:02); *The Canterville Ghost* (1:03); *Who's Afraid of the Big Bad Wolf?* (1:04); *The Flying Dutchman* (1:05); *The Dummy's Revenge* (1:06); *A Worthless Gauze* (1:07); *Which Witch is Which?* (1:08); *They Went Thataway* (1:09); *The Vampire's Apprentice* (1:10); *Jekyll & Hyde: Together, for the First Time!* (1:11); *Only Ghosts Have Wings* (1:12); *The Vikings Have Landed* (1:13); *Merlin the Magician* (1:14); *The Abominable Snowman* (1:15).

Ghostbusters (1984) [Film]

Premiere: June 7, 1984; Main Cast: Bill Murray as Dr. Peter Venkman, Dan Aykroyd as Dr. Raymond Stanz, Harold Ramis as Dr. Egon Spengler, Ernie Hudson as Winston Zeddemore, Sigourney Weaver as Dana Barrett, Annie Potts as Janine Melnitz, Rick Moranis as Louis Tully, William Atherton as Walter Peck, David Margulies as Mayor Lenny Clotch, Michael Ensign as Hotel Manager, Slavitza Jovan as Gozer, Paddi Edwards as Voice of Gozer; Executive Producer: Bernie Brillstein; Story: Dan Aykroyd, Harold Ramis; Director: Ivan Reitman; 105 min.; Columbia-Delphi Productions; Black Rhino-Bernie Brillstein Productions; Columbia Pictures; Color.

Three disgraced Columbia University paranormal scientists create a ghostbusting agency in an abandoned New York City firehouse. With their proton packs and containment unit they capture the ghost known as Slimer and attract their first client. Dana Barrett's apartment is haunted, but Peter Venkman is more interested in Barrett's physical charms. Complications arise when Barrett and her neighbor Louis Tully are possessed by demons. Soon New York City is under demonic attack and only the ghostbusters can save the day by closing a gateway and destroying the gigantic Stay Puft Marshmallow Man.

The box-office hit spawned the successful animated television series *The Real Ghostbusters* (1986) and the live-action sequel *Ghostbusters II* (1989) with the original cast reprising their roles. A 2016 reboot featuring a female cast as the lead characters was a box-office failure.

Ghost Detective (Myron Vale Investigation Book #1) [Novel]

Author: Scott William carter; First publication: Flying Raven Press, 2013.

Portland detective Myron Vale has seen ghosts ever since he recovered from a coma with a bullet lodged in his brain. He has one major problem. He can't distinguish between the living and the dead. Vale's case takes a dramatic turn when he realizes the husband of his ghost client is the same man responsible for the bullet in his brain.

A short story prequel *The Haunted Breadbox* (2013) was published prior to the release of *Ghost Detective*.

Followed by: *The Ghost Who Said Goodbye* (2015); *The Ghost, the Girl and the Gold* (2016).

Ghost Detectives; The Lost Bride (Book #1) [Juvenile book]

Author: Emily Mason; First publication: London: Puffin, 2012.

A ghost bride is haunted by her own past. The Ghost Detectives, Abi, Sarah, Hannah and Grace investigate why she was left at the altar over a century ago.

Ghost Detectives; The Missing Dancer (Book #2) [Juvenile book]

Author: Emily Mason; First publication: London: Puffin, 2013.

The Ghost Detectives help the ghost of a young girl who must perform one last time before her soul can rest in peace.

Ghost Hunt [Novel; Manga; Anime; Japan]

First publication: 1989; Creator-Writer: Fuyumi Ono; Publisher: Kodansha.

Shibuya Psychic Research (SPR), headed by teenager Kazu Shibuya, nicknamed "Naru." Members of SPR include 16-year-old high school student Mai Taniyama who possesses ESP powers, a Catholic priest who performs exorcisms, a spirit medium, a Buddhist monk and a shrine maiden. The SPR investigates paranormal events in Japan.

[Manga] First publication: *Nakayoshi* (July 7, 1998); Story & Art: Shiho Inada; Publisher: Kodansha.

12-volume manga series based on the novels by Fuyumi Ono.

[Anime] Premiere: October 3, 2006; Voice Cast: ; Story: Reiko Yoshida, Rika Nakase; Director: Rei Mano; 25 × 25 min.; JC Staff; Avex Entertainment; Marvelous Entertainment; TV Tokyo: Color.

Based on the manga series by Shiho Inada. Episodes include stories of a haunted school, voodoo dolls, spirit possession, will-o-the-wisps and a death spell.

Episodes

File 1: Evil Spirits All Over!?: Part 1 (1:01); *File 1: Evil Spirits All Over!?: Part 2* (1:02); *File 1: Evil Spirits All Over!?: Part 3* (1:03); *File 2: The Doll House: Part 1* (1:04); *File 2: The Doll House: Part 2* (1:05); *File 2: The Doll House: Part 3* (1:06); *File 3: The After School Hexer: Part 1* (1:07); *File 3: The After School Hexer: Part 2* (1:08); *File 3: The After School Hexer: Part 3* (1:09); *File 3: The After School Hexer: Part 4* (1:10); *File 4: Ghost Story in the Park!?* (1:11); *File 5: Silent Christmas: Part 1* (1:12); *File 5: Silent Christmas: Part 2* (1:13); *File 6: The Forbidden Pastime: Part 1* (1:14); *File 6: The Forbidden Pastime: Part 2* (1:15); *File 6: The Forbidden Pastime: Part 3* (1:16); *File 6: The Forbidden Pastime: Part 4* (1:17); *File 7: The Bloodstained Labyrinth: Part 1* (1:18); *File 7: The Bloodstained Labyrinth: Part 2* (1:19); *File 7: The Bloodstained Labyrinth: Part 3* (1:20); *File 7: The Bloodstained Labyrinth: Part 4* (1:21); *File 8: The Cursed House: Part 1* (1:22); *File 8: The Cursed House: Part 2* (1:23); *File 8: The Cursed House: Part 3* (1:24); *File 8: The Cursed House: Part 4* (1:25).

The Ghost, Master Magician [Comic book character]

First appearance: *Thrilling Comics* #3 (April 1940); Story: Richard Hughes; Art: August Froehlich; Publisher: New York: Better Publications.

Following the death of his father in India young George Chance is raised by yogis. They teach him the magic arts which he puts to good use as an adult in America. His first case sees him investigating the suicide of Leonard Van. Chance is convinced it was murder as Van was in excellent spirits the night before his death. Disguising himself as a sinister skull-face figure with the power of levitation and invisibility Case gets to the truth of Van's death.

"At his make-up table George Chance disappears. A sinister face stares back at him. The Ghost is ready to strike!"

The comic book character is a variation of the pulp character *The Ghost, Super-Detective* a.k.a. *The Ghost Detective* a.k.a. *The Green Ghost* with a new origin story and actual mystical powers. As the series progresses George Chance drops his skull-face disguise but maintains his mystical powers and adds a magic cape and crystal ball of his yogi teacher as he tackles cases with his wife Betty. His final appearance is in *Thrilling Comics* #52 (August 1946). Although the readers are promised a new adventure next month *The Ghost* is replaced with *The Phantom Detective*. *The Ghost* resurfaces again as The Green Ghost in America's Best Comics (DC) *Tom Strong* #11 (January 2001) and the miniseries spin-off *Terra Obscura* (2003).

Ghost of a Chance (Ghost Finders Book #1) [Novel]

Author: Simon R. Green; First publication: London: Jo Fletcher Books, 2015.

The supernatural investigators for the Carnacki Institute comprise of charming but arrogant team leader J. C. Chance, techno-wizard Melody Chambers and the melancholy telepath known as Happy Jack Palmer. The team must investigate an apparent haunting at a London underground tube station, but they have nefarious opposition in their rivals the Crowley Project.

The team's adventures continue as they investigate the Phantom of the Hayburn Theatre, the haunted King's Arms Inn, a poltergeist threatening university students, and the evil entity known as the Flesh Undying.

Ghost Finders series: *Ghost of a Chance* (2015); *Ghost of a Smile* (2015); *Ghost of a Dream* (2016); *Spirits From Beyond* (2016); *Voices From Beyond* (2016); *Forces From Beyond* (2016).

"The Ghost of the Grate" [Short story]

Author: Sarah P. E. Hawthorne; First publication: *Ballou's Monthly Magazine* (February 1888); Publisher: Boston, MA: Thomes & Talbot.

Detective Curtis visits Rothmore Lodge in Orange County where he investigates the case of the missing widower Solomon Rothmore, who has bequeathed his vast wealth to brother James and a small legacy to his eighteen-year-old daughter. Jabez the gardener reports finding Solomon's hat in the summer-house next to a blood stain. Miss Rothmore tells Curtis, "I know papa was murdered; and I do not know where his poor body is laid! I do not believe papa made that will. It was forged."

Later that fall Curtis poses as an artist in order to obtain permission to occupy a few rooms in James Rothmore's house, the residence of his late brother. One evening while enjoying a cigar in the library Curtis falls asleep reading his book and awakes with a start. "I look at the fire. It had burned down to coals. From those dying embers arose a thin, gray vapor. Faint at first, it rose in sinuous curves, like a sea-serpent, higher, higher! Now faint, now dark in hue, until widening it took a shape. From the ghostly veil of vapor the form of a man was evolved. A man past the prime of life, with gray hair dabbled in blood, and a gaping wound in the throat…. Never can I forget the expression in that face, the anxiety in those sunken eyes."

When Curtis cleans the grate for evidence of human remains, he finds "indisputable proof that a human being had been cut to pieces and buried there." Reading Solomon's will Curtis notices the water-mark in the paper is only two-years-old but the date on the will is six-years-old. He arrests the brother, but not without a fight. Detective Curtis marries the lonely Edwina Rothmore and learns Solomon and James had been estranged ever since their father left most of the property to Solomon. James was also in love with Edwina, but she chose Solomon. James then murdered Solomon in a fit of rage and reduced the body to ashes.

Detective Curtis concludes, "Explain it as you will, savants or students of psychometry. I know that he came to justice by the aid of, not a fabrication of my disordered brain, but through the agency of the soul of the owner of the Lodge, the facsimile of whose corporeal frame rose, phoenix-like, from its own ashes.

I had never been a believer in the supernatural, and this was my first and only experience with the great unexplainable. Neither do I wish to make any converts to that faith."

Ghost Story (The Dresden Files Book #13)
Author: Jim Butcher; Publisher: New York: Roc, 2011.

Harry Dresden has been murdered by a mystery assailant. Now he finds himself powerless, surrounded by dark spirits who hold grudges against him. To move on he must find his murderer and save his friends in peril. All without the use of magic.

See: **Cold Days**

The Ghost, Super-Detective [Pulp fiction]
Author-Creator: G.T. Fleming-Roberts; Publisher: New York: Better Publications.

In his first story "Calling the Ghost" young George Chance is taught the skills of a magician by Marko following the death of his circus performer parents. As an adult he fights crime behind the ghoulish disguise of a skull-faced "ghost" while his lookalike Glenn Saunders provides cover for him. Police Commissioner Standish and medical examiner Robert Demarest also know George Chance's secret disguise.

His stories were initially published in *The Ghost, Super-Detective* magazine before changing title to *The Ghost Detective* in 1940 and *The Green Ghost Detective* in 1941. With the cancellation of the pulp magazine the character transferred to his own comic strip **The Ghost, Master Magician** where he was given a new origin story and mystical powers.

Ghost Sweeper Mikami a.k.a. ***Gosuto suipa Mikami*** (1993) [Anime; Japan]
Premiere: April 11, 1993; Voice Cast: Tsuru Hiromi as Reiko Makimi, Ryo Horikawaa as Tadao Yokoshima, Kumiko Nishihara as Meiko Rokudo, Kazuyuki Sogabe as Karasu Kazuhiro; Producer: Hiromi Seki; Creator: Takashi Shiina; Story: Aya Matsui, Nobuaki Kishima, Masaharu Amiya; Director: Atsutoshi Umezawa; 45 × 24 min.; Sentai Filmworks; Toei; TV Asahi; Color.

Tokyo has a ghost epidemic created by urban sprawl. Ghost Sweepers are private exorcists for hire to the highest bidder. First-class Ghost Sweeper Reiko Makimi runs "The Mikami Ghost Sweeper Company" with underpaid teenage assistant Tadao Yokoshima and ghost girl Okinu. Tadao lusts after Reiko and Reiko's lusts after money.

The anime TV series was followed by the anime movie *GS Mikami: War in Heaven* (1994).

The Green Ghost Detective (Summer 1941). Published by Better Publications.

SEASON ONE

First Appearance of the Exorcist! (1:01); *There is No Tomorrow for the Burglar!* (1:02); *Empire of the Cursed Dolls!* (1:03); *The Extermination of the Space-Ghost* (1:04); *Howl of the Haunted House!* (1:05); *The Girl is an Exorcist!* (1:06); *Challenge From Dr. Kaos!* (1:07); *Love Transcends Time!* (1:08); *Please, Kiss!!* (1:09); *The Search for Shikigami!* (1:10); *Let's Go on the Spirited Train!* (1:11); *Beware to Yakuchindo!?* (1:12); *Rival, Ogasawara Emi!* (1:13); *The Summer, the Pool, the Demon* (1:14); *All-Ensemble in the Mediterranean* (1:15); *Make the Vampire Sleep!* (1:16); *The Allurement of the Summer Sea* (1:17); *The Shrinking Mikami!!* (1:18); *After the Ghost Submarine!* (1:19); *Paradise Smash!!* (1:20); *Everyone Has Become Children!!* (1:21); *Counterattack of the Devil Viper* (1:22); *Road to the Dragon!!* (1:23); *Outburst of the Dragon's Wrath* (1:24); *Himoko of Yamatai* (1:25); *Hero, Mikami's Adventure!* (1:26); *Maria's Devotion!* (1:27); *The Dragon Prince!!* (1:28); *Crisis of the Dragon!!* (1:29); *The Devil Sword, Shimesabamaru* (1:30); *Department of Sky and Magic Broom* (1:31); *Reiko is Married!?* (1:32); *To Invite the Mannequin Doll* (1:33); *The Demon High School* (1:34); *Santa's Gift!* (1:35); *Okinu's Christmas* (1:36); *The Battle's Celebration for the New Year!!* (1:37); *Examinee's Blues* (1:38); *Maria's Sister* (1:39); *Maria and Teresa* (1:40); *Showdown! The Snow Queen* (1:41); *Give You the Choco!!* (1:42); *Into the Dream!* (1:43); *Hellish Nightmare* (1:44); *Love Overflows* (1:45).

Ghost Sweeper Mikami Gokuraku Daisakusen!! [Manga; Japan]

First publication: *Weekly Shonen Sunday* (April 17, 1991); Story & Art: Takashi Shiina; Publisher: Shogakukan.

The inspiration for the anime TV series ran to 39 volumes.

Ghost Talker's Daydream a.k.a. **Teizokurei Daydream** (2004) [OVA; Japan]

Premiere: June 25, 2004; Voice Cast: Masumi Asano as Misaki Saiti, Yukari Tamura as Ai Kunugi, Tomokazu Sugita as Souichiro Kadotake, Michiko Neya as Detective Anzai, Tetsuo Kanao as Detective Yamazake; Producers: Minori Takanashi, Atsushi Yukawa, Katsunori Haruta; Story: Katsuma Kanazawa; Director: Osamu Sekita; 4 × 24 min.; HAL Film Maker; Geneon; Bandai Visual; Color.

Albino Misaki Saiki shares her time between work as a dominatrix at an S&M gentlemen's club and a spiritual medium solving supernatural cases for the Livelihood Preservation Group. Helping with her investigations is psychic school girl Ai Kunugi who is introduced to Misaki when she investigates the death of Ai's sister and her baby niece.

EPISODES

Ghost Talker (1:01); *Bindweed* (1:02); *Mad Bones* (1:03); *Water Spirit* (1:04).

[Manga] First publication: *Shonen Ace* (August 2000); Story: Saki Okuse; Art: Sankichi Meguro; Publisher: Kadokawa Shoten.

This 10-volume manga was adapted into the OVA Anime, although only the first two episodes follow the original manga chapters.

Ghost Trick: Phantom Detective [Video game]

Release date: June 19, 2010; Creator/Director: Shu Takumi; Developer: Capcom; Platforms: Nintendo DS, iOS, Android; Perspective: Side View; Publisher: Capcom Entertainment Ltd.

The player controls Sissel, a ghost who must recover his own identity and discover who murdered him. Sissel can possess corpses four minutes before their death and restore them to life by changing the future. He employs many "Ghost Tricks" manipulating inanimate objects during his time in the "Land of the Living." Sissel has until dawn to unravel the mystery of his death or he will be confined to the Ghost World where time has ceased. Various detectives populate the game including Detective Jowd and young female police detective Lynne who Sissel saves from death. Blue Detective and Green Detective are both investigating Sissel's murder.

Ghosted (2017) [TV series]

Premiere: October 1, 2017; Main Cast: Craig Robinson as Leroy Wright, Adam Scott as Max Jennifer, Ally Walker as Captain Ava

Lafrey, Adeel Akhtar as Barry Shaw, Amber Stevens West as Annie Carver; Producer: Steve Burgess; Creator: Tom Gormican; 16 × 22 min.; Crowley Etten Productions; Getting' Rad Productions; TYPO Inc.; Afternoonnap; Additional Dialogue; 3 Arts Entertainment; 20th Century–Fox Television; Fox Network; Color.

Former police detective Leroy Wright is teamed up with former Stanford professor Max Jennifer as they investigate the paranormal for The Bureau Underground organization. Cases range from ghosts to UFOs to psychics to zombies.

This sitcom failed to attract an audience and was canceled after 16 episodes.

SEASON ONE

Pilot (1:01); *Bee-Mo* (1:02); *Whispers* (1:03); *Lockdown* (1:04); *The Machine* (1:05); *Sam* (1:06); *Ghost Studz* (1:07); *Haunted Hayride* (1:08); *Snatcher* (1:09); *The Wire* (1:10); *The Demotion* (1:11); *The Premonition* (1:12); *The Article* (1:13); *Unbelievable* (1:14); *The Airplane* (1:15); *Hello Boys* (1:16).

Ghosts of Mars (20010 [Film]

Premiere: August 24, 2001; Main Cast: Natasha Henstridge as Lieutenant Melanie Ballard, Ice Cube as Desolation Williams, Jason Statham as Sgt. Jericho Butler, Pam Grier as Commander Helena Braddock, Clea DuVall as Bashira Kincaid, Joanna Cassidy as Whitlock, Richard Cetrone as Big Daddy Mars, Rosemary Forsyth as Inquisitor, Liam Waite as Michael Descanso, Duane Davis as Uno, Lobo Sebastian as Dos, Rodney A. Grant as Tres; Producer: Sandy King; Story: Larry Sulkis, John Carpenter; Director: John Carpenter; 98 min.; Screen Gems; Storm King Productions; Animationwerks; Color.

Police Lieutenant Melanie Ballard and her team arrive at a remote mining outpost on Mars to transport a dangerous prisoner from a city compound. But upon arrival they encounter miners possessed by ancient evil spirits.

Gilda Joyce: The Bones of the Holy (Book #5) [Juvenile book]

Author: Jennifer Allison; First publication: New York: Dutton Children's Books, 2011.

Gilda feels uneasy about her mother's engagement to Eugene Pook, a man who seems to be more connected to his former fiancé. As the couple prepare for their wedding in St. Augustine, Florida Gilda feels herself surrounded by ghosts and investigations into her future step-father's past only complicate matters further.

Gilda Joyce: The Dead Drop (Book #4) [Juvenile book]

Author: Jennifer Allison; First publication: New York: Dutton Books for Young Readers, 2009.

Psychic investigator Gilda Joyce is enjoying a summer internship at the International Spy Museum in Washington, D.C. She soon puts her psychic skills to the test when she experiences dreams of Abraham Lincoln and sees the ghost of a mystery woman in the museum exhibits. The connection to the increased psychic activity appears to be KGB artifacts that were recently donated to the museum.

Gilda Joyce: The Ghost Sonata (Book #3) [Juvenile book]

Author: Jennifer Allison; First publication: New York: Dutton Children's Books, 2007.

Gilda joins her best friend Wendy Choy who has qualified for the International Young Virtuoso Piano Competition in Oxford, England. Gilda investigates the meaning behind the Tarot cards depicting the nine of swords placed in their bedrooms and the strange haunting melody only Wendy can hear. Wendy fears she is haunted by the ghost of Charles Drummond who died in a car accident four years ago and was a former student of one of the judges in the piano competition.

Gilda Joyce: The Ladies of the Lake (Book #2) [Juvenile book]

Author: Jennifer Allison; First publication: New York: Dutton Children's Books, 2006.

Gilda investigates the drowning of freshman student Dolores Lambert at Our Lady of Sorrows Catholic High School. The student's ghost is said to haunt the bridge overlooking the lake where she drowned.

Gilda Joyce: Psychic Investigator (Book #1) [Juvenile book]

Author: Jennifer Allison; First publication: New York: Sleuth/Dutton, 2005.

Mr. Splinter and his teenage daughter Juliet live in a San Francisco mansion with an imposing Gothic tower. The tower holds a terrible secret and thirteen-year-old Gilda Joyce is ready to help her cousin Juliet using her budding psychic powers, Ouija board and magic typewriter bequeathed by her late father in the first case of her career.

God Told Me To a.k.a. ***Demon*** (1976) [Film]

Premiere: October 22, 1976; Main Cast: Tony Lo Bianco as Detective Peter J. Nicholas, Deborah Raffin as Casey Forster, Sandy Dennis as Martha Nicholas, Sylvia Sidney as Elizabeth Mullin, Richard Lynch as Bernard Phillips, Sam Levene as Everett Lukas, Sammy Williams as Harold Gorman, Robert Drivas as David Morten, Alf Kellin as Deputy Commissioner; Producer/Screenplay/Director: Larry Cohen; 91 min.; Big Hit Productions; New World Pictures; Metrocolor-b/w.

New York police detective Peter Nicholas investigates a series of murders with one factor in common. Each of the killer's claim "Gold told me to" before dying. Further investigation by devout Catholic Peter Nicholas leads to cult figure Bernard Phillips and the astounding truth about his own past, the source of his supernatural powers.

Goober and the Ghost Chasers (1973) [Animated TV series]

Premiere: September 8, 1973; Voice Cast: Jerry Dexter as Ted, Jo Ann Harris as Tina, Ronnie Schell as Gillie, Paul Winchell as Goober; Executive Producers: William Hanna, Joe Barbera; 16 × 25 min.; Hanna-Barbera Productions; American Broadcasting Company (ABC); Color.

Teenage reporters Ted, Tina and photographer Gillie are aided by Goober the dog in their pursuit of ghosts for their "Ghost Chasers" magazine. Their Anti-Apparition Kit consisting of the Specter Detector, Poltergeist Powder and Post-Ghost Scanner confirms if a ghost is real or fake. Whenever Goober senses fear he becomes temporarily invisible and while he doesn't talk to his fellow Ghost Chasers he does occasionally talk directly to the viewer.

The "Partridge Kids" made regular guest appearances in the early episodes, with *Partridge Family* cast members Danny Bonaduce, Susan Dey, Suzanne Crough and Brian Forster providing the voice-overs.

SEASON ONE

Assignment: The Ahab Apparition (1:01); *Brush Up Your Shakespeare* (1:02); *The Galloping Ghost* (1:03); *The Singing Ghost* (1:04); *The Ghost Ship* (1:05); *Mummy Knows Best* (1:06); *The Haunted Wax Museum* (1:07); *Aloha Ghost* (1:08); *The Wicked Witch Dog* (1:09); *Venice Anyone?* (1:10); *Go West Young Ghost, Go West* (1:11); *A Hard Day's Knight* (1:12); *Is Sherlock Holme?* (1:13); *That Snow Ghost* (1:14); *Inca Dinka Doo* (1:15); *Old MacDonald Had a Ghost—Ei, Ei, Eeyow* (1:16).

Gotham (2014) [TV series]

Premiere: September 24, 2014; Main Cast: Ben McKenzie as Detective James Gordon, Donal Logue as Harvey Bullock, David Mazouz as Bruce Wayne/Batman, Sean Pertwee as Alfred Pennyworth, Robin Lord Taylor as Oswald Cobblepot/Penguin, Camren Bicondova as Selian Kyle, Cory Michael Smith as Edward Nygma/Riddler, Erin Richards as Barbara Kean, Morena Baccarin as Leslie Thompkins, Alexander Siddig as Ra's al Ghul; Executive Producers: Danny Cannon, Bruno Heller, John Stephens; Developer: Bruno Heller; Based on characters created by Bill Finger, Bob Kane; 100 × 42 min.; Primrose Hill Productions; DC Comics; Warner Bros. Television; Fox Network; Color.

The formative years of young Bruce Wayne and the quest to find the killers of Thomas and Martha Wayne by Detective James Gordon and his cynical partner Harvey Bullock. A Gotham City underworld is gradually uncovered that includes psychotic criminals who will play a major part in Bruce Wayne's future as The Batman.

The occult figure of Ra's al Ghul makes his entrance in the final two episodes of Season Three.

Gotham by Midnight [Comic book]
First publication: December 2014; 5-issue mini-series; Writer: Ray Fawkes; Art: Ben Templesmith; Publisher: DC Comics.

The Gotham City Police Department's Detailed Case Task Force a.k.a. the Midnight Shift tackles cases of the supernatural out of Precinct Thirteen. Founded by Commissioner Gordon as a personal project the Shift consists of Commanding Officer Lieutenant Weaver, Detective Jim Corrigan, alias **The Spectre**, forensics expert Dr. Szandor Tarr, religious consultant Sister Justine and Detective Lisa Drake. Sergeant Rook of Internal Affairs has been given the task of observing the Task Force in action with the objective of ultimately shutting them down as they investigate a case of children speaking in tongues.

Grave Peril (The Dresden Files Book #3)
Author: Jim Butcher; Publisher: New York: Roc, 2001.

Chicago is under attack from tormented and violent ghosts. Who or what is responsible for the upsurge in activity and why do so many of the ghosts have connections to wizard and paranormal investigator Harry Dresden?

See: **Summer Night**

Gravity Falls (2012) [Animated TV series]
Premiere: June 15, 2012; Voice Cast: Jason Ritter as Dipper Pines, Kristen Schaal as Mabel Pines, Alex Hirsch as Grunkle Stan, Linda Cardellini as Wendy Corduroy. Kevin Michael Richardson as Sheriff Blubs, John DiMaggio as Manly Dan; Creator-Executive Producer: Alex Hirsch; 40 × 23 min.; Disney Television Animation; Color.

While spending the summer with Grunkle Stan youngsters Dipper Pines and his twin sister Mabel discover a strange journal in the forest. This results in them investigating supernatural forces and beings in the peculiar town of Gravity Falls, Oregon.

SEASON ONE

Tourist Trapped (1:01); *The Legend of the Gobblewonker* (1:02); *Headhunters* (1:03); *The Hand That Rocks the Mabel* (1:04); *The Inconveniencing* (1:05); *Dipper vs. Manliness* (1:06); *Double Dipper* (1:07); *Irrational Treasure* (1:08); *The Time Traveler's Pig* (1:09); *Fight Fighters* (1:10); *Little Dipper* (1:11); *Summerween* (1:12); *Boss Mabel* (1:13); *Bottomless Pit* (1:14); *The Deep End* (1:15); *Carpet Diem* (1:16); *Boyz Crazy* (1:17); *Land Before Swine* (1:18); *Dreamscaperers* [Part 1] (1:19); *Gideon Rises* [Part 2] (1:20).

SEASON TWO

Scary-Oke (2:01); *Into the Bunker* (2:02); *The Golf War* (2:03); *Sock Opera* (2:04); *Soos and the Real Girl* (2:05); *Little Gift Shop of Horrors* (2:06); *Society of the Blind Eye* (2:07); *Blendin's Game* (2:08); *The Love God* (2:09); *Northwest Mansion Mystery & Northwest Mansion Noir* (2:10); *Not What He Seems* (2:11); *A Tale of Two Stans* (2:12); *Dungeons, Dungeons & More Dungeons* (2:13); *The Stanchurian Candidate* (2:14); *The Last Mabelcorn* (2:15); *Roadside Attraction* (2:16); *Dipper and Mabel vs. the Future* (2:17); *Weirdmageddon* [Part 1] (2:18); *Weirdmageddon 2: Escape From Reality* (2:19); *Weirdmageddon 3: Take Back the Falls* (2:20).

Grey Shapes [Novel]
Author: Jack Mann (E. Charles Vivian); First publication: London: Wright & Brown, 1937.

The son of a general who is disappointed he didn't follow him into military life, former policeman Gregory George Gordon Green goes by the nickname of Gees. He runs "Gee's Confidential Agency for everything, from mumps to murder." with his secretary Eve Madeleine Brandon who acts as his transcriber and researcher. Gees agrees to investigate the killing of sheep on Mr. Tyrrell's property in Cumberland when he suspects the paranormal is a factor. All clues lead to inhuman werewolves who aren't at the mercy of the full moon.

Novels in the series: *Gee's First Case* (1936); *Grey Shapes* (1937); *Nightmare Farm* (1937); *The Kleinert Case* (1938); *Maker of Shadows* (1939);

The Ninth Life (1939); *Her Ways Are Death* (1940); *The Glass Too Many* (1940).

Greywalker [Novel]

Author: Kat Richardson; First publication: New York: Ace Books, 2006.

Private investigator Harper Blaine is viciously attacked and left for dead. When she recovers in hospital Harper discovers she was clinically dead for two minutes. She experiences weird shapes in a foggy mist and menacing creatures. Harper Blaine can now travel between the world of the living and the supernatural world known as the Grey. She is a Greywalker.

Greywalker book series: *Greywalker* (2006); *Poltergeist* (2007); *Underground* (2008); *Vanished* (2009); *Labyrinth* (2010); *Downpour* (2011); *Seawitch* (2012); *Possession* (2013); *Revenant* (2014).

Grimm (2011) [TV series]

Premiere: October 28, 2011; Main Cast: David Giuntoli as Nick Burkhardt, Russell Hornsby as Hank Griffin, Silas Weir Mitchell as Monroe, Sasha Roiz as Captain Sean Renard, Reggie Lee as Sgt. Wu, Elizabeth Tulloch as Juliette Silverton, Bree Turner as Rosalee Calvert, Claire Coffee as Adalind Schade; Executive Producers: David Greenwalt, Jim Kouf, Todd Milner, Sean Hayes, Norberto Barba; Creators: Stephen Carpenter, David Greenwalt; 123 × 45 min.; GK Productions; Hazy Mill Productions; Universal Television; National Broadcasting Company (NBC); Color.

When Portland homicide detective Nick Burkhardt begins to see outwardly ordinary people turning into terrifying monsters, he learns from his dying aunt that he is one of the last Grimms. "We have the ability to see what no one else can. When they lose control, they can't hide, and we see them for what they are." Burkhardt discovers the monsters he sees are from fairy tales and folklore and it is his duty as a Grimm to keep them under control. And he must discover why his aunt left him a mysterious key.

Season One

Pilot (1:01); *Bears Will Be Bears* (1:02); *Beeware* (1:03); *Lonelyhearts* (1:04); *Danse Macabre* (1:05); *The Three Bad Wolves* (1:06); *Let Your Hair Down* (1:07); *Game Ogre* (1:08); *Of Mouse and Man* (1:09); *Organ Grinder* (1:10); *Tarentella* (1:11); *Last Grimm Standing* (1:12); *Three Coins in a Fuchsbau* (1:13); *Plumed Serpent* (1:14); *Island of Dreams* (1:15); *The Thing with Feathers* (1:16); *Love Sick* (1:17); *Cat and Mouse* (1:18); *Leave it to Beavers* (1:19); *Happily Ever Aftermath* (1:20); *Big Feet* (1:21); *Woman in Black* (1:22).

Season Two

Bad Teeth (2:01); *The Kiss* (2:02); *Bad Moon Rising* (2:03); *Quill* (2:04); *The Good Shepherd* (2:05); *Over My Dead Body* (2:06); *The Bottle Imp* (2:07); *The Other Side* (2:08); *La Llorona* (2:09); *The Hour of Death* (2:10); *To Protect and Serve Man* (2:11); *Season of the Hexenbiest* (2:12); *Face Off* (2:13); *Natural Born Wesen* (2:14); *Mr. Sandman* (2:15); *Nameless* (2:16); *One Angry Fuchsbau* (2:17); *Volcanis* (2:18); *Endangered* (2:19); *Kiss of the Muse* (2:20); *The Waking Dead* (2:21); *Goodnight, Sweet Grimm* (2:22).

Season Three

The Ungrateful Dead (3:01); *PTZD* (3:02); *A Dish Best Served Cold* (3:03); *One Night Stand* (3:04); *El Cucuy* (3:05); *Stories We Tell Our Young* (3:06); *Cold Blooded* (3:07); *Twelve Days of Krampus* (3:08); *Red Menace* (3:09); *Eye of the Beholder* (3:10); *The Good Soldier* (3:11); *The Wild Hunt* (3:12); *Revelation* (3:13); *Mommy Dearest* (3:14); *Once We Were Gods* (3:15); *The Show Must Go On* (3:16); *Synchronicity* (3:17); *The Law of Sacrifice* (3:18); *Nobody Knows the Trubel I've Seen* (3:19); *My Fair Wesen* (3:20); *The Inheritance* (3:21); *Blond Ambition* (3:22).

Season Four

Thanks for the Memories (4:01); *Octopus Head* (4:02); *The Last Fight* (4:03); *Dyin' on a Prayer* (4:04); *Cry Luison* (4:05); *Highway of Tears* (4:06); *The Grimm Who Stole Christmas* (4:07); *Chupacabra* (4:08); *Wesenrein* (4:09); *Tribunal* (4:10); *Death Do Us Part* (4:11); *Marechausee* (4:12); *Trial by Fire* (4:13); *Bad Luck* (4:14); *Double Date* (4:15); *Heartbreaker* (4:16); *Hibernaculum* (4:17); *Mishipeshu* (4:18); *Iron Hans* (4:19); *You Don't Know Jack* (4:20); *Headache* (4:21); *Cry havoc* (4:22).

SEASON FIVE

The Grimm Identity (5:01); *Clear and Wesen Danger* (5:02); *Lost Boys* (5:03); *Maiden Quest* (5:04); *Rat King* (5:05); *Wesen Nacht* (5:06); *Eve of Destruction* (5:07); *A Reptile Dysfunction* (5:08); *Star-Crossed* (5:09); *Map of the Seven Knights* (5:10); *Key Move* (5:11); *Into the Scharzwald* (5:12); *Silence of the Slams* (5:13); *Lycanthropia* (5:14); *Skin Deep* (5:15); *The Believer* (5:16); *Inugami* (5:17); *Good to the Bone* (5:18); *The Taming of the Wu* (5:19); *Bad Night* (5:20); *Beginning of the End: Part 1* (5:21); *Beginning of the End: Part 2* (5:22).

SEASON SIX

Fugitive (6:01); *Trust Me Knot* (6:02); *Oh Captain, My Captain* (6:03); *El Cuegle* (6:04); *The Seven Year Itch* (6:05); *Breakfast in Bed* (6:06); *Blind Love* (6:07); *The Son Also Rises* (6:08); *Tree People* (6:09); *Blood Magic* (6:10); *Where the Wild Things Were* (6:11); *Zerstorer Shrugged* (6:12); *The End* (6:13).

Guinea PIG: Pet Shop Private Eye [Graphic novel series]

First publication: April 2010; Author: Colleen AF Venable; Art: Stephanie Yue; Publisher: Graphic Universe.

When Hamisher the hamster, who thinks he's a koala, sees a sign that says "GUINEA PI" he hires Sasspant the guinea pig to find his missing sandwich. What he doesn't realize is the letter "G" fell off Sasspant's cage when Mr. Venezi the short-sighted owner of "Pets and Stuff" slammed the cage door. Book loving Sasspant reluctantly agrees to take the case and becomes a private investigator by night.

In the second book in the series *And Then There Were Gnomes* Sasspants and junior investigator Hamisher investigate a case of missing mice and suspected ghosts when Mr. Venezi puts up a sign in the store that says "Please Enjoy the Rest of Our Shop. This Aisle is Currently HAUNTED."

The Harrowing (2018) [Film]

Premiere: December 25, 2018; Main Cast: Detective Matthew Tompkins as Ryan Calhoun, Michael Ironside as Lt. Logan, Arnold Vosloo as Dr. Franklin Whitney, Arianne Martin as Anne Calhoun, Damon Carney as Jack Myers, James Cable as Roy Greenbaum, Susana Gibb as Nurse Decker, Michael Crabtree as Dr. Hoch, Hayden Tweedie as Ella, Erin Marie Garrett as Bethany, John Walpole as Karl, Morgana Shaw as Jessica; Producers: John Keeyes, Matthew Tompkins; Writer-Director: John Keeyes; Wolfclan Productions; Highland Myst Entertainment, Cableye Cinematics; Film Mode Entertainment (FME); Color.

Vice Detective Ryan Calhoun is wrongly accused of the ritualistic killing of his best friend. Going undercover in a forensic hospital Calhoun discovers the truth behind a demonic myth while experiencing his own personal demons.

Harry Absalom [Comic book character; UK]

First appearance: *2000 A.D.* #1446 (July 2005); Story: Gordon Rennie; Art: Tiernen Trevallion; Publisher: Rebellion Developments.

Despite suffering from terminal cancer, Detective Inspector Harry Absalom heads a special squad that enforces a centuries old treaty between the Royal Crown and Hell known as The Accord. In his latest mission Absalom puts together a squad consisting of "misfits, psychos and brainwashed demon killers" to rescue his grandchildren who are being held hostage by a religious fanatic.

Harry Absalom appears in the *2000 A.D.* strip *Absalom*, a **Caballistics Inc**. spin-off. The strip is collected in the graphic novels *Absalom: Ghosts of London* (2012) and *Absalom: Under a False Flag* (2017).

Harry Escott [Short story character]

Author-Creator: Fitz James O'Brien; First appearance: "The Pot of Tulips" *Harper's New Monthly Magazine* (November 1855).

One of the first paranormal detectives, Harry Escott is an expert in the occult who investigates the supernatural with a logical mind. In "The Pot of Tulips" Escott and his companion Jasper Joyce investigate a case of a missing fortune. The late Mr. Van Koeren was an abusive husband and father who was determined that no blood relative should inherit his wealth. Escott has a double motive for accepting the case for he is in love with the daughter Alice Van Koeren. Together with Jasper Joyce he spends the summer at the Old Dutch villa owned by the late husband. It isn't long before strange events take place.

"The luminous cloud now began to grow brighter and brighter as I gazed. The horrible odor of which I have spoken did not cease to oppress me, and gradually I could discover certain lines making themselves visible in the midst of this lambent radiance. These lines took the form of a human figure, a tall man, clothed in a long dressing-robe, with a pale countenance, burning eyes, and a very bold and prominent chin. At a glance I recognized the original of the picture of old Van Koeren that I had seen with Alice. My interest was now aroused to the highest point; I felt that I stood face to face with a spirit, and doubted not that I should learn the fate of the old man's mysteriously concealed wealth."

"The spirit presented a very strange appearance. He himself was not luminous, except some tongues of fire that seemed to proceed from the tips of his fingers, but was completely surrounded by a thin gauze of light, so to speak, through which his outlines were visible. His head was bare, and his white hair fell in huge masses around his stern, saturnine face. As he moved on the floor, I distinctly heard a strange crackling sound, such as one hears when a substance has been overcharged with electricity. But the circumstance that seemed to me most incomprehensible connected with the apparition was that Yan Koeren held in both hands a curiously painted flower-pot, out of which sprang a number of the most beautiful tulips in full blossom. He seemed very uneasy and agitated, and moved about the room as if in pain, frequently bending over the pot of tulips as if to inhale their odor, then holding it out to me, seemingly in the hope of attracting my attention to it. I was, I confess, very much puzzled. I knew that Mr. Van Koeren had in his lifetime devoted much of his leisure to the cultivation of flowers, importing from Holland the most expensive and rarest bulbs; but how this innocent fancy could trouble him after death I could not imagine. I felt assured, however, that some im-portant reason lay at the bottom of this spectral eccentricity, and determined to fathom it if I could."

After another night of ghostly apparitions that also includes Van Koeren's late wife the solution to the mystery of the pot of tulips and the missing fortune is solved.

Harry Escott makes one final appearance in *Harper's New Monthly Magazine* in "What Was It? A Mystery" (March 1859). Escott is attacked in his bed by a muscular invisible creature. His friend Dr. Hammond helps Escott uncover the truth behind the mysterious assailant.

Haven (2010) [TV series; Canada-U.S.]

Premiere: July 9, 2010; Main Cast: Emily Rose as Audrey Parker/Lexie DeWitt/Paige, Lucas Bryant as Nathan Wuornos, Nicholas Campbell as Garland Wuornos, Eric Balfour as Duke Crocker, Richard Donat as Vince Teagues, John Dunsworth as Dave Teagues, Stephen McHattie as Ed Driscoll, Adam "Edge" Copeland as Dwight Hendrickson, Vinessa Antoine as Evidence "Evi" Ryan, Jason Priestley as Chris Brody, Maurice Dean Wint as Agent Byron Howard, Jayne Eastwood as Gloria Verrano; Executive Producers: Shawn Piller, David MacLeod; Developed by Jim Dunn, Sam Ernst; Based on *The Colorado Kid* by Stephen King; 78 × 43 min.; Entertainment One; Big Motion Pictures; Piller/Segan/Shepherd; Universal Networks; CanWest Global Television Network International; Showcase; Color.

FBI agent Audrey Parker tracks an escaped prisoner to the Maine village of Haven little knowing she will become a pivotal figure in the life of the small harbor town. Together with local detective Nathan Wuornos they investigate supernatural and paranormal events known as "The Troubles" that plague Haven and provide a link to Audrey Parker's past.

A loose connection to Stephen King's novel *The Colorado Kid* is the unsolved murder of "The Colorado Kid" in Haven which is referenced in the opening title sequence and certain episodes of the series. The murder may be the source of all "The Troubles" in Haven.

Season One

Welcome to Haven (1:01); *Butterfly* (1:02); *Harmony* (1:03); *Consumed* (1:04); *Ball and Chain* (1:05); *Fur* (1:06); *Sketchy* (1:07); *Ain't No Sunshine* (1:08); *As You Were* (1:09); *The Hand You're Dealt* (1:10); *The Trial of Audrey Parker* (1:11); *Resurfacing* (1:12); *Spiral* (1:13).

Season Two

A Tale of Two Audreys (2:01); *Fear & Loathing* (2:02); *Love Machine* (2:03); *Sparks and Recreation* (2:04); *Roots* (2:05); *Audrey Parker's Day Off* (2:06); *The Tides That Bind* (2:07); *Friend or Faux* (2:08); *Lockdown* (2:09); *Who, What, Where, Wendigo?* (2:10); *Business as Usual* (2:11); *Sins of the Father* (2:12); *Silent Night* (2:13).

Season Three

301 (3:01); *Stay* (3:02); *The Farmer* (3:03); *Over My Head* (3:04); *Double Jeopardy* (3:05); *Real Estate* (3:06); *Magic Hour* (3:07); *Magic Hour: Part 2* (3:08); *Sarah* (3:09); *Burned* (3:10); *Last Goodbyes* (3:11); *Reunion* (3:12); *Thanks for the Memories* (3:13).

Season Four

Fallout (4:01); *Survivors* (4:02); *Bad Blood* (4:03); *Lost and Found* (4:04); *The New Girl* (4:05); *Countdown* (4:06); *Lay Me Down* (4:07); *Crush* (4:08); *William* (4:09); *The Trouble with Troubles* (4:10); *Shot in the Dark* (4:11); *When the Bough Breaks* (4:12); *The Lighthouse* (4:13).

Season Five

See No Evil (5:01); *Speak No Evil* (5:02); *Spotlight* (5:03); *Much Ado About Mara* (5:04); *The Old Switcheroo: Part 1* (5:05); *The Old Switcheroo: Part 2* (5:06); *Nowhere Man* (5:07); *Exposure* (5:08); *Morbidity* (5:09); *Mortality* (5:10); *Reflections* (5:11); *Chemistry* (5:12); *Chosen* (5:13); *New World Order* (5:14); *Power* (5:15); *The Trial of Nathan Wuornos* (5:16); *Enter Sandman* (5:17); *Wild Card* (5:18); *Perditus* (5:19); *Just Passing Trough* (5:20); *Close to Home* (5:21); *A Matter of Time* (5:22); *Blind Spot* (5:23); *The Widening Gyre* (5:24); *Now* (5:25); *Forever* (5:26).

Hellbound (1994) [Film]

Premiere: January 21, 1994; Main Cast: Chuck Norris as Sergeant Frank Shatter, Calvin Levels as Detective Calvin Jackson, Christopher Neame as Professor Malcolm Lockley/Prosatanos, Sheree J. Wilson as Leslie Hawkins, David Robb as King Richard I, Cherie Franklin as Captain Hull, Jack Adalist as Reinhard Kreiger, Ori Levy as Rabbi Mordechai Shindler, Ezere Atar as Bezi, Jack Messinger as Mahoney, Elki Jacobs as Mort, Nico Nitai as Friar; Executive Producers: Yoram Globus, Christopher Pearce; Story: Ian Rabin, Anthony Ridio, Brent Friedman; Screenplay: Brent Friedman, Donald G. Thompson; Director: Aaron Norris; 95 min.; Cannon Pictures; The Cannon Group; Anthony Ridio Productions; Globus Pictures; Color.

While investigating the murder of a rabbi Chicago police detectives Frank Shatter and Calvin Jackson are called to Israel. Rather than tracking down a human killer their main suspect is an agent of Satan. Trapped in a tomb by King Richard I of England during the Crusades he is now free again in human form. Shatter and Jackson must stop him before he gains control of the world.

Hellboy [Comic book character]

First appearance: *San Diego Comic-Con Comics* #2 (August 1993); Creator: Mike Mignola; Publisher: Dark Horse Comics.

The demon Hellboy wasn't born but was summoned from Hell by Nazi occultists on December 23, 1944. Although a demon, Hellboy hates the Nazis and actively works against evil forces as a paranormal investigator for the Bureau of Paranormal Research (BRPD).

Hellboy (2004) [Film]

Premiere: April 2, 2004; Main Cast: Ron Perlman as Hellboy, John Hurt as Professor Trevor "Broom" Bruttenholm, Selma Blair as Liz Sherman, Rupert Evans as John Myers, Jeffrey Tambor as Tom Manning, Karel Roden as Grigori Rasputin, Bridget Hodson as Ilsa Haupstein; Doug Jones as Abe Sapien; Executive Producer: Patrick Palmer; Story: Guillermo del Toro, Peter Briggs. Based on the comic book characters created by Mike Mignola; Director: Guillermo del

Toro; 122 min.; Dark Horse Entertainment, Starlite Films, Lawrence Gordon Productions, Revolution Studios; Columbia Pictures; Color.

As World War II reaches its conclusion Nazis turn to the occult to defeat the enemy. The demon Hellboy is summoned but is taken by the Allies when they raid the Nazi ritual. Raised by Professor Bruttenholm, Hellboy grows to maturity and joins the Bureau of Paranormal Research where he attempts to rid the world of evil.

See: ***BRPD: 1946***

Hellboy: The Science of Evil [Videogame]
Release date: August 15, 2008; Platforms: PlayStation 3, Xbox 360; Developer: Krome Studios; Publisher: Konami Digital Entertainment.

Hellboy travels through six different settings in his efforts to track down insane Nazi Hermann Von Klempt, clockwork Nazis, cyborg Nazis and zombie Nazis.

Hellraiser: Judgment (2018) [Film]
Premiere: February 3, 2018; Main Cast: Damon Carney as Detective Sean Carter, Randy Wayne as Detective David Carter, Alexandra Harris as Detective Christine Egerton, Paul T. Taylor as Pinhead, Gary J. Tunnicliffe as The Auditor, Heather Langenkamp as Landlady, Rheagan Wallace as Alison Carter, Helena Grace Donald as Jophiel, Grace Montie as Crystal Lanning, Jeff Fenter as carl Watkins, John Walpole as Hodges; Executive Producer: Bob Weinstein; Story/Director: Gary J. Tunnicliffe; 81 min.; Dimension Films; Puzzle Box Pictures; Color.

Detective brothers Sean and David Carter and Detective Christine Egerton investigate a serial killer who looks to the Ten Commandments for his inspiration. Their investigations take them down a dark path that leads to Hell.

Hellsing (2001) [Anime; Manga; Japan]
Premiere: October 11, 2001; Voice Cast: Jouji Nakata as Arucard, Fumiko Orikasa as Seras Victoria, Yoshiko Sakakibara as Integra Fairbrook Wingates Hellsing, Nachi Nozawa as Alexander Anderson; Producer: Satoshi Fujii; Story: Kohta Hirano, Taliesin Jaffe, Chiaka Konata; Directors: Manabu Ono, Umanosuke Iida; 13 × 23 min; Gonzo; Fuji TV; Pioneer LDC; Color.

The Royal Order of Religious Knights, also known as Hellsing is a secret government organization based in the U.K. Its purpose to protect the population from the undead. Integra Wingates Hellsing, daughter of vampire hunter Professor Van Hellsing, heads the military paranormal investigation unit with the help of Alucard, a vampire who works with humans. Working alongside Alucard is police girl turned vampire Seras Victoria.

The anime TV Series was followed by the 10 episode OVA, *Hellsing: Ultimate* (2006).

SEASON ONE

The Undead (1:01); *Club M* (1:02); *Sword Dancer* (1:03); *Innocent as a Human* (1:04); *Brotherhood* (1:05); *Dead Zone* (1:06); *Duel* (1:07); *Kill House* (1:08); *Red Rose Vertigo* (1:09); *Master of Monster* (1:10); *Transcend Force* (1:11); *Total Destruction* (1:12); *Hellfire* (1:13).

[Manga] First publication: Young King OURs (1997); Story & Art: Kouta Hirano; Publisher:

The manga that inspired the anime TV series and its sequels ran to 10 volumes. Dark Horse Comics published the title in the U.S. from December 2003 to May 2010.

Help for the Haunted [Novel]
First publication: 2014; Author: John Searles; Publisher: London: Sphere.

Young Sylvie Mason's parents help haunted souls find peace. But when they are brutally murdered in an old church Sylvie must find her own peace by searching for the murderer.

Hex-Rated (Brimstone Files Book #1) [Novel]
Author: Jason Ridler; First publication: New York: Night Shade Books, 2017.

Private investigator James Brimstone works out of Los Angeles. A Korean War veteran he is also adept in the martial arts and magic. The year is 1970 and Brimstone is representing a facially scarred actress from the San Fernando Valley's porn industry. His investigations lead him to Nazi occultists, dark magic and demons.

Followed by *Black Lotus Kiss* (2018).

Hoax Hunters [Comic book]

First publication: March 2012; Story: Michael Moreci, Steve Seeley; Art: JM Ringuet, Axel Medellin Machain; Publisher: Image.

Hoax Hunters is a reality TV show that debunks the paranormal in all its forms. But the focus of the group away from the TV cameras is to cover-up the genuine cases of the paranormal.

Holy Ghost: a Virgil Flowers Novel [Novel]

Author: John Sandford; First publication: New York: G.P. Putnam's Sons, 2018.

News of a floating apparition of the Virgin Mary attracting thousands of pilgrims gives the mayor of small-town Pinion, Minnesota an idea. If he can duplicate the visions, he can boost tourism. But when visitors to the town are being shot by a sniper investigator Virgil Flowers is called upon to find those responsible.

Hope … for the Future [Graphic novel; UK]

Story: Guy Adams; Art: Jimmy Broxton; First publication: 2000 A.D. Prog #2011 (December 14, 2016); Publisher: Rebellion.

In an alternate reality former New York cop turned Hollywood private investigator Mallory Hope returns home from World War II to find his wife and young child have disappeared. Now he has a case that strikes close to home investigating missing Hollywood child star Joey Fabrizzi a.k.a. Buster Ritz. In this post-war timeline magic exists but is covered up by the government. Mallory can create illusions but is hampered by the demon Cade who became attached to Mallory's soul after he delved too deep into the dark arts.

Originally serialized as a 12-part strip in *2000 A.D.*

"The Horror at Red Hook" [Short story]

Author: H.P. Lovecraft; First publication: *Weird Tales* (January 1927).

We are introduced to New York police detective Thomas F. Malone as he takes a long leave of absence due to a traumatic local case in Red Hook, Brooklyn that has left him under medical treatment. Now he has an acute fear of old brick buildings thanks to the strange case of Robert Suydam.

Malone recalls that Suydam's relatives had noted his shabby appearance and nonsensical speech invoking mystical powers. His basement flat was home to nocturnal rites behind the green window blinds. Malone was assigned to watch Suydam and assist private detectives when Suydam began to entertain the worst criminals and illegal immigrants in Red Hook.

His engagement and marriage to a "young woman of excellent position" came as a surprise to Malone. But their marital bliss was short-lived when both were found viciously murdered in the stateroom of the ocean liner that had recently left the harbor. The doctor attending the bodies noted that just before he turned on the lights the porthole "was clouded for a second with a certain phosphorescence, and for a moment there seemed to echo in the night outside the suggestion of hellish tittering…"

Two men claimed Suydam's body at his request in a final message he had written before his death. Malone decided to check out Suydam's basement flat but upon opening the cellar door encountered a hellish sight that has led to his present state of nervous agitation.

Houdini and Doyle (2016) [TV series; Canada-UK]

Premiere: March 13, 2016; Main Cast: Michael Weston as Harry Houdini, Stephen Mangan as Arthur Conan Doyle, Rebecca Liddiard as Adelaide Stratton, Emily Carey as Mary Conan Doyle, Noah Jupe as Kingsley Conan Doyle; Executive Producers: Luke Alkin, Kenton Allen, Scott Garve, Christina Jennings, Matthew Justice, Maggie Murphy, David N. Titcher, David Hoselton, David Shore, Kate Garwood, Stephen Hopkins; Creators: David Hoselton, David N. Titcher; 10 × 44 min.; Shore Z Productions; Shaw Media; Big Talk Productions; Shaftesbury; ITV Studios; Sony Pictures Television; Fox Network; Color.

Renowned stage magician and escapologist Harry Houdini joins forces with Sherlock Holmes' creator Arthur Conan Doyle to solve mysterious and bizarre crimes. Cases include a dead nun tormenting the living, a boy taking revenge for his own murder in a past life, a demonic entity, vampire hunters and the inexplicable death of all the townsfolk of a village except for the minister. Real life characters Bram Stoker and Thomas Edison make guest appearances.

SEASON ONE

The Maggie's Redress (1:01); *A Dish of Adharma* (1:02); *In Manus Dei* (1:03); *Spring-Heel'd Jack* (1:04); *The Curse of Korzha* (1:05); *The Monsters of Nethermoor* (1:06); *Bedlam* (1:07); *Strigoi* (1:08); *Necromanteion* (1:09); *The Pall of LaPier* (1:10).

The Hound of the Baskervilles (1939)
[Film]

Premiere: March 31, 1939: Main Cast: Basil Rathbone as Sherlock Holmes, Nigel Bruce as Dr. Watson, Richard Greene as Sir Henry Baskerville, Wendy Barrie as Beryl Stapleton, Lionel Atwill as James Mortimer M.D., Ralph Forbes as Sir Hugo Baskerville, E.E. Clive as John Clayton the Cabby, Beryl Mercer as Mrs. Jennifer Mortimer, Morton Lowry as John Stapleton, Barlowe Bortland as Mr. Frankland, John Carradine as Barryman the butler, Eily Malyon as Mrs. Barryman, Mary Gordon as Mrs. Hudson; Executive Producer: Darryl F. Zanuck; Screenplay: Ernest Pascal; Adapted from the story by Sir Arthur Conan Doyle; Director: Sidney Lanfield; 80 min.; Twentieth Century–Fox; b/w.

1889—the desolate, fog-shrouded moors of Dartmoor in Devonshire. Sir Charles Baskerville dies of heart failure running in fear from the eerie howling of a "supernatural" hound. Sir Henry Baskerville arrives from Canada as the young heir to the Baskerville title and estates to take up residence at Baskerville Hall. At 221b Baker Street Doctor Mortimer tells Sherlock Holmes that every Baskerville who has inherited the estates has met with a sudden, violent death.

The Hound of the Baskervilles (1939), starring Nigel Bruce as Dr. Watson (left) and Basil Rathbone as Sherlock Holmes (Twentieth Century–Fox).

He believes Sir Henry's life is in danger from a gigantic hound that first killed Sir Hugo Baskerville in 1650.

Sir Arthur Conan Doyle's story first serialized in *The Strand Magazine* between August 1901 and April 1902 has been adapted numerous times for stage and screen. The 1939 film is generally considered to be the best film adaptation.

The House That Dripped Blood (1971)
[Film; UK]

Premiere: February 21, 1971; Main Cast: John Bennett as Detective Inspector Holloway, John Bryans as A.J. Stoker, John Malcolm as Sergeant Martin, Denholm Elliott as Charles Hillyer, Joanna Dunham as Alice Hillyer, Tom Adams as Richard/Dominic, Peter Cushing as Philip Grayson, Joss Ackland as Neville Rogers, Christopher Lee as John Reid, Nyree Dawn Porter as Ann Norton, Chloe Franks as Jane Reid, Jon Pertwee as Paul Henderson, Ingrid

Pitt as Carla Lynde, Geoffrey Bayldon as Theo von Hartmann; Producers: Max J. Rosenberg, Milton Subotsky; Writers: Robert Bloch, Russ Jones; Director: Peter Duffell; 102 min.; Amicus Productions; Cinerama Releasing; Color.

Scotland Yard Detective Inspector Holloway investigates the disappearance of horror movie actor Paul Henderson. An estate agent tells Holloway about the macabre history of the house Henderson rented before he went missing. Each of the four tales recalls previous tenants who met strange fates. Holloway decides to check out the house for himself and discovers a transformed Paul Henderson.

The Howling (1981) [Film]
Premiere: April 10, 1981; Main Cast: Dee Wallace as Karen White, Patrick Macnee as Dr. George Waggner, Robert Picardo as Eddie Quist, Christopher Stone as R. William Neill, Dennis Dugan Chris Halloran, Belinda Balaski as Terry Fisher, Kevin McCarthy as Fred Francis, John Carradine as Erie Kenton, Slim Pickens as Sam Newfield, Elisabeth Brooks as Marsha Quist; Executive Producers: Daniel H. Blatt, Steven A. Lane; Screenplay; John Sayles, Terence H. Winkless; Based on the novel by Gary Brandner; Director: Joe Dante; 91 min.; AVCO Embassy Pictures; Wescom Productions; Color.

The Los Angeles police use television anchor Karen White as bait to trap and kill serial killer Eddie Quist at a peep show theater. The trauma of confronting the serial killer who had been stalking her results in amnesia for White. Her therapist recommends a country retreat for White and her husband. But the retreat only adds to her anxiety when she encounters Eddie Quist returned from the dead and a colony of werewolves.

The Humbug Murders: An Ebenezer Scrooge Mystery [Novel]
Author: L. J. Oliver; First publication: New York: Pocket Books, 2015.

The week before Christmas 1833. A thirty-something Ebenezer Scrooge receives a visit from the ghost of his friend Fezziwig. He claims he was murdered and three more will die before Scrooge is also slain. At the crime scene Scrooge's calling card is found in the hand of Fezziwig's corpse and the word "Humbug" written in blood. With Scrooge the prime suspect investigative reporter Charles Dickens, and young clerk Adelaide Owen joins Scrooge in his quest to discover the truth behind the murder.

The Hypnotist (The Reincarnationist #3) [Novel]
Author: M. J. Rose; First publication: Don Mills, Ont.: Mira Books, 2010.

FBI Art Crime Team agent Lucan Glass is still haunted by the murder of a beautiful young artist he failed to prevent, a crime he cannot solve and a long-lost love. When a stolen Matisse painting is defaced beyond recognition with the warning four more paintings by the masters will be destroyed, the thief demands the sculpture Hypnos that can grant a person paranormal power. The case provides a link to Lucan's first love, Solange, who was killed during the theft of the Matisse twenty years ago. When Lucan undertakes past-life regression at the Phoenix Foundation the connections between past and present take on new significance.

See: ***Past Life***

I Was a Teenage Weredeer (*Bright Falls Mysteries* Book 1) [Novel]
Authors: C.T. Phipps, Michael Suttkus; First publication: Hertford, NC: Mystique Press–Crossroad Press 2017.

Jane Doe waits tables at her mother's 1950s-style Deerlighter Diner in Bright Falls, Michigan. She also happens to be a shapeshifter who becomes a weredeer with the psychic ability to read objects and solve supernatural crimes. Her eighteenth birthday celebrations are interrupted by news of the death of the sister's best friend Victoria O'Henry. Worse news awaits when Jane discovers her death is an occult murder and Jane's brother Jeremy is the main suspect. Jane turns detective to find the real killer along with her werewolf friend Emma O'Henry, unconventional FBI Special Agent Alex Timmons, local crime lord Lucien Lyons and a werecrow.

See: ***An American Weredeer in Michigan***

The Idylls of the Queen [Novel]

Author: Phyllis Ann Karr; First publication: New York, NY: Ace Books, 1982.

Fifth century Britain in the mythical time of King Arthur and Camelot where necromancy is a fact of life. Queen Guenevere is accused of murder when her dinner guest Sir Patrise dies suddenly from poison. The Queen's fate depends on the outcome of trial by combat. But her champion and lover Sir Lancelot has gone missing. Sir Kay turns detective as he investigates the facts behind the death of Sir Patrise and joins the search for Sir Lancelot with Sir Gawaine, Sir Gareth and Mordred.

In the Electric Mist (2009) [Film; France-U.S.]

Premiere: February 7, 2009; Main Cast: Tommy Lee Jones as Dave Robicheaux, John Goodman as Julie "Baby Feet" Balboni, Peter Sarsgaard as Elrod Sykes, Kelly Macdonald as Kelly Drummond, Mary Steenburgen as Bootsie Robicheaux, Levon Helm as General John Bell Hood, Ned Beatty as Twinky LeMoyne, Buddy Guy as Sam "Hogman" Patin, Justina Machado as Rosie Gomez, James Gammon as Ben Hebert; Producers: Frederic Bourboulon, Michael Fitzgerald; Screenplay: Jerry Kromolowski, Mary Orson-Kromolowski;; Director: Bertrand Tavernier; 117 min.; Ithaca Pictures; Little Bear; TFI International; Color.

Based on the novel ***In the Electric Mist with Confederate Dead*** by James Lee Burke.

In the Electric Mist with Confederate Dead [Novel]

Author: James Lee Burke; First publication: London: Phoenix, 1993.

New Iberia police detective and Vietnam vet Dave Robicheaux hunts a serial prostitute killer he links to New Orleans mobster "Baby Feet" Balboni. Balboni also happens to be co-producing a Civil War movie in New Iberia, Louisiana. The murders bring back bad memories of a black man who was chained and murdered in the swampland thirty-five years ago. Robicheaux failed to report the murder and was engulfed in guilt for his lack of action. As Robicheuax delves deeper into the prostitute murders he begins to have visions of the Confederate dead and talks to the spirit of General John Bell Hood of the Confederacy.

In the Mouth of Madness (1994) [Film]

Premiere: December 10, 1994; Main Cast: Sam Neill as John Trent, Julie Carmen as Linda Styles, Jurgen Prochnow as Sutter Cane, David Warner as Dr. Wrenn, Charlton Heston as Jackson Harglow, Peter Jason as Mr. Paul, Bernie Casey as Robinson, John Glover as Saperstein, Frances Bay as Mrs. Pickman, Wilhelm von Homburg as Simon; Executive Producer-Story: Michael De Luca; Director: John Carpenter; 95 min.; New Line Cinema; Color.

Private investigator John Trent specializes in false insurance claims. His latest case is the disappearance of famous horror novelist Sutter Cane. Trent believes his disappearance may be part of a publicity campaign for his latest book. His investigations lead to the sleepy New England town Hobb's End that should only exist in Cane's books. What is fact and what is fiction?

The Incredible Adventures of Dog Mendonça and PizzaBoy a.k.a. ***As Incríveis Aventuras de Dog Mendonça e PizzaBoy*** (Graphic novel; Portugal)

First publication: (February 2010); Story: Filipe Melo; Art: Juan Cava, Santiago Villa; Publishers: Tinta-da-China (Portugal); Dark Horse Books (U.S.).

Joao Vincente "Dog" Mendonça is an overweight occult detective who also happens to be a werewolf. Dog's partner is Pazuul, a six-thousand-year-old demon trapped inside the body of an eight-year-old girl. When pizza delivery boy Eurico's scooter is stolen by gargoyles he turns to Dog Mendonça for help. Together they discover somebody is kidnapping children in World War II Lisbon.

The first in a trilogy of graphic novels featuring Dog Mendonça and Pizzaboy.

See: ***The Interactive Adventures of Dog Mendonça and Pizzaboy.***

"The Inmost Light" [Novelette]

Author: Arthur Machen; First publication:

The Great God Pan and the Inmost Light; Publisher: London: John Lane, 1894.

The reader is first introduced to amateur occult detective Dyson in the mysterious case of Dr. Black from Harlesden. The doctor is often seen walking out with his pretty wife on summer evenings. Gradually over time Mrs. Black is nowhere to be seen and rumors of her untimely death circulate. But Dyson tells his friend Mr. Salisbury that he has seen her alive, albeit it in a transformed state.

"As I glanced up I had looked straight towards the last house in the row before me, and in an upper window of that house I had seen for some small fraction of a second a face. It was the face of a woman and yet it was not human…. I knew I had looked into another world—looked through the window of a commonplace, brand new house, and seen hell open before me."

When Dyson later discovers Mrs. Black is dead and the autopsy shows her brain has been altered to resemble "the brain of a devil" Dyson's curiosity is piqued. He uncovers sinister occult experiments by Dr. Black on his wife where he transfers her soul to an opal gem and in doing so invites demonic forces to enter her vacant shell.

The Interactive Adventures of Dog Mendonça and Pizzaboy [Video game]

Release date: March 4, 2016; Developer: OKAM Studio; Platforms: Windows; Linux; Mac OSX; Perspective; 1st-Person; Publisher: Ravenscourt.

The play controls Pizzaboy Eurico in the first in a series of episodic self-contained stories. After being hired by a woman who believes she is cursed occult werewolf detective Dog Mendonça disappears. Eurico must search for clues, solve puzzles, remove obstacles and interrogate witnesses and subjects in the supernatural city of Lisbon, Portugal.

Based on the characters from popular trilogy of graphic novels.

See: ***The Incredible Adventures of Dog Mendonça and Pizzaboy.***

Invader Zim (2001) [Animated TV series]

Premiere: March 30, 2001; Voice Cast: Andy Berman as Dib, Richard Steven Horvitz as ZIM; Rikki Simmons as GIR, Melissa Fahn as Gaz, Jhonen Vasquez as Computer, Roger Bumpass as Professor Membrane, Lucille Bliss as Ms. Bitters, Mo Collins as Zeta, Wally Wingert as Almighty Tallest Red; Executive Producers: Mary Harrington, Jhonen Vasquez; Creator: Jhonen Vasquez; 27 × 24 min.; Nicktoons Productions; Nickelodeon Network; Color.

Dib has a credibility problem. The world thinks he's crazy because of his love for all things paranormal and spooky. But only Dib knows ZIM is an alien from the planet Irk, disguised as a schoolboy with a skin problem. He's green but nobody seems to care, except Dib.

"Am I the only one here seeing the alien sitting in class?" states an exasperated Dib. And worse still ZIM has plans to destroy Earth.

SEASON ONE

Pilot (1:0) *The Nightmare Begins* (1:01); *Parent Teacher Night/Walk of Doom* (1:02); *Bestest Friend/Nanozim* (1:03); *Germs/Dark Harvest* (1:04); *Attack of the Saucer Morons/The Wettening* (1:05); *Career Day/Battle-Dib* (1:06); *A Room With a Moose/Hamstergeddon* (1:07); *Invasion of the Idiot Dog Brain/Bad, Bad Rubber Piggy* (1:08); *Planet Jackers/Rise of the Zitboy* (1:09); *Plague of Babies/Bloaty's Pizza Hog* (1:10); *Bolognius Maximus/Game Slave 2* (1:11); *Halloween Spectacular of Spooky Doom* (1:12).

SEASON TWO

Mysterious Mysteries/Future Dib (2:01); *Door to Door/FBI Warning of Doom* (2:02); *Battle of the Planets* (2:03); *Abducted/The Sad, Sad Tale of Chickenfoot* (2:04); *Megadoomer/Lice* (2:05); *TAK: The Hideous New Girl* (2:06); *Dib's Wonderful Life of Doom/GIR Goes Crazy and Stuff* (2:07); *HOBO 13/Walk For Your Lives* (2:08); *Backstreet Drivers From Beyond the Stars* (2:09); *Mortos Der Soulstealer/ZIM Eats Waffles* (2:10); *The Frycook What Came From All That Space* (2:11); *The Girl Who Cried Gnome/Dibship Rising* (2:12); *Vindicated/The Voting of the Doomed* (2:13); *Gaz, Taster of Pork* (2:14); *The Most Horrible Xmas Ever* (2:15).

Invisible Avenger a.k.a. ***Bourbon Street Shadows*** (1958) [Film]

Premiere: December 2, 1958; Main Cast: Richard Derr as Lamont Cranston/The Shadow, Marc Daniels as Jogendra, Helen Westcott as Tara O'Neill, Jack Doner as Billy Sanchez, Jeanne Neher as Felicia Ramirez, Steve Dano as Tony Alcade, Dan Mullin as Pablo/Victor Ramirez, Leo Bruno as Ramon 'Rocco' Martinez, Lee Edwards as The Colonel, Sam Page as Charlie; Producers: Emanuel Demby, Eric Sayers; Screenplay adaptation: George Bellak, Betty Jeffries; Directors: James Wong Howe, Ben Parker, John Sledge; 60 min.; Republic Pictures; MPA Feature Films Inc.; b/w.

While investigating the death of a jazz band leader in New Orleans Lamont Cranston becomes involved in stopping the fascist Victor Ramirez from assassinating his brother Pablo who plans a coup d'état in Santa Cruz. Cranston's partner Jogendra teaches Cranston the power of the mind.

"The mind is capable of transmitting and receiving images. When you become the Shadow you send a powerful image into the mind of another and he sees not you but a shadow."

Jogendra communicates telepathically with Cranston warning him of impending danger ahead.

The film is a re-edited version of a failed pilot for a television series loosely based on ***The Shadow*** pulp fiction character and radio drama. It was subsequently re-released with added scenes in 1962 under the new title *Bourbon Street Shadows*.

The Invisible Detective [Juvenile book series]

Author: Justin Richards; First publication: London: Simon & Schuster UK Ltd., 2003.

The antiques shop in London's Cannon Street has a reputation for being haunted. Fourteen-year-old Arthur Drake thinks it to be superstitious nonsense. One fateful day Art finds shelter from the rain in the shop. Browsing through the books he comes across the antique casebook of the Invisible Detective. Written in 1936 the handwriting appears to match Arthur's handwriting in the present day. He soon finds himself sharing the memories and dreams of the person who wrote in the book many decades ago.

In the 1930s Art forms his own group of super-sleuths, "The Cannoniers" with his three friends. Margaret "Meg" Wallace can detect when someone isn't telling the truth, Jonny Levin can run at speed and Flinch can squeeze into small spaces by dislocating her bones. Art disguises himself as the fictional Brandon Lake, the Invisible Detective, who can only be seen in silhouette by his clients. The four "Cannoniers" investigate crimes and strange happenings ranging from an army of mutant soldiers to ancient Egyptian curses. Meanwhile in the 21st century Art's grandson Arthur Drake II investigates mysteries with his friend Sarah.

Books in the series: *The Paranormal Puppet Show* a.k.a. *Double Life* [U.S.] (2003); *Shadow Beast* (2003); *Ghost Soldiers* (2003); *Killing Time* (2003); *Faces of Evil* (2004); *Web of Anubis* (2004); *Stage Fright* (2005); *Legion of the Dead* (2005).

iZombie (2015) [TV series]

Premiere: March 17, 2015; Main Cast: Rose McIver as Olivia Moore, Malcolm Goodwin as Detective Clive Babineaux, Rahul Kohli as Ravi Chakrabarti, Robert Buckley as Major Lilywhite, David Anders as Blaine DeBeers, Aly Michalka as Peyton Charles; Executive Producers: Dan Etheridge, Diane Ruggiero, Danielle Stokdyk, Rob Thomas; 64 × 42 min.; Spondoolie Entertainment; Vertigo Productions; Warner Bros. Television; DC Entertainment; Color.

Liv Moore is a medical student turned zombie who takes a job at the King County morgue to be near human brains. Her appetite for brains is fed by her desire to stay human. But when she eats the brains Liv gains access to the memories and personality traits of the deceased person. She puts her psychic abilities to good use helping Seattle Police Detective Clive Babineaux solve murder cases. Liv hopes her boss Dr. Ravi Chakrabarti can find a cure to return her to normal.

Season One

Pilot (1:01); *Brother, Can You Spare a Brain?* (1:02); *The Exterminator* (1:03); *Live and Let

Clive (1:04); *Flight of the Living Dead* (1:05); *Virtual Reality Bites* (1:06); *Maternity Liv* (1:07); *Dead Air* (1:08); *Patriot Brains* (1:09); *Mr. Berserk* (1:10); *Astroburger* (1:11); *Dead Rat, Live Rat, Brown Rat, White Rat* (1:12); *Blaine's World* (1:13).

SEASON TWO

Grumpy Old Liv (2:01); *Zombie Bro* (2:02); *Real Dead Housewife of Seattle* (2:03); *Even Cowgirls Get the Black and Blues* (1:04); *Love & Basketball* (2:05); *Max Wager* (2:06); *Abra Cadaver* (2:07); *The Hurt Stalker* (2:08); *Cape Town* (2:09); *Method Head* (2:10); *Fifty Shades of Grey Matter* (2:11); *Physician, Heal Thy Selfie* (2:12); *The Whopper* (2:13); *Eternal Sunshine and the Caffeinated Mind* (2:14); *He Blinded Me.... With Science* (2:15); *Pour Some Sugar, Zombie* (2:16); *Reflections of the Way Liv Used to Be* (2:17); *Dead Beat* (2:18); *Salivation Army* (2:19).

SEASON THREE

Heaven Just Got a Little Bit Smoother (3:01); *Zombie Knows Best* (3:02); *Eat, Pray, Liv* (3:03); *Wag the Tongue Slowly* (3:04); *Spanking the Zombie* (3:05); *Some Like It Hot Mess* (3:06); *Dirt Nap Time* (3:07); *Eat a Knievel* (3:08); *Twenty-Sided, Die* (3:09); *Return of the Dead Guy* (3:10); *Conspiracy Weary* (3:11); *Looking for Mr. Goodbrain, Part 1* (3:12); *Looking for Mr. Goodbrain, Part 2* (3:13).

SEASON FOUR

Are You Ready for Some Zombies? (4:01); *Blue Bloody* (4:02); *Brainless in Seattle, Part 1* (4:03); *Brainless in Seattle, Part 2* (4:04); *Goon Struck* (4:05); *My Really Fair Lady* (4:06); *Don't Hate the Player, Hate the Brain* (4:07); *Chivalry is Dead* (4:08); *Mac-Liv-Moore* (4:09); *Yippee Ki Brain, Motherscratcher* (4:10); *Insane in the Germ Brain* (4:11); *You've Got to Hide Your Liv Away* (4:12); *And He Shall Be a Good Man* (4:13).

SEASON FIVE

Thug Death (5:01); *Dead Lift* (5:02); *Five, Six, Seven, Ate!* (5:03); *Dot Zom* (5:04); *Death Moves Pretty Fast* (5:05); *The Scratchmaker* (5:06); *Filleted to Rest* (5:07); *Death of a Car Salesman* (5:08); *The Fresh Princess* (5:09); *Night and the Zombie City* (5:10); *Killer Queen* (5:11); (5:12); (5:13).

Jackaby [Juvenile book]

Author: William Ritter; First publication: Chapel Hill, NC: Algonquin Young Readers, 2014.

New Fiddleham, New England, 1892. Abigail Rock becomes the assistant to psychic investigator R. F. Jackaby. Their first case is a serial killer who Jackaby believes has supernatural connections. Jackaby's detective agency residence is also home to the ghost of Jenny Cavanaugh who was murdered on the property.

Jackaby and Abigail Rock's supernatural investigations continue in *Beastly Bones* (2016), *Ghostly Echoes* (2017) and *The Dire King* (2018).

Jake Helman Files [Book series]

First publication: 2009; Author: Gregory Lamberson; Publisher: St. Charles Ill.: Medallion Press.

The series details the supernatural cases of New York private investigator Jake Helman who is first introduced as an elite member of the New York Special Homicide Task Force. When he refuses to take a drug test, the cocaine addicted Helman resigns and takes a position at a genetic-engineering company. But Helman discovers the CEO oversees an unethical business that trades in human souls.

In subsequent cases Helman tackles zombie assassins, voodoo practitioners, a curse that has turned his former partner into a raven and the Storm Demon, also known as Lilith.

Jake Helman novels: *Personal Demons* (2009); *Desperate Souls* (2010); *Cosmic Forces* (2011); *Tortured Spirits* (2012); *Storm Demon* (2013); *Human Monsters* (2015).

Jeffery Wren [Pulp fiction character]

Author-Creator: G.T. Fleming-Roberts; First appearance: "No Haunting Allowed" *Dime Detective* (April 1944); Publisher: Popular Publications.

Former vaudeville magician Jeffery Wren owns a novelty and magic shop in Indianapolis.

As a sideline he enjoys detective work that often involves the supernatural which he loves to debunk. Helping Wren capture fake practitioners of the paranormal is outspoken policewoman Zoe Osbourn. Wren occasionally utilizes his store assistant Horace in his detective work. Homicide detective Sergeant Tom Hogan considers Wren to be an annoyance despite the fact Wren solves cases that elude him.

Wren prefers to use his magician skills than handling a gun when confronting his foes who are often murderers set against an occult backdrop.

Short stories: "No Haunting Allowed" (April 1944); The Spirit Was Willing" (August 1944); "A Sleight Case of Murder" (October 1944); "Scare a Man to Death" (January 1945); "He Couldn't Stay Dead" (May 1945); "Medium Dead" (November 1945); "Feather Your Coffin" (October 1946).

Jim Butcher's the Dresden Files [Comic book]

"WELCOME TO THE JUNGLE"

First publication: March 2008; Four-issue mini-series; Story: Jim Butcher; Art: Ardian Syaf; Inks: Joe Pimentel; Publisher: Dabel Brothers Publishing.

Lieutenant Murphy of Chicago Special Investigations asks professional wizard Harry Dresden for help in solving the grisly death of Maurice Sandbourne at the Lincoln Park Zoo. Sergeant Carmichael believes a gorilla is responsible, but Murphy and Dresden know better. And when a group of big cats with glowing green eyes attack Dresden he knows the supernatural is at work. But who is controlling the wild animals at the zoo?

This original comic book story by Jim Butcher is followed by comic book adaptations of *Storm Front* and *Fool Moon*.

Jimmy Holm and the Secret Twelve [Pulp fiction characters]

Author: Harold Ward (Zorro); First appearance: "12 Must Die" *Doctor Death* (February 1935); Publisher: Dell Magazines.

Dr. Rance Mandarin, former Yale professor and scientist, hates the modern world and seeks a return to the Stone Age. As Doctor Death, master of the black arts, he invokes elementals and an army of zombies in his quest to destroy modern society and most of the population. Opposing him is millionaire supernatural detective Jimmy Holm, the head of the Secret Twelve, comprising business and political leaders, including the President of the United States of America.

Harold Ward wrote three *Doctor Death* novels under the pseudonym of "Zorro." The *Doctor Death* magazine folded after three issues leaving two completed Harold Ward novels

Dime Detective (November 1945) featuring magician-detective Jeffery Wren in "Medium Dead." Cover art by Sam Cherry. Published by Popular Publications.

"Waves of Madness" and "The Red Mist of Death" unpublished until they resurfaced in the late 1980s in the fanzine publications *Nemesis* and *Pulp Vault*.

Short stories: "12 Must Die" (February 1935); "The Gray Creatures" (March 1935); The Sniveling Murders (April 1935).

Joe Golem and the Drowning City: An Illustrated Novel (Novel)

First publication: March 2012; Authors: Mike Mignola, Christopher Golden; New York: St. Martin's Press.

Lower Manhattan first began to sink in 1925 following a series of natural disasters. Now, fifty years later the drowning Downtown is home to scavengers and water rats while Uptown continues to thrive. Former stage magician Orlov the Conjurer now makes a living as a psychic medium with the ability to speak with the dead. But a botched séance leads to his abduction by creatures in gas masks and rubber suits under the control of Dr. Cocteau.

Orlov's fourteen-year-old friend Molly McHugh flees the scene and is rescued by Detective Joe Golem, whose own mysterious past is highlighted through his nightmares of golems and witches in 15th century Europe.

Joe Golem: Occult Detective [Comic book]

First publication: November 2015; Writers: Mike Mignola, Christopher Golden; Art: Patric Reynolds; Publisher: Dark Horse Comics.

New York Detective Joe Golem works with elderly Detective Simon Church, who unknown to Golem, has been making certain Golem remains oblivious of his past with a mixture of magic and chemistry. Golem's recurring nightmares of a Golem and witches are doorways to his own past as a Golem.

The comic book series is based on the novel *Joe Golem and the Drowning City*. While investigating a case of missing children from the Hudson Home for Children Joe Golem encounters an underwater creature known as the Rat Catcher.

John Constantine [Comic book character]

First appearance: *Swamp Thing* Vol. 2 #37 (June 1985); Creators: Alan Moore, Steve Bissette, John Totleben; Publisher: DC Comics/Vertigo.

John Constantine is a streetwise, antisocial, working-class occult detective from Liverpool, England who is also a master sorcerer, exorcist and expert con artist. His magical and mystical powers include divination, curses, mind control, necromancy and the ability to summon demons and cast illusions. Constantine is also adept at stage magic and often uses deception to help defeat his enemies.

Constantine made his official debut in the *Swamp Thing* story "Growth Patterns" (June 1985) before becoming the regular title character in the long-running DC-Vertigo title *Hellblazer* (January 1988). The DC incarnation and the Vertigo Universe character took different paths with Constantine aging in real-time in the Vertigo version. An anonymous non-speaking character resembling the singer-actor Sting, who according to creator Alan Moore was the original visual inspiration for

Matt Ryan as occult detective John Constantine. Ryan has portrayed the character in the TV series *Constantine* (2015) and *Legends of Tomorrow* (2016).

Constantine, appeared briefly in *The Saga of Swamp Thing* # 25 (June 1984).

John Constantine has also featured in the film **Constantine** (2005) starring Keanu Reeves and the TV series **Constantine** (2014), ***DC's Legends of Tomorrow*** (2016), a single episode of *Arrow* (2012), the animated film ***Justice League Dark*** (2017) and the animated web series **Constantine: City of Demons** (2018).

John Silence: Physician Extraordinary
[Short story anthology]

Author: Algernon Blackwood; First publication: London: Eveleigh Nash, 1908.

Independently wealthy philanthropist Dr. John Silence is in his forties, sparsely built with striking brown eyes and a close beard.

He has devoted his life to treating economically challenged patients free of charge. Known as the "Psychic Doctor" Silence has submitted himself to physical, mental and spiritual training for five years, isolated from the world. Possessing the power of clairvoyance Dr. Silence stresses the importance of thought. "Learn how to think … and you have learned to tap power at its source."

In his first case "PSYCHICAL INVASION" writer and humorist Felix Pender, after experimenting with a drug, has become the victim of a mysterious malady in the "psychical region" that threatens to destroy his talent. Mrs. Pender declares to Dr. Silence, "What frightens me is that he assumes there is someone else in the house all the time—someone I never see."

After interviewing Felix in his Putney Hill home, Dr. Silence comes to the conclusion, "You are now in touch with certain violent emotions, desires, purposes, still active in this house, that were produced in the past by some powerful and evil personality that lived here…. In this case I think there has been an unusual and dreadful aggrandizement of the thoughts and purposes left behind long ago by a woman of consummate wickedness and great personal power of character and intellect."

Silence tells Felix, "You are a victim of psychical invasion. It is very simple. You must leave this house at once."

Meanwhile Dr. Silence, part-time occult detective, Plans to conduct an experiment "with a view to drawing out this evil, coaxing it from its lair, so to speak, in order that it may exhaust itself through me and become dissipated forever."

The second story in the anthology "ANCIENT SORCERIES" sees timid English man Arthur Vezin travelling through France by train. Tiring of the noisy behavior of his fellow "holiday English" he decides to leave the train and stay overnight in the local small town until he can resume his journey on a quieter train. An elderly French man hands Vezin his bag from the departing train and warns him about the town.

Vezin finds the little town to be quiet, reminding him of a bygone century. At first, he feels he has made no impression on the local people, "feeling delightfully insignificant and unimportant and unselfconscious. It was like becoming part of a softly colored dream which he did not even realize to be a dream."

Vezin continues with his strange story to Dr. Silence. "Everybody as a matter of fact was watching me closely. Every movement made was known and observed. Ignoring me was all a pretense—an elaborate pretense. The whole town, I suddenly realized, was something other than I so far saw it. The real activities and interests of the people were elsewhere and otherwise than appeared. Their true lives lay somewhere out of sight behind the scenes."

Despite his reservation Vezin decides to stay in the town.

"Can it be that these people are people of the twilight, that they live only at night their real life, and come out honestly only with dusk? That during the day they make a sham through pretense, and after the sun is down their true life begins? Have they the souls of night-things, and is the whole blessed town in the hands of the cats?"

Vezin finds himself bewitched by a young, attractive girl. "The real life I speak of … is the old, old life within, the life of long ago, the life to which you, too, once belonged and to which you still belong…. I possess the spell to conquer you and hold you; the spell of old love. I can win you back and make you live the old life with me, for the force of the ancient tie between us, if I choose to use it, is irresistible. And I choose to use it. I still want you.... You came here because I called you. I have called you for years, and you came with the whole force of the past behind you. You had to come, for I own you, and I claim you."

Supernatural forces are tempting Vezin to stay. "A great lithe cat had leaped softly up from the shadows below on the sill close to his face and was staring fixedly at him with the eyes of a human. "Come," it seemed to say, "come with us to the Dance! Change as of old! Transform yourself swiftly and come!"

The girl declares, "Satan has come. The Sacraments call us! Come, with your dear apostate soul, and we will worship and dance till the moon dies and the world is forgotten!"

Vezin escapes the grasp of the girl and the "many dark flying forms crowding upwards out of the sky" fleeing to safety.

After listening to Vezin's story Dr. Silence investigates further and discovers Vezin's ancestors have lived in the town for generations. Two witches were burnt at the stake on the spot where Vezin stayed at the inn.

"The whole adventure seems to have been a very vivid revival of the memories of an earlier life.... But that entire affair took place subjectively in the man's own consciousness. I have no doubt," concludes Silence.

The third case for Dr. Silence, titled "THE NEMESIS OF FIRE" sees Dr. Silence investigate two simultaneous and baffling deaths that occurred twenty years ago at Twelve Acres Plantation. Confidential secretary Mr. Hubbard, who possesses limited psychic powers, accompanies Silence to the Manor House of Colonel Wragge. Wragge's brother was one of the victims, along with the gamekeeper.

The Colonel recalls the traumatic events. "My brother's face, they said, looked as if it had been scorched. It had been swept, as it were, by something that burned—blasted. It was, I am told, quite dreadful. The bodies were found lying side by side, face downwards, both pointing away from the wood, as though they had been in the act of running, an not more than a dozen yards from its edge."

The Colonel continues to tell Silence of strange lights "like globes of fire" coming from the plantation, and blazing stars "as though the ground was alight."

In the last three weeks the fires in the plantation have spread to the house and the room of the Colonel's sister.

The next morning Dr. Silence, Mr. Hubbard and the Colonel explore the woods of the plantation. Soon Silence is on the trail of a mysterious presence that heads toward the house. He defines it as "a fire-elemental." Only a blood sacrifice will bring the evil spirit to the surface.

The Colonel slaughters one of his pigs and covers a bowl containing its blood with a cloth. Taking the cloth from the bowl reveals an invisible presence in the room accompanied by an oppressive heat. The Colonel is possessed by the dark spirit who speaks through him.

"Even as Colonel Wragge spoke, it seemed that the invisible presence began to increase.... Then out of this rising sea of shadows, issued a pale and spectral light that gradually spread itself about us.... And these were not human shapes ... but outlines of fire that traced globes, triangles, crosses and the luminous bodies of various geometrical figures."

The fire elementals precede their master who takes shape in a sudden roar of flame before dissipating into the air. Silence concludes that the dead brother desecrated the mummy of an Egyptian priest and in doing so released the elemental of fire. Now they must unearth the mummy located in a tunnel beneath the grounds of the plantation and replace its stolen green jasper scarabaeus presently worn by the Colonel's sister. But it comes at a dreadful price when Miss Wragg restores the scarabaeus.

"...the silent figure before us moved in its grave of lead and sand. Slowly, before our eyes, it writhed, and, through sightless and bandaged eyes, stared across the yellow candlelight at the woman who had violated it ... the mummy was lying once more upon its back, motionless, the shrunken and painted face upturned towards the ceiling, and the old lady had tumbled forward and was lying in the semblance of death with her head and arms upon its crumbling body."

Case number four, "SECRET WORSHIP" begins with English silk merchant Harris travelling to his old school in southern Germany after an interval of more than thirty years. He departs the train and feels his youth return as his surroundings bring forth memories of the past. At the inn he finds himself in the company of a fellow English man and a Catholic priest who warns him he will find his old school to be very different.

Harris is filled with joy when he finally sees the Bruderstube again. He is met at the door by a former master, who in turn introduces him to a room full of Brothers. All of them seem familiar. "...he saw that all the Brothers about him had the faces he had known and lived with long ago."

Feeling ill at ease Harris begins to see the truth of the situation. "The motives of their secret souls rose to the eyes, and mouths, and foreheads, and hung there for all to see like the black banners of an assembly of ill-starred and fallen creatures. Demons—was the horrible word that flashed through his brain like a sheet of fire.... He was playing a part in some horrible masquerade, he was among men who cloaked their lives with religion in order to follow their real purposes unseen of men."

Unable to escape, Harris finds himself part of a devil-worshipping cult. "Then at the end of the room ... there rose into view far up against the night sky, grand and terrible, the outline of a man ... immense, imposing, horrific in its distant splendor."

Harris is to be the Brother's offering to this dark, evil being. But in the presence of his own death Harris sees the face of the English man he met at the inn. His countenance comforts him and gives him the strength to repel the Brothers who scream, "A man of power is among us! A man of God!"

When Harris recovers consciousness, the English man is by his side among the rubble of the school building and informs him, "That school building has long been in ruins ... it was burnt down by the orders of the Elders of the community at least ten years ago ... the simulacra of certain ghastly events that took place under that roof in past days still continue."

The next day Harris reflects on the English man. "The presence of this quiet stranger, the man with the wonderful eyes which he felt now, rather than saw, applied a soothing anodyne to his shattered spirit that healed him through and through."

Harris ponders the man's final words before his departure. "And if thought and emotion can persist in this was so long after the brain that sent them forth has crumbled into dust, how vitally important it must be to control their very birth in the heart, and guard them with the keenest possible restraint."

But who is this man with his words and actions of wisdom? Harris peruses the visitor book and reads the signature, "John Silence, London."

The final case in the anthology is "CAMP OF THE DOG." While camping on one of the numerous Swedish islands, Mr. Hubbard, confidential secretary to Dr. Silence, and a party of friends experience a mysterious hostile intruder.

That night Hubbard encounters the beast. "It was about the size of a large dog, but at the same time it was utterly unlike any animal that I had ever seen.... Foolish as it may sound, and impossible as it is for me to deduce proof, I can only say that the animal seemed to me then to be—not real."

Dr. John Silence arrives on the island the following evening as if sensing danger by "some secret telepathic method." Silence immediately concludes that lycanthropy is to blame in the form of a werewolf. "One of you has gone wild.... Gone a savage."

Silence explains that the Double, or astral body, "can often assume a form that gives impression to the overwhelming desire that molds it; for it is composed of such tenuous matter that it lends itself readily to the molding by thought and wish."

In certain persons of poor health, "...it is easy for the Double to dissociate itself during sleep from their system, and, driven forth by some consuming desire, to assume an animal form and seek fulfilment of that desire."

That desire being the repressed feelings of Canadian Peter Sangree for Joan Maloney, the wife of the Reverend Timothy Maloney. His deep love for her can only be expressed in astral, animal form. One fateful evening Sangree approaches her in werewolf form while she sleepwalks. Timothy Maloney lays in wait, shooting and injuring Sangree in the face. But the incident awakens Joan's love for Sangree as he returns to human form with the scars on his face a permanent reminder of the animal body he has finally relinquished.

"Underneath those remote regions of consciousness where the emotions, unknown to their owners, do secretly mature, and owe thence their abrupt revelation to some abrupt psychological climax, there can be no doubt that Joan's love for the Canadian had been growing steadily and irresistibly all the time. It had now rushed to the surface so that she recognized it…"

John Thunstone [Pulp fiction character]
Author: Manly Wade Wellman; First appearance: "The Third Cry to Legba" *Weird Tales* (November 1943); Publisher: Weird Tales Inc.

Manhattan playboy John Thurston is an expert in the occult. His strong physique serves him well in physical battles with the supernatural but more potent is the sapphire and steel amulet that protects his old flame Sharon and the silver bladed sword-cane forged by Saint Dunstan and passed down from **Judge Pursuivant**. Recurring foes include sorcerer Rowley Thorne and the ancient Shonokin who predate humans in America.

Manly Wade Wellman's John Thunstone stories were published in the pulp magazine *Weird Tales* between November 1943 and May 1951.

Short stories: "The Third Cry to Legba" (November 1943); "The Golden Goblins" (January 1944); "Hoofs" (March 1944); "The Letters of Cold Fire" (May 1944); John Thunstone's Inheritance" (July 1944); "Sorcery from Thule" (September 1944); "The Dead Man's Hand" (November 1944); "Thorne on the Threshold" (January 1945); "The Shonokins: (March 1945); "Blood from a Stone" (May 1945); "The Dai Sword" (July 1945); "Twice Cursed" (March 1946); "Shonokin Town" (July 1946); "The Leonardo Rondache" (March 1948); "The Last Grave of Lill Warren" (May 1951); "Rouse Him Not" (1982).

Novels: *What Dreams May Come* (1983); *The School of Darkness* (1985).

Jonathan Creek (1997) [TV series; UK]
Premiere: May 10, 1997; Main Cast: Alan Davies as Jonathan Creek, Caroline Quentin as Maddy Magellan, Stuart Milligan as Adam Klaus, Julia Sawalha as Carla Borrego, Sheridan Smith as Joey Ross, Sarah Alexander as Polly Creek; Executive Producers: David Renwick, Peter Thornton, Rexal Ford, Steven Canny; Writer: David Renwick; 12 × 50 min.; 13 × 60 min.; 5 × 90 min.; 2 × 120 min.; British Broadcasting Corporation (BBC); BBC One; Color.

Jonathan Creek leads a quiet life designing illusions for stage magician Adam Klaus, until investigative journalist Maddy Magellan enters his life. Now they have joined forces to solve bizarre crimes that border on the supernatural—until Creek provides the logical conclusion.

SEASON ONE

The Wrestler's Tomb (1:01); *Jack in the Box* (1:02); *The Reconstituted Corpse* (1:03); *No Trace of Tracy* (1:04); *The House of Monkeys* (1:05).

SEASON TWO

Danse Macabre (2:01); *Time Waits for Norman* (2:02); *The Scented Room* (2:03); *The Problem at Gallows Gate: Part 1* (2:04); *The Problem at Gallows Gate: Part 2* (2:05); *Mother Redcap* (2:06); *Black Canary* (2:07).

SEASON THREE

The Curious Tale of Mr. Spearfish (3:01); *The Eyes of Tiresias* (3:02); *The Omega Man* (3:03); *Ghost's Forge* (3:04); *Miracle in Crooked Lane* (3:05); *The Three Gamblers* (3:06); *Satan's Chimney* (3:07).

SEASON FOUR

The Coonskin Cap (4:01); *Angel Hair* (4:02); *The Tailor's Dummy* (4:03); *The Seer of the Sands* (4:04); *The Chequered Box* (4:05); *Gorgon's Wood* (4:06); *The Grinning Man* (4:07); *The Judas Tree* (4:08); *The Clue of the Savant's Thumb* (4:09).

SEASON FIVE

The Letters of Septimus Noone (5:01); *The Sinner ad the Sandman* (5:02); *The Curse of the Bronze Lamp* (5:03); *Daemon's Roost* (5:04).

Judge Pursuivant [Pulp fiction character]

Author: Gans T. Field (Manly Wade Wellman); First appearance: "The Hairy Ones Shall Dance" *Weird Tales* (January 1938); Publisher: Weird Tales Inc.

Retired Judge Keith Hilary Pursuivant investigates the supernatural with the aid of his silver bladed sword-cane inscribed with the Old Testament text "thus perish all your enemies." In his declining years Judge Pursuivant will hand over his sword-cane to fellow occult investigator **John Thunstone**.

Judge Pursuivant originally featured in four stories published in *Weird Tales* where he encounters a werewolf, the vampire Lord Byron, demon rabbits and ghosts. He also appeared as a supporting character to Silver John, John Thunstone and Lee Cobbett.

Short stories: "The Hairy Ones Shall Dance"–Serialized in three parts (January–March 1938); "The Black Drama"–Serialized in three parts (June–August 1938); "The Dreadful Rabbits" (July 1940); "The Half Haunted" (September 1941).

Jules de Grandin (Pulp fiction character)

Author: Seabury Quinn; First appearance: "The Horror on the Links" *Weird Tales* (October 1925).

Renowned French physician Jules de Grandin and his assistant and friend Dr. Samuel Trowbridge work out of the town of Harrisonville, New Jersey, home to all manner of weird events. De Grandin's time working for the French *Sûreté* has prepared him for his role as occult detective. The influence of Hercule Poirot is evident in author Seabury Quinn's description of an enthused De Grandin "his little blond mustache twitching like the whiskers of an excited cat." Dr. Trowbridge by comparison owes much to Conan Doyle's Dr. Watson with both characters chronicling the tales of their detective superiors. Despite De Grandin and Trowbridge's numerous encounters with the supernatural which includes confrontations with werewolves, vampires, ghosts and demons Dr. Trowbridge remains skeptical of the paranormal.

The case files of Jules de Grandin ran to ninety-three stories from October 1925 to September 1951 in *Weird Tales* pulp magazine. "The Devil's Bride" serialized in six-parts between February and July 1932 was later collected and published by Popular Library as a novel in 1976. The story centers around young Alice Hume who is kidnapped by Satanists known as the Yezidees who are in part financed by Russia.

Selected short stories: "The Horror on the Links" (October 1925); "The Tennants of Broussac" (December 1925); "The House of Horror" (July 1926); "The Great God Pan" (October 1926); "The Grinning Mummy" (November 1926); "The Curse of Everand Maundy" (July 1927); "The White lady of the Orphanage" (September 1927); "The Poltergeist" (October 1927); "The Serpent Woman" (June 1928); "The Chapel of Mystic Horror" (December 1928); "The Devil-People" (April 1929); "The Corpse-Master" (July 1929); "The Wolf of St. Bonnot" (December 1930); "The Ghost-Helper" (February 1931); "Satan's Stepson" (September 1931); "The Devil's Bride" (February–July 1932);

"The Dark Angel" (August 1932); "The Mansion of Unholy Magic" (October 1933); "The Children of the Bat" (January 1937); "Incense of Abomination" (March 1938); "The House Where Time Stood Still" (March 1939); "Lords of the Ghostlands" (March 1945); "Vampire Kith and Kin" (May 1949); "The Ring of Bastet" (September 1951).

Justice Inc. (Comic book)

First publication: May 1975; Story: Dennis O'Neill; Art: Al McWilliams; Jack Kirby; Joe Kubert; Al Milgrom; Michael Royer; Publisher: DC Comics.

The first two issues of the four-issue series featured adaptations of Paul Ernst's pulp fiction stories "Justice Inc." and "The Sky Walker" starring "the man of a thousand faces," **The Avenger**.

The title was revived in 1989 (DC Comics) and 2014 (Dynamite Entertainment).

Justice League Action (2016) [Animated TV series]

Premiere: November 26, 2016; Voice cast: Damian O'Hare as John Constantine/Abnegazar/Mr. Anderson, Lacey Chabert as Zatanna, Jon Cryer as Felix Faust, Paula Rhodes as Kid Constantine, Dayci Brookshire as Kid Zatanna, Kevin Conroy as Batman/Bruce Wayne, Jason J. Lewis as Superman/Clark Kent, Rachel Kimsey as Wonder Woman/Diana Prince, Chris Diamantopoulos as Green Arrow/Oliver Queen, Mark Hamill as Swamp Thing, James Woods as Lex Luthor, Charlie Schlatter as The Flash, Patrick Seitz as Etrigan the Demon/Jason Blood/Merlin, Joanne Spracklen as Supergirl; Executive Producers: Sam Register, Jay Bastian, Tramm Wigzell, Tatania Krokar; Based on the original *Justice League* concept by Gardner Fox; 52 × 11 min.; Warner Bros. Animation; DC Entertainment; Cartoon Network; CITV; Color.

This animated series contains episodes featuring occult detective **John Constantine**.

Episodes

"SHAZAM SLAM" (1:01–1:04); Air date: December 16, 2016; Story: Jake Castorena, Doug Murphy; Directors: Patrick Reiger, Heath Corson.

After Black Adam usurps the Wizard from his throne he releases the Brothers Djinn from the Rock of Eternity to wreak havoc upon the Earth. The Wizard enlists the help of the Justice League to combat the Djinns and John Constantine joins the action.

John Constantine appears in (1:04) of the four-part story.

"ZOMBIE KING" (1:07); Air date: February 4, 2017; Story: Paul Dini; Director: Jake Castorena.

Solomon Grundy raises a zombie army with a mystical diamond known as the Star of the Dead. Batman, Zatanna, Swamp Thing and John Constantine join forces to stop Grundy and his undead army before they reach New Orleans to raise more lost souls under the Crimson Moon.

"TRICK OR THREAT" (1:19); Air date: December 24, 2017; Story: Paul Dini; Director: Doug Murphy.

Klarion the Witch Boy turns Batman, Zatanna, John Constantine and Doctor Fate into witless ten-year-old children. Trapped in the House of Mystery at Halloween the children come under attack from werewolves and vampires and must return to normal size by midnight or vanish into thin air.

"SUPERNATURAL ADVENTURES IN BABYSITTING" (1:30); Air date: July 29, 2017; Story: Ernie Altbacker; Director: Shaun Nigoghossian.

Stargirl babysits Professor Anderson's young son Timmy in a house full of antiquities. This attracts the attention of Klarion the Witch Boy who wants to steal the Magadelene Grimoire. Klarion possesses Timmy as his demon cat searches for the book. Stargirl calls Batman for help. He in turn turns to John Constantine to fight Klarion's magic.

Justice League Dark (2017) [Animated film]

Premiere: January 14, 2017; Voice cast: Jason O'Mara as Batman/Bruce Wayne, Jerry O'Connell as Superman, Matt Ryan as Constantine, Camilla Luddington as Zatanna, Rosario Dawson as Wonder Woman, Nicholas Turturro as Boston Brand/Deadman, Enrico Colantoni as Felix Faust, Alfred Molina as Destiny, Jeremy Davies as Ritchie Simpson, Fred Tatasciore as Ghast, Roger R. Cross as Alec Holland/Swamp Thing/John Stewart/Green Lantern, JB Blanc as Abnegazar/Merlin, Ray Chase as Jason Blood, Colleen O'Shaughnessey as Alba Garcia/Black Orchid, Sachie Alessio as Lady Shiva, Brian T. Delaney as Shroud Leader; Executive Producer: Sam Register; Story: Ernie Altbacker, J.M. DeMatteis; Teleplay: Ernie Altbacker; Director: Jay Oliva; 75 min.; Warner Bros. Animation; DC Entertainment; DR Movie; Color.

When demons invade the Earth the Justice League calls on occult detective **John Constantine** to combat the supernatural threat. Joining Constantine's team is Zatanna, Deadman, Etrigan the Demon and Swamp Thing.

Kindaichi Case Files a.k.a. ***Kindaichi Shounen no Jikenbo*** [Manga; Japan]

First publication: *Weekly Shonen Magazine* (1992); Creator: Seimaru Amagi; Story: Yozaburo Kanari; Art: Fumiya Sato; Publisher: Kodansha.

Despite a terrible high school attendance record seventeen-year-old Hajime Kindaichi has a gift for sleight of hand and solving murders. Grandson of the famous detective Kosuke Kindaichi, Hajime is helped in his criminal investigations by Fudo High School friend Miiyuki Nanase and Tokyo homicide detective Isamu Kenmochi.

The cases often border on the supernatural in the long-running manga series which has run to 71 volumes and spawned animated and live-action TV series, anime films and novels.

A Kiss Before the Apocalypse (Remy Chandler Book #1) [Novel]

Author: Thomas E. Sniegoski; First publication: New York: Ace, 2008.

Boston private investigator Remy Chandler is the angel Remiel. Remiel, who can never reveal he has taken the human form of Chandler is able to talk with and understand his dog Marlowe and other animals, make himself invisible and hear thoughts. His latest assignment is to locate the Angel of Death and the missing scrolls that could initiate the apocalypse.

Book series: *A Kiss Before Dying* (2008); *Dancing on the Head of a Pin* (2009); *Where Angels Fear to Tread* (2010); *A Hundred Words for Hate* (2011); *In the House of the Wicked* (2012); *Walking in the Midst of Fire* (2013); *A Deafening Silence in Heaven* (2015).

Kolchak: The Night Stalker (1974) [TV series]

Premiere: September 13, 1974; Main Cast: Darren McGavin as Carl Kolchak, Simon Oakland as Tony Vincenzo, Jack Grinnage as Ron Updyke, Ruth McDevitt as Emily Cowles; Executive Producer: Darren McGavin; Producers: Cy Chermak, Paul Playdon; Creator: Jeff Rice; 20 × 51 min.; Francy Productions; Universal Television; American Broadcasting Company (ABC); Color.

Following the success of the telefilms ***The Night Stalker*** (1972) and ***The Night Strangler*** (1973) ABC commissioned a weekly series based on the main character Carl Kolchak.

Working as an investigative reporter out of Chicago the single-minded and stubborn Kolchak tracks down various monsters and paranormal creatures. His brand of detective journalism places him at odds with his editor and the police, but Kolchak must get his story, no matter the consequences.

Darren McGavin who portrayed Kolchak in the telefilms and TV series stated, "The truth of the matter is I love Kolchak. He's terrific. What he's saying to the world is beautiful—the heck with you brother. I'll get my story anyway."

In the course of the series Kolchak tackles a variety of paranormal entities and monsters. The first episode brings him face-to-face with the original Victorian Jack the Ripper who now possesses super-human powers. In *Bad Medicine* (1:08) Kolchak encounters the Native American spirit Diablero who desires priceless gems. *Horror in the Heights* (1:11) features a Rakshasah who can control people's minds and appear as a person the victim knows and trusts. It's goal to colonize the Earth and destroy humanity. In *Chopper* (1:15) a headless motorcyclist with a sword beheads the gang members who killed him. *Demon in Lace* (1:16) features a female demon known as a succubus who seduces young male students on a college campus, scaring them to death.

Kolchak also confronts a female vampire from Las Vegas, a werewolf on a singles cruise ship, a Rottweiler from Hell, a zombie raided from the dead by voodoo, an invisible creature that gains power from electricity, a rampaging robot, mannequins commanded by a witch, a resurrected mummy, a 12th-century knight's bewitched armor and a reptilian monster.

Canceled after 20 episodes due to low ratings the show gained a cult following and influenced Chris Carter the creator of ***The X-Files***.

SEASON ONE

The Ripper (1:01); *The Zombie* (1:02); *They Have Been, They Are. They Will Be …* (1:03); *The Vampire* (1:04); *The Werewolf* (1:05); *Firefall* (1:06); *The Devil's Platform* (1:07); *Bad Medicine* (1:08); *The Spanish Moss Murders*

(1:09); *The Energy Eater* (1:10); *Horror in the Heights* (1:11); *Mr. R.I.N.G.* (1:12); *Primal Scream* (1:13); *The Trevi Collection* (1:14); *Chopper* (1:15); *Demon in Lace* (1:16); *Legacy of Terror* (1:17); *The Knightly Murders* (1:18); *The Youth Killer* (1:19); *The Sentry* (1:20).

Laced: A Regan Reilly Mystery [Novel]
Author: Carol Higgins Clark: First publication: New York: Scribner, 2007.

Private investigator Regan Reilly and her husband Jack Reilly, head of New York City's Major Crime Squad, are spending their honeymoon at Hennessey Castle in Ireland. May Reilly is rumored to haunt the castle after failing to receive payment for her work on a beautiful lace tablecloth in the 19th century.

When Regan sees a ghost outside of the hotel window and a rare lace tablecloth is stolen during a fire alarm Reagan and Jack investigate further. A note left at the castle by a pair of jewel thieves Jack had been tracking in New York leads to a chase across County Galway.

Lady Mechanika [Comic book]
First publication: October 2010; Creator-Art: Joe Benitez; Publisher: Benitez Productions, Aspen MLT Inc.

Half-human, half-robot investigator Lady Mechanika has no memory of her past or how she acquired her mechanical limbs. Her quest to uncover her origins leads to paranormal cases in a Victorian steampunk setting.

"The Last Illusion" [Short story]
Author: Clive Barker; First publication: *Books of Blood, Volume 6*; Publisher: Sphere Books, 1985.

Occult detective Harry D'Amour is hired by the wife of recently deceased magician Swann to protect his body at his cremation. Demons want to claim Swann's body in order to gain the magical powers Swann promised them in a deal.

The first appearance of New York private investigator Harry D'Amour whose body tattoos protect him from the forces of darkness. Author Clive Barker states, "His antecedents are the troubled, weary and often lovelorn heroes of film noir."

The character also features in the short story "Lost Souls" (1985) and the novels *The Great & Secret Show: The First Book of the Art* (1989) and *Everville: The Second Book of the Art* (1994). Scott Bakula portrays Harry D'Amour in *Lord of Illusions* (1995).

Last Shift (2014) [Film]
Premiere: October 6, 2014; Main Cast: Juliana Harkavy as Jessica Loren, Joshua Mikel as John Michael Paymon, Hank Stone as Grip Cohen, J. LaRose as Patrick Black, Sarah Sculco as Kitty Paymon, Kathryn Kilger as Dorthea Paymon, Natalie Victoria as Marigold, Mary Lankford as Birdie, Matt Doman as Officer Ryan Price, Lindsi Jetter as Bashed Face Betty/Ghost Girl, Randy Molanar as Steve Loren, Jeremy S, Brock as Detective; Producers: Mary Lankford Poiley, Scott Poiley; Story: Anthony DiBlasi, Scott Poiley; Director: Anthony DiBlasi; 90 min.; Skyra Entertainment; Magnet Releasing; Color.

Alone in a dying police station rookie cop Jessica Loren awaits a Hazmat team scheduled to pick up bio-hazardous waste. But as the night progresses Officer Loren is threatened by a Satanic cult and their dead leader John Michael Paymon.

"The Leather Funnel" [Short story]
Author: A. Conan Doyle; Illustrator: A. Castaigne; First publication: *McClure's Magazine* Vol. 20 #1 (November 1902); Publisher: New York, NY: S. S. McClure.

The late Lionel Dacre owned a library of occult literature with a unique collection of Talmudic, cabalistic and magical works. A wealthy and somewhat eccentric man, Dacre's interest in his collection "was intellectual rather than spiritual" although he experimented in the black arts. Of peculiar interest to Dacre was the psychology of dreams "from Albertus Magnus onward" and his ownership of a brass-rimmed black leather funnel from the Middle Ages.

On this occasion Dacre invited his guest and "psychic subject" to go to sleep with the funnel by his pillow. Falling into a deep sleep the guest found himself in a vaulted room. A small woman draped in a loose white gown was being questioned by three men dressed in black. The woman was being prepared for a dreadful water torture shackled to a wooden horse. A leather funnel was thrust into the woman with force when the guest awoke with a shriek. Hearing the scream Dacre rushed to the room. Both Dacre and his guest had shared the same dream. A dream of real-life events from long ago. The trial of Marie Madeleine D'Aubray, Marquise de Brinvilliers. A woman who tortured her sick father and murdered her brothers for monetary gain. Her initials were still engraved in the brass rim of the leather funnel and now her story had been preserved across time.

Legends of Tomorrow (2016) [TV series]
Premiere: January 21, 2016; Main Cast: Brandon Routh as Ray Palmer/The Atom, Caity Lotz as Sara Lance/White Canary, Dominic Purcell as Mick Rory/Heat Wave/Chronos, Amy Louise Pemberton as Gideon, Nick Zano as Nate Heywood/Steel, Franz Drameh as Jefferson Jackson/Firestorm, Victor Garber as Dr. Martin Stein/Firestorm, Tala Ashe as Zari Tomaz, Arthur Darvill as Rip Hunter, Jess Macallan as Ava Sharpe, Matt Ryan as John Constantine, Wentworth Miller as Leonard Snart/Captain Cold, Courtney Ford as Nora Dahrk, Neal McDonough as Damien Dark, Adam Tsekhman as Agent Gary Green, Ciara Renee as Kendra Saunders/Hawkgirl; Executive Producers: Greg Berlanti, Matt Guggenheim, Phil Klemmer, Sarah Schechter, Andrew Kreisberg, Grainne Godfree, Chris Fedak; Developers: Phil Klemmer, Greg Berlanti, Marc Guggenheim, Andrew Kreisberg; Based on DC Comics characters; 73 × 42 min.; Berlanti Productions, Bonanza Productions; DC Entertainment; Warner Bros. Television. The CW Network; Color.

Time traveler Rip Hunter recruits an assorted team of super-heroes and super-villains to save the Earth from catastrophe. Matt Ryan as occult detective **John Constantine** joins the cast in *Daddy Darhkest* (3:10) before becoming a regular team member in Season Four.

The series includes many storylines with supernatural elements including Confederate zombies, Jonah Hex, Damien and Nora Dahrk, the Spear of Destiny, totems and magic.

SEASON ONE

Pilot: Part 1 (1:01); *Pilot: Part 2* (1:02); *Blood Ties* (1:03); *White Knights* (1:04); *Fail-Safe* (1:05); *Star City 2046* (1:06); *Marooned* (1:07); *Night of the Hawk* (1:08); *Left Behind* (1:09); *Progeny* (1:10); *The Magnificent Eight* (1:11); *Last Refuge* (1:12); *Leviathan* (1:13); *River of Time* (1:14); *Destiny* (1:15); *Legendary* (1:16).

SEASON TWO

Out of Time (1:01); *The Justice Society of America* (1:02); *Shogun* (1:03); *Abominations* (1:04); *Compromised* (1:05); *Outlaw Country* (1:06); *Invasion!* (1:07); *The Chicago Way* (1:08); *Raiders of the Lost Art* (1:09); *The Legion of Doom* (1:10); *Turncoat* (1:11); *Camelot/3000* (1:12); *Land of the Lost* (1:13); *Moonshot* (1:14); *Fellowship of the Spear* (1:15); *Doomworld* (1:16); *Aruba* (1:17).

SEASON THREE

Aruba-Con (1:01); *Freakshow* (1:02); *Zari* (1:03); *Phone Home* (1:04); *Return of the Mack* (1:05); *Helen Hunt* (1:06); *Welcome to the Jungle* (1:07); *Crisis on Earth-X: Part 4* (1:08); *Beebo the God of War* (1:09); *Daddy Darhkest* (1:10); *Here I Go Again* (1:11); *The Curse of the Earth Totem* (1:12); *No Country for Old Dads* (1:13); *Amazing Grace* (1:14); *Necromancing the Stone* (1:15); *I, Ava* (1:16): *Guest Starring John Noble* (1:17); *The Good, the Bad and the Cuddly* (1:18).

SEASON FOUR

The Virgin Gary (1:01); *Witch Hunt* (1:02); *Dancing Queen* (1:03); *Wet Hot American Bummer* (1:04); *Tagumo Attacks!!!* (1:05); *Tender is the Nate* (1:06); *Hell No, Dolly!* (1:07); *Legends of To-Meow-Meow* (1:08); *Lucha de Apuestas* (1:09); *The Getaway* (1:10); *Séance & Sensibility* (1:11); *The Eggplant, the Witch & the Wardrobe* (1:12); *Egg MacGuffin* (1:13); *Nip/Stuck* (1:14); *Terms of Service* (1:15); *Hey, World!* (1:16); (1:17); (1:18); (1:19); (1:20).

The Leopard Man (1943) [Film]
Premiere: June 25, 1943; Main Cast: Dennis O'Keefe as Jerry Manning, Margo as Clo-Clo, Jean Brooks as Kiki Walker, Isabel Jewell as Maria, Fortune Teller, Ben Bard as Police Chief Roblos, James Bell as Dr. Gailbraith, Abner Biberman as Charlie How-Come, Tula Parma as Consuelo Contreras, Margaret Landry as Teresa Delgado; Producer: Val Lewton; Screenplay: Ardel Wray; Based on the novel by Cornel Woolrich; Director: Jacques Tourneur; 66 min.; RKO Radio Pictures, Inc.; b/w.

A tame leopard used as part of a publicity stunt to promote singer Kiki Walker, escapes captivity during a nightclub act. Female corpses showing signs of being mauled allude to the leopard. Theatrical agent Jerry Manning, Kiki Walker and the local police investigate the deaths. But who is responsible? Man, or beast or both? The trailer hints at a man-beast at work. "Death stalks the panic-stricken people.... Hunted by a killer who is half-cat, half-man!"

This adaptation of **Black Alibi** by Cornel Woolrich substitutes a leopard for the original jaguar, changes the locale from South America to New Mexico and features a different conclusion.

Let Us Prey (2014) [Film; UK/Ireland]
Premiere: April 17, 2014; Main Cast: Liam Cunningham as Six, Pollyanna McIntosh as PC Rachel Heggie, Bryan Larkin as PC Jack Warnock, Hanna Stanbridge as PC Jennifer Mundie, Douglas Russell as Sgt. MacReady, Niall Greig Fulton as Dr. Duncan Hume, Jonathan Watson as Ralph Beswick, Brian Vernel as Caesar Sargison, James McCreadie as Mulvey; Executive Producers: John Brady, Lee Brazier, James Daly, Chris Hainsworth, Nick Munday; Story: Fiona Watson, David Cairns; Director: Brian O'Malley; 92 min.; Dark Sky Films; Creative Scotland; Fantastic Films; Greenhouse Media Investment; Makar Productions; Irish Film Board; Color.

A drifter named Six creates mayhem in a Sottish police station when he exposes the dark secrets of the people in the station by supernatural means—with the destination of their journey being Hell.

London Falling (Shadow Police #1) [Novel]
Author: Paul Cornell; First publication; New York: Tor Books, 2012.

London police officers Quill, Costain and Sefton and intelligence operative Lisa Ross form a task force to investigate the strange death of mob boss Rob Toshack. When they come across a mysterious artifact they develop "The Sight" allowing them to see the evil occult underbelly of London.

Now they can connect the death of the mob boss to a witch which in turn connects to child sacrifice, Anne Boleyn, and the West Ham soccer team.

Shadow Police series: *London Falling* (2012); *The Severed Streets* (2016); *Who Killed Sherlock Holmes?* (2017).

"Loot of the Vampire" [Novella]
Author: Thorp McClusky; First publication: *Weird Tales* (June 1936).

Police Commissioner Charles B. Ethredge and Detective Lieutenant Peters of the Homicide Squad investigate the theft of a string of pearls valued at $400,000 and the strange death of renowned jeweler David Eichelman. Ethredge declares, "He looks awfully pale! You'd say all the blood had been drained out of him."

That night in the County Hospital morgue the attendant Derwin sees a tall figure moving from slab to slab until he uncovers Eichelman's corpse. After giving the dead man a transfusion of his blood Eichelman stirs and is engaged in conversation with the weird visitor. They both depart by squeezing "between bars so closely spaced that they would not admit the body of a full-grown cat..."

The next day Eichelman is sitting at his desk in the jeweler's store, alive and well. And so, his reign of terror begins with Count Woerz in control.

Novellas in the Ethredge & Peters series: *Loot of the Vampire* (June 1936); *The Woman in Room 607* The (January 1937); *The Thing on the Floor* (March 1938); *Monstrosity of Evolution* (November 1938); *Slaves of the Gray Mold* (March 1940).

The cover for *Weird Tales* (June 1936) featuring the short story "Loot of the Vampire" introducing Police Commissioner Charles B. Ethredge and Detective Lieutenant Peters. Cover art by Margaret Brundage.

Lord Darcy [Short story character]
Author: Randall Garrett; First appearance: "The Eyes Have It" *Analog Science Fact-Science Fiction* (January 1964); Publisher: Conde Nast.

"In a sense, this is a story of here-and-now. This Earth, this year … but on a history-line slipped slightly sidewise. A history in which a great man acted differently, and Magic, rather than physical science, was developed…."

Lord Darcy lives in an alternate history ruled by the Plantagenets who continue their rule into 1963 and beyond when Darcy's first story begins. The Anglo-French Empire is ruled by King John IV and Lord Darcy is the Chief Forensic Investigator to Richard, Duke of Normandy and Special Investigator for the High Court of Chivalry. Together with his assistant Master Sorcerer Sean O'Lochlainn they investigate crimes that involve magic.

Too Many Magicians was collected in novel form and published by Doubleday in 1967. Following Randall Garrett's death after a prolonged illness in 1987 his friend Michael Kurland wrote two Lord Darcy novels, *Ten Little Wizards* (1988) and *A Study in Sorcery* (1989).

Short stories/novellas: "The Eyes Have It" (1964); "A Case of Identity" (1964); "The Muddle of the Woad" (1965); "A Stretch of the Imagination" (1973); "Matter of Gravity" (1974); "The Ipswich Phial" (1976); "The Sixteen Keys" (1976); "The Bitter End" (1978); "The Napoli Express" (1979); "The Spell of War" (1979).

Serialized novel in four parts: *Too Many Magicians* (August to November 1966; *Analog*).

Short story collections: *Murder and Magic* (1979); *Lord Darcy Investigates* (1981).

Lord of Illusions (1995) [Film]
Premiere: August 25, 1995; Main Cast: Scott Bakula as Harry D'Amour, Famke Janssen as Dorothea Swann, Ashley Lyn Cafagna as Young Dorothea, Daniel von Bargen as Nix, Kevin J. O'Connor as Philip Swan, Joseph Latimore as Caspar Quaid, Sheila Tousey as Jennifer Desiderio, Barry Del Sherman as Butterfield, Trevor Edmond as Young Butterfield, Wayne Grace as Loomis, Jordan Marder as Ray Miller, Joel Swetow as Valentin, Vincent Schiavelli as Vinovich; Executive Producers: Steve Golin, Sigurjon Sighvatsson; Screenplay/Di-

rector: Clive Barker; 109 min.; Seraphim Films; MGM/UA; Color.

New York occult investigator Harry D'Amour encounters members of a cult who await the resurrection of their leader Nix, who was buried alive thirteen years ago.

See: **"The Last Illusion"**

Lord Syfret [Short story character]

Author: Arabella Kenealy; Illustrator: R. Savage; First appearance: *The Ludgate* (June 1896); Publisher: London: W. J. Monckton.

Part-time occult detective Lord Syfret investigates the strange case of widow Lady Deverish in "A Beautiful Vampire." Dr. Andrew has twice failed in his efforts to kill Lady Deverish but she refuses to press charges. Lord Syfret decides to investigate further by sending Nurse Marian to spy on Lady Deverish. What she uncovers is beyond belief. Deverish is feeding on the blood of her human victims to maintain her vitality.

Lord Syfret appeared in eight short stories published in *The Ludgate* magazine between June 1896 and January 1897 under the banner "Some Experiences of Lord Syfret." The final three stories "The Metamorphosis of Peter Humby," "The Beautiful Mrs. Tompkyns" and "An Ogre in Tweeds" didn't feature Lord Syfret.

Short stories: "The Haunted Child" (June 1896); "In a Terrible Grip" (July 1896); "The Villa of Simpkins" (August 1896); "The Wolf and the Stork" (September 1896); "Stronheim's Extremity" (October 1896); "A Beautiful Vampire" (November 1896); "Honorias Hero" (December 1896); "Prince Ranjichatterjee's Vengeance" (January 1897).

The Lost Room (2006) [TV series]

Premiere: December 11, 2006; Main Cast: Peter Krause as Police Detective Joe Miller, Elle Fanning as Anna Miller,

Julianna Margulies as Jennifer Bloom, Peter Jacobson as Wally Jabrowski, Dennis Christopher as Dr. Martin Ruber, April Grace as Lee Bridgewater, Kevin Pollack as Karl Kreutzfeld, Benjamin Petry as Isaac Kreutzfeld, Jason Douglas as Anthony, Chris Bauer as Lou Desefano, Margaret Cho as Suzie Kang, Ann Cusack as Helen Ruber, Harriet Sansom Harris as Margaret Milne, Roger Bart as Howard 'The Weasel' Montague, Tim Guinee as Eddie McCleister, Chris Monberg as Little Jim; Executive Producer: Richard Hatem; Story: Laura Harkcom, Christopher Leone, Paul Workman; Directors; Craig R. Baxley, Michael W. Watkins; 270 min.; Lions gate Films; Lionsgate Productions; Motel Man Productions; Sci-Fi Channel; Color.

In this three-episode mini-series police detective Joe Miller and his partner Lou investigate two burnt corpses connected to a magical motel key that opens portals to alternate realities. Before he dies from his gunshot wounds the owner of the key passes it to Joe Miller. The detective finds himself transported to different locations when he opens doors. But a motel room that contains one hundred objects with unique powers attracts people who will kill Miller and his young daughter for the key.

Episodes

The Key and the Clock (1:01); *The Comb and the Box* (1:02); *The Eye and the Prime Object* (1:03).

Love Is the Law [Novel]

First publication: 2013; Author: Nick Mamatas; Publisher: Milwaukie, OR: Dark Horse Books.

Long Island, NY 1989. Black magic student and punk rocker, "Golden" Dawn discovers her mentor shot in the head, an apparent suicide. But Dawn is convinced it was murder and bypasses the police to investigate his death herself.

Lucifer (2016) [TV series]

Premiere: January 25, 2016; Main Cast: Tom Ellis as Lucifer Morningstar, Lauren German as Detective Chloe Decker, Kevin Alejandro as Detective Daniel "Dan" Espinoza, D. B. Woodside as Amenadiel, Lesley-Ann Brandt as Mazikeen, Scarlett Estevez as Trixie, Rachael Harris as Linda Martin, Tricia Helfer as Charlotte, Aimee Garcia As Ella Lopez, Tom Welling as Marcus Pierce; Executive Producers: Jerry Bruckheimer, Jonathan Littman, Ildy Modrovich, KristieAnne Reed, Sheri Ellwood, Joe

Henderson, Len Wiseman; Developed by Tom Kapinos; Based on the DC/Vertigo characters created by Neil Gaiman, Sam Keith, Mike Drinkenberg; 67 × 42 min.; Aggressive Mediocrity; Jerry Bruckheimer Television; DC Entertainment; Vertigo; Warner Bros. Television; Fox Network; Netflix; Color.

Bored with his life as the Lord of Hell Lucifer Morningstar incarnates in human form on Earth and settles in Los Angeles where he enjoys his retirement as owner of the upscale piano bar Lux. When a beautiful singer is murdered outside of his club Lucifer finds himself experiencing feelings and joins LAPD homicide detective Chloe Decker in trying to solve the pop star's murder. Meanwhile the angel Amanadiel is on a mission to send Lucifer back to Hell. But Lucifer has other ideas including employment as a consultant to the LAPD where he works alongside Chloe Decker.

Canceled by Fox Network after three seasons the show was picked up by Netflix.

Season One

Pilot (1:01); *Lucifer, Stay, Good Devil* (1:02); *The Would-Be Prince of Darkness* (1:03); *Manly Whatnots* (1:04); *Sweet Kicks* (1:05); *Favorite Son* (1:06); *Wingman* (1:07); *Et Tu, Doctor?* (1:08); *A Priest Walks Into a Bar* (1:09); *Pops* (1:10); *St. Lucifer* (1:11); *#TeamLucifer* (1:12); *Take Me Back to Hell* (1:13).

Season Two

Everything's Coming Up Lucifer (2:01); *Liar. Liar, Slutty Dress on Fire* (2:02); *Sin-Eater* (2:03); *Lady Parts* (2:04); *Weaponizer* (2:05); *Monster* (2:06); *My Little Monkey* (2:07); *Trip to Shabby Town* (2:08); *Homewrecker* (2:09); *Quid Pro Ho* (2:10); *Stewardess Interruptus* (2:11); *Love Handles* (2:12); *A Good Day to Die* (2:13); *Candy Morningstar* (2:14); *Deceptive Little Parasite* (2:15); *God Johnson* (2:16); *Sympathy for the Goddess* (2:17); *The Good, the Bad, and the Crispy* (2:18).

Season Three

They're Back Aren't They? (3:01); *The One with the Baby Carrot* (3:02); *Mr. and Mrs. Mazikeen Smith* (3:03); *What Would Lucifer Do?* (3:04); *Welcome Back, Charlotte Richards* (3:05); *Vegas With Some Radish* (3:06); *Off the Record* (3:07); *Chloe Does Lucifer* (3:08); *The Sinnerman* (3:09); *The Sin Bin* (3:10); *City of Angels?* (3:11); *All About Her?* (3:12); *Til Death Do Us Part* (3:13); *My Brother's Keeper* (3:14); *High School Poppycock* (3:15); *Infernal Guinea Pig* (3:16); *Let Pinhead Sing!* (3:17); *The Last Heartbreak* (3:18); *Orange is the New Maze* (3:19); *The Angel of San Bernardino* (3:20); *Anything Pierce Can Do I Can Do Better* (3:21); *All Hands on Decker* (3:22); *Quintessential Deckstar* (3:23); *A Devil of My Word* (3:24); *Boo Normal* (3:25); *Once Upon a Time* (1:26).

Season Four

Everything's Okay (4:01); *Somebody's Been Reading Dante's Inferno* (4:02); *O. Ye of Little Faith, Father* (4:03); *All About Eve* (4:04); *Expire Erect* (4:05); *Orgy Pants to Work* (4:06); *Devil as Devil Does* (4:07); *Super Bad Boyfriend* (4:08); *Save Lucifer* (4:09); *King of Hell?* (4:10).

Lucius Leffing [Short story character]
Author: Joseph Payne Brennan; First appearance: "The Haunted Housewife" *Macabre XII* (Winter 1962–1963).

Occult detective, psychic investigator and antique glass collector Lucius Leffing works out of his home in New Haven, Connecticut. Author Joseph Payne Brennan serves as his chronicler, adopting a Dr. Watson type role. Leffing is a reserved scholarly type who prefers a glass of sarsaparilla to bourbon and is a calming presence to his clients.

Leffing appeared in approximately forty short stories published in a variety of magazines including *Alfred Hitchcock's Mystery Magazine* and *Mike Shayne Mystery Magazine*. Stories from this period are low on supernatural elements but by the late 1970s and early 1980s the supernatural returns in full force.

Selected short stories: "The Haunted Housewife" (Winter 1962–63); "In the Very Stones" (1963); "Apparition in the Sun" (1963); "In the Death of Life" (1963); "The Strange Case of Peddler Phelps" (September 1965); "Death Mask" (October 1965); "The Dead of Winter Apparition" (February 1975); "The Nursing Home

Horror" (1981); "The Haunting at Juniper Hill" (1985); "The Spruce Valley Monster" (1990); "The Swamp Horror" (1990); "The Vanning Case" (1990).

Novel: *Act of Providence* (1979).

Collections: *The Casebook of Lucius Leffing* (1973); The Chronicles of Lucius Leffing (1977); The Adventures of Lucius Leffing (1990).

The Lurkers [Comic book]

First publication: October 2004; Four-part mini-series; Story: Steve Niles; Art: Hector S. Casanova; Publisher: IDW Publishing.

Los Angeles detective Jack Dietz investigates a serial killer with a taste for human flesh. When Dietz notices a mob of ghouls, he realizes this may be the work of zombies.

Manifest (2018) [TV series]

Premiere: September 24, 2018; Main Cast: Melissa Roxburgh as Detective Michaela Stone, Josh Dallas as Ben Stone, Athena Karkanis as Grace Stone, J.R. Ramirez as Jared Vasquez, Luna Blaise as Olive Stone, Jack Messina as Cal Stone, Pareveen Kaur as Saanvi Bahl, Daryl Edwards as NSA Director Vance, Alfredo Narciso as Captain Rojas; Executive Producers: Jeff Rake, Jaqueline Levine, Robert Zemeckis, Jack Rapke, Len Goldstein, David Frankel; Creator: Jeff Rake; 16 × 43 min.; Compari Entertainment; Jeff Rake Productions; Universal Television; Warner Bros. Television; NBC; Color.

Montego Air Flight 828 lands safely after a turbulent flight. But the world is five years older and friends and families have moved on believing the plane crashed. As the passengers adjust to their new life, they begin to hear voices that point to future events that need to be stopped. Detective Michaela Stone is one of the passengers who searches for the truth behind the missing years.

SEASON ONE

Pilot (1:01); (1:01); *Reentry* (1:02); *Turbulence* (1:03); *Unclaimed Baggage* (1:04); *Connecting Flights* (1:05); *Off Radar* (1:06); *S.N.A.F.U.* (1:07); *Point of No Return* (1:08); *Dead Reckoning* (1:09); *Crosswinds* (1:10); *Contrails* (1:11); *Vanishing Point* (1:12); *Cleared for Approach* (1:13); *Upgrade* (1:14); *Hard Landing* (1:15); *Estimated Time of Departure* (1:16).

"The Mark of the Beast" [Short story]

Author: Rudyard Kipling; First publication: *The Pioneer: A Literary and Critical Magazine* (July 1890); Publisher: Boston, MA: Leland and Whiting.

"My friend Strickland of the Police, who knows as much of natives of India as is good for any man, can bear witness to the facts of the case."

Fleete is a big genial man who has come to India to finance properties left to him. New Year's Eve is a riotous affair with an excess of drinking. Strickland decides to escort a drunken Fleete home. On their journey they make a stop at the Temple of Hanuman, the monkey-god. Before he can be stopped Fleete runs past two priests and proceeds to grind his cigar-butt into the forehead of the stone image of Hanuman. Strickland warns Fleete of the dangers of polluting gods but Fleete takes little notice until a naked Silver man "a leper as white as snow" with no face leaps from behind a recess. The leper grabs hold of Fleete and drops his head on Fleete's breast. A priest approaches Strickland telling him to take his friend away. "He has

Manifest (2018), starring Melissa Roxburgh as NYPD Detective Michaela Stone (Universal-WB Television).

done with Hanuman, but Hanuman has not done with him."

The following morning Fleete notices a black mark on his left breast that resembles black rosettes. He also finds he has an unhealthy appetite for rare pork chops which he devours like a beast. In the stables the horses rear and scream in the presence of Fleete. Returning that evening from a ride Strickland finds Fleete "on his hands and knees under the orange-bushes." Fleete then asks to dine outside on a freezing winter evening "and have some more chops … bloody ones with gristle."

Refusing his request and taking Fleete inside to his room Strickland waits for him to prepare for dinner but only hears "the long-drawn howl of a wolf" coming from his room. Entering the room Strickland notes, "Fleete could not speak, he could only snarl. And his snarls were those of a wolf, not of a man. The human spirit must have given way all day and have dried out with the twilight. We were dealing with a beast that once had been Fleete."

Doctor Dumoise arrives and after examining the bound and gagged Fleete declares that he is dying from hydrophobia. Hearing a cry from the shrubbery at the front of the house Strickland and his friend investigate. The leper is captured and brought face-to-face with the beast. "The beast doubled backwards into a bow as though he had been poisoned with strychnine and moaned in the most pitiable fashion." Strickland tells the leper to remove the evil spirit. Laying his hands on the left breast of the beast the soul of Fleete returns as the leper departs. The rosette has disappeared.

Strickland tells his friend to record the story for the public. "…no one will believe a rather unpleasant story, and … it is well known to every right-minded man that the gods of the heathen are stone and brass, and any attempt to deal with them otherwise is justly condemned."

Mark of the Demon (Kara Gillian book #1) [Novel]
Author: Diana Rowland; First publication: New York: Bantam Books, 2009.

The Symbol Man is back again after an absence of three years. A serial killer versed in the occult. Rookie Louisiana homicide detective Kara Gillian has occult skills of her own as a demon summoner and conjures up the demonic lord Rhyzhahl. Can she stop the Symbol Man, and should she enlist the aid of Rhyzhahl?

Kara Gillian series: *Mark of the Demon* (2009); *Blood of the Demon* (2010); *Secrets of the Demon* (2011); *Sins of the Demon* (2012); *Touch of the Demon* (2012); *Fury of the Demon* (2014); *Vengeance of the Demon* (2015); *Legacy of the Demon* (2016)

Mark of the Vampire (1935) [Film]
Premiere: April 26, 1935; Main Cast: Lionel Barrymore as Professor Zelin, Elizabeth Allen as Irena Borotyn, Bela Lugosi as Count Mora, Lionel Atwill as Inspector Neumann, Jean Her-

Mark of the Vampire (1935), starring Donald Meek as Dr. Doskil (left) Lionel Atwill as Inspector Neumann (MGM).

sholt as Baron Otto, Henry Wadsworth as Fedor Vincente, Donald Meek as Dr. Doskil, Carrol Borland as Luna, Holmes Herbert as Sir Karell Borotyn; Producers: Tod Browning, E.J. Mannix; Screenplay; Guy Endore, Bernard Schubert; Director: Tod Browning; 60 min.; Metro-Goldwyn-Mayer (MGM); b/w.

Sir Karell Borotyn is murdered in his castle home and drained of his blood. When two bite marks on his neck are found the townsfolk become fearful a vampire is at large. Count Mora and his deathly pale daughter Luna are seen near the castle by superstitious villagers who claim they turned into bats. Inspector Neumann from Prague is called upon but dismisses any idea of any supernatural connection. Neumann suspects those who might profit financially from Borotyn's death.

Sir Karell's daughter Irena prepares for her wedding only to see her fiancé Fedor badly affected by two wounds on his neck. Soon Irena is attacked by Luna. When Inspector Neumann finds Sir Karell's coffin empty and sees him walking the castle grounds with Count Mora he finally comes to terms with the fact vampires are real. They must destroy the vampires to save the souls of Irena and Fedor.

A lookalike of Sir Karell is used as bait for the killer and the vampires are revealed to be vaudeville actors. All have played their part in Inspector Neumann's elaborate plan.

Martian Manhunter [Comic book character]

First appearance: *Detective Comics* #225 (November 1955); Creators: Joseph Samachson, Joe Certa; Publisher: DC Comics.

The last surviving Martian following the death of his wife and daughter in fires that engulfed his planet. He was brought to Earth accidentally on a teleportation beam by scientist Saul Erdel. As police detective John Jones a.k.a. J'onn J'onzz working out of Middletown he resumes the career he had on Mars. His detective work is greatly enhanced with his ability to shape-shift and fly. Added powers of telekinesis, telepathy, super-vision, super- hearing, super-strength, super-speed is counterbalanced with a vulnerability to fire in his native form.

John Jones eventually discards his human identity as a police detective after he is apparently killed in action but goes undercover as Marco Xavier to bring down an international crime cartel. After an absence of twenty years John Jones resurfaces as a private detective.

The Martian Manhunter is a recurring character portrayed by David Harewood on the live-action TV series *Supergirl* (2015).

Martin Mystery (2003) [Animated TV series]

Premiere: October 1, 2003; Voice Cast: Samuel Vincent as Martin Mystery/Billy, Kelly Sheridan as Diana Lombard, Teryl Rothery as M.O.M, Dale Wilson as Java the Caveman, Tabitha St. Germain as Jenni Anderson; Executive Producers: Sylvain Viau, Jisoo Han, Myun Young Jung; Creators: Vincent Chalvon-Demersay, David Michel; Based on the comic book by Alfredo Castelli; Director: Stephen Berry; 66 × 22 min.; Marathon Animation; Image Entertainment Corporation. Inc.; DPS; CJ E&M; Infinity-Comic Korea Entertainment; Color.

Torrington Academy, Sherbrooke, Quebec acts as the gateway to 'The Center' where teenage step-siblings Martin Mystery and Diana Lombard are assigned their latest paranormal missions. Helping them in their cases is Neanderthal caveman Java. The skeptical Diana is often in conflict with Martin, who displays a lack of personal hygiene and a flippant approach to their assignments. Creatures they've encountered include, werewolves, witches, zombies, vampires, living garden gnomes, a leprechaun, djinni and various evil spirits.

SEASON ONE

It Came from the Bog (1:01); *Terror from the Sky* (1:02); *The Creeping Slime* (1:03); *Curse of the Deep* (1:04); *Mark of the Shapeshifter* (1:05); *Mystery of the Vanishing* (1:06); *It Came from Inside the Box* (1:07); *Attack of the Sandman* (1:08); *Shriek from Beyond* (1:09); *Eternal Christmas* (1:10); *Return of the Dark Druid* (1:11); *Nightmare of the Coven* (1:12); *They Lurk Beneath* (1:13); *Curse of the Necklace* (1:14); *Haunting of the Blackwater* (1:15); *Mystery of* the Hole Creature (1:16); *Fright from the Ice* (1:17); *Beast from Within* (1:18); *Revenge of the Doppelganger* (1:19); *The Return of the Beasts* (1:20); *Attack of the Mothman* (1:21); *Summer Camp Nightmare* (1:22); *The Sewer Thing* (1:23); *Scream from the Forest* (1:24); *The Amazon Vapor* (1:25); *The Awakening* (1:26).

Season Two

They Came from Outer Space: Part 1 (2:01); *They Came from Outer Space: Part 2* (2:02); *Attack of the Slime People* (2:03); *The Vampire Returns* (2:04); *Crypt of the Djinni* (2:05); *You Do Voodoo* (2:06); *Zombie Island* (2:07); *The Lost Tribe* (2:08); *Monster Movie Mayhem* (2:09); *The Third Eye* (2:10); *The Body-Swapper* (2:11); *Germs from Beyond* (2:12); *The Came from the Gateway: Part 1* (2:13); *The Came from the Gateway: Part 2* (2:14).

Season Three

Curse of the Looking Glass (3:01); *Mystery of Teen Town* (3:02); *Attack of the Evil Roommate* (3:03); *Web of the Spider Creature* (3:04); *Attack of the Lawn Gnomes* (3:05); *Rise of the Sea Mutants* (3:06); *Hairier and Scarier* (3:07); *Wrath of the Torrington Worm* (3:08); *The Warlock Returns* (3:09); *Return of the Imaginary Friend* (3:10); *Night of the Scarecrow* (3:11); *The House of Zombies* (3:12); *Rise of the Secret Society* (3:13); *Day of the Shadows: Part 1* (3:14); *Day of the Shadows: Part 2* (3:15); *Return of the Djinni* (3:16); *Tale of the Enchanted Keys* (3:17); *All I Want for X-Mas* (3:18); *Lovespell from the Underworld* (3:19); *Journey Into Terrorland* (3:20); *Curse of the Six-String Serenade* (3:21); *Wrath of the Venus Flytrap* (3:22); *Pirates of Doom* (3:23); *Rage of the Leprechaun* (3:24); *It's Alive: Part 1* (3:25); *It's Alive: Part 2* (3:26).

The Master Mystery [Film Serial; Novel]

[Film Serial] Premiere: November 18, 1918; Main Cast: Houdini as Quentin Locke, Marguerite Marsh as Eva Brent, Ruth Stonehouse as Zita Dane, Edna Britton as De Luxe Dora, William Pike as Paul Balcom, Charles E. Graham as Herbert Balcom, Floyd Buckley as Q the Automaton, Jack Burns as Peter Brent; Producer: B.A. Rolfe; Story: Arthur B. Reeve, Charles A, Logue; Directors: Harry Grossman, Burton King; 330 min. approx.; B.A. Rolfe Productions; Octagon Films, Inc.; Silent; b/w.

International Patents Inc. is a firm whose vast fortune has been made by inducing inventors to trust the marketing of inventions to their care. After obtaining sole rights they suppress the manufacture of the inventions much to the financial gain of the owners of the already existing patents. Federal agent Quentin Locke, working for the Department of Justice, infiltrates the firm working undercover as an employee but must contend with Q the Automaton guided by a human brain and the Madagascan Madness gas which makes its victims laugh uncontrollably.

The serial highlights Harry Houdini's skills as an escape artist as Quentin Locke finds himself in various physical constraints in each episode.

Chapter Titles: 1. *Living Death*; 2. *The Iron*

***The Master Mystery* (1918), film serial starring (Harry) Houdini as Quentin Locke and Marguerite Marsh as Eva Brent (Octagon Films).**

Terror; 3. *The Water Peril*; 4. *The Test*; 5. *The Chemist's Shop*; 6. *The Mad Genius*; 7. *Barbed Wire*; 8. *The Challenge*; 9. *The Madagascan Madness*; 10. *The Binding Ring*; 11. *The Net*; 12. *The Death Noose*; 13. *The Flash of Death*; 14. *The Tangled Web*; 15. *Bound at Last or The Unmasking of the Automaton*.

[Novel] Authors: Arthur B. Reeve and John W. Grey; From Scenarios by Arthur B. Reeve in collaboration with John W. Grey and C.A. Logue; Publisher: New York: Grosset & Dunlap, 1919.

The novelization of the film includes a detailed description of the automaton.

"Suddenly came a dull metallic clank through the passage, strangely echoing. At once all leaped to their feet, at attention, not unmixed with awe and fear that sat strangely on their desperate features. What was it that they, who feared neither God nor man, feared?

They strained their eyes, looking into the passage that led darkly away into blackness.

Dimly down it now could be seen two gleaming spots of light, points in the Cimmerian darkness. They seemed to be growing larger and coming nearer as with each hollow reverberation the dull metallic thuds increased.

Faintly now could be made out in the blackness a huge, stalking figure, having the shape of a man, with gigantic, powerful shoulders, powerful arms, a thick body, hips, and thighs that spelled terrific strength, legs and feet that suggested irresistible force.

"'The Automaton!' escaped involuntarily from all lips.

Slowly, irresistibly, the horrendous figure stalked forth into the dim light. There it paused for a moment—a figure of steel, larger than most men, yet not so large but that it might have incased a man. And yet its motions, its every action, were like nothing mortal. Even these hardened denizens of the underworld shuddered."

Medium (2005) [TV series]
Premiere: January 3, 2005; Main Cast: Patricia Arquette as Allison DuBois, Jake Weber as Joe Dubois, Miguel Sandoval as D.A. Manuel Devalos, David Cubitt as Detective Lee Scanlon, Sofia Vassilieva as Ariel Dubois, Maria Lark as Bridgette Dubois, Miranda Carabello/Madison Carabello as Marie Dubois; Executive Producers: Glenn Gordon Caron, Kelsey Grammar, Ronald L. Schwary, Steve Stark; Creator: Glenn Gordon Caron; 130 × 45 min.; Picturemaker Productions; Grammnet Productions; Paramount Network Television; CBS Television Studios; Pointe Studios; National Broadcasting Company (NBC); Columbia Broadcasting System (CBS); Color.

In the pilot episode we are introduced to wife, mother of two young daughters and law intern Allison DuBois. When she begins to see visions of crime scenes in her dreams and spirits of the dead in her waking life Allison becomes uncomfortable. She just wants to be a normal law student with a normal family life. Attracting the attention of the Texas Rangers in the case of a missing child DuBois' psychic talents are met with hostility. But her talents are recognized by the District Attorney who hires DuBois as a consultant.

In later episodes DuBois often works alongside skeptical Detective Lee Scanlon. Her psychic gifts create conflict and frustration within DuBois and balancing her job with her family life is often a struggle.

The character of Allison DuBois is based on the real-life medium of the same name who worked as a consultant on the series. In an interview for *Sci Fi Weekly* (January 3, 2005) actress Patricia Arquette stated, "The way I play Allison ... is a little different from the real Allison. I'm more self-doubting and skeptical of myself." Allison DuBois responded, "I actually encourage people to be skeptical, and I think you can be a skeptic and watch it."

SEASON ONE

Pilot (1:01); *Suspicions and Certainties* (1:02); *A Couple of Choices* (1:03); *Night of the Wolf* (1:04); *In Sickness and Adultery* (1:05); *Coming Soon* (1:06); *Jump Start* (1:07); *Lucky* (1:08); *Coded* (1:09); *The Other Side of the Tracks* (1:10); *I Married a Mind Reader* (1:11); *A Priest, a Doctor and a Medium Walk into an Execution Chamber* (1:12); *Being Mrs. O'Leary's Cow* (1:13); *In the Rough* (1:14); *Penny for Your*

Thoughts (1:15); When Push Comes to Shove (Part I) (1:16).

Season Two

When Push Comes to Shove (Part II) (2:01); The Song Remains the Same (2:02); Time Out of Mind (2:03); Light Sleeper (2:04); Sweet Dreams (2:05); Dead Aim (2:06); Judge, Jury & Executioner (2:07); Too Close to Call (2:08); Still Life (2:09); The Reckoning (2:10); Method to His Madness (2:11); Doctor's Orders (2:12); Raising Cain (2:13); A Changed Man (2:14); Sweet Child O' Mine (2:15); Allison Wonderland (2:16); Lucky in Love (2:17); S.O.S. (2:18); Knowing Her (2:19); The Darkness is Light Enough (2:20); Death Takes a Policy (2:21); Twice Upon a Time (2:22).

Season Three

Four Dreams (Part I) (3:01); Four Dreams (Part II) (3:02); Be Kind, Rewind (3:03); Blood Relations (3:04); Ghost in the Machine (3:05); Profiles in Terror (3:06); Mother's Little Helper (3:07); The Whole Truth (3:08); Better Off Dead (3:09); Very Merry Maggie (3:10); Apocalypse Push (3:11); The One Behind the Wheel (3:12); Second Opinion (3:13); We Had a Dream (3:14); The Boy Next Door (3:15); Whatever Possessed You (3:16); Joe Day Afternoon (3:17); 1–900-Lucky (3:18); No One to Watch Over Me (3:19); Head Games (3:20); Heads Will Roll (3:21); Everything Comes to a Head (3:22).

Season Four

About Then (4:01); But for the Grace of God (4:02); To Have and to Hold (4:03); Do You Hear What I Hear? (4:04); Girls Ain't Nothing But Trouble (4:05); Aftertaste (4:06); Burn, Baby Burn (Part I) (4:07); Burn, Baby Burn (Part II) (4:08); Wicked Game (Part I) (4:09); Wicked Game (Part II) (4:10); Lady Killer (4:11); Partners in Crime (4:12); A Cure For What Ails You (4:13); Car Trouble (4:14); Being Joey Carmichael (4:15); Drowned World (4:16).

Season Five

Soul Survivor (5:01); Things to Do in Phoenix When You're Dead (5:02); A Person of Interest (5:03); About Last Night (5:04); A Taste of Her Own Medicine (5:05); Apocalypse, Now? (5:06); A Necessary Evil (5:07); Truth Be Told (5:08); All in the Family (5:09); Then and Again (5:10); The Devil Inside (Part I) (5:11); The Devil Inside (Part II) (5:12); How to Make a Killing in Big Business (Part I) (5:13); How to Make a Killing in Big Business (Part II) (5:14); How to Make a Killing in Big Business (Part III) (5:15); The Man in the Mirror (5:16); The First Bite is the Deepest (5:17); The Talented Ms. Boddicker (5:18); Bring Me the Head of Oswaldo Castillo (5:19).

Season Six

Déjà Vu All Over Again (6:01); Who's That Girl? (6:02); Pain Killer (6:03); The Medium is the Message (6:04); Baby Fever (6:05); Bite Me (6:06); New Terrain (6:07); Once in a Lifetime (6:08); The Future's So Bright (6:09); You Give Me Fever (6:10); An Everlasting Love (6:11); Dear Dad (6:12); Psych (6:13); Will the Real Fred Rovick Please Stand Up? (6:14); How to Beat a Bad Guy (6:15); Allison Rolen Got Married (6:16); There Will Be Blood: Type A (Part I) (6:17); There Will Be Blood: Type B (Part II) (6:18); Sal (6:19); Time Keeps on Slipping (6:20); Dead Meat (6:21); It's a Wonderful Death (6:22).

Season Seven

Bring Your Daughter to Work Day (7:01); The Match Game (7:02); Means and Ends (7:03); How to Kill a Good Guy (7:04); Talk to the Hand (7:05); Where Were You When? (7:06); Native Tongue (7:07); Smoke Damage (7:08); The People in Your Neighborhood (7:09); Blood on the Tracks (7:10); Only Half Lucky (7:11); Labor Pains (7:12); Me Without You (7:13).

Millennium (1996) [TV series]
Premiere: October 25, 1996; Main Cast: Lance Henriksen as Frank Black, Megan Gallagher as Catherine Black, Terry O'Quinn as Peter Watts, Brittany Tiplady as Jordan Black, Klea Scott as Agent Emma Hollis, Stephen J. Lang as Detective Bob Giebelhouse; Executive Producers: Chris Carter, Chip Johannessen, Glen Morgan, James Wong, Michael Duggan; Creator: Chris Carter; 67 × 45 min.; 20th Century–Fox Television; Ten Thirteen Productions; Fox Network; Color.

Former FBI profiler agent Frank Black works as a consultant for the private investigation organization based in Seattle known as the Millennium Group. He has a special ability to see inside the minds of criminals and serial killers. Black's time with the Millennium Group is short-lived when his wife dies from a virus created by the group who have an apocalyptic agenda. Returning to the FBI he works alongside partner Emma Hollis. His daughter Jordan has inherited some of her father's psychic abilities, despite his initially claiming to have no paranormal gifts.

Following the conclusion of the series Frank Black makes one final appearance in *The X-Files* episode *Millennium* (7:04).

SEASON ONE

Pilot (1:01); *Gehenna* (1:02); *Dead Letters* (1:03); *The Judge* (1:04); *5-2-2-6-6-6* (1:05); *Kingdom Come* (1:06); *Blood Relatives* (1:07); *The Well-Worn Lock* (1:08); *Wide Open* (1:09); *The Wild and the Innocent* (1:10); *Weeds* (1:11); *Loin Like a Hunting Flame* (1:12); *Force Majeure* (1:13); *The Thin White Line* (1:14); *Sacrament* (1:15); *Covenant* (1:16); *Walkabout* (1:17); *Lamentation* (1:18); *Powers, Principalities, Thrones and Dominions* (1:19); *Broken World* (1:20); *Maranatha* (1:21); *Paper Dove* (1:22).

SEASON TWO

The Beginning and the End (2:01); *Beware of the Dog* (2:02); *Sense and Antisense* (2:03); *Monster* (2:04); *A Single Blade of Grass* (2:05); *The Curse of Frank Black* (2:06); *19:19* (2:07); *The Hand of Saint Sebastian* (2:08); *Jose Chung's 'Doomsday Defense'* (2:09); *Midnight of the Century* (2:10); *Goodbye Charlie* (2:11); *Luminary* (2:12); *The Mikado* (2:13); *The Pest House* (2:14); *Owls* (2:15); *Roosters* (2:16); *Siren* (2:17); *In Arcadia Ego* (2:18); *Anamnesis* (2:19); *A Room with No View* (2:20); *Somehow, Satan Got Behind Me* (2:21); *The Fourth Horseman* (2:22); *The Time is Now* (2:23).

SEASON THREE

The Innocents (3:01); *Exegesis* (3:02); *TEOTWAWKI* (3:03); *Closure* (3:04); *…Thirteen Years Later* (3:05); *Skull and Bones* (3:06); *Through a Glass Darkly* (3:07); *Human Essence* (3:08); *Omerta* (3:09); *Borrowed Time* (3:10); *Collateral Damage* (3:11); *The Sound of Snow* (3:12); *Antipas* (3:13); *Matryoshka* (3:14); *Forcing the End* (3:15); *Saturn Dreaming of Mercury* (3:16); *Darwin's Eye* (3:17); *Bardo Thodol* (3:18); *Seven and One* (3:19); *Nostalgia* (3:20); *Via Dolorosa* (3:21); *Goodbye to All That* (3:22).

Mistry, P.I. [Comic book]

First publication: July 2015; Five-part mini-series; Story: Ashwan Pande; Art: Arjuna Susini; Publisher: Graphic India.

Indian paranormal investigators for hire Darius Mistry and his friend Amos Golem work in the underworld of the supernatural. Their cases include a female ghost who hires the sleuths to solve her own murder, recovering the soul of the police commissioner's daughter from soul smugglers and stopping the citywide destruction of the demon Ahrimaan and his colossal metal golem.

Mona the Vampire (1999) [Animated TV series]

Premiere: September 13, 1999; Voice Cast: Emma Taylor-Isherwood as Mona Parker, Carrie Finlay as Lily "Princess Giant" Duncan, Justin Bradley/Evan Smirnow as Charley Bones, Tia Caroleo as Angela Smith, Jennifer Seguin as Miss Gotto, Al Gravelle as Big Al; Executive Producers: Ian Lewis, Micheline Charest, Ronald A. Weinberg, Steven Ching, David Ferguson, Peter Moss, Louis Fournier; Based on the books by Sonia Holleyman and Hiawyn Oram; 65 × 23 min.; Gaumont-Alphanim; Cinar; Color.

Ten-year-old Mona Parker is "an ordinary girl in an extraordinary world" who loves to dress as a vampire and solve supernatural mysteries with her pet cat Fang.

Moon of the Wolf (1972) [Telefilm]

Premiere: September 26, 1972; Main Cast: David Janssen as Sheriff Aaron Whitaker, Barbara Rush as Louis Rodanthe, Bradford Dillman as Andrew Rodanthe, John Beradino as Dr. Druten, Geoffrey Lewis as Lawrence Burrifors; Executive Producer: Edward S. Feldman; Teleplay: Alvin Sapinsley; Based on the novel by Leslie H. Whitten; Director: Daniel Petrie; 75 min.; Filmways; Color.

Investigating the savage murder of a pregnant young woman, Louisiana bayou Sheriff Whitaker uncovers a dark secret connecting a member of the Rodanthe family to a case of lycanthropy.

Moonlight (2007) [TV series]

Premiere: September 28, 2007; Main Cast: Alex O'Loughlin as Mick St. John, Sophia Miles as Beth Turner, Jason Dohring as Josef Kostan, Shannyn Sossamon as Coraline/Morgan, Chris Krauser as Guard, Tami Roman as Maureen 'Mo' Williams, Brian White as Lt. Carl Davis, Jordan Belfi as Josh Lindsey; Executive Producers: Gerard Bocaccio, Ron Koslow, Joel Silver, Rod Holcomb, Chip Johannessen, David Greenwalt; Creators: Ron Koslow, Trevor Munson; 16 × 43 min.; Silver Pictures Television, Warner Bros. Television; CBS; Color.

Mick St. John, working out of Los Angeles as a private investigator, has a secret. On his wedding night he was transformed into a vampire by his bride, but rather than seek out victims for their blood he has chosen to solve crimes. His romantic feelings toward reporter Beth Turner are a source of conflict knowing vampires and humans don't make for compatible partners. And his life is further complicated when he encounters a woman who looks exactly like his former vampire wife Coraline but appears to be human.

The stories feature vampires who can tolerate limited sunlight, have psychic abilities and are immune to the traditional garlic and holy relics. Only decapitation and fire can destroy them.

SEASON ONE

No Such Thing as Vampires (1:01); *Out of the Past* (1:02); *Dr. Feelgood* (1:03); *Fever* (1:04); *Arrested Development* (1:05); *B.C.* (1:06); *The Ringer* (1:07); *12:04 AM* (1:08); *Fleur De Lis* (1:09); *Sleeping Beauty* (1:10); *Love Lasts Forever* (1:11); *The Mortal Cure* (1:12); *Fated to Pretend* (1:13); *Click* (1:14); *What's Left Behind* (1:15); *Sonata* (1:16).

Moris Klaw (Short story character)

First appearance: *The New Magazine* (April 1913); Author: Sax Rohmer.

Psychic detective Moris Klaw made his debut in the short story, "The Case of the Tragedies in the Greek Room" (1913). The owner of a dilapidated antique store in Wapping, Klaw is described in detail by Mr. Searles, the narrator of his stories.

"A tall man who stooped ... a very old man who carried his many years lightly; or a younger man prematurely aged; none could say which. His skin, brows, his scanty beard were so toneless as to defy classification in terms of color. He wore an archaic brown bowler, smart, gold rimmed pince-nez and a black silk muffler. A long, caped black cloak completely enveloped the stooping figure; from beneath its mud-splattered edge peeped long-toed continental boots."

Arriving at the scene of a murder Klaw requests that he spend the night sleeping on the floor at the spot where the victim was slain. Klaw talks of "the odic force" which he claims, "carries the message ... the supreme thought preceding death" which is "imprinted on the surrounding atmosphere, like a photograph." With the help of his "odically sterilized" pillow Klaw can reach the victim's final, unpolluted mental emotion.

Helping Klaw in his detection work is his beautiful daughter, Isis, who possesses a charming French accent.

Moris Klaw short stories by Sax Rohmer: "The Potsherd of Anibis" (May 1913); "The Crusader's Ax" (June 1913); "The Ivory Statue" (July 1913); "The Blue Rajah" (August 1913); "The Whispering Poplars" (September 1913); "The Chord in G" (October 1913); "The Headless Mummies" (November 1913); "The Haunting of Grange" (December 1913); "The Case of the Veil of Isis" (January 1914).

Morris and Chastain Supernatural Investigations [Book series]

First publication: 2009; Author: Justin Gustainis; Publisher: Nottingham: Solaris.

Texan occult investigator Quincey Harker Morris is the great-grandson of Dracula's killer. Helping him in his paranormal investigations

Moris Klaw in "The Mysteries of the Greek Room" published in the *Washington Herald*, Sunday, October 24, 1915 (author's personal collection).

is white witch Elizabeth "Libby" Catherine Chastain. Assisting Morris and Chastain in their cases are two Special Agents in the FBI Behavioral Science Section, Dale Fenton and Colleen O'Donnell. Their cases range from Salem witch family curses to a demon possessed U.S. Senator to stopping a deadly djinn striking at the heart of America.

Morris and Chastain novels: *Black Magic Woman* (2011); *Evil Ways* (2011); *Sympathy for the Devil* (2011); *Play with Fire* (2012); *Midnight at the Oasis* (2013)

The Mothman Prophecies (2002) [Film]

Premiere: January 25, 2002; Main Cast: Richard Gere as John Klein, Debra Messing as Mary Klein, Laura Linney as Connie Mills, Will Patton as Gordon Smallwood, Lucinda Jenney as Denise Smallwood, Yvonne Erickson as Dr. McElroy, David Eigenberg as Ed Fleischman, Bob Tracey as Cyrus Bills; Executive Producers: Terry A. McKay, Ted Tannebaum, Richard S. Wright; Screenplay: Richard Hatem; Based on the novel by John A. Keel; Director: Mark Pellington; 119 min.; Lakeshore Entertainment; Sony Pictures Entertainment (SPE); Color.

Investigative reporter John Klein investigates a weird creature known as the Mothman following the death of his wife in a car accident. In Point Pleasant the mystery of the Mothman deepens as Klein learns the creature's appearances point to future disasters. And one of those disasters is about to claim many lives in Point Pleasant.

Muhyo and Roji's Bureau of Supernatural Investigation (2018) [Anime; Manga; Japan]

Premiere: August 3, 2018; Voice Cast: Ayumi Murase as Toru Muhyo, Yuu Hayashi as Jirou "Roji" Kusano, Hiroshi Kamiya as Soratsugu Madoka, Iori Nomizu as Nana Takenouchi, Mitsuki Saiga as ReikorImai; Creator: Yoshiyuki Nishi; Animation Directors: Hiromi Matsushita, Kazuko Tadano; Director: Nobuhiro Kondou; 12 × 23 min.; Studio Deen; Animax; Bandai Namco Arts; JY Animation; Muhyoroji Production Committee; Color.

Youngsters Turo Muhyo and Jirou "Roji" Kusano, experts in Magic Law, work out of the "Muhyo Bureau of Supernatural Investigations." Muhyo acts as the Executor and chief exorcist. Roji is his less than confident assistant. In their first case high school student Inoue Rie seeks the help of Muhyo and Roji. Track 5 at Hashiki train station is haunted by the vengeful spirit of Rie's former best friend Taeko. Rie feels responsible for her death and seeks peace for Taeko's spirit.

First Season

Rie and Taeko (1:01); *Kenji and Nana* (1:02); *Talent* (1:03); *Omen* (1:04); *Insanity* (1:05); *The Butterfly of the Night* (1:06); *Magic Prison* (1:07); *Becoming Someone Else* (1:08); *Sophie* (1:09); (1:10); (1:11); (1:12).

[Manga] First publication: *Weekly Shonen Jump* (November 29, 2004); Story-Art: Yoshiyuki Nishi; Publisher: Shueisha.

The inspiration for the anime TV series ran to 18 volumes.

Murdered: Soul Suspect [Video game]

Release date: June 3, 2014; Voice Cast: Jason Brooks as Ronan O'Connor, Cassidy Lehrman as Joy Foster, Travis Willingham as Javier 'Rex' Reyes, Tiffany Espensen/Laura Harrison as Abigail Williams, Hannah Telle as Iris Campbell/Rose Campbell, Bruno Amato as Baxter, Steve Braun as Officer Robinson, Tim DeZarn as Officer Stewart/Father McCauley, Don Fischer as Officer Broyles/Priest, Producer: Naoto Sugiyama; Writers: Chris Faiella, Anna Megill; Director: Yosuke Shiokawa; Developer: Airtight Games; Platforms: Windows, PS3, PS4, Xbox One; Xbox 360; Perspective: 3rd-Person; Publisher: Square Enix.

When Salem police detective Ronan O'Connor is murdered by the serial killer known as the Bell Killer, he finds himself trapped in the limbo of the "Dusk." Now he must discover the identity of his killer so he can be released into the after-life where his wife Julia awaits.

The player navigates the ghost of Ronan through various levels as he searches for his killer by collecting clues in the town of Salem, Massachusetts.

Murdoch Mysteries a.k.a. ***The Artful Detective*** (2008) [TV Series; Canada-UK]

Premiere: January 24, 2008; Main Cast: Yannick Bisson as Detective William Murdoch, Helene Joy as Dr. Julia Ogden, Thomas Craig as Inspector Thomas Brackenreid, Jonny Harris as Constable George Crabtree, Lachlan Murdoch as Constable Henry Higgins, Georgina Reilly as Dr. Emily Grace, Arwen Humphreys as Margaret Brackenreid; Executive Producers: Christina Jennings, Scott Garvie, Peter Mitchell, Yannick Bisson, Noel Hedges, Samantha McMillon, Cal Coons, Kate Barnes, Philip Bedard, Larry Lalonde, David Clarke, Richard Life; Creator: Maureen Jennings; Developers: Alexandra Zarowny, Cal Coons, Bob Carney; 189 × 48 min.; Shaftesbury Films; Bell Broadcast and New Media Fund; ITV; Citytv; Canadian Broadcasting Corporation (CBC); Color.

Initially set in the 1890s police Detective William Murdoch is also an inventor who tackles crime with a scientific approach. He is often accompanied by Constable George Crabtree who prefers to view crimes with an open mind that wanders into fantasy which he expresses in his self-published books. Dr. Julia Ogden is the coroner who eventually becomes Murdoch's wife. In charge of the station house is the down-to-earth Inspector Brackenreid originally from Yorkshire, England who is henpecked by his wife Margaret.

The following is a sample of episodes that feature supernatural or paranormal themes.

"Elementary, My Dear Murdoch" (1:04)

Air date: February 14, 2008; Guest Cast: Geraint Wyn Davies as Arthur Conan Doyle, Maria Del Mar as Sarah Pensell, Dan Lett as Fredrick Waters, Tom Barnett as Conrad Hunt, Kerry Ann Doherty as Ida Winston, Natalie Roy as Liza; Story: Jason Sherman; Director: Don McBrearty.

Arthur Conan Doyle is in Toronto promoting spiritualism when the medium Sarah Pensell appears to locate the body of a recently murdered woman. A skeptical Murdoch is moved when the medium contacts his deceased girlfriend Liza.

"Werewolves" (2:12)

Air date: May 20, 2009; Guest Cast: Nathaniel Arcand as Jimmy McLeod, Sarah Allen as Enid Jones, Dakota Goyo as Alwyn Jones, Paul Amos as Dr. Roberts, Jeff Douglas as Reginald Poundsett, Paul Essiembre as Jacob Summers, Hamish McEwan as Frank Jenson; Story: Paul Aitken; Director: Kelly Makin.

When corpses turn up with their throats torn to shreds Constable Crabtree suspects a werewolf may be on the rampage.

"Bloodlust" (4:11)

Air date: August 17, 2011; Guest Cast: Jonathan Watton as Dr. Darcy Garland, Ephraim Ellis as Paddy Glenn, Leah Pinsett as Mrs. Irvin, Holly Deveaux as Arlene Dennet, Kyle Mac as Daniel Irvin, Britanny Bristow as Lara McFarlane, Vivien Endicott-Douglas as Olivia Cornell, Hannah Endicott-Douglas as Dorothy Cornell, Sarah Grey as Amy Goldham, Scott Wentworth as Dr. Harwick; Teleplay: Paul Aitken, Graham Clegg, Phil Bedard, Larry Lalonde; Director: Gail Harvey.

A young female student is discovered drowned in a school fountain with two bite marks on her neck and the loss of three pints of blood. Constable Crabtree's theory of a vampire appears to be confirmed when other female students tell Murdoch they have been willingly meeting an attractive vampire each night.

"Evil Eye of Egypt" (5:03)

Air date: June 21, 2012; Guest Cast: Aidan Devine as Desmond Rutherford, Athena Karkanis as Dr. Iris Bajjali, Julian Richings as Phillip Uxbridge, Keon Mohajeri as Fouad Sharif, Jill Frappier as Mrs. Xavier McAllister, Mike Petersen as Professor Alger Greenwood; Story: Michelle Ricci; Director: Don McCuthcheon.

Constable Crabtree believes a mummy's curse may be behind a series of deaths that coincide with an exhibition of Egyptian antiquities.

"Staircase to Heaven" (5.10)

Air date: August 7, 2012; Guest Cast: Christopher Jacot as Russell Chisholm, Victor

A. Young as Magnus MacDonald, Deborah Odell as Hannah Beaumont, Kate Ross as Fanny Glover, Evert Houston as Jacob Oliver, Jamie Robinson as Ned Watts, Peter Graham-Gaudreau as Randall the Razor; Story: Peter Mitchell; Director: Harvey Crossland.

Murdoch discovers that Dr. Emily Grace and her friends have been involved in a dangerous card game. Inducing temporary death in the hope of experiencing the afterlife before returning the person to life. But one of the players has been murdered.

"The Ghost of Queen's Park" (6:07)

Air date: February 25, 2013; Guest Cast: Chris Britton as Thaddeus Walsh, Drew Carnwatch as Samuel Jenkins, Keith Kemps as Professor Paul Monteith, Taylor Trowbridge as Lorraine Monteith, Les Carlson as Dr. Ansel Fraser, Lynne Deragon as Mrs. Imogene Fraser, Robert Clarke as Howard Biggs; Story; Lori Spring; Director: Harvey Crossland.

When Howard Briggs, the guard at Queen's Park blames a ghost for the death of politician Reginald Chilton, Constable Crabtree sees an opportunity for some ghost hunting with Dr. Emily Grace.

The Mystery of the Blazing Cliffs (The Three Investigators Mystery Series #32) [Juvenile book]

Author: M.V. Carey; Based on characters created by Robert Arthur; First publication: New York: Random House, 1981.

Wealthy Charles Barron, owner of Rancho Valverde, believes aliens are about to transport him to another planet. Even the President of the United States has acknowledged their presence. The Three Investigators must prove if the claims of UFO's and aliens are true or a part of an elaborate hoax.

Murdoch Mysteries (2008), starring (left to right) Thomas Craig as Inspector Thomas Brackenreid, Yannick Bisson as Detective William Murdoch, Helene Joy as Dr. Julia Ogden, and Jonny Harris as Constable George Crabtree (CBC).

The Mystery of the Coughing Dragon
(Alfred Hitchcock and the Three Investigators Book #14) [Juvenile book]

Author: Nick West (Kin Platt); Based on characters created by Robert Arthur; Illustrator: Harry Kane; First publication: New York: Random House, 1970.

The Three Investigators are hired to find a missing dog, supposedly eaten by a dragon according to Henry Allen, the dog's owner. The clues lead the boy detectives to hidden caves and an abandoned underground railway before confronting the coughing dragon.

The Mystery of the Cranky Collector
(The Three Investigators Mystery Series #43) [Juvenile book]

Author: M.V. Carey; Based on characters created by Robert Arthur; First publication: New York: Random House, 1987.

The Three Investigators attempt to discover why a mean-spirited book collector has disappeared and find a ghost who returns to haunt an employer's mansion.

The final book in the long-running series.

The Mystery of the Dancing Devil
(Alfred Hitchcock and the Three Investigators Book #25) [Juvenile book]

Author: William Arden (Dennis Lynds); Based on characters created by Robert Arthur; Illustrator: Jack Hearne; First publication: New York: Random House, 1976.

During their search for a stolen statue that belongs to the Chinese government the Three Investigators come to realize the "dancing devil" statue must be protected by a guardian spirit.

"The Mystery the Djara Singh: A Spiritual Detective Story" [Short story]

Author: Alexander M. Reynolds; Illustrator: D.J. Blakistan; First publication: *Overland Monthly* Vol. 30 #179 (November 1897).

A series of high-profile bank robberies in New York City coincides with the arrival of Tibetan prince Djara Singh. A bank clerk recalls, "…he had seen a gold coin in a tray vanish before his eyes." A dumbfounded Chief of police is assigned to the case.

One morning the Chief greets the professor of Oriental Philosophies at Columbia College. He informs the Chief of occult practices by Orientals who have "the power of not only freeing the spirit from the body, but also of dissolving into their original etheric atoms, many forms of matter. A vault would not be the slightest protection against such a being, who could enter where he willed, after dissolving into its etheric elements such as gold as he desired, carry it off, to be returned to its original form."

The Chief discovers similar robberies occurred when the prince stayed in London and that despite his reported lack of wealth he was living in luxury. Now he has news of a new bank robbery at the Bartholdi Bank in New York where "a tray of gold, containing something over seven thousand dollars, had mysteriously disappeared."

The Chief decides to visit Djara Singh at the Hotel Riche where he finds him. "ghastly pale and apparently in a deep sleep." Frustrated by his investigations the detective realizes there is no way "by which a warrant could be served upon a spook." He must find a way to capture the spirit. Consulting the spiritualist and fortune-teller known as "The Peerless Colonna" the Chief knows he possesses some spiritual gifts despite being a charlatan. Colonna agrees to help track Singh using his astral body. "I am perfectly willing to enter your service as a 'spiritual detective.'"

Colonna prepares for his task fasting for thirty days on public view at the New Anatomical Museum. But into the fast the state of his body alarms the medical staff and is examined. It is pronounced that "the unfortunate man had been dead for two days." Following the news of the death Djara Singh announces his departure from New York City. The bank robberies cease. Sometime later the Chief receives a letter from Japan cautioning the Chief not to experiment with forces he doesn't know the power of and to recognize the strength of the opposition.

The Chief of police is currently "studying occult philosophy and speculating upon the advisability of introducing into the police department a corps of trained spiritualists."

The Mystery of the Green Ghost (Alfred Hitchcock and the Three Investigators Book #4) [Juvenile book]

Author: Robert Arthur; Illustrator: Harry Kane; First publication: New York: Random House, 1965.

A green ghost is seen at a house due for demolition and at various sites around town including the grave of Mathias Green. The Three Investigators decide to search the house where Mathias Green died long ago and discover the grinning skeleton of Green's wife wearing Chinese Ghost Pearls. Pete Crenshaw and Bob Andrews investigate further when the pearls disappear but soon find themselves in greater danger. Jupiter Jones must discover why Pete, Bob and Chang, the nephew of the woman who inherited the house have gone missing.

The Mystery of the Invisible Dog (Alfred Hitchcock and the Three Investigators Book #23) [Juvenile book]

Author: M.V. Carey; Based on characters created by Robert Arthur; Illustrator: Jack Hearne; First publication: New York: Random House, 1975.

While investigating a haunted house a burglar steals an expensive crystal sculpture of a Carpathian Hound belonging to Fenton Prentice. The Three Investigators are hired to retrieve the sculpture and encounter the ghost of a parish priest and a mysterious mystic who can walk through walls in their astral body while asleep.

The Mystery of the Magic Circle (Alfred Hitchcock and the Three Investigators Book #27) [Juvenile book]

Author: M.V. Carey; Based on characters created by Robert Arthur; Illustrator: Jack Hearne; First publication: New York: Random House, 1978.

The Three Investigators are teenage amateur detectives Jupiter Jones, Pete Crenshaw and Bob Andrews working out of Rocky Beach, California, located near Hollywood.

In their latest case the sleuths encounter a witch performing secret rites and agonizing over an accident from times past that may have been murder by magic.

The Mystery of the Monster Mountain (Alfred Hitchcock and the Three Investigators Book #20) [Juvenile book]

Author: M.V. Carey; Based on characters created by Robert Arthur; Illustrator: Jack Hearne; First publication: New York: Random House, 1973.

On a camping trip the Three Investigators explore the legend of Monster Mountain and discover Bigfoot.

The Mystery of the Scar-Faced Beggar (The Three Investigators Mystery Series #31) [Juvenile book]

Author: M.V. Carey; Based on characters created by Robert Arthur; First publication: New York: Random House, 1981.

Mrs. Denicola has dreams of future and past events in this case involving a blind scar-faced beggar who loses his wallet outside a bank that is being robbed. But when the Three Investigators attempt to track him down the sleuths find themselves confronting terrorists.

With the death of Alfred Hitchcock in 1980 the series dropped his name from the title. In this story the Three Investigators acknowledge Hitchcock's real-life death and introduce the fictional Hector Sebastian as Hitchcock's replacement.

The Mystery of the Singing Serpent (Alfred Hitchcock and the Three Investigators Book #17) [Juvenile book]

Author: M.V. Carey; Based on characters created by Robert Arthur; Illustrator: Ed Vebell; First publication: New York: Random House, 1972.

The Three Investigators encounter witchcraft when a neighbor's aunt joins a cult who worship snakes and can summon a singing serpent. Young Allie Jamison hires the boy sleuths to help her eccentric aunt and uncover the truth behind the cult's occult activities.

The Mystery of the Sinister Scarecrow (Alfred Hitchcock and the Three Investigators Book #29) [Juvenile book]

Author: M.V. Carey; Based on characters created by Robert Arthur; First publication: New York: Random House, 1979.

Beautiful heiress Letitia Radford is being terrorized by a ghostly scarecrow and an army of mutant ants. Nobody will believe her until the Three Investigators come to her aid. And after the scarecrow tries to behead the sleuths, they know Letitia is telling the truth.

The Mystery of the Vanishing Treasure
(Alfred Hitchcock and the Three Investigators Book #5) [Juvenile book]
Author: Robert Arthur; Illustrator: Harry Kane; First publication: New York: Random House, 1966.

A friend of film director Alfred Hitchcock asks the Three Investigators for help in solving the case of garden gnomes with fiery eyes staring into windows. Their investigations uncover a link between the gnomes and the theft of a priceless jeweled golden belt recently stolen from the local Petersen Museum.

The Mystery of the Wandering Caveman
(The Three Investigators Mystery Series #34) [Juvenile book]
Author: M.V. Carey; Based on characters created by Robert Arthur; First publication: New York: Random House, 1982.

The Three Investigators attempt to find out who stole the caveman's bones from Newt McAfee's museum. Their investigations lead them to a trio of strange and sinister scientists and an encounter with a man who should have been dead for centuries.

The Mystery of the Whispering Mummy
(Alfred Hitchcock and the Three Investigators Book #3) [Juvenile book]
Author: Robert Arthur; Illustrator: Harry Kane; First publication: New York: Random House, 1965.

The 3,000-year-old mummy Ra-Orkon has been whispering to Professor Yarborough in a strange language that may be a curse. Film director Alfred Hitchcock asks the Three Investigators to contact the Professor to find what is behind the strange whispering. Meanwhile the boys discover the mummy is connected to another case involving Mrs. Banfry's missing cat.

Mythical Detective Loki Ragnarok a.k.a. ***Matentei Loki Ragnarok*** (2003) [Anime; Japan]
Premiere: April 5, 2003; Voice Cast: Takahiro Sakurai as Loki, Yui Horie as Mayura Daidouji, Shinichiro Miki as Ryuusuke Yamino, Romi Park as Heimdall, Junko Asami as Freya; Executive Producers: Yoshihiro Hosaka, Naoki Nakamura; Story: Kenichi Kanemaki, Sakura Kinoshita; Director: Horoshi Watanabe; 26 × 24 min.; Studio Deen; MediaNet; TV Tokyo; Rakuosha; Color.

Loki, the trickster Norse god has been banished to Earth by Odin. Taking the form of a young child Loki establishes Enjanku Detective Agency to collect evil auras from human hearts, allowing him to return to his home among the gods. But various Norse gods are intent on making certain he never returns. Helping Loki at his detective agency is Mayura Daidouji, a schoolgirl who loves paranormal mysteries and Loki's assistant Ryusuke Yamino.

SEASON ONE

Presenting! The Mythical Detective! (1:01); *The Allies of Justice Are Totally Broke?!* (1:02); *The Assassin Descends* (1:03); *My Dad's a Great Detective?!* (1:04); *Challenge of the Mystery Thief, Frey!* (1:05); *The Targeted Girl* (1:06); *The Goddess Freya Awakens!* (1:07); *Onward Yamino Detective Agency?!* (1:08); *Mayura's Surefire Way to Pass Tests* (1:09); *Twilight Coffee Shop* (1:10); *Transfer Student in Love* (1:11); *The Traps of Castle Dracula* (1:12); *Fantastic Flower* (1:13); *Little Dog, Dark Dog, Black Dog* (1:14); *The Beautiful Assassins* (1:15); *Bell of Evil* (1:16); *Crashing Into Kitchen Sanctuary!* (1:17); *The Multi-Faceted Detective Appears?!* (1:18); *The Tale of Narugami's Devotion* (1:19); *The Red Shoes* (1:20); *Heimdall, God of the Dawn* (1:21); *The Goddesses' Reality* (1:22); *Summer Girl of the Lake* (1:23); *The Shadow of Solitude* (1:24); *The Dream's Final Stop* (1:25); *The Gods Depart* (1:26).

Necropath [Bengal Station Trilogy #1] [Novel]
Author: Eric Brown; First publication: Nottingham, UK: Solaris, 2008.

Jeff Vaughn is a telepath detective who

can read the minds of the dead. He works for the interstellar port Bengal Station situated over the ocean spanning India and Thailand. When Vaughn's friend overdoses on the drug Rhapsody he connects the death to the alien cult Church of the Adoration of the Chosen One. Meanwhile a psychopath is intent on killing him.

See: *Xenopath*

Neils Orsen [Short story character]
Author-Creator: Dennis Wheatley; First appearance: *Gunmen, Gallants and Ghosts*; Publisher: London: Hutchinson, 1943.

Swedish psychic detective Neils Orsen "The Ghost Hunter" aided by assistant Bruce Hemmingway investigates paranormal cases worldwide. "The Case of the Thing that Whimpered" takes place in New York City. Nightwatchmen at a warehouse are being attacked and murdered by an unknown force despite all the windows and doors being locked. One of the surviving watchmen describes hearing a curious whining sound before "the whole place seemed to dissolve."

Fiona Clyde is allegedly being haunted at Stuart Castle in "The Case of the Long Dead Lord" while "The Case of the Red-Headed Woman" sees Orsen investigate a spate of suicides in a South Kensington flat. In "The Case of the Haunted Chateau" an abandoned chateau is said to be haunted by the Vicomte de Cheterau who was crucified by peasants who rebelled against his sadistic ways during the French Revolution.

The character of Neils Orsen is based on Dennis Wheatley's real-life acquaintance Henry Dewhurst who Wheatley was convinced could foretell the future.

Neuro: Supernatural Detective a.k.a. ***Majin Tantei Nougami Neuro*** (2007) [Anime; Manga; Japan]
Premiere: October 2, 2007; Voice Cast: Takehito Koyasu as Neuro Nougami, Kana Ueda as Yako Katsuragi, Romi Park as Sai, Kouji Yusa as Eishi Sasazuka, Hiroyuki Yoshino as Shinobu Godai; Story: Ryo Tumura, Satoshi Suzuki; Director: Hiroshi Kojina; 25 × 25 min.; Madhouse; D/N/Dream Partners; NYV; Shueisha; VAP; Color.

Neuro is a demon living in the human world who feeds on the energy created by criminals. 16-year-old high school detective Yako Katsuragi teams up with Neuro to help solve the mystery behind her father's 'suicide.' Although Neuro is the real genius behind Yako's detective agency, she takes all the credit, thus ensuring Neuro maintains a low profile.

SEASON ONE

Eat (1:01); *Community* (1:02); *Poison* (1:03); *Dog* (1:04); *Office* (1:05); *Long Friends* (1:06); *Box* (1:07); *Future* (1:08); *Tie* (1:09); *Alone* (1:10); *Limelight* (1:11); *Statue* (1:12); *Sai* (1:13); *Dream-Like* (1:14); *Dragon* (1:15); *Spring* (1:16); *Chase* (1:17); *Key* (1:18); *Two* (1:19); *Woman* (1:20); *Beauty* (1:21); *Witch* (1:22); *Sai* (1:23); *Sai (Sealed)* (1:24); *Sai (Final)* (1:25).

[Manga] First publication: *Weekly Shonen Jump* (February 21, 2005); Creator: Yusei Matsui; Publisher: Shueisha.

The inspiration for the anime TV series ran to 23 volumes.

Nick Knight (1989) [Telefilm]
Premiere: August 20, 1989; Main Cast: Rick Springfield as Detective Nick Knight, John Kapelos as Detective Don Schanke, Robert Harper as Dr. Jack Brittington, Richard Fancy as Captain Brunetti, Laura Johnson as Dr. Alyce Hunter, Craig Richard Nelson as Fenner, Fran Ryan as Jeannie, Cec Verrell as Janette, Jack Murdock as Topper, Michael Nader as LaCroix, Gregory Wagrowski as Detective Jessell; Executive Producers: Barry Weitz, Roberta Becker Ziegel; Story: James Parriott, Barney Cohen; Teleplay: James Parriott; Director: Farhad Mann; 92 min.; Barry Weitz Films; Robirdie Pictures; New World Television; Columbia Broadcasting System (CBS); Color.

Detective Nick Knight is a homicide cop who drives a classic Cadillac, collects Aztec art and does his best work after dark. Now Knight is tracking a bloodthirsty killer from his past. Lacroix, the person who transformed him into a vampire many centuries ago, is using a stolen goblet to lure Knight into a confrontation that can either cure him of his vampirism or turn him to the dark side.

This failed pilot later resurfaced in 1992 with a new cast in ***Forever Knight***.

The Night Stalker (1972) [Telefilm]

Premiere: January 11, 1972; Main Cast; Darren McGavin as Carl Kolchak, Carol Lynley as Gail Foster, Simon Oakland as Tony Vincenzo, Ralph Meeker as Bernie Jenks, Claude Akins as Sheriff Warren Butcher, Charles McGraw as Police Chief Ed Masterson, Kent Smith as D. A. Tom Payne, Elisha Cook, Jr., as Mickey Crawford, Barry Atwater as Janos Skorzeny, Jordan Rhodes as Dr. O'Brien, Larry Linville as Mazurji, Stanley Adams as Fred Hurley; Producer: Dan Curtis; Teleplay: Richard Matheson; From a story by Jeff Rice; Director: John Llewellyn Moxey; 74 min.; ABC Circle Films; Dan Curtis Productions; Color.

Las Vegas showgirls are being terrorized by a serial killer who drains the blood from his victims. When Kolchak discovers blood-plasma is missing from a local hospital he links the murders to a vampire. Kolchak's editor is driven to distraction by what he views as ridiculous claims.

This highest rated telefilm at the time of broadcast spawned a second pilot, ***The Night Strangler*** and the short-lived, but influential television series. ***Kolchak: The Night Stalker***.

Nightstalkers [Comic book]

First appearance: *Ghost Rider* Vol. 3 #28 (August 1992); Publisher: Marvel Comics.

Operating as Borderline Investigations, vampire hunters Blade, Frank Drake and supernatural detective Hannibal King are the Nightstalkers. Together they fight supernatural threats. King was confined to investigations by night after he was turned into a vampire, but Dr. Strange partially cured him with a blood transfusion. King still has a thirst for blood and a zero tolerance for direct sunlight. He also possesses many paranormal talents including the ability to become a werewolf and to transform into mist. King can also regenerate, stop the aging process and operate with superhuman strength and speed.

The Night Strangler (1973) [Telefilm]

Premiere: January 16, 1973; Main Cast; Darren McGavin as Carl Kolchak, Simon Oakland as Tony Vincenzo, Jo Ann Pflug as Louise Harper, Scott Brady as Capt. Roscoe Schubert, Wally Cox as Titus Berry, Margaret Hamilton as Professor Crabtree, John Carradine as Llewellyn Crossbinder, Richard Anderson as Dr. Richard Malcolm; Producer: Dan Curtis; Teleplay: Richard Matheson; Based on characters created by Jeff Rice; Director: Dan Curtis; 74 min.; ABC Circle Films; Color.

Carl Kolchak is now working out of Seattle, investigating a series of grisly murders of young women. Kolchak uncovers similar murders going back to 1889 that lasted for a period of 18 days. Kolchak fears the same killer may still be lurking in the Seattle "underground."

Originally titled "The Time Killer" this successful second pilot resulted in the cult TV series ***Kolchak: The Night Stalker***.

Nightwalker: The Midnight Detective a.k.a. Mayonaka no Tantei Nightwalker [Video Game; Anime; Japan]

[Video Game]; Released: December 22, 1993; May 25, 2001; Developer: TomBoy; Arieroof; Platform: NEC PC98/PC 9801; Windows 2000.

[Anime] Premiere: July 8, 1998; Voice Cast: Takumi Yamazaki as Shido Tatsuhiko. Emi Shinohara as Yayoi Matsunaga, Maaya Sakamoto as Riho Yamazaki; Creator: Iyana Itsuki; Producer: Hiroaki Inoue; Directors: Kiyotoshi Sasano, Yutaka Kagawa; 12 × 25min.; AIC; Bandai Visual; Mitsubishi Corp.; BeSTACK; d-rights; Studio Gazelle; TV Tokyo; Color.

Private eye Shido Tatsuhiko, alongside NOS government agent Yayoi Matsunaga, encounters the demonic Nightbreed and the creature who made him a vampire. Teenage assistant Riho, who has a crush on Shido is jealous of his affection for Yayoi, not realizing their "affair" is based on Shido drinking Yayoi's blood.

SEASON ONE

A Visitor in the Night (1:01); *The Terms of Stardom* (1:02); *A Man on the Run* (1:03); *The

Golden Dawn (1:04); *Medicine for the Dead* (1:05); *The Bottom of A Well* (1:06); *A Mother & Her Son* (1:07); *A Soul Lost in Darkness* (1:08); *Someone Else's Face* (1:09); *Tears of an Angel* (1:10); *A Witch in the Forest* (1:11); *Eternal Darkness* (1:12).

Nocturne [Video game]

Release date: October 1999; Voice Cast: Lynn Mathis as The Stranger/Baron Samedy, Candace Evans as Elspeth "Doc" Holliday/Svetlana Lupescu, John Gait as Hiram Mottra/Scat Dazzle/Ken Rigzin/Moloch, Brazos MacDonald as Colonel Cedric Feldspar Hapscomb, Dell Johnson as Sammy "Haystack" Kayo, Jeremy Schwartz as Vincenco "Icepick" Gasparro/General Seymore Biggs; Developer: Terminal Reality; Platform: Microsoft Windows; Perspective: 3rd-Person; Publisher: Gathering of Developers.

"Spookhouse" is a secret organization founded by President Theodore Roosevelt to investigate and confront the supernatural.

The player controls the "Spookhouse" operative known as The Stranger in four cases involving the supernatural. In "Dark Reign of the Vampire King" his mission is to retrieve a potent artifact from a German castle occupied by vampires. "Tomb of the Underground God" sees The Stranger fighting a zombie outbreak in the western town of Redeye in 1931. "Windy City Massacre" is set in 1932 Chicago. The Stranger battles mobsters restored to life by a German scientist working for Al Capone. In "The House on the Edge of Hell" The Stranger finds himself part of a game devised by retired Spookhouse agent Hamilton Killian. He must survive in a mansion filled with numerous death traps and monsters.

The Norliss Tapes (1973) [Telefilm]

Premiere: February 21, 1973; Main Cast: Roy Thinnes as David Norliss, Angie Dickinson as Ellen Sterns Cort, Don Porter as Sanford Evans, Claude Akins as Sheriff Hartley, Michele Carey as Marsha Sterns, Hurd Hatfield as Charles Langdon; Executive Producer: Charles Fries; Teleplay: William F. Nolan; Director: Dan Curtis; 75 min.; Metromedia; Color.

Investigative reporter David Norliss finds himself in the grip of a demonic spirit as he explores supernatural events involving the walking dead.

A pilot that failed to sell from *Night Stalker* producer Dan Curtis.

The Nun (2018) [Film]

Premiere: September 7, 2018; Main Cast: Demian Bichir as father Burke, Taissa Farmiga as Sister Irene, Jonas Bloquet as Frenchie, Bonnie Aarons as The Nun, Ingrid Bisu as Sister Ona, Vera Farmiga as Lorraine Warren, Lili Taylor as Carolyn Perron, Charlotte Hope as Sister Victoria, Sandra Teles as Sister Ruth, Maria Obretin as Sister Abigail, Ani Sava as Sister Jessica, Lynette Gaza as Mother Superior; Executive Producers: Richard Brener, Michael Clear, Gary Dauberman, Walter Hamada, Dave Neustadter, Hans Ritter, Todd Williams; Story: James Wan, Gary Dauberman; Screenplay: Gary Dauberman; Director: Corin Hardy; 96 min.; Atomic Monster; New Line Cinema; The Safran Company; Warner Bros.; Color.

When Father Burke and novice Sister Irene are summoned by the Vatican to investigate the suicide of a nun at a Romanian monastery, they encounter a demon posing as a nun and a portal to hell.

Occult Academy a.k.a. *Seikimatsu Occult Gakuin* (2010) [Anime; Japan]

Premiere: July 6, 2010; Voice Cast: Yoko Hikasa as Maya Kumashiro, Takahiro Mizushima as Fumiaki Uchida, Ayahi Takagaki as Ami Kuroki, Hiroki Takahashi as Smile, Kana Hanazawa as Kozue Naruse, Minori Chihara as Mikaze Nakagawa, Sayuri Yahagi as Bunmeikun, Takehito Koyasu as JK, Yu Kobayashi as Chihiro Kawashima; Art Director: Yusuke Takeda; Director: Tomohiko Ito; 13 × 24 min.; Aniplex; TV Tokyo 7; Color.

The Waldstein Academy a.k.a. the Occult Academy located in Matsushiro, Nagano Prefecture, specializes in studying the paranormal in its many forms. While attending the funeral of her father, the former principal of the Academy, Maya and the students are attacked by his possessed body. Despite hating the occult Maya reluctantly teams up with a time agent from the future to find the Key of Nostradamus and prevent the dimensional rift that will destroy the Occult Academy in July 1999 and lead to the destruction of humanity.

SEASON ONE

Maya's Prophecy (1:01); *The Advent of Bunmei* (1:02); *Mikaze Blows Through* (1:03); *The Collapse of Bunmei* (1:04); *The Kozue of Summer* (1:05); *Bunmei's Distance* (1:06); *Maya's Amigo* (1:07); *Mama Ami-ya* (1:08); *Akari of Snow* (1:09); *Akari of Fireplace* (1:10); *Maya's Death* (1:11); *A Thousand Wind, the Search for Beauty* (1:12); *Maya's Bunmei* (1:13).

Occult Detective Club: Doll Cemetery a.k.a. ***Okaruto tanteidan: Shiningyou no hakaba*** (2006) [Film; Japan]

Premiere: September 12, 2006; Main Cast: Hitomi Miwa as Occult Detective Club leader, Sayaka Hosaka, Kazunori Tani; Story: Hideshi Hino; Director: Kiyoshi Yamamoto; 54 min.; Pony Canyon; Color.

A group of Japanese students create a club to study the paranormal. Nanami and Daisuke join the club out of curiosity and become involved in a case of student suicide and a cemetery of demonic dolls.

The Occult Files of Dr. Spektor (Comic book)

First appearance: *Mystery Comics Digest* #5 (July 1972); Creator: Donald F. Glut; Art: Dan Spiegle, Jesse Santos; Publisher: Western Publishing (Gold Key).

The introduction to "Cult of the Vampire" in *The Occult Files of Dr. Spektor* # 1 (May 1973): "I am Dr. Spektor … and the weird and the supernatural is my life."

Dr. Spektor investigates the supernatural with the aid of his part Sioux, part Apache secretary Lakota Rainflower. His detective work has led to encounters with werewolves, the ghost of Dr. Howard Jekyll, vampires and mummies.

O.C.T.: Occult Crimes Taskforce [Comic book]

First publication: July 2006; Four-issue mini-series; Story: David Atchison, Rosario Dawson; Art: Tony Shasteen; Publishers: 12 Gauge Comics/Image Comics.

Formed in the 1800s the covert police unit known as the Occult Crimes Taskforce (O.C.T.) is a small, elite taskforce of officers protecting Manhattan, the gateway to another realm, from

The Occult Files of Dr. Spektor # 15 (August 1975). Cover art by Jesse Santos (Gold Key-Western).

magic, monsters and witches. The force consists of human detectives and supernatural creatures known as Ceteri. The O.C.T. Officer Shield, forged from the inter-dimensional metal Firon protects members of the taskforce against magical attacks, spells and curses and allows officers to cast spells by reciting incantations.

Detective Sophia Ortiz is modeled on the likeness of actress Rosario Dawson, who co-created the comic book series.

Odd Thomas (2013) [Film]

Premiere: April 6, 2013; Main Cast: Anton Yelchin as Odd Thomas, Ashley Sommers as Penny Kalisto, Leonor Varela as Odd's Mother, Matthew Daniel Page as Harlo Anderson, Casey Messer as Pool Mom, Barney Lanning as Stevie, Nico Tortorella as Officer Simon Varner, Kyle McKeever as Officer Bern Eckles, Willem Dafoe as Chief Wyatt Porter, Addison Timlin as Stormy Llewellyn, Gugu Mbatha-Raw as Viola Peabody, Maisha Diata As Nicolina, Carmen Corley as Levanna, Jack Justice Brown as Young Odd, Robin Lanning as Young Stormy; Producers: John Baldecchi, Howard Kaplan, Stephen Sommers; Screenplay: Stephen Soomers; Based on the novel by Dean R. Koontz; Director: Stephen Sommers; 97 min.; Fusion Films; Future Films; The Sommers Company; Image Entertainment; Color.

Odd Thomas is a short-order cook in small town Pico Mundo who can see and talk to ghosts. Thomas works with Chief of Police Wyatt Porter on cases and the latest involves Fungus Bob Robertson. When he walks into Thomas' diner surrounded by ghostly bodachs who love causing misery Odd Thomas knows trouble lies ahead. When Thomas' girlfriend Stormy tells him Fungus Bob worships the Prince of Darkness it's time for Odd Thomas, Stormy and Chief Porter to put a stop to Fungus Bob's evil and murderous plans.

Out of the Shadows (2017) [Film; Australia]

Premiere: April 29, 2017; Main Cast: Kendal Rae as Katrina Hughes, Blake Northfield as Eric Hughes. Lisa Chappell as Linda Dee. Jake Ryan as Charles Winter, Goran D. Klut as Mr. Augusta, Helmut Bakaitis as Father Joe Phillips, Fiona Press as Helen. Jim Robison as Robert Long, Miyuki Lotz as Doctor Khoen, Milan Pulvermacher as Terry, Veronica Sywak as Ada Horrace, Anna Demidova as Olga Katerinovic, Madison Haley as Chloe Richardson. Barbara Hastings as Katerina's Mother; Producers: Tim Maddocks, Blake Northfield, Jim Robison; Story: Eric C. Nash; Writers: Dee McLachlan, Rena Owen; Director: Dee McLachlan; 78 min.; Bronte Pictures; Head Gear Films; Kreo Films FZ; Maddfilms; Metrol Technology; Red Hound Films; Color.

Crystal Springs, Australia. When newly-wed detective Eric Hughes and his pregnant wife Katrina move into their dream home Katrina believes malevolent supernatural forces are at work on her baby. Eric must investigate the history of the house to get to the truth.

Pall in the Family (A Family Fortune Mystery #1) [Novel]

Author: Dawn Eastman; First publication: New York: Berkley Prime Crime, 2013.

Crystal Haven, Michigan is home to numerous psychics including the Fortune family. Rose reads tarot cards; her sister Vi is a pet psychic and Rose's daughter Clyde works for the Ann Arbor police department. On leave to escape the stress of her job and reluctant to use her psychic gifts Clyde soon finds herself called into action when a local psychic is murdered. The only eyewitness is a traumatized Shih Tzu named Tuffy. Clyde's life is further complicated when she discovers her former love interest heads the murder investigation.

Book series: *Pall in the Family* (2013); *Be Careful What You Witch For* (2014); *A Fright to the Death* (2015).

Parascientific Escape: Gear Detective a.k.a. ***Chou Kagaku Dasshutsu: Gear Detective*** [Video game; Japan]

Release date: December 2, 2015; Developer: Intense; Platform: Nintendo 3DS; Perspective: 1st-Person; Publisher; Circle Entertainment.

Detective Kyosuke Ayana has the psychic ability to view up to five days back in time and manipulate the past. One day Tsukiko Nagise turns up at the Ayana Detective Agency requesting the detective investigate a serial killer who is threatening her life and stalking the Camelia Hills neighborhood.

The player employs Detective Ayana's chronokenisis using his prosthetic arm and eye to find clues and solve puzzles. He is aided by his female assistant and romantic interest Mari Sasamine and close friend Yukiya Ousaka. In the Adventure Section the player can choose from multiple endings and in the Investigation section they can use PSI to change the past.

Detective Ayana returns in *Crossing at the Farthest Horizon* (2017) where he travels to Witsarock with Mari Sasamine to meet a psychic connected to the Camelia Hills serial killer case.

Past Life (2010) [TV series]

Premiere: February 9, 2010; Main Cast: Kelli Giddish as Dr. Kate McGinn, Nic Bishop as Price Whatley, Richard Schiff as Dr. Malachi Talmadge, Ravi Patel as Dr. Rishi Karna; Executive Producers: David Hudgins, Lou Pitt; Creator: David Hudgins; Inspired by *The Reincarnationist* book series by M. J. Rose; 8 × 43 min.; Hudgins Productions; Lou Pitt Productions; Bonanza Productions Inc.; Warner Bros. Television; Fox Network; Color.

At New York's Talmadge Center for Behavioral Health past-life regression therapist Dr. Kate McGinn and cynical former NYPD homicide detective Price Whatley investigate current crimes through their patient's past-life memories. Helping them is McGinn's mentor Dr. Malachi Talmadge and Calcutta therapist Dr. Rishi Karna

The series was canceled after three episodes due to failing ratings. Five of the eight completed episodes eventually aired.

Season One

Pilot (1:01); *Dead Man Talking* (1:02); *Soul Music* (1:03); *Saint Sarah* (1:04); *Gone Daddy Gone* (1:05); *Running on Empty* (1:06); *All Fall Down* (1:07); *Regressing Henry* (1:08).

Penny Dreadful (2014) [TV series]

Premiere: April 28, 2014; Main Cast: Rory Kinnear as John Clare/The Creature/Dr. Peter Craft, Reeve Carney as Dorian Gray, Timothy Dalton as Sir Malcolm Murray, Eva Green as Vanessa Ives, Billie Piper as Lily/Brona Croft, Harry Treadway as Dr. Victor Frankenstein, Josh Harnett as Ethan Chandler, Danny Sapani as Sembene, Simon Russell Beale as Ferdinand Lyle, Douglas Hodge as Bartholomew Rusk, Sarah Greene as Hecate Poole, Olivia Llewellyn as Mina Harker, Helen McCrory as Madame Kali, Patti LuPone as Dr. Seward/Joan Clayton, Shazad Latif as Dr. Henry Jekyll; Executive Producers: Pippa Harris, John Logan, Sam Mendes, Michael Aguilar; Creator: John Logan; 27 × 60 min.; Desert Wolf Productions; Neal Street Productions; Showtime Networks; Color.

The series title refers to the 19th century British publications that were the equivalent of the American Dime Novels. Episodes feature fictitious characters from celebrated novels of the era including, Dorian Gray, Dr. Victor Frankenstein, his monster and Dr. Henry Jekyll. Also featured is Scotland Yard police inspector Bartholomew Rusk who is introduced in the premiere episode of the second season. Investigating the Mariner's Inn massacre in Victorian London, he soon deduces Ethan Hawke, who leads a double life as werewolf Ethan Lawrence Talbot, is responsible for the killings. Hawke confesses to his crimes, but escapes capture in America. Inspector Rusk assists federal marshals in hunting him down with deadly results.

Season One

Night Work (1:01); *Séance* (1:02); *Resurrection* (1:03); *Demimonde* (1:04); *Closer Than Sisters* (1:05); *What Death Can Join Together* (1:06); *Possession* (1:07); *Grand Guignol* (1:08).

Season Two

Fresh Hell (2:01); *Verbis Diablo* (2:02); *The Nightcomers* (2:03); *Evil Spirits in Heavenly Places* (2:04); *Above the Vaulted Sky* (2:05); *Glorious Horrors* (2:06); *Little Scorpion* (2:07); *Momento Mori* (2:08); *And Hell Itself My Only Foe* (2:09); *And They Were Enemies* (2:10).

Season Three

The Day Tennyson Died (3:01); *Predators Near and Far* (3:02); *Good and Evil Braided Be*

(3:03); *A Blade of Grass* (3:04); *This World Is Our Hell* (3:05); *No Beast So Fierce* (3:06); *Ebb Tide* (3:07); *Perpetual Night* (3:08); *The Blessed Dark* (3:09).

Phantom Quest Corp a.k.a. ***Yuugen Kaisha*** (1994) [OVA; Japan]

Premiere: August 25, 1994; Voice Cast: Rica Matsumoto as Ayaka Kisaragi, Kouchi Yamadera as Kozu Karina, Yoko Kawanami as Ruriko Asakaga, Naoko Watanabe as Madame Suimei, Kotono Mitsuishi as Nanami Rokugo, Koichi Yamadera as Lt. Kozo Karino, Kotono Ikura as Mamoru Shimesu; Producer: Hiroaki Inoue; Story: Mami Watanabe, Tatsuhiko Urahata, Satoshi Kimura; Directors: Morio Asaka, Kouichi Chigira, Takuji Endo; 4 × 30 min.; Madhouse; Color.

Ayaka Kisaragi and her team tackle the paranormal as the Phantom Quest Corp. Lieutenant Karino, working for the government's paranormal Section U Division, is often more of a hindrance than a help and has a crush on Ayaka. In her first "Incident File" Ayaka tracks down Dracula in the streets of Tokyo with the help of an anemic vampire.

EPISODES

Incident File 01: *Kiss of Fire*; Incident File 02: *End of World*; Incident File 03: *Love Me Tender*; Incident File 04: *Lover Come Back To Me*.

Plastic Man [Comic book character]

First appearance: *Police Comics* #1 (August 1941); Creator: Jack Cole; Publisher: Quality Comics/DC Comics.

Notorious criminal Eel O'Brian is wounded during a chemical factory raid. As his fellow hoodlums make their escape by automobile Eel is covered in acid from an overturned chemical vat. He awakens in a monastic retreat attended by a monk whose kindness has a life-changing affect on Eel. No longer pursuing a life of crime, Eel decides to fight crime.

To his amazement Eel discovers he can stretch his body like rubber. The acid has entered his bloodstream and altered his body chemistry. Now he assumes a dual identity. As Eel O'Brian he maintains contact with the criminal underworld but as the costumed Plastic Man he thwarts their activities.

In later adventures Plastic Man is joined by stumbling sidekick Woozy Winks and joins the police force and the F.B.I.

Poe [Comic book]

Story: J. Barton Mitchell; Art: Dean Kotz; 4-issue mini-series; First publication: July 2009; Publisher: Boom! Studios.

1847. Horror and mystery writer Edgar Allan Poe plays detective tracking the killer of his brother's friend in Baltimore. What he finds is his brother and wife captured by the Red Death. But the recent death of Poe's beloved wife Virginia is used as a bargaining chip when the Red Death claims he can return her to life in exchange for his brother and wife.

Pokemon Detective Pikachu (2019) [Film; Japan/USA]

Premiere: May 10, 2019; Main Cast: Ryan Reynolds as Detective Pikachu (voice), Kathryn Newton as Lucy, Ken Watanae as Detective Toshida, Justice Smith as Tim Goodman, Karan Soni as Jack, Bill Nighy, Suki Waterhouse, Rita Ora, Chris Geere; Executive Producers: Joseph M. Caracciolo Jr., Tsunekazu Ishihara; Screenplay: Nicole Perlman, Rob Letterman; Director: Rob Letterman; Original story: Tomokazu Ohara, Haruka Utsui; Based on "Pokemon" created by Satoshi Tajiri, Ken Sugimori, Junichi Masuda; Director: Rob Letterman; Legendary Entertainment, Nintendo, The Pokemon Company, Warner Bros.; Color.

A talking Pikachu discovers he can communicate with Tim Goodman, son of missing private eye Harry Goodman. Together they attempt to find Goodman among the sprawling metropolis of Ryme City, home to both humans and the Pokemon. But there is a plot that threatens the harmony of Ryme City and the future of the Pokemon.

The first live-action Pokemon adventure is based on the video game ***Detective Pikachu***.

Poltergeist: The Legacy (1996) [TV series; Canada]

Premiere: April 21, 1996; Main Cast: Derek de Lint as Derek Rayne, Helen Shaver as Rachel Corrigan, Martin Cummins as Nick Boyle, Robbi Chong as Alexandra Moreau, Kristin Lehman as Kristin Adams, Alexander Purvis as Katherine "Kat" Corrigan, Patrick Fitzgerald as Father Philip Callaghan, Daniel J. Travanti as William Sloan; Executive Producers: Pen Densham, Richard Barton Lewis, John Watson, Grant Rosenberg; Creator: Richard Barton Lewis; 87 × 45 min. 1 × 90 min; Trilogy Entertainment Group; PMP Legacy Productions; Showtime Networks, Sci-Fi Channel; MGM Worldwide Television Group; Color.

"Since the beginning of time, mankind has existed between the world of light and the world of darkness. This journal chronicles the work of our secret society known as the Legacy, created to protect the innocent from those creatures that inhabit the shadows and the night."

Operating out of the private Angel Island in San Francisco Bay the Legacy team consists of psychiatrist Dr. Rachel Corrigan, Father Philip Callaghan, former Navy SEAL Nick Boyle and psychic researcher Alexandra Moreau. Dr. Derek Rayne is the Precept of the San Francisco House which works under the guise of the charitable Luna Foundation. William Sloan heads the Ruling Legacy House in London. Kristin Adams from the Boston Legacy House joins the San Francisco House in season three.

Season One

Pilot (1:01); *Sins of the Father* (1:02); *Town Without Pity* (1:03); *The Tenement* (1:04); *Twelfth Cave* (1:05); *Man in the Mist* (1:06); *Ghost in the Road* (1:07); *Doppelganger* (1:08); *The Substitute* (1:09); *Do Not Go Gently* (1:10); *Crystal Scarab* (1:11); *The Bell of Girardius* (1:12); *Fox Spirit* (1:13); *Thirteenth Generation* (1:14); *Dark Priest* (1:15); *Revelations* (1:16); *Bones of St. Anthony* (1:17); *Inheritance* (1:18); *The Signalman* (1:19); *The Reckoning* (1:20); *Traitor Among Us* (1:21).

Season Two

The New Guard (2:01); *Black Widow* (2:02); *Lights Out* (2:03); *Spirit Thief* (2:04); *The Gift* (2:05); *Transference* (2:06); *Dark Angel* (2:07); *Lives in the Balance* (2:08); *Rough Beast* (2:09); *Ransom* (2:10); *Finding Richter* (2:11); *Repentance* (2:12); *Devil's Lighthouse* (2:13); *Lullaby* (2:14); *Silent Partner* (2:15); *Shadow Fall* (2:16); *Mind's Eye* (2:17); *Fear* (2:18); *Someone to Watch Over Me* (2:19); *Let Sleeping Demons Lie* (2:20); *Trapped* (2:21); *The Choice* (2:22).

Season Three

Darkness Falls (3:01); *Light of Day* (3:02); *Enlightened One* (3:03); *Stolen Hearts* (3:04); *Father to Son* (3:05); *Fallen Angel* (3:06); *Dream Lover* (3:07); *Debt of Honor* (3:08); *The Light* (3:09); *Hell Hath No Fury* (3:10); *Irish Jug* (3:11); *Metamorphosis* (3:12); *La Belle Dame Sans Merci* (3:13); *The Prodigy* (3:14); *The Human Vessel* (3:15); *The Covenant* (3:16); *The Internment* (3:17); *Seduction* (3:18); *Out of Sight* (3:19); *Last Good Knight* (3:20); *Armies of Night* (3:21); *Darkside* (3:22).

Season Four

Song of the Raven (4:01); *Bird of Prey* (4:02); *Vendetta* (4:03); *The Painting* (4:04); *The Possession* (4:05); *The Traitor* (4:06); *Double Cross* (4:07); *Brother's Keeper* (4:08); *Initiation* (4:09); *Wishful Thinking* (4:10); *Still Waters* (4:11); *Unholy Congress* (4:12); *Sacrifice* (4:13); *She's Got the Devil in Her Heart* (4:14); *Body and Soul* (4:15); *Forget Me Not* (4:16); *The Portents* (4:17); *Gaslight* (4:18); *Sabbath's End* (4:19); *Mephisto Strain* (4:20); *Internal Affairs* (4:21); *The Beast Within* (4:22).

The Possessed (1977) [Telefilm]

Premiere: May 1, 1977; Main Cast: James Farentino as Kevin Leahy; Joan Hackett as Louise Gelson, Claudette Nevins as Ellen Sumner; Eugene Roche as Sgt. Taplinger; Diana Scarwid as Lane, Harrison Ford as Paul Winjam, Ann Dusenberry as Weezie Sumner; Executive Producer: Jerry Thorpe; Teleplay: John Sacret Young; Director: Jerry Thorpe; 76 min.; Warner Bros. Television; National Broadcasting Company (NBC); Color.

When Father Kevin Leahy is killed in an automobile accident he is told in the afterlife that he has lost his faith and failed as God's servant. His only hope for salvation is to return to life to seek out evil and fight it. Now working as an exorcist, Leahy battles Satanic forces at a girl's school.

Professor Arnold Rhymer M.D. [Short story character]

Author-Creator: Uel Key (Samuel Whittell Key); First appearance: "The Broken Fang" *Pearson's Magazine* (1917); Publisher: London: Arthur Pearson.

A young medical doctor is employed on occasion by Scotland Yard to help them investigate weird cases involving the supernatural. Professor Rhymer a.k.a. the Spook Doctor, uses a scientific approach to solve the mysteries.

Samuel Whittell Key, writing under his pen-name Uel Key wrote seven short stories between 1917 and February 1922 for the London based Pearson's Magazine.

Short stories: "The Broken Fang"; "The Shrouded Dome"; "A Post-Mortem Reversal"; "A Prehistoric Vendetta"; "A Sprig of Sweet Briar"; "The Inaudible Sound"; "Buried Needles."

Novel: *Yellow Death (A Tale of Occult Mysteries) Recording a Further Experience of Professor Rhymer the "Spook" Doctor* (London: Hodder & Stoughton, 1920)

Short story collection: *Broken Fang and Other Experiences of a Specialist in Spooks* (London: Books Limited, 1921).

Professor Nathan Enderby [Short story character]

Author-Creator: Manly Wade Wellman; First appearance: "Vigil" *Strange Stories* (December 1939).

"Slender savant and unassuming authority on the supernatural, aided by his sharp wits and his Chinese servant Quong, His cabin in rural Pennsylvania is a retreat from the frenetic social life of New York City—and a fortress against the powers of black magic."

Proven Guilty (The Dresden Files Book #8)

Author: Jim Butcher; Publisher: New York: Roc, 2006.

After years of being under suspicion by the White Council Wardens Dresden is now a Warden himself. When movie monsters come to life the pressure is on Dresden to succeed or suffer the consequences of his client, the White Council.

See: *White Night*

PSI Factor: Chronicles of the Paranormal (1996) [TV series; Canada]

Premiere: October 12, 1996; Main Cast: Dan Ackroyd as the Host, Nancy Anne Sakovich as Lindsay Donner, Barclay Hope as Peter Axon, Colin Fox as Professor Anton Hendricks, Soo Garay as Dr. Claire Davison, Matt Frewer as Matt Prager, Peter MacNeill as Ray Donahue, Nigel Bennett as Frank Elsinger, Maurice Dean Wint as Dr. Curtis Rollins, Paul Miller as Professor Conner Doyle, Joanne Vannicola as Mia Stone, Peter Blais as Lennox "LQ" Cooper, Michael Moriarty as Michael Kelly; Executive Producers/Creators: David Ackroyd, Christopher Chacon; 88 × 45 min.; Alliance Atlantis Communications; Atlantis Films; First Television; Paranormal Productions; CanWest Global Communications; Color.

A science research team working for the Office of Scientific Investigation and Research (O.S.I.R.) investigate cases of the paranormal and supernatural phenomena. Stories are allegedly based on "Anomalous Phenomena" handled by the real-life clandestine organization.

Cases investigated in the series include poltergeist activity, alien abductions, demons, ghosts, psychokinesis, teleportation, a dybbuk possession, reincarnation, Sasquatch, killer plants, doppelgangers, astral projection, human combustion, forest trolls, black magic, time traveling cowboys, a wendigo, dead zones, angels, witchcraft, mind control, vampires and telepathy.

SEASON ONE

Dream House/UFO Encounter (1:01); *Possession/Man Out of Time* (1:02); *Reptilian Revenge/Ghostly Voice s*(1:03); *The Creeping Darkness/Power* (1:04); *The Freefall/Presence* (1:05); *The Infestation/Human Apportation* (1:06); *The Underneath/Phantom Limb* (1:07); *The Tran-*

sient/Two Lost Old Men (1:08); *UFO Duplication; Clara's Friend* (1:09); *The Hunter/The Healer* (1:10); *The Curse/Angel on a Plane* (1:11); *Anasazi Cave/Devil's Triangle* (1:12); *The Undead/Stalker Moon* (1:13); *The Forbidden North/Reincarnation* (1:14); *The Greenhouse Effect/The Buzz* (1:15); *The Light* (1:16); *The 13th Floor/The Believer* (1:17); *The Fog/House on Garden Street* (1:18); *Second Sight/Chocolate Soldier* (1:19); *Fire Within/Fate* (1:20); *Death at Sunset/Collision* (1:21); *Perestroika* (1:22).

SEASON TWO

Threads (2:01); *Donor* (2:02); *Wish I May* (2:03); *Communion* (2:04); *Frozen in Time* (2:05); *Devolution* (2:06); *The Warrior* (2:07); *The Grey Men* (2:08); *Man of War* (2:09); *Hell Week* (2:10); *The Edge* (2:11); (2:12); *Bad Dreams* (2:13); *Kiss of the Tiger* (2:14); *The Haunting* (2:15); *The Night of the Setting Sun* (2:16); *The Labyrinth* (2:17); *Pentimento* (2:18); *Frozen Faith* (2:19); *Map to the Stars* (2:20); *The Endangered* (2:21); *The Egress* (2:22).

SEASON THREE

Jaunt (3:01); *Comings & Goings* (3:02); *Heartland* (3:03); *Palimpsest* (3:04); *The Kiss* (3:05); *Absolution* (3:06); *Little People* (3:07); *Return* (3:08); *All Hallow's Eve* (3:09); *Chango* (3:10); *The Winding Cloth* (3:11); *Harlequin* (3:12); *Old Wounds* (3:13); *Solitary Confinement* (3:14); *Valentine* (3:15); *The Observer Effect* (3:16); *School of Thought* (3:17); *Y2K* (3:18); *Tribunal* (3:19); *John Doe* (3:20); *Forever and a Day: Part 1* (3:21); *Forever and a Day: Part 2* (3:22).

SEASON FOUR

Shocking (4:01); *Sacrifices* (4:02); *Happy Birthday, Matt Praeger* (4:03); *Soul Survivor* (4:04); *883* (4:05); *Once Upon a Time in the West* (4:06); *Body and Soul* (4:07); *Temple of Light* (4:08); *Inertia* (4:09); *Nocturnal Cabal* (4:10); *'Til Death Do Us Part* (4:11); *Tyler/Tim* (4:12); *Super Sargasso Sea* (4:13); *Persistence of Vision* (4:14); *GeoCore* (4:15); *Gone Fishing* (4:16); *Chiaroscuro* (4:17); *Regeneration* (4:18); *Wendigo* (4:19); *Elevator* (4:20); *Force Majeure* (4:21); *Stone Dreams* (4:22).

Psych (2006) [TV series]
Premiere: July 7, 2006; Main Cast: James Roday as Shawn Spencer, Dulé Hill as Burton Guster, Timothy Omundson as Carlton Lassiter, Maggie Lawson as Juliet O'Hara, Corbin Bernsen as Henry Spencer, Kirsten Nelson as Karen Vick, Liam James/Skyler Gisondo as Young Shawn, Carlos McCullers II as Young Gus, Sage Brocklebank as Buzz McNab; Executive Producers: Steve Franks, Chris Henze, Kelly Kulchak, Mel Damski; Creator: Steve Franks; 121 × 44 min.; GEP Productions, NBC Universal Television Studio, Pacific Mountain Pictures, Tagline Pictures, Universal Cable Productions; USA Network; Color.

Shawn Spencer and his best friend Gus are owners of the Psych Detective Agency. The only problem is neither one of them possesses psychic powers. Thanks to a photographic memory and acute powers of observation Shawn is so effective pretending to be psychic he is regularly employed as a consultant on cases for the Santa Barbara Police Department. Shawn's psychic abilities fail to impress Detective Carlton "Lassie" Lassiter who is often wound up by the mischievous Shawn. Other regulars include Shawn Spencer's romantic interest detective Juliet "Jules" O'Hara, the Police Chief Karen Vick and Shawn's father Henry Spencer who taught his son all the skills he puts to use as an adult.

The cast reunited in 2017 for the telefilm *Psych: The Movie.*

SEASON ONE

Pilot (1:01); *Spellingg Bee* (1:02); *Speak Now or Forever Hold Your Piece* (1:03); *Woman Seeking Dead Husband: Smokers Okay. No Pets* (1:04); *9 Lives* (1:05); *Weekend Warriors* (1:06); *Who Ya Gonna Call?* (1:07); *Shawn vs. the Red Phantom* (1:08); *Forget Me Not* (1:09); *From the Earth to Starbucks* (1:10); *He Loves Me, He Loves Me Not, He Loves Me, Oops He's Dead!* (1:11); *Cloudy.... With a Chance of Murder* (1:12); *Game, Set.... Muuurder?* (1:13); *Poker? I Barely Know Her* (1:14); *Scary Sherry: Bianca's Toast* (1:15).

SEASON TWO

American Duos (1:01); *65 Million Years Off* (2:02); *Psy vs. Psy* (2:03); *Zero to Murder in*

Sixty Seconds (2:04); *And Down the Stretch Comes Murder* (2:05); *Meat is Murder, But Murder Is Also Murder* (2:06); *If You're So Smart, Then Why Are You Dead?* (2:07); *Rob-a-Bye Baby* (2:08); *Bounty Hunters!* (2:09); *Gus' Dad May Have Killed an Old Guy* (2:10); *There's Something About Mira* (2:11); *The Old and the Restless* (2:12); *Lights, Camera.... Homicidio* (2:13); *Dis-Lodged* (2:14); *Black and Tan: A Crime of Fashion* (2:15); *Shawn (and Gus) of the Dead* (2:16).

Season Three

Ghosts (3:01); *Murder? ... Anyone? ... Anyone? ... Bueller?* (3:02); *Daredevils!* (3:03); *The Greatest Adventure in the History of Basic Cable* (3:04); *Disco Didn't Die. It Was Murdered!* (3:05); *There Might Be Blood* (3:06); *Talk Derby to Me* (3:07); *Gus Walks into a Bank* (3:08); *Christmas Joy* (3:09); *Six Feet Under the Sea* (3:10); *Lassie Did a Bad, Bad Thing* (3:11); *Earth, Wind and.... Wait for It* (3:12); *Any Given Friday Night at 10 pm, 9pm Central* (3:13); *Truer Lies* (3:14); *Tuesday the 17th* (3:15); *An Evening with Mr. Yang* (3:16).

Season Four

Extradition: British Columbia (4:01); *He Dead* (4:02); *High Noon-ish* (4:03); *The Devil's in the Details ... and the Upstairs Bedroom* (4:04); *Shawn Has the Yips* (4:05); *Bollywood Homicide* (4:06); *High Top Fade Out* (4:07); *Let's Get Hairy* (4:08); *Shawn Takes a Shot in the Dark* (4:09); *You Can't Handle This Episode* (4:10); *Thrill Seekers & Hell Raisers* (4:11); *A Very Juliet Episode* (4:12); *Death is in the Air* (4:13); *Think Tank* (4:14); *The Head, the Tail, the Whole Damn Episode* (4:15); *Mr. Yin Presents ...* (4:16).

Season Five

Romeo and Juliet and Juliet (5:01); *Feet Don't Kill Me Now* (5:02); *Not Even Close.... Encounters* (5:03); *Chivalry is Not Dead.... But Someone Is* (5:04); *Shawn & Gus in Drag (Racing)* (5:05); *Viagra Falls* (5:06); *Ferry Tale* (5:07); *Shawn 2.0* (5:08); *One, Maybe Two, Ways Out* (5:09); *Extradition II: The Actual Extradition Part* (5:10); *In Plain Fright* (5:11); *Dual Spires* (5:12); *We'd Like to Thank the Academy* (5:13); *The Polarizing Express* (5:14); *Dead Bear Walking* (5:15); *Yang 3 in 2D* (5:16).

Season Six

Shawn Rescues Darth Vader (6:01); *Last Night Gus* (6:02); *This Episode Sucks* (6:03); *The Amazing Psych-Man & Tap Man, Issue #2* (6:04); *Dead Man's Curve Ball* (6:05); *Shawn Interrupted* (6:06); *In for a Penny ...* (6:07); *The Tao of Gus* (6:08); *Neil Simon Lover's Retreat* (6:09); *Indiana Shawn and the Temple of the Kinda Crappy, Rusty Old Dagger* (6:10); *Heeeeere's Lassie* (6:11); *Shawn and the Real Girl* (6:12); *Let's Doo-Wop It Again* (6:13); *Autopsy Turvy* (6:14); *True Grits* (6:15); *Santabarbaratown* (6:16).

Season Seven

Santabarbaratown 2 (7:01); *Juliet Takes a Luvvah* (7:02); *Lassie Jerky* (7:03); *No Country for Two Old Men* (7:04); *100 Clues* (7:05); *Cirque du Soul* (7:06); *Deez Nups* (7:07); *Right Turn or Left for Dead* (7:08); *Juliet Wears the Pantsuit* (7:09); *Santa Barbarian Candidate* (7:10); *Office Space* (7:11); *Dead Air* (7:12); *Nip and Suck It* (7:13); *No Trout About It* (7:14); *Psych the Musical* (7:15).

Season Eight

Lock, Stock, Some Smoking Barrels and Burton Guster's Goblet of Fire (8:01); *S.E.I.Z.E. the Day* (8:02); *Remake A.K.A. Cloudy.... With a Chance of Improvement* (8:03); *Someone's Got a Woody* (8:04); *Cog Blocked* (8:05); *1967: A Psych Odyssey* (8:06); *Shawn and Gus Truck Things Up* (8:07); *A Touch of Sweevil* (8:08); *A Nightmare on State Street* (8:09); *The Break-Up* (8:10).

Psychic Detective [Video game]
Release date: November 30, 1995; Main Cast: Beata Pozniak as Laina Pozok, Kevin Breznahan as Eric Fox, Marcia Pizzo as Sylvia Bourget, Jarion Moore as Lexi Golitsyn/Max Mirage, Zachary Barton as Monica Pozok, Sharon Lockwood as madam Tikunov, Luis Oropeza as Moki Valdez, Eric Beavers as Sergei Nosenko, Rob Nilsson as Vladimir Pozok; Executive Producer: Jim Simmons; Writer: Michael Kaplan; Director: John Sanborn; Developers: Colossal Pictures,

Electronic Arts (EA); Platforms: 3DO, DOS, PlayStation; Perspective: 1st-Person; Publisher: Electronic Arts, Inc.

An interactive movie game centered on San Francisco psychic and magician Eric Fox. Laina Pozok hires Fox as a private detective to find out how her father died by probing the minds of the people who attend his wake.

The Psychic Detective [Novel]

Author: R. Chetwynd-Hayes; First publication: London: Robert Hale, 1993.

Occult authority Francis St Clare meets gifted medium Frederica Masters, commonly known as Fred, and asks her to become his assistant in order to achieve her potential. But their partnership places both of their lives in danger as they encounter dark, malevolent forces.

Psychic Detective Yakumo a.k.a. ***Shinrei Tantei Yakumo*** [Novel Series; TV Series; Manga; Anime; Japan]

[Novel Series] First Publication: 2004; Author: Manabu Kaminga; Illustrator: Katoh Akatsuki; Publisher: Nihon Bungeisha.

[TV Series] Premiere: March 3, 2006; Main Cast: Atae Shinjiro as Yakumo Saito, Nagasawa Nao as Asami Inoue; Directors: Kiyoshi Yamamoto, Koutarou Terauchi; 13 × 30 min.; TV Tokyo; Color.

College student Yakumo Saito was born with a red left eye, enabling him the ability to see ghosts and communicate with them. The head of the police department asks for Yakumo's help in rescuing his daughter who is under the spell of evil.

[Manga] First publication: *Hana to Yume* (2007); Story: Manabu Kaminaga; Art: Ritsu Miyako; Publisher: Hakusensha.

The original manga published in two volumes was followed by a 14-volume manga in *Asuka Magazine* (2009).

[Anime] Premiere: October 3, 2010; Voice Cast: Daisuke Ono as Yakumo Saito, Ayumi Fujimura as Haraka Ozawa, Akimutsu Takase as Unkai Saito, Ami Koshimizu as Miki Sasaki, Takuya Kirimoto as Takaoka-sensei; Producer: Ken Suekawa; Story: Hiroyuki Kawasaki; Animation Directors: Manamu Amasaki, Yukiko Ban; Director: Tomoyuki Kurokawa; 13 × 24 min.; Bee Train; NHK; Sogo Vision; Color.

In the first episode we are introduced to sophomore student Haraka Ozawa who seeks the help of Yakumo Saito. After visiting the forbidden room of an old school building Haraka's friend Miki is possessed by spirits of the dead. Other friends have committed suicide. Yakumo sees the ghosts surrounding Miki and realizes they are murder victims. Now Yuko must find the murderer and the truth behind the suicides.

Season One

The Forbidden Room (1:01); *The Curse of the White Fox* (1:02); *The Tunnel's Darkness* (1:03); *Connecting Spirits: Possession* (1:04); *Connecting Spirits: Rebirth* (1:05); *Bargain Property* (1:06); *Sentiments that Bind: Trap* (1:01); *Sentiments that Bind: Fate* (1:01); *Sentiments that Bind: Light* (1:01); *Beyond Despair: The Omen* (1:01); *Beyond Despair: Assassin's Dagger* (1:01); *Beyond Despair: Animosity* (1:01); *Beyond Despair: Eternity* (1:01).

Psychic Squad a.k.a. ***Zettai Karen Children*** (2008) [Anime; Manga; Japan]

Premiere: April 6, 2008; Voice Cast: Aya Hirano as Kaoru Akashi, Haruka Tomatsu as Shiho Sannomiya, Ryko Shiraishi as Aoi Nogami, Yuichi Nakamura as Koichi Minamoto; Producers: Shin'ichi Iwata, Naohiko Furuichi; Story: Kazuyuki Fudeyasu, Shinichi Inotsume, Satoru Nishizoni, Masanao Akahoshi; Director: Keiichiro Kawaguchi; 51 × 25 min.; Shogakukan-Shueisha Productions; TV Tokyo; Color.

Three ten-year-old schoolgirls, collectively known as The Children, work for B.A.B.E.L., an organization that works to stop crime before it occurs. Kaoru Akashi is psychokinetic. Shiho Sannomiya can read minds and the vibrations from inanimate objects. Aoi Nogami can teleport herself and others. Their operation leader, Kouichi Minamoto must keep Level 7 children under control in a world where ESP is common.

A 12-episode sequel series *Unlimited Psychic Squad* began broadcasts in January 2013.

[Manga] First publication: *Shonen Sunday Cho Zoka* (July 2003); Story & Art: Takashi Shiina; Publisher: Shogakuken.

The manga *Zettai Karen Children* ran to 49-volumes between 2005 and 2017.

Pushing Daisies (2007) [TV series]

Premiere: October 3, 2007; Main Cast: Lee Pace as Ned, Anna Friel as Charlotte "Chuck" Charles, Chi McBride as Emerson Cod, Jim Dale as Narrator, Ellen Greene as Vivian Charles, Swoosie Kurtz as Lily Charles, Kristin Chenoweth as Olive Snook, Field Cate as Young Ned, Sy Richardson as Coroner; Executive Producers: Bruce Cohen, Bryan Fuller, Dan Jinks, Barry Sonnenfeld, Peter Ocko, Brooke Kennedy; Creator: Bryan Fuller; 22 × 44 min.; Jinks/Cohen Company; Living Dead Guy Productions; Warner Bros. Television; American Broadcasting Company (ABC); Color.

Pie-maker Ned, owner of the Pie Hole restaurant bring the dead back to life with his touch and make them dead again forever with his second touch. But if he lets the person live for longer than one minute another living person must die in their place. When he resurrects Charlotte, his childhood sweetheart they work together to solver her murder. But he cannot touch her, or she will die again.

Private detective Emerson Cod, the only person to know Ned's secret, proposes a partnership. Ned will help him solve murders by touching the corpses of victims and questioning them about their violent murders before returning them back to the land of the dead. Pie Hole waitress Olive Snook, who has a crush on Ned joins him in the occasional murder investigation.

Season One

Pie-lette (1:01); *Dummy* (1:02); *The Fun in Funeral* (1:03); *Pigeon* (1:04); *Girth* (1:05); *Bitches* (1:06); *Smell of Success* (1:07); *Bitter Sweets* (1:08); *Corpsicle* (1:09).

Season Two

Bzzzzzzzz! (2:01); *Circus, Circus* (2:02); *Bad Habits* (2:03); *Frescorts* (2:04); *Dim Sum Lose Some* (2:05); *On Oh Oh.... It's Magic* (2:06); *Robbing Hood* (2:07); *Comfort Food* (2:08); *The Legend of Merle McQuoddy* (2:09); *The Norwegians* (2:10); *Window Dressed to Kill* (2:11); *Water & Power* (2:12); *Kerplunk* (2:13).

Question [Comic book character]

First appearance: *Blue Beetle* #1 (June 1967); Creator: Steve Ditko; Publisher: Charlton.

The original Question a.k.a. Vic Sage works as a crusading investigative reporter for television who has a secret life as a vigilante detective in Hub City. He tackles the criminal underworld behind the disguise of a faceless mask made of psuedoderm, invented by his mentor Aristotle "Tot" Rodor. A spray of gas from a canister on his belt buckle combined with a chemical rubbed on the face make the mask stick to Sage's now featureless face. The gas also possesses the ability to change the color of his hair and clothing. The Question is often ruthless with criminals, his blank expres-

***Pushing Up Daisies* (2007),** starring Anna Friel as Charlotte "Chuck" Charles (Warner Bros. Television-ABC).

sionless face-hugging mask mirroring his lack of compassion for those who break the law. His signature blank calling card releases a smoky question mark when touched.

Writer-artist Steve Ditko created a character who reflected his own interest in Ayn Rand and Objectivism. Ditko stated, "I worked up the Question, using the basic idea of a man who was motivated by basic black-and-white principles." Subsequent versions of the Question at DC Comics would take him in directions at odds with Ditko's original vision including a change of name to Charles Victor Szasz, an interest in Zen philosophy and martial arts and the ability to create illusions.

Question II [Comic book character]

First appearance: *Batman* #475 (March 1992); Creators: Paul Dini, Greg Rucka, Bruce Timm, Alan Grant, Norman Breyfogle; Publisher: DC Comics.

Before he dies of lung cancer Vic Sage trains Renee Montoya to succeed him. As the Question Montoya applies the same psuedoderm faceless mask to fight crime and wears the trademark fedora and trenchcoat. A former detective who resigned from the Gotham City Police Department, Montoya works as a private investigator who can be contacted through her website. Enemies include the Religion of Crime and the agents of S.H.A.D.E. (Super Human Advanced Defense Executive).

Raines (2007) [TV series]

First broadcast: March 15, 2007: Main Cast: Jeff Goldblum as Michael Raines, Matt Craven as Captain Dan Lewis, Nicole Sullivan as Carolyn Crumley, Linda Park as Sally Lance, Dov Davidoff as Remi Boyer, Malik Yoba as Charlie Lincoln, Madeleine Stowe as Dr. Samantha Kohl; Executive Producers: Graham Yost, Frank Darabont; Creator: Graham Yost; 7 × 45 min.; Nemo Films; NBC Universal Television. National Broadcasting Company (NBC); Color.

LAPD detective Michael Raines suffers hallucinations of dead crime victims following the death of his partner in a shootout. His unique interaction with his visions help Raines solve criminal cases. His unusual crime fighting methods bring him into conflict with fellow detectives who question his sanity and force him to see a psychiatrist.

The show was canceled after only seven episodes.

SEASON ONE

Pilot (1:01); *Meet Juan Doe* (1:02); *Reconstructing Alice* (1:03); *Stone Dead* (1:04); *5th Step* (1:05); *Inner Child* (1:01); *Closure* (1:01).

Randall and Hopkirk (Deceased) a.k.a. **My Partner the Ghost** (1969) [TV series; UK]

First broadcast: September 21, 1969; Main Cast: Mike Pratt as Jeff Randall, Kenneth Cope as Marty Hopkirk, Annette Andre as Jeannie Hopkirk; Producer: Monty Berman; Creator: Dennis Spooner; 26 × 50 min.; Incorporated Television Company (ITC); Independent Television (ITV); Color.

In the premiere episode, *My Late Lamented Friend and Partner* (1:01) while investigating a murder Jeff Randall becomes a marked man. But Jeff's partner Marty Hopkirk is mistaken for Jeff by the hit-man and kills Marty in a hit-and-run incident. Following his funeral Marty appears to Jeff as a white-suited ghost vowing to bring justice to those responsible for his death.

But Marty makes a major blunder in not returning to his grave before daylight. Now he is trapped by an ancient curse that dooms him to roam the Earth as a ghost for the next 100 years. With only Jeff able to see him the detective duo decide to continue their work as private detectives. Marty's widow Jean Hopkirk continues her secretarial duties at the detective agency unaware that her late husband is at her side.

The one-season UK show failed to find distribution in the U.S. until 1973 when it went into syndication as *My Partner the Ghost*.

SEASON ONE

[Original UK Titles and Order of Broadcast]

My Late Lamented Friend and Partner (1:01); *But What a Sweet Little Room* (1:02); *For the Girl Who Has Everything (1:03); A Sentimental Journey (1:04); You Can Always Find a Fall Guy (1:05); Who Killed Cock Robin? (1:06); The Smile Behind the Veil (1:07); The Trouble With Women (1:08); It's Supposed to Be Thicker Than Water (1:09); That's How Murder Snowballs (1:10); Vendetta For a Dead Man (1:11); Whoever Heard of a Ghost Dying? (1:12) Never Trust a Ghost (1:13); Money to Burn (1:14); The Ghost Talks (1:15); All Work and No Pay (1:16); When the Spirit Moves You (1:17); Just For the Record (1:18); Could You Recognise The Man Again? (1:19); The Man From Nowhere (1:20); The Ghost Who Saved the Bank at Monte Carlo (1:21); A Disturbing Case (1:22); When Did You Start to Stop Seeing Things? (1:23); The House on Haunted Hill (1:24); Murder Ain't What It Used To Be (1:25); Somebody Just Walked Over My Grave (1:26).

Randall and Hopkirk (Deceased) (2000) [TV series; UK]

First broadcast: March 18, 2000; Main Cast: Vic Reeves as Marty Hopkirk, Bob Mortimer as Jeff Randall, Emilia Fox as Jeannie, Charlie Higson as Bulstrode, Tom Baker as Professor Wyvern, Melissa Knatchbull as Wendy Gill, Jessica Hynes as Felia Siderova; Executive Producer: Simon Wright; Based on characters created by Dennis Spooner; 13 × 50 min.; Ghost Productions; Working Title Television; Universal Pictures; Color.

This remake of the 1969 TV series features the comedy team of Reeves and Mortimer in the title roles and updates the original concept with slight revisions and additions. Marty Hopkirk's widow Jeannie is his fiancée in this version after he dies on their wedding day before the ceremony takes place. In the afterlife elderly ghost Professor Wyvern teaches Marty the essentials of being a ghost. Meanwhile Jeannie becomes Jeff Randall's new partner at the detective agency and they become entangled in a romantic relationship but feel guilty about betraying Marty.

SEASON ONE

Drop Dead (1:01); Mental Apparition Disorder (1:02); The Best Years of Your Death (1:03); Paranoia (1:04); A Blast From the Past (1:05); A Man of Substance (1:06).

SEASON TWO

Whatever Possessed You? (2:01); Revenge of the Bog People (2:02); O Happy Isle (2:03); Painkillers (2:04); Marshall and Snellgrove (2:05); The Glorious Butranekh (2:06); Two Can Play at That Game (2:07).

The Reaping (2007) [Film]

Premiere: April 5, 2007; Main Cast: Hilary Swank as Katherine Winter, David Morrissey as Doug, Idris Elba as Ben, Stephen Rea as Father Costigan, William Ragsdale as Sheriff Cade, AnnaSophia Robb as Loren McConnell, Andrea Frankle as Maddie McConnell; Executive Producers: Bruce Berman, Erik Olsen, Steve Richards; Story: Brian Rousso; Screenplay: Carey W. Hayes, Chad Hayes; Director: Stephen Hopkins; 99 min.; Warner Bros.; Dark Castle Entertainment; Chime Productions LLC; Eyetronics; Chime Films; Village Roadshow Pictures; Color.

Katherine Winter has lost her faith. The former Christian missionary and her personal assistant investigate religious paranormal events to debunk them. But her cynicism is tested when she investigates strange happening in the small town of Haven, Louisiana. The mysterious death of a child appears to be connected to the ten Biblical plagues as the town is overrun by locusts, frogs and a river of blood.

Regression (2015) [Film]

Premiere: October 2, 2015; Main Cast: Ethan Hawke as Detective Bruce Kenner, Emma Watson as Angela Gray, David Thewlis as Kenneth Raines, Lothaire Bluteau as the Reverend Beaumont, Dale Dickey as Rose Gray, David Dencik as John Gray, Devin Bostick as Roy Gray, Aaron Ashmore as George Nesbitt, Peter MacNeill as Police Chief Cleveland, Adam Butcher as Brody; Executive Producers: Gabriel Arias-Salgado, Ghislain Barrois, Simon de Santiago, Axel Kuschevatzky, Alex Lalonde, Noah Segal, Bob Weinstein, Harvey Weinstein; Story/Director: Alejandro Amenabar; 106 min.; Mod Productions; First Generation Films; FilmNation Entertainment; Himenoptero, Telecino Cinema, Telefonica Studios; Color.

Detective Bruce Kenner is assigned to a case of a father sexually abusing his seventeen-year-old daughter. The father who admits to the abuse but claims to have no memory of it is regressed by hypnosis along with his daughter Angela. What it reveals is a Satanic cult at work that is so distressing it begins to psychologically affect Detective Kenner.

The Return of Chandu (1934) [Film serial]
Premiere: October 1, 1934; Main Cast: Bela Lugosi as Frank Chandler/Chandu, Maria Alba as Princess Naji of Egypt, Clara Kimball Young as Dorothy Regent, Deane Benton as Bob Regent, Phyllis Ludwig as Betty Regent, Lucien Prival as High Priest Vindhyan, Murdock MacQuarrie as Supreme Voice of Ubasti, Wilfred Lucas as Captain Wilson, Jack J. Clark as Vitras, Josef Swickard as Tyba; 208 min.; 12 Chapters; Producer: Sol Lesser; Adaptation: Barry Barringer; Based on the radio show by Harry A. Earnshaw, Vera M. Oldham, R.R. Morgan; Director: Ray Taylor; Principal Pictures Corp.; B/W.

Following her previous exploits at the hands of Roxor Princess Nadji of Egypt has relocated to the safety of California. But she is pursued by members of the Black Magic cult Ubasti. To restore high priestess Ossana to life they must sacrifice Princess Hadji. Even Chandu the Magician's mystical powers are tested by high priest Vindyhan and the Voice of Ubasti as he attempts to save the Princess from a deadly fate.

Chapter titles: 1. *The Chosen Victim*; 2. *The House in the Hills*; 3. *On the High Seas*; 4. *The Evil Eye*; 5. *The Invisible Circle*; 6. *Chandu's False Step*; 7. *Mysterious Magic*; 8. *The Edge of the Pit*; 9. *The Terror Invisible*; 10. *The Crushing Rock*; 11. *The Uplifted Knife*; 12. *The Knife*

The serial was edited to form two feature films. **The Return of Chandu** (1935) comprises of the first four chapters. *Chandu and the Magic Island* (1935) features chapters five through twelve.

The Return of Doctor X (1939) [Film]
Premiere: November 23, 1939; Main Cast: Humphrey Bogart as Kane, Wayne Morris as Walter Garrett, Rosemary Lane as Joan Vance, Dennis Morgan as Michael Rhodes, John Litel as Dr. Francis Flegg, Lya Lys as Angela Merrova. Charles Wilson as Detective Roy Kincaid; Story: William J. Makin; Screenplay: Lee Katz; Director: Vincent Sherman; 62 min.; First National; Warner Bros.; b/w.

New York Morning Dispatch reporter Walter Garrett discovers the body of stage actress Angela Merrova at her apartment. But when the police arrive no corpse can be found. When she turns up alive at the Dispatch offices Garrett is fired for making a fool of the newspaper with a fake death headline. Garrett and his friend Michael Rhodes sense a connection to Merrova when blood donor Stanley Rogers is murdered and his blood drained.

While visiting Doctor Flegg to tell him of Rogers' death the pair meet Flegg's assistant Kane. His deathly pallor and strange manner lead Garrett to investigate further. In the newspaper archives he comes across a photograph of Kane under the name of Dr. Maurice J. Xavier and discovers he was a convicted murderer executed in the electric chair. Digging up Xavier's grave Garrett and Rhodes find it empty. Dr. Flegg has found a way to bring the dead back to life, but Kane must kill to feed on the blood that sustains his life.

The Ring (2002) [Film]
Premiere: October 18, 2002; Main Cast: Naomi Watts as Rachel Keller, David Dorfman as Aidan Keller, Martin Henderson as Noah Clay, Daveigh Chase as Samara Morgan, Brian Cox as Richard Morgan, Shannon Cochran as Anna Morgan, Jane Alexander as Dr. Grasnik, Lindsay Frost as Ruth Embry, Amber Tamblyn as Katie Embry, Rachael Bella As Becca Kotler, Pauley Perrette as Beth; Executive Producers: Roy Lee, Mike Macari, Michele Weisler; Screenplay: Ehren Kruger; Based on the novel by Koji Suzuki; Director: Gore Verbinski; 115 min.; DreamWorks; MacDonald/Parkes Productions; BenderSpink; Color.

This financially successful remake of the Japanese film *Ringu* moves the location from Japan to Seattle, Washington.

Ringu a.k.a. ***Ring*** (1998) [Film; Japan]

Premiere: January 31, 1998; Main Cast: Nanako Matsushima as Reiko Asakawa, Hiroyuki Sanada as Ryuji Takayama, Miki Nakatani as Mai Takano, Yuko Takeuchi as Tomoko Oishi, Hitomi Sato as Masami Kurahashi, Yoichi Numata As Takashi Yamamura, Daisuke Ban as Dr. Heihachiro Ikuma, Rie Ino as Sadako Yamamura, Masako as Shizuko Yamamura; Executive Producer: Masato Hara; Screenplay: Hiroshi Takahashi; Based on the novel by Koji Suzuki; Director: Hideo Nakata; 96 min.; Basara Pictures; Imagica; Asmik Ace Entertainment; Kadokawa Shoten Publishing; Omega Project; Pony Canyon; Toho Company; Ace Pictures; Color; b/w.

Female reporter Reiko Asakawa investigates a series of untimely deaths including that of her niece, connected to an allegedly cursed video. Anyone watching it is said to die within seven days. With the help of her former husband Ryuji, the couple attempt to solve the mystery of the tape that can be traced to psychic Shizuko Yamamura and her child Sadako.

R.I.P.D. [Comic book; SFW]

First publication: October 1999; 4-part mini-series; Creator-Story: Peter Lenkov; Art: Lucas Marangon, Randy Emberlin; Publisher: Dark Horse Comics.

Nick Cruz is murdered by an unknown assailant. Now thanks to the R.I.P.D. (Rest in Peace Department) he is offered the opportunity to find his killer, even if it takes him to Hell and back. Helping Cruz is Old West Sheriff Roy Powell who has been tracking murderers for the last century.

R.I.P.D.: Rest in Peace Department (2013) [Film; SFW]

Premiere: July 17, 2013; Main cast: Jeff Bridges as Roycephus "Roy" Pulsipher, Ryan Reynolds as Nick Walker, Kevin Bacon as Bobby Hayes. Mary-Louise Parker as Mildred Proctor, Stephanie Szostak as Julia Walker, James Hong as Grandpa Jerry Chen (Nick Walker's avatar), Marisa Miller (Roy Pulsipher's avatar); Producers: David Dobkin, Peter M. Lenkov, Neal H. Moritz, Mike Richardson; Story: David Dobkin, Phil Hay, Matt Manfreddi; Based on *Rest in Peace Department* by Peter M. Lenkov; Director: Robert Schwentke; 96 min.; Dark Horse Entertainment, Original Film, Relativity Media, Universal Pictures; Color.

The Rest in Peace Department partners murdered detective sergeant Nick Walker with United States Marshal and former American Civil War soldier Roycephus "Roy" Pulsipher. Walker's Boston police partner Bobby Hayes killed him after Walker decided stealing gold while on duty wasn't a good idea. And while Walker's task in the afterlife is to gather souls who won't move on, Walker is obsessed with avenging his murder. In their investigations Walker and Roy have human avatars on earth. Walker is an old Asian man, while Roy attracts wolf whistles as a sexy female model.

The film failed to recover its $130 million budget after receiving negative reviews. Stephanie Merry of *The Washington Post* (July 19, 2013) declared: "The comic book-based 'R.I.P.D.' is a dud that squanders a decent cast and succeeds neither as the comedy nor the action film it purports to be."

Ritual of Evil (1970) [Telefilm]

Premiere: February 23, 1970; Main Cast: Louis Jordan as David Sorell, Wilfred Hyde-White as Harry Snowden, Anne Baxter as Jolene Wiley, Diana Hyland as Leila Barton, Belinda Montgomery as Loey Wiley, Carla Borelli as Aline Wiley, John McMartin as Edward Bolander, Georg Stanford Brown as Larry Richmond; Producer: David Levinson; Teleplay: Robert Presnell, Jr.; Based on characters created by Richard Alan Simmons; Director: Robert Day; 98 min.; Universal Television; Color.

In this sequel to *Fear No Evil* (1969) Louis Jordan and Wilfred Hyde-White reprise their roles. Psychiatrist David Sorell investigates the death of the parents of young heiress Loey Wiley and uncovers a devil worshipping cult.

The Rivals of Sherlock Holmes (1971) [TV series; UK]

Anthology series of stories featuring Sherlock Holmes' contemporary literary rivals.

"The Horse of the Invisible" (1:05)
Air date: October 18, 1971; Main Cast: Donald Pleasance as Carnacki, Tony Steadman as Captain Hisgins, Michele Dotrice as Mary Hisgins, Michael Johnson as Charles Beaumont, Geoffrey Whitehead as Harry Parsket, Aimee Delamain as Miss Hisgins, Arthur White as March; Executive Producer: Lloyd Shirley; Adapted by Philip Mackie from the short story by William Hope Hodgson; Director: Alan Cooke; 50 min.; Thames Television; Pearson Television International; Color.

Miss Hisgins, the eldest child of the Hisgins family of East Lancashire is the first to be the eldest female for seven generations. According to the family legend she is cursed to be haunted by the Horse if she marries her fiancé. Ghost detective **Carnacki** has seen photographs of the girl with a half-formed hoof above her head and has been invited to investigate further.

Rivers of London a.k.a. Midnight Riot [Novel]

Author: Ben Aaronovitch; Publisher: London; Gollancz, 2011.

Following an encounter with a deceased witness probationary Constable Peter Grant is assigned to a division of the Metropolitan Police Department known as the Folly, dealing with supernatural cases. Apprenticed to Inspector Thomas Nightingale, the last wizard in London, Grant is promoted to Detective Police Constable as the first trainee wizard in fifty years. Now he must investigate vampires, malicious spirits, the warring god and goddess of the River Thames and bring order to chaos in London.

Followed by: *Moon Over Soho* (2011); *Whispers Under Ground* (2012); *Broken Homes* (2014); *Foxglove Summer* (2015); *The Hanging Tree* (2017); *The Furthest Station: A PC Grant Novella* (2018).

Rivers of London: Detective Stories [Comic book]

First publication: 2017; Writers: Ben Aaronovitch, Andrew Cartmel; Art: Lee Sullivan; Publisher: Titan Comics.

Four-part limited series based on the novel by Ben Aaronovitch.

Romeo Spikes [Novel]

Author: Joanne Reay; First publication: New York: Gallery Books, 2011.

Homicide detective Alexis Bianco joins forces with Lola who hunts demons known as Tormenta who look, sound and act like everyday humans. But they have an evil agenda for they torment their victims until they commit suicide and feed on their life force. But an even greater menace awaits in the form of the Mosca. Bianco and Lola must find a way to end the threat to the future of mankind.

Rotten [Comic book; WW]

First publication: June 2009; Story: Mark Rahner; Art: Dan Dougherty; Publisher: Moonstone.

The year, 1877. William Wade, secret agent for President Rutherford B. Hayes is assigned, along with partner J.J. Flynn, to travel the Old West to investigate reported outbreaks of the living dead.

Route 666 (2001) [Film]

Premiere: October 30, 2001; Main Cast: Lou Diamond Phillips as Jack La Roca, Lori Petty as Steph, Steven Williams as Rabbit/Fred, L.Q. Jones as Sheriff Bob Conaway, Dale Midkiff as P.T., Alex McArthur as Nick, Mercedes Colon as Mary, Rob Roy Fitzgerald as Joe, Adam Vernier as Deputy Gil Conaway, Chester E. Tripp III as Deputy Tim Conaway, Rhino Michaels as John La Roca, Gary Roberts as Pickaxe/Miles Hackman, Peewee Piemonte as Jackhammer/Steve Pikowski, Michael Chance as Sledgehammer/Frank Slater; Executive Producer: Cami Winikoff; Story: Scott Fivelson, Thomas Weber, William Wesley; Director: William Wesley; 86 min.; Lions Gate Films; Color.

"On the road to nowhere lies a forgotten highway where secrets are buried, souls are lost, and the dead come to life." Federal Marshals encounter zombies while escorting a mob informer on the abandoned Route 666.

Sapphire and Steel [TV series; Comic book characters; Audio drama; UK]

[TV series] First broadcast: July 10, 1979; Main Cast: Joanna Lumley as Sapphire, David McCallum as Steel, David Collings as Silver; Executive Producer: David Reid; Creator: Peter J. Hammond; Writers: P. J. Hammond, Anthony Read, Don Houghton; Directors: Shaun O'Riordan, David Foster; 34 × 25 min.; Associated Television (ATV); Central TV; Independent Television (ITV); Color.

Interdimensional operatives are assigned to Earth in human form to investigate and solve cases involving the distortion of time. Sapphire's eyes turn blue when she displays her powers which include the ability to manipulate time in limited ways and read the history of objects by touch. Steel lacks the empathy of Sapphire but has his own unique powers. These range from freezing himself to absolute zero to combat ghosts, enormous strength and telekinetic skills. Telepathy and the ability to teleport are shared by Sapphire and Steel and other elemental operatives.

Within the constraints of a limited budget the show managed to convey an uneasy, claustrophobic atmosphere, aided by enigmatic plots that could be viewed as inspired or confusing.

SEASON ONE

Serial 1 (1:01–1:06); *Serial 2* (1:07–1:15)

SEASON TWO

Serial 3 (2:01–2:06); *Serial 4* (2:07–2:10)

SEASON THREE

Serial 5 (3:01–3:06)

SEASON FOUR

Serial 6 (4:01–4:04)

[Comic book characters] First publication: *Look-in* # 33 (August 11, 1979); Story; Angus P. Allen; Art: Arthur Ranson; Publisher: Independent Television Publications Ltd.

This color comic strip adaptation of the television series ran to 76 weekly installments between 1979 and 1983.

[Audio drama] Release date: May 2005; Voice Cast: Susannah Harker as Sapphire, David Warner as Steel, Mark Gatiss as Gold, David Collings as Silver, Lisa Bowerman as Ruby; Producers-Directors: Nigel Fairs, Jason Haigh-Ellery; Writers: Steve Lyons, Joseph Lidster, David Bishop, Nigel Fairs, Simon Guerrier, Richard Dinnick, John Dorney, John Ainsworth; Big Finish Productions.

Released on CD this updated version of the television series features new actors in the lead roles. Each episode is divided into 25-minute segments to mimic the serial nature of the television episodes.

SEASON ONE

The Passenger (1:01); *Daisy Chain* (1:02); *All Fall Down* (1:03); *The Lighthouse* (1:04); *Dead Man Walking* (1:05)

SEASON TWO

The School (2:01); *The Surest Poison* (2:02); *Water Like a Stone* (2:03); *Cruel Immortality* (2:04); *Perfect Day* (2:05); *The Mystery of the Missing Hour* (2:06)

SEASON THREE

Second Sight (3:01); *Remember Me* (3:02); *Zero* (3:03); *The Wall of Darkness* (3:04)

Satan Returns a.k.a. ***666: Mo gui fu huo*** (1996) [Film; Hong Kong]

Premiere: May 17, 1996; Main Cast: Donnie Yen as Mo Ti Nam, Chingmy Yau as Officer Chan Shou-Ching, King-Tan Yuen as Rose, Francis Ng as Judas, Chi Wah Wong as Ka-Ming, Spencer Lam as The Reverend; Executive Producers: Jing Wong, Teng-Kuei Yang; Story: Jing Wong; Director: Wai-Lun Lam; 95 min.; Upland Films Corp. Ltd.; Wong Jing's Workshop Ltd.; Newport Entertainment; Color.

Royal Hong Kong Police Force Officer Chan Shou-Ching is told by a serial killer named Judas that she is the daughter of Satan—and he sets out to prove it.

Satan's School for Girls (1973) [Telefilm]

Premiere: September 19, 1973; Main Cast: Pamela Franklin as Elizabeth Sayres; Roy Thinnes as Dr. Clampett, Kate Jackson as Roberta Lockhart, Lloyd Bochner as Dr.

Delacroix, Jo Van Fleet as Mrs. Williams, Cheryl Jean Stoppelmoor (Cheryl Ladd) as Jody Kelly, Jamie Smith-Jackson as Debbie Jones; Producers: Aaron Spelling, Leonard Goldberg; Teleplay: Arthur A. Ross; Director: David Lowell Rich; 75 min.; Spelling/Goldberg Productions; Color.

Elizabeth Sayres enrolls at a girl's school in New England to investigate the suspicious suicide of her sister. But her investigations lead her to the same Satanic influences that caused her sister's death.

Saving Grace (2007) [TV series]

Premiere: July 23, 2007; Main Cast: Holly Hunter as Detective Grace Hanadarko, Leon Rippy as Earl, Kenny Johnson as Ham Dewey, Bailey Chase as Butch Ada, Laura San Giacomo as Rhetta Rodriguez, Gregory Cruz as Detective Bobby Stillwater, Lorraine Toussaint as Kate Perry, Dylan Minnette as Clay Norman, Bokeem Woodbine as Leon Cooley, Mark L. Taylor as Henry Silver, Yaani King Mondschein as Neely Lloyd, Tom Irwin as Father John Hanadarko; Executive Producers: Holly Hunter, Artie Mandelberg, Nancy Miller, Gary A. Randall; Creator: Nancy Miller; 46 × 43 min.; Fox Television Studios; TNT; Color.

After yet another night of heavy drinking Oklahoma police detective Grace Hanadarko accidentally hits and kills a man while driving her car. An angel named Earl comes to her emotional aid and tells her to renounce her self-destructive lifestyle and turn to God. Miraculously the dead man disappears, and she is granted the chance of a fresh start. But Grace finds turning her back on her promiscuous lifestyle to be almost impossible and Earl must keep a watch on her.

SEASON ONE

Pilot (1:01); *Bring It On, Earl* (1:02); *Bless Me Father, For I Have Sinned* (1:03); *Keep Your Damn Wings Off My Nephew* (1:04); *Would You Want Me to Tell You?* (1:05); *And You Wonder Why I Lie* (1:06); *Yeehaw, Geepaw* (1:07); *Everything's Got a Shelf Life* (1:08); *A Language of Angels* (1:09); *It's Better When I Can See You* (1:10); *This Is Way Too Normal for You* (1:11); *Is There a Scarlet Letter on My Breast?* (1:12); *Taco, Tulips, Duck and Spices* (1:13).

SEASON TWO

Have a Seat, Earl (2:01); *A Survivor Lives Here* (2:02); *A Little Homestead Love* (2:03); *It's a Fierce, White-Hot, Mighty Love* (2:04); *Do You Love Him?* (2:05); *Are You an Indian Princess?* (2:06); *You Are My Partner* (2:07); *The Heart of a Cop* (2:08); *Do You Believe in Second Chances?* (2:09); *Take Me Somewhere, Earl* (2:10); *The Live Ones* (2:11); *But There's Clay* (2:12); *So What's the Purpose of a Platypus?* (2:13); *I Believe in Angels* (2:14).

SEASON THREE

We're Already Here (3:01); *She's a Lump* (3:02); *Watch Siggybaby Burn* (3:03); *What Would You Do?* (3:04); *Moooooooo* (3:05); *Am I Going to Lose Her?* (3:06); *That Was No First Kiss* (3:07); *Popcorn* (3:08); *Looks Like a Lesbian Attack to Me* (3:09); *Am I Gonna Die Today?* (3:10); *Let's Talk* (3:11); *Hear the Birds?* (3:12); *You Can't Save Them All, Grace* (3:13); *I Killed Kristin* (3:14); *So Help You God* (3:15); *Loose Men in Tight Jeans* (3:16); *You Think I'm Gonna Eat My Gun?* (3:17); *I Need You to Call Earl* (3:18); *I'm Gonna Need a Big Night Light* (3:19).

The Scarlet Claw (1944) [Film]

Premiere: May 26, 1944; Main Cast: Basil Rathbone as Sherlock Holmes, Nigel Bruce as Dr. Watson, Gerald Hamer as Potts/Tanner/Ramson, Paul Cavanagh as Lord Penrose, Arthur Hohl as Emile Journet, Miles Mander as Judge Brisson, Kay Harding as Marie Journet, David Clyde as Sergeant Thompson, Ian Wolfe as Drake, Victoria Horne as Nora; Producer: Roy William Neill; Story: Paul Gangelin, Brenda Weisberg; Screenplay: Edmund L. Hartmann, Roy William Neill; Based on characters created by Sir Arthur Conan Doyle; Director: Roy William Neill; 74 min.; Universal Pictures; b/w.

Sheep's throats are ripped apart and a strange light is seen on the Quebec marshes. Now the phantom is killing humans. At a meeting of the Royal Canadian Occult Society Lord Penrose discusses murders at La Morte Rouge that date back 100 years. His wife has become the latest victim.

When Sherlock Holmes receives a letter from the late Lady Penrose stating she is in fear of her life Holmes decides to investigate. He tells Dr. Watson, "For the first time we've been retained by a corpse." Holmes soon discovers the late Lady Penrose was the famous actress Lillian Gentry and the murders are linked to her past and an actor who is a master of disguise.

Scooby Doo Where Are You! (1969) [Animated TV series]

Premiere: September 13, 1969; Voice Cast: Casey Kasem as Norville "Shaggy" Rogers, Don Messick as Scooby-Doo, Frank Welker as Freddy Jones, Nicole Jaffe/Rosalinda Galli/Carmen Onorati as Velma Dinkley, Stefanianna Christopherson/Emanuela Fallini/Heather North as Daphne Blake; Creators: Joe Ruby, Ken Spears; Original Character Designs: Iwao Takamoto; Writers: Bill Lutz, Larz Bourne, Tom Dagenais, John Strong; Producers-Directors: William Hanna, Joseph Barbera; 25 × 30 min.; Hanna-Barbera Productions; Taft Broadcasting; Columbia Broadcasting System (CBS); American Broadcasting Company (ABC); Color.

Lovable Great Dane Scooby-Doo joins Shaggy and his teenage friends in their "Mystery Machine" van as they investigate all manner of paranormal mysteries. The supernatural events are usually revealed by the "meddling kids" as ordinary criminals using scare tactics. Scooby-Doo and Shaggy provide the humor with their voracious appetites and cowardly ways when confronted with spooky happenings.

Dobie Gillis, Maynard G. Krebs, Thalia and Zelda on *The Many Loves of Dobie Gillis* (1959) served as the inspiration for Freddy, Shaggy, Daphne and Velma.

This successful and influential animated series has spawned numerous spin-offs including live action and direct-to-video films, video games and a revival of ***Scooby Doo Where are You!*** on the ABC network in 1978. Listed under Season Three, the revival show lasted for nine episodes under the original title with the final seven segments broadcast on *Scooby's All-Stars*.

SEASON ONE

What a Night for a Knight (1:01); *A Clue for Scooby Doo* (1:02); *Hassle in the Castle* (1:03); *Mine Your Own Business* (1:04); *Decoy for a Dognapper* (1:05); *What he Hex Going On?* (1:06); *Never Ape an Ape Man* (1:07); *Foul Play in Funland* (1:08); *The Backstage Rage* (1:09); *Bedlam in the Big Top* (1:10); *A Gaggle of Galloping Ghosts* (1:11); *Scooby Doo and a Mummy Too* (1:12); *Which Witch is Which?* (1:13); *Go Away Ghost Ship* (1:14); *Spooky Space Kook* (1:15); *A Night of Fright is No Delight* (1:16); *That's Snow Ghost* (1:17).

SEASON TWO

Nowhere to Hyde (2:01; *Mystery Mask Mix-Up* (2:02); *Scooby's Night with a Frozen Fright* (2:03); *Jeepers, it's the Creeper* (2:04); *Haunted House Hang-Up* (2:05); *A Tiki Scare is No Fair* (2:06); *Who's Afraid of the Big Bad Werewolf?* (2:07); *Don't Fool with a Phantom* (2:08).

SEASON THREE

Watch Out! The Willawaw! (3:01); *A Creepy Tangle in the Bermuda Triangle* (3:02); *A Scary Night with a Snow Beast Fright* (3:03); *To Switch a Witch* (3:04); *The Tar Monster* (3:05); *A Highland Fling with a Monstrous Thing* (3:06); *The Creepy Case of Old Iron Face* (3:07); *Jeepers, It's the Jaguaro* (3:08); *Make a Beeline Away From that Feline* (3:09); *The Creepy Creature of Vulture's Claw* (3:10); *The Diabolical Disc Demon* (3:11); *Scooby's Chinese Fortune Kooky Caper* (3:12); *A Menace in Venice* (3:13); *Don't Go Near the Fortress of Fear* (3:14); *The Warlock of Wimbledon* (3:15); *The Beast is Awake at Bottomless Lake* (3:16).

See: ***The 13 Ghosts of Scooby Doo***

Scoop, Vol. 1: Breaking News [Graphic novel]

First publication: June 2018: Story: Richard Hamilton; Art: Joseph Cooper; Publisher: Insight Comics.

Fourteen-year-old Cuban American Sophie Cooper accepts an internship at her local news station to clear her father's name. Her investigations concentrate on the Matheson Savings and Trust bank that accuses her father of money laundering. But a journey into conspiracy and the paranormal awaits young Sophie Cooper.

The Screaming Staircase (Lockwood & Co. #1) [Juvenile book]

Author; Jonathan Stroud; First publication: New York: Disney Hyperion, 2013.

Teenagers Lucy Carlyle, George Cubbins and Anthony Lockwood comprise Lockwood & Co., an agency specializing in the paranormal. "The Problem" has spread throughout the United Kingdom. Visitors are malicious ghosts that only children with psychic abilities can see. Lockwood & Co.'s latest assignment is Combe Carey Hall, renowned as the most haunted house in England. But their adversaries include humans as well as ghosts.

Lockwood & Co. series; *The Screaming Staircase* (2013); *The Whispering Skull* (2014); *The Hollow Boy* (2015); *The Creeping Shadow* (2016); *The Empty Grave* (2017).

The Secret of Skeleton Island (Alfred Hitchcock and the Three Investigators Book #6) [Juvenile book]

Author: Robert Arthur; Illustrator: Harry Kane; First publication: New York: Random House, 1966.

Alfred Hitchcock offers the Three Investigators acting roles in a short film about three boys on vacation on Skeleton Island who dive for pirate treasure. Meanwhile Pete Crenshaw's father is working on the main movie being filmed at an abandoned amusement park on the island in Atlantic Bay, off the southeastern coast of the United States. Recently movie equipment has gone missing and local workers have been spooked by the ghost of a girl who died when she was hit by lightning on the merry-go-round ride.

Hitchcock tells the boys that on their time off from shooting their film they can work in secret finding out who is disturbing the equipment.

The book was adapted with major revisions into the feature length film *The Three Investigators and the Secret of Skeleton Island* (2007).

The Secret of Terror Castle (Alfred Hitchcock and the Three Investigators Book #1) [Juvenile book]

Author: Robert Arthur; First publication: New York: Random House, 1964.

Film director Alfred Hitchcock sets the three boys known as the Three Investigators the task of proving a castle is haunted. If they succeed, he'll consider using the haunted castle as a location in his next film. The trio soon discover the castle is apparently haunted by former silent horror film actor Stephen Terrill. When sound replaced the silent film Terrill's lisp and shrill voice ruined his career and he reportedly took his own life in a fit of despair.

This first book in the long-running series introduces the reader to the Three Investigators. Jupiter Jones, the stocky leader of the team has an acute memory and an incredible talent for deduction but can be pompous. His friends refer to him as Jupe. Pete Crenshaw is quick, athletic and cautious. The third member Bob Andrews is studious with a talent for research. The trio who reside in Rocky Beach, California work out of an old mobile home trailer located in a salvage yard managed by Jupiter's uncle Titus Jones and Aunt Mathilda. Hidden among mounds of debris the headquarters comes complete with secret passageways, a lab and a darkroom. The cases of the Three Investigators often involve a natural explanation for apparent supernatural events, although the paranormal is sometimes the only explanation possible.

See: *The Three Investigators and the Secret of Terror Castle*

The Secret of the Haunted Mirror (Alfred Hitchcock and the Three Investigators Book #21) [Juvenile book]

Author: M.V. Carey; Based on characters created by Robert Arthur; Illustrator: Jack Hearne; First publication: New York: Random House, 1974.

Elderly Mrs. Dabney has spent her lifetime collecting antique mirrors. "That's the fascinating thing about mirrors. They've held so many images and it's easy to imagine a little bit of each person stays in the mirror."

At her home she leads the boys known as

the Three Investigators to her prize possession—a giant enchanted mirror decorated with carved goblins that once belonged to the Spanish magician Chiavo. A mirror that others want to possess and that Mrs. Dabney believes is home to a terrifying ghost.

Semi Dual [Short story character]

Authors-Creators: J.U. Giesy and Junius B. Smith: First Appearance: "The Occult Detector" *The Cavalier* (February 17, 1912).

Semi Dual alias Prince Abdul Omar of Persia is a mystic, telepath, astrologer, psychologist and psychic investigator. Dual assists "Glace and Bryce, Private Investigators" located in the same Urania building where Dual resides in his white cube tower penthouse on the roof of the twenty-story New York City office building. While many early cases don't directly involve the supernatural later stories feature the devil-worshipping Black Brotherhood and their leader Otho Khan.

Short stories-novellas: "The Occult Detector" (February 17–March 2, 1912); "The Significance of the High D" (March 9–23, 1912); "The Wisteria Scarf" (June 1–15, 1912); "The Purple Light" (October 5–19, 1912); "The Master Mind" (January 25, 1913); "Rubies of Doom" (July 5–12, 1913); "The House of the Ego" (September 20–October 4, 1913); "The Ghost of a Name" (December 20, 1913); "The Curse of Quetzal" (November 28, 1914); "The Web of Destiny" (March 20–27, 1915); "Snared" (December 11–25, 1915); "Box 991" (June 3–17, 1916); "The Killer" (April 7–28, 1917); "The Storehouse of Past Events" (February 10, 1918); "The Moving Shadow" (June 10, 1918); "The Stars Were Looking" (July 1, 1918); "The Black Butterfly" (September 14–October 5, 1918); "The Trail in the Dust" (October 25, 1918); "Stars of Evil" (January 25–February 8, 1919); "The Ivory Pipe" (September 20–October 4, 1919); "House of the Hundred Lights" (May 22–June 12, 1920); "Black and White" (October 2–23, 1920); "Wolf of Erlik" (October 22–November 12, 1920); "Poor Little Pigeon" (August 9–September 13, 1924); "The House of Invisible Bondage" (September 18–October 9, 1926); "The Wooly Dog" (March 23–April 13, 1929); "The Green Goddess" (January 31–March 7, 1931); "The Ledger of Life" (June 30–July 21, 1934).

Sergeant Spook [Comic book character]

First appearance: *Blue Bolt* #1 (June 1940); Story-Art: Malcolm Kildale; Publisher: New York, NY: Novelty Press, Inc.

Police Sergeant Spook is working on a chemical analysis connected to the murder of elderly Carrie Carter when his lit pipe sets off an explosion that kills him. Unphased by his new state as a transparent ghost that nobody can see he decides to continue working on the Carrie Carter case. To his amazement he discovers she was the leader of a spy ring who was murdered because she kept 60 percent of the money made from stolen plans of a super tank.

Now Riga Majesky is the new leader of the spy ring. Spook notices he can interact with the living despite being invisible and swiftly brings Majesky and his gang to justice, dumping him outside of the police station with a signed note from "Sergeant Spook."

In later adventures Sergeant Spook teams up with young Jerry who is the only person able to see him.

The Shadow [Pulp fiction character; Radio drama; Film]

Author-Creator: George C. Jenks a.k.a. Frank S. Lawton; First appearance: *Fame and Fortune* "The Shadow of Wall Street" (February 1929); Publisher: Street & Smith.

The original *Shadow* bears only a passing resemblance to the later creation by Walter B. Gibson. His real identity is Compton Moore, a hooded masked figure in green who protects the interests of honest investors from the crooks on Wall Street. But the beginnings of his sinister laugh are there. "Then from behind the mask sounded a hollow laugh!"

When *Fame and Fortune* folded *The Shadow* transferred to *Detective Story Magazine* which announced a contest to coincide with the premiere of *The Shadow* CBS radio drama. Maxwell Grant was now the official author of *The Shadow*. In truth it was thirty-three-year-old Walter Brown Gibson chronicling his exploits in *The Shadow Magazine*. Now he is World War I aviator Kent Allard who assumes various identities after faking his death. These include playboy Lamont Cranston and businessman Henry Arnaud. *The Shadow* stories by Gibson come under the category of weird menace with teasing titles such as: "The Ghost Makers" (October 15, 1942); "The Ghost of the Manor" (June 15, 1933); "The House That Vanished" (October 15, 1935); "The Ghost Murders" (January 1, 1936); "The Voodoo Master (March 1, 1936); "The Gray Ghost" (May 1, 1936); "Voodoo Trail" (June 1, 1938); "City of Ghosts" (November 15, 1939); "The Vampire Murders" (September 1, 1942); "The Murdering Ghost" (November 15, 1942); "House of Ghosts" (September 1, 1943); "Voodoo Death" (June 1, 1944).

The Shadow has been adapted for newspaper strips, comic books, film and radio. The radio show which had no input from Gibson would introduce his ability "to cloud men's minds so that they could not see him." The film adaptations are played as straight crime dramas except for **Invisible Avenger** (1958) and **The Shadow** (1994) which both utilize the mystic backstory.

2. [Radio drama] First broadcast: July 31, 1930; *Detective Story Hour*; Columbia Broadcasting System (CBS).

"Who knows what evil lurks in the hearts of men? The Shadow knows!"

The Shadow was initially used as a narrator and host for various radio shows from 1930–1935 voiced by Jack LaCurto, Frank Readick, George Earle and Robert Hardy Andrews. He began his dramatic radio career on September 26, 1937, on the Mutual Broadcasting System. The 30-minute show ran until December 26, 1954, completing 677 episodes in total. In that time the Shadow was voiced by many different actors including William Johnstone, Bret Morrison, John Archer and Steve Cortleigh but the classic version belongs to Orson Welles who provided the voice for the character from September 1937 to October 1938.

Amateur criminologist Lamont Cranston solves cases beyond the scope of the police. Able to cloud men's minds so he is heard but never seen he is aided by his companion Margo Lane who alone knows his identity.

Each episode concludes with the sound of menacing laughter and the words, "The weed of crime bears bitter fruit. Crime does not pay. The Shadow knows!"

3. [Film] Premiere: July 1, 1994; Main Cast: Alec Baldwin as Lamont Cranston/The Shadow,

The cover for *The Shadow Detective Monthly* (March 1932). Cover art by George Rozen (Street & Smith).

John Lone as Shiwan Khan, Penelope Ann Miller as Margo Lane, Peter Boyle as Moe Shrevnitz, Ian McKellen as Reinhardt Lane, Tim Curry as Farley Claymore, Jonathan Winters as Barth, Sab Shimono as Dr. Tam, Andre Gregory as Burbank, James Hong as Li Peng, Joseph Maher as Isaac Newboldt, John Kapelos as Duke Rollins, Max Wright as Berger; Executive Producers: Rolf Deyhle, Louis A. Stroller; Story: David Koepp; Director: Russell Mulcahy; 108 min.; Bregman/Baer Productions; Universal Pictures; Color.

Former drug lord Lamont Cranston learns mind altering skills from a Tibetan mystic. "I will use your black shadow to fight evil." Back in 1930s New York City Cranston attempts to atone for his past sins by fighting for justice as *The Shadow*. "I do what I do to fight the evil inside me." He confronts his greatest foe in Shiwan Khan, the descendant of Genghis Khan who also possesses mind-altering powers and threatens New York with an atomic bomb. Meanwhile Cranston is charmed by socialite Margo Lane whose psychic abilities threaten to reveal his secret identity.

Shadow Chasers (1985) [TV series]

Premiere: November 14, 1985; Main Cast: Trevor Eve as Dr. Jonathan MacKenzie, Dennis Duggan as Edgar "Benny" Benedek, Nina Foch as Dr. Julian Moorhouse; Executive Producers: Brian Grazer, Kenneth Johnson; Creator: Kenneth Johnson; 14 × 50 min.; Warner Bros. Television; ABC; Color.

Dr. Jonathan MacKenzie, British professor of anthropology at the Georgetown Institute of Science and Technology is threatened with the grant for his research being cut unless he works on cases for Dr. Moorhouse's Paranormal Research Unit. The reluctant studious and skeptical professor teams up with brash tabloid reporter Edgar "Benny" Benedeck. Despite their contrasting personalities the duo continues to investigate the paranormal for Dr. Moorhouse.

Season One

Shadow Chasers: Part 1 (1:01); *Shadow Chasers: Part 2* (1:02); *Spirit of St. Louis* (1:03); *Amazing Grace* (1:04); *The Middle of Somewhere* (1:05); *Parts Unknown* (1:06); *The Many Lives of Jonathan* (1:07); *Phantom of the Galleria* (1:08); *How Green Was My Murder* (1:09); *Let's Make a Deal* (1:10); *Cora's Stranger* (1:11); *Curse of the Full Moon* (1:12); *Blood and Magnolias* (1:13); *Ahead of Time* (1:14).

Shadows Over Baker Street [Short story anthology]

Editors Michael Reaves, John Phelan; First publication: New York; Del Rey Books, 2003.

This anthology features stories by various authors blending the world of Sherlock Holmes and the universe of H.P. Lovecraft's Cthulhu Mythos in a timeline ranging from 1881 to 1915. Authors include (in short story order), Neil Gaiman, Elizabeth Bear, Steve Perry, Steven Elliot Altman, James Lowder, Brain Stableford, Poppy Z. Brite, David Ferguson, Barbara Hambly, John Phelan, Paul Finch, Tim Lebbon, Michael Reaves, Caitlin R. Kiernan, John B. Vourlis, Richard A. Lupoff, David Niall Wilson, Patricia Lee Macomber, Simon Clark.

Short stories: **"A Study in Emerald"**; "Tiger! Tiger!"; "The Case of the Wavy Black Dagger"; "A Case of Royal Blood"; "The Weeping Masks"; 'Art in the Blood"; "The Curious Case of Miss Velvet Stone"; "The Adventure of the Antiquarian's Niece"; "The Mystery of the Worm"; "The Mystery of the Hanged Man's Puzzle"; "The Horror of the Many Faces"; "The Adventures of the Arab's Manuscript"; "The Drowned Geologist"; "A Case of Insomnia"; "The Adventure of the Voorish Sign"; "The Adventure of Exham Priory"; "Death Did Not Become Her"; "Nightmare in Wax."

Sheila Crera (Short story character)

First appearance: *The Blue Magazine* (May 1920); Author: Ella Scrymsour; Publisher: Walbrook & Co., London.

One of the first female psychic detectives. Sheila Crera is introduced in the short story "The Eyes of Doom."

"She was sitting in the gardens of Lincoln's Inn one day, when she suddenly became aware of a quaint little figure beside her—a wizened man of perhaps sixty years, in a dark, claret-colored suit, with a black three-cornered hat upon his knee...."

"You are a sad and lonely little lady," he said suddenly. "Why not help those that are sad and lonely too?" You have a gift—a most wonderful gift of sight. Use that sight for your own benefit and the benefit of mankind. I promise you, you will not fail."

"But how?" she began, but the quaint little figure had gone...

Sheila felt dazed. She rose and looked round. No, she was still in the bustling world of taxis and motor-buses. The picturesque past had vanished. She smiled a little, and went *home, but her brain was working hard. She slept well that night, and when morning came her mind was made up.*

For the next three days, an advertisement appeared in the agony column of The Times.

Lady of gentle birth, Scottish, young, penniless, possessing strong psychic powers, will devote her services to the solving of uncanny mysteries or the "laying of ghosts." Offer quite genuine. Reply, with particulars and remuneration offered, to S.C. c/o Mrs. Barker, 14b Air Street, Regent's Park, London.

Sheila Crera features in six short stories by Ella Scrymsour including: "The Death Vapour" (June 1920), "The Room of Fear" (July 1920), "The Phantom Isle" (August 1920), "The Werewolf of Rannoch" (September 1920) and "The Wraith of Fergus McGinty" (October 1920).

Sherlock Holmes (2009) [Film]

Premiere: December 25, 2009; Main Cast: Robert Downey, Jr., as Sherlock Holmes, Jude Law as Dr. John Watson, Rachel McAdams as Irene Adler, Mark Strong as Lord Henry Blackwood, Eddie Marsan as Inspector Lestrade, Robert Maillet as Dredger, Geraldine James as Mrs. Hudson, Kelly Reilly as Mary Morstan, William Houston as Constable Clark, Hans Matheson as Lord Coward, James Fox as Sir Thomas Rotheram, William Hope as Ambassador Standish, Clive Russell as Captain Tanner; Executive Producers: Bruce Berman, Michael Tadros, Dana Goldberg; Story: Lionel Wigram, Michael Robert Johnson; Screenplay: Michael Robert Johnson, Anthony Peckham,

Sherlock Holmes (2009), starring Mark Strong as Lord Henry Blackwood (left) and Robert Downey, Jr., as Sherlock Holmes (Warner Bros.).

Simon Kinberg; Based on characters created by Sir Arthur Conan Doyle; Director: Guy Ritchie; 128 min.; Warner Bros.; Village Roadshow Pictures; Silver Pictures; Wigram Productions; Internationale Filmproduktion Blackbird Dritte; Color.

London, England, 1890. Occultist Lord Henry Blackwood apparently rises from the grave after being sentenced to hang for his crime spree of serial killings. Now Holmes and Watson are approached by members of the secret magical fraternity known as the Temple of the Four Orders to stop Blackwood before he kills members of Parliament.

Sherlock Holmes and the Servants of Hell [Novel]

Author; Paul Kane; First publication: Oxford, UK; Solaris, 2016.

London, 1895. An investigation into how a person vanished from a locked room leads to similar events. Sherlock Holmes and Dr. Watson trace the peculiar incidents to the mysterious "Order of the Gash" and ultimately to the Cenobites from Hell.

Sherlock Holmes: The Awakened [Video game]

Release date: February 16, 2007; Developer: Frogwares; Platform: Microsoft Windows; Perspective: 3rd-Person; Publisher: Focus Home Interactive.

In this 3D adventure Sherlock Holmes and Dr. John Watson investigate strange activities and search for clues that appear to be related to a secret sect which worships the ancient god Cthulhu.

Sherlock Holmes: The Breath of God
[Novel]

Author: Guy Adams; First publication; London: Titan Books, 2011.

Socialite Hilary De Montfort is seen running in terror in the windswept, snow covered streets surrounding Grosvenor Square. When his bloated and bruised body is found there is "scarcely a bone left intact." His cause of death is beyond explanation.

Sherlock Holmes' latest client is renowned psychical doctor John Silence. He tells Holmes and Watson of a possessed girl who passed along three names. The late Hilary De Montfort, the Laird of Bolskine a.k.a. Aleister Crowley and Sherlock Holmes.

Holmes and Watson decide to pay Crowley a visit and meet occult detective Thomas Carnacki on their travels. Crowley claims a rebel branch of the Hermetic Order of the Golden Dawn wants to instill fear in the public as Holmes and Watson come under attack from dark forces.

Silent Mobus a.k.a. *Sairento mebiusu*
[Manga; Anime film; Anime TV series; Japan]

[Manga] First publication: *Comic Dragon* (1989); Story-Art: Kia Asamiya; 12 volumes; Publisher: Fujimi Shobo.

The Attacked Mystification Police Department (AMP) is a division of the Tokyo police defending the Earth against the demonic Lucifer Hawks who originates from another dimension. The female officers of AMP, each possessing paranormal gifts, are Earth's best hope. The officers consist of their half-human leader Rally Cheyenne, cybernetic medium Lebia Maverick, Australian cyborg Kiddy Phenil, Japanese mystic Nami Yamigumo and psychic Yuki Saiko.

The manga has been adapted as two animated films and an animated TV series.

[Anime film a.k.a. *Silent Mobius: The Motion Picture 1*] Premiere: August 17, 1991; Voice Cast: Naoko Matsui as Katsumi Liqueur, Toshiko Fujita as Rally Cheyenne, Gara Takashima as Lebia Maverick, Hiromi Tsuru as Kiddy Phenil, Chieko Honda as Nami Yamigumo, Maya Okamoto as Yuki Saiko, Masako Ikeda as Fuyuka Liqueur, Kiyoshi Kawakubo as Grospoliner, Kouji Nakata as Lucifer Hawke; Executive Producers: Takashi Komatsu, Tsunemitsu Shirai; Creator: Kia Asamiya (a.k.a. Michitaka Kikuchi); Story: Kei Shigema, Michitaka Kikuchi; Directors: Michittaka Kikuchi, Kazuo Tomisawa; 54 min.; Anime International Company (AIC); Kadokawa Shoten Company, Anime Roman; Imagica; Studio Egg; Color.

Followed by the sequel *Silent Mobius: The Motion Picture 2* (1992).

[Anime TV series] Premiere: January 29, 1998; Voice Cast: Naoko Matsui as Katsumi Liqueur, Toshiko Fujita as Rally Cheyenne, Gara Takashima as Rosa Cheyenne, Miho Nagahori as Lebia Maverick, Hiromi Tsuru as Kiddy Phenil, Chieko Honda as Nami Yamigumo, Maya Okamoto as Yuki Saiko, Mami Koyama as Mana Isozaki, Kiyoshi Kawakubo as Grospoliner, Akiko Hiramatsu as Lum Cheng, Kaneto Shiozawa as Ganossa Maximillian, Koichi Hashimoto as Robert DeVice, Yasunori Matsumoto as Ralph Bowmers; Producers: Ikou Saito, Makiko Iwata, Shinjiro Yokoyama, Toru Shimose; Based on the manga by Kia Asamiya; Director: Hideki Tonokatsu; 26 × 23 min.; Radix; Sotsu Eizo; TV Tokyo; Color.

Season One

Awake (1:01); *Decide* (1:02); *Tokyo Underground* (1:03); *Break-In* (1:04); *Let's Have a Party* (1:05); *Endless Battle* (1:06); *Behind the Façade* (1:07); *The Succession* (1:08); *Tokyo Antique* (1:09); *Memories of a Labyrinth* (1:10); *Alice in Logic Space* (1:11); *Sister* (1:12); *Category-IV* (1:13); *Mobius Klein* (1:14); *Lum Chang* (1:15); *The Labyrinth of Time* (1:16); *Destiny* (1:17); *The Night of Separation* (1:18); *The End of the Wanderings* (1:19); *Love* (1:20); *Dark Side of the Moon* (1:21); *Crying* (1:22); *Life Again*

(1:23); *The Road to Hell* (1:24); *Battle to the Death* (1:25); *Hope* (1:26).

Silent Mobius: Case: Titanic a.k.a. ***Silent Mobius*** [Video game; Japan]
Release date: August 10, 1990; Developer: Gainax Co. Ltd.; Platforms: FM Towns, PC-98, PlayStation, Sharp X68000; Perspective: 1st-person; Publisher: Gainax Co. Ltd.

A ship identical to the RMS Titanic that sank after hitting an iceberg in 1912 is sighted above the clouds over Tokyo in 2023. The Attacked Mystified Police Department (AMP) investigate and encounter zombies on board.

Simon Ark [Short story character]
Author-Creator: Edward D. Hoch; First appearance: "Village of the Dead" *Famous Detective Stories* (February 1955).

Simon Ark claims to be a two-thousand-year-old Coptic priest doomed to walk the earth forever in the hope that one day he will encounter and defeat Satan. Meanwhile he makes a hobby "…of investigating any strange and unexplained happenings in the world."

In his first case "Village of the Dead" the small population of the village of Gidaz are found dead at the bottom of a cliff. Simon Ark arrives at the scene and learns of a charismatic leader named Axidus who may be linked to a centuries old evil force.

Selected short stories: "The Village of the Dead" (1955); "The Hoofs of Satan" (1956); "The Witch is Dead" (1956); "The Man from Nowhere" (1956); "The Vicar of Hell" (1956); "The Judges of Hades" (1957); "The Hour of None" (1957); "Sword for a Sinner" (1959); "City of Brass" (1959); "Funeral in the Fog" (1973); "The Treasure of Jack the Ripper" (1978); "The Mummy from the Sea" (1979); "The Vultures of Malabar" (1980); "The Unicorn's Daughter" (1982); "The Witch of Park Avenue" (1982); "The Stalker of Souls" (1989).

Simon Iff [Short story character]
Author-Creator: Edward Kelly (Aleister Crowley); First appearance: "Big Game" *The International* (September 1917).

Simon Iff is an occult detective, magician, mystic and psychologist. Following his adventures in six short stories he appears in the novel *Moonchild* (1929) under Edward Kelly's real name the British occultist Aleister Crowley. Simon Iff's initial short stories published in *The International* were collected as *The Scrutines of Simon Iff*. Three short story collections were then published totaling seventeen stories.

Short stories: "Big Game" (September 1917); "The Artistic Temperament" (October 1917); "Outside the Bank's Routine" (November 1917); "The Conduct of John Briggs" (December 1917); "Not Good Enough" (January 1918); "Ineligible" (February 1918).

Short story collections: The Scrutinies of Simon Iff; Simon Iff in America; Simon Iff Abroad; Simon Iff, Psychoanalyst.

Sir Edward Grey Witchfinder: In the Service of Angels [Comic book]
First publication: July 2009; 5-issue mini-series; Writer: Mike Mignola; Art: Ben Stenbeck; Publisher: Dark Horse Comics.

In the streets of Victorian London Solicitor Bernard T. Hopkins is found ripped apart by a savage beast without a trace of blood present. Enter Sir Edward Grey, Witchfinder and master of the occult, knighted by Queen Victoria for saving her from the evil witches of Farnham.

Hopkins is the latest in a string of identical murders whose victims were all members of the same archaeological expedition that discovered and disturbed an unearthly skeleton. Now a supernatural beast is on the loose as Grey finds himself at odds with the occult society the Heliopic Brotherhood of Ra.

The Sixth Sense (1972) [TV series]
Premiere: January 15, 1972; Main Cast: Gary Collins as Dr. Michael Rhodes, Catherine Ferrar as Nancy Murphy; Producer: Stanley Shpetner; Creator: Anthony Lawrence; 24×50 min.; 1×75 min.; Universal Television; American Broadcasting Company (ABC); Color.

"Move down the darkest corridor of the inner mind, across the comprehensions of reality. Beyond the shroud of the subconscious and into the Sixth Sense."

College professor Dr. Michael Rhodes explores his interest in the paranormal and extrasensory perception as a psychic investigator. His assistant Nancy Murphy assists him with his cases on occasion. Joan Crawford made her final acting appearance in the only feature-length episode of the series, "Dear Joan: We're Going to Scare You to Death" (2:02). Joan Fairchild (Joan Crawford) seeks refuge after crashing her car following a vision of her daughter who died prematurely in a boating accident. But the inhabitants of the house who offer Fairchild shelter are practitioners of the occult and intend to scare Fairchild to death. Actor Gary Collins interviews the real-life Joan Crawford at the conclusion of the story, despite not appearing in the actual episode.

The Sixth Sense is based on the 1971 pilot **Sweet, Sweet Rachel**. The series struggled to find an audience and was canceled halfway into Season Two. In syndication, episodes were edited down to 30-minutes with new introductions by Rod Serling for inclusion in the syndicated version of his *Night Gallery* series.

SEASON ONE

I Do Not Belong to the Human World (1:01); *The Heart That Wouldn't Stay Buried* (1:02); *Lady, Lady, Take My Life* (1:03); *The House That Cried Murder* (1:04); *The Man Who Died at Three and Nine* (1:05); *Can a Dead Man Strike from the Grave?* (1:06); *With This Ring, I Thee Kill* (1:07); *Witch, Witch, Burning Bright* (1:08); *Eye of the Haunted* (1:09); *Echo of a Distant Scream* (1:10); *Whisper of Evil* (1:11); *Shadow in the Well* (1:12); *Face of Ice* (1:13).

SEASON TWO

Coffin, Coffin, in the Sky (2:01); *Dear Joan: We're Going to Scare You to Death* (2:02); *Witness Within* (2:03); *With Affection. Jack the Ripper* (2:04); *Once Upon a Chilling* (2:05); *Through a Flame Darkly* (2:06); *I Do Not Mean to Slay Thee* (2:07); *And Scream by the Light of the Moon, the Moon* (2:08); *If I Should Die Before I Wake* (2:09); *Five Widows Weeping* (2:10); *Gallows in the Wind* (2:11); *The Eyes That Wouldn't Die* (2:12).

Skin Game (The Dresden Files Book #15)
Author: Jim Butcher; Publisher: New York: Roc, 2014.

Still under the control of Mab, the Queen of Air and Darkness, Harry Dresden a.k.a. White Knight must help Nicodemus Archleone and his supernatural felons steal the Holy Grail in the possession of Hades, Lord of the Underworld.

Skulduggery Pleasant (Book #1) [Juvenile book]
Author: Derek Landy; First publication: London: HarperCollins's Children's Books, 2007.

When twelve-year-old Stephanie Edgley a.k.a. Valkyrie Cain is attacked in the home she has just inherited from her late Uncle Gordon a mysterious stranger comes to her rescue. That stranger is the sharp-dressed 400-year-old skeleton-detective Skulduggery Pleasant. He believes her uncle was murdered and she is next in line. Stephanie and Skulduggery's investigations lead them to the evil Nefarian Serpine who seeks the Scepter of the Ancients that will enable him to reign over the world and restore the Faceless Ones.

First series: *Skulduggery Pleasant* (2007); *Playing with Fire* (2008); *The Faceless Ones* (2009); *Dark Days* (2010); *Mortal Coil* (2010); *Death Bringer* (2011); *Kingdom of the Wicked* (2012); *Last Stand of Dead Men* (2013); *The Dying of the Light* (2014).

Second series: *Resurrection* (2017); *Midnight* (2018).

Short story-novella collection: *Armageddon Outta Here* (2014).

Sleepy Hollow [Film; TV series]
[Film] Premiere: November 19, 1999; Main Cast: Johnny Depp as Ichabod Crane, Christina Ricci as Katrina Van Tassel, Miranda Richardson as Lady Van Tassel, Michael Gambon as Baltus Van Tassel, Casper Van Dien as Brom Van Brunt, Jeffrey Jones as the Reverend Steenwyck, Richard Griffiths as Magistrate Philipse, Ian McDiarmid as Doctor Lancaster, Michael Gough as Notary Hardenbrook, Christopher Walken as Hessian Horseman, Lisa Marie as Lady Crane, Christopher Lee as Burgomaster; Executive Producers: Francis Ford Coppola, Larry Franco; Story: Kevin

Yagher, Andrew Kevin Walker; Screenplay: Andrew Kevin Walker; Based on the story "The Legend of Sleepy Hollow" by Washington Irving; Director: Tim Burton; 105 min.; Paramount Pictures; Mandalay Pictures; American Zoetrope; Karol Film Productions; Color.

Constable Ichabod Crane is assigned from New York to investigate the death of three murders in the small town of Sleepy Hollow. All the victims have been decapitated by an alleged headless horseman riding a giant black steed. Crane is convinced there is an ordinary man hiding behind the guise of the headless horseman.

[TV series] Premiere: September 16, 2013; Main Cast: Tim Mison as Ichabod Crane, Lyndie Greenwood as Jenny Mills, Nicole Beharie as Abbie Mills, Orlando Jones as Frank Irving, Katia Winter as Katrina Crane, John Noble as Henry Parrish, Nikki Reed as Betsy Ross, Zach Appleman as Joe Corbin, Shannyn Sossamon Pandora, Lance Gross as Daniel Reynolds; Executive Producers: Heather Kadin, Alex Kurtzman, Roberto Orci, Len Wiseman, Albert Kim, Mark Goffman, Clinton Campbell, Ken Olin; Creators: Phillip Iscove, Alex Kurtzman, Roberto Orci, Len Wiseman; Based on characters created by Washington Irving; 62 × 43 min.; Mark Goffman Productions; Sketch Films; K/O Paper Products; 20th Century–Fox Television; Fox Network; Color.

A headless horseman is at large in present day Sleepy Hollow. Now Ichabod Crane has returned to life and traveled through time to 2013. With his partner, Sheriff's Lieutenant and FBI agent Abbie Mills, Crane sets about investigating the truth behind the surge in supernatural events in Sleepy Hollow.

Season One

Pilot (1:01); *Blood Moon* (1:02); *For the Triumph of Evil* (1:03); *The Lesser Key of Solomon* (1:04); *John Doe* (1:05); *The Sin Eater* (1:06); *The Midnight Ride* (1:07); *Necromancer* (1:08); *Sanctuary* (1:09); *The Golem* (1:10); *The Vessel* (1:11); *The Indispensable Man* (1:12); *Bad Blood* (1:13).

Season Two

This Is War (2:01); *The Kindred* (2:02); *Root of All Evil* (2:03); *Go Where I Send Thee ...* (2:04); *The Weeping Lady* (2:05); *And the Abyss Gazes Back* (2:06); *Deliverance* (2:07); *Heartless* (2:08); *Mama* (2:09); *Magnum Opus* (2:10); *The Akeda* (2:11); *Paradise Lost* (2:12); *Pittura Infamante* (2:13); *Kali Yuga* (2:14); *Spellcaster* (2:15); *What Lies Beneath* (2:16); *Awakening* (2:17); *Tempus Fugit* (2:18).

Season Three

I, Witness (3:01); *Whispers in the Dark* (3:02); *Blood and Fear* (3:03); *The Sisters Mills* (3:04); *Dead Men Tell No Tales* (3:05); *This Red Lady from Caribee* (3:06); *The Art of War* (3:07); *Novus Ordo Seclorum* (3:08); *One Life* (3:09); *Incident at Stone Manor* (3:10); *Kindred Spirits* (3:11); *Sins of the Father* (3:12); *Dark Mirror* (3:13); *Into the Wild* (3:14); *Incommunicado* (3:15); *Dawn's Early Light* (3:16); *Delaware* (3:17); *Ragnarok* (3:18).

Season Four

Columbia (4:01); *In Plain Sight* (4:02); *Heads of State* (4:03); *The People v. Ichabod Crane* (4:04); *Blood From a Stone* (4:05); *Homecoming* (4:06); *Loco Parentis* (4:07); *Sick Burn* (4:08); *Child's Play* (4:09); *Insatiable* (4:10); *The Way of the Gun* (4:11); *Tomorrow* (4:12); *Freedom* (4:13).

Sleepy Hollow (1999), starring Johnny Depp as Ichabod Crane and Christina Ricci as Katrina Van Tassel (Paramount).

Small Favor (The Dresden Files Book #10)

Author: Jim Butcher; Publisher: New York: Roc, 2008.

Harry Dresden's period of calm comes to a sudden end when Mab, monarch of the Winter Court of Sidhe calls in a small favor. He is literally in her debt and has little choice but to help her. But in doing so he places himself in mortal danger.

See: *Turn Coat*

Snake Agent (Detective Inspector Chen #1) [Novel]

Author: Liz Williams; First publication: Portland, OR: Night Shade, 2006.

Detective inspector Wei Chen of Singapore Three's 13th precinct is a snake agent, allowing him to travel between Earth, Heaven and Hell. Chen and his aide Zhu Irzh, Hell's vice detective, search for the recently deceased teenager Pearl Tang who failed to arrive in Heaven. All clues point to the father who murdered her in order to supply righteous souls, including his daughter, to Hell.

Detective Chen series: *Snake Agent* (2006); *The Demon and the City* (2007); *Precious Dragon* (2007); *The Iron Khan* (2009); *The Shadow Pavilion* (2009).

Solange Fontaine [Short story character]

Author-Creator: F. Tennyson Jesse; First appearance: "Mademoiselle of the Mantles" *The Metropolitan Magazine* (August 1918).

Psychic detective Solange Fontaine "has an extraordinarily delicate mechanism for becoming aware of evil." Solange works as an assistant to her French father who is a criminologist working out of his laboratory in their home in the south of France. Her gift for detecting evil is so finely balanced she rejects love out of fear of losing "that instinct."

Following the introductory story (August 1918) published in *The Metropolitan Magazine* the first series of stories (November 1918–June 1919) was published in *The Premier Magazine*. The second series (August 1929–December 1929) was published in *The London Magazine*. The final story (November 1931) was published in *The Strand*.

Short stories: "Mademoiselle of the Mantles" (August 1918); "Emma-Brother and Susie-Sister" (November 1918); "The Green Parakeet" (December 1918); "The Lovers of St. Lys" (February 1919); "The Mother's Heart" (March 1919); "What Happened at Bout-du-Monde" (April 1919); "The Sanatorium" (June 1919); "The Canary" (August 1929); "The Black Veil" (September 1929); "The Reprieve" (October 1929); "Lot's Wife" (November 1929); "The Pedlar" (December 1929); "The Railway Carriage" (November 1931).

Something From the Nightside (Nightside Book #1) [Novel]

Author: Simon R. Green; First publication: New York: Ace, 2003.

When detective John Taylor is hired by Joanna Barrett to locate her teenage runaway daughter, he ends up in the Nightside. A secret square mile in the middle of London where monsters and inhumans exist at an ever-present 3 A.M.

As the series progresses Taylor discovers his mother is the biblical Lilith who created the Nightside.

Book series: *Something From the Nightside* (2003); *Agents of Light* (2004); *Nightingale's Lament* (2004); *Hex and the City* (2005); *Paths Not Taken* (2005); *Sharper Than a Serpent's Tooth* (2006); *Hell to Pay* (2006); *The Unnatural Inquirer* (2008); *Just Another Judgement* (2009); *The Good, the Bad, and the Uncanny* (2010); *A Hard Day's Knight* (2011); *The Bride Wore Black Leather* (2012).

Special Unit 2 (2001) [TV series]

Premiere: April 11, 2001; Main Cast: Michael Landes as Detective Nicholas O'Malley, Alexondra Lee Detective Kate Benson, Richard Gant as Captain Richard Page, Danny Woodburn as Carl the Gnome, Jonathan Togo as Jonathan; Executive Producer/Creator: Evan Katz; 19 × 44 min.; Paramount Television; Rego Park; United Paramount Network (UPN); Color.

Special Unit 2, a division of the Chicago Police Department, has been formed to tackle "Links" who fill the gap between animals and humans. Operating out of a dry-cleaning store, recruit Kate Benson is assigned to Detective

Nick O'Malley to hunt gargoyles who are kidnapping humans for food. The interplay between the gun-happy O'Malley and kleptomaniac Carl the Gnome provides the comic relief.

"Links" investigated and confronted by Benson and O'Malley include a shape-shifting Japanese mummy with a taste for beautiful women, black widow spider mutants, a monster that feeds on human fat, a year witch that sucks the youth out of its victims, beautiful female gorgons who turn male victims to stone, an ogre who feeds on strippers and hookers, and a scarecrow who scares people to death.

The series was brought to a premature end when the creator of the RPG *Bureau 13: Stalking the Night Fantastic* claimed similarities between the game and the series. Rather than contest a lawsuit UPN canceled the show.

SEASON ONE

The Brothers (1:01); *The Pack* (1:02); *The Wraps* (1:03); *The Web* (1:04); *The Waste* (1:05); *The Depths* (1:06).

SEASON TWO

The Grain (2:01); *The Skin* (2:02); *The Years* (2:03); *The Invisible* (2:04); *The Eve* (2:05); *The Rocks* (2:06); *The Drag* (2:07); *The Beast* (2:08); *The Wall* (2:09); *The Straw* (2:10); *The Love* (2:11); *The Piper* (2:12); *The Wish* (2:13).

Spectacle [Web comic; Comic book]

First digital publication: October 11, 2017; Story-Art: Megan Rose Gedris; Publisher: Oni Press Inc.

Anna is a fortune teller who doesn't believe in the supernatural—until her twin sister Kat is murdered and returns as a ghost. Now Anna must share her body with Kat and look for clues in tracking Kat's killer among her troupe at Samson Brothers Circus.

The webcomic was collected in printed editions beginning May 23, 2018.

"Specter of the Yellow Quarter" [Short story]

Author: Alan Van Hoesen; First publication: *Ghost Stories* Vol.2 #1 (January 1927); Publisher: Macfadden Publications Inc.; Constructive Publishing Corp.

Deputy police commissioner "John Smith" is assigned to direct the fight against the distribution of contraband narcotics in New York's Chinatown. On a December morning in a raging snow storm Smith comes across veteran cop Clancy in a panicked state.

"Listen Chief. I'm telling you on the square. I was slipping along here looking for an unlocked door so's I could get in out of the storm for a few minutes. I stepped in the hall. I had just removed my coat to shake off the snow, when I heard a sound and looked up. There was old Tsing Lai Low—standing on the stairs. You know, the fellow they call the 'wise one.' I nearly took a flop. Just as I was raising my club to give him a crack, he suddenly pointed up then—just disappeared into the air, right before my eyes…"

Smith and Clancy then discover the body of Tsing in his apartment, still warm but dead, a dagger in his heart. Tsing had refused Bow Ming's hand in marriage to Chino Joe and Tsing paid the price. Now Cho has kidnapped the girl, forcing her to tell him where Tsing hid his will protecting Bow Ming from Chino. But when the police track Chino down and confront him he chooses suicide by dagger.

Spectre (1977) [Telefilm]

Premiere: May 21, 1977; Main Cast: Robert Culp as William Sebastian, Gig Young as Dr. Hamilton, John Hurt as Mitri Cyon, Gordon Jackson as Inspector Cabell, Ann Bell as Anitra Cyon, James Villiers as Sir Geoffrey Cyon, Majel Barrett as Lilith, Jenny Runacre as Sydna; Executive Producer: Gene Roddenberry; Teleplay Gene Roddenberry and Samuel B. Peebles; Director: Clive Donner; 120 min.; 20th Century–Fox; NBC; Technicolor.

World renowned American criminologist William Sebastian accepts an invitation to Cyon House in England. Sebastian's task, as an expert in the occult, is to prove supernatural evil exists in the house with Sir Geoffrey Cyon under its influence. Accompanying Sebastian is his friend Dr. Hamilton, a recovering alcoholic who is skeptical of the supernatural. Events soon test the Doctor's skepticism as the

Cyon family appears to be in the grip of demonic activity.

This failed pilot from *Star Trek* creator Gene Roddenberry marked the final television appearance of Gig Young before his untimely death one year later. He murdered his young wife before turning the gun on himself.

The Spectre [Comic book character]

First appearance: *More Fun Comics* #52 (February 1940); Creators: Jerry Siegel, Bernard Bailey; Publisher: Detective Comics Inc. (DC).

On a date with his fiancée Clarice Frets police detective Jim Corrigan is captured by Gat Benson and his thugs, his unconscious body dumped into a barrel filled with cement and thrown into the water. The spirit of the deceased Corrigan is told by a disembodied voice to return to earth as an earthbound ghost fighting crime. Corrigan protests but to no avail.

The cover for *More Fun Comics* #60 (October 1940) featuring the supernatural detective The Spectre. Art by Bernard Bailey (DC).

"Now doomed to haunt crime and the world forever, The Spectre begins his lone battle against the underworld in earnest!"

Corrigan quickly adjusts to his new existence and powers. These include flying, invisibility, the ability to grow to gigantic proportions, shrinking, transforming matter so bullets pass through him and walking through walls.

Despite being officially dead Jim Corrigan can fool everyone into thinking he's still alive. He alternates between his human form and his crime-fighting disguise as the cloaked Spectre, evoking fear in criminals with his grim skull-like visage.

In the mini-series *Day of Judgment* (November 1999) former Green Lantern Hal Jordan replaces Jim Corrigan as the Spectre, finally allowing Corrigan to be released from his earthbound existence.

Spell Blind (The Case Files of Justis Fearsson Book #1) [Novel]

Author; David B. Coe; First publication: Riverdale, NJ: Baen Publishing Enterprises, 2015.

Private investigator Justis Fearsson is a weremyste, a person with the gifts of a wizard who can enter the world of the paranormal. He also temporarily loses his mind every cycle of the full moon. The serial killer known as the Blind Angel is back on the streets of Phoenix, Arizona. Fearsson know the killer from his days as a police detective—his trademark calling card burning out his victim's eyes using magic.

Followed by: *His Father's Eyes* (2015); *Shadow's Blade* (2016).

The Spiritglass Charade (Stoker & Holmes Book #2) [Juvenile book]

Author: Colleen Gleason; First publication: San Francisco: Chronicle Books, 2014.

Princess Alexander calls upon Evaline, daughter of Bram Stoker and Mina, niece of Sherlock Holmes for help involving a friend. Seventeen-year-old Willa Ashton is being manipulated by a fake spiritualist into thinking she's in contact with her dead mother.

The goal is to make her appear to be losing her mind. Meanwhile vampires may be on the lose again in Victorian London.
See: **The Clockwork Scarab**

Stalin's Ghost [Novel]
Author: Martin Cruz Smith; First publication: New York: Simon & Schuster, 2007.

Investigator Arkady Renko's latest assignment is finding the truth behind sightings of the ghost of former Soviet dictator Joseph Stalin on the platform of the Chistye Prudy Metro station in Moscow.

Stan Against Evil (2016) [TV series]
Premiere: October 31, 2016; Main Cast: John C. McGinley as Stanley Miller, Janet Varney as Sheriff Evie Barret, Nate Mooney as Deputy Leon Drinkwater, Deborah Baker, Jr., as Denise Miller, Dana Gould as Kevin; Executive Producers: Dana Gould, Tom Lassally, Frank Scherma, Justin Wilkes; Creator; Dan Gould; 24 × 22 min.; 3 Arts Entertainment; Radical Media; IFC; Color.

Disgraced former sheriff Stan Miller joins forces with new sheriff Evie Barret to protect their New Hampshire town from supernatural entities who have a hatred for authority figures.

SEASON ONE

Dig Me Up, Dig Me Down (1:01); *Know, Know, Know Your Goat* (1:02); *Let the Love Groan* (1:03); *Life Orr Death* (1:04); *Ouija Bored* (1:05); *I'm Gleaning My Coven* (1:06); *Spider Walk With Me* (1:07); *Level Boss* (1:08).

SEASON TWO

The Black Hat Society: Part 1 (2:01); *The Black Hat Society: Part 2* (2:02); *Curse of the Werepony* (2:03); *Girl's Night* (2:04); *The Eyes of Evie Barret* (2:05); *Hex Marks the Tot* (2:06); *Mirror Mirror* (2:07); *A Hard Day's Night* (2:08).

SEASON THREE

Hell Is What You Make It (3:01); *The Hex Files* (3:02); *Larva My Life* (3:03); *The Demon Who Came in From the Heat* (3:04); *Nubbin But Trouble* (3:05); *Vampire Creek* (3:06); *Intensive Scare Unit* (3:07); *Stan Against Evie* (3:08).

Stan Lee's Lucky Man (2016) [TV series; UK]
Premiere: January 22, 2016; Main Cast: James Nesbitt as Detective Inspector Harry Clayton, Sienna Guillory as Eve, Darren Boyd as Detective Constable Orwell, Amara Karan as Detective Superintendent Suri Chohan, Stephen Hagan as Rich Clayton, Eve Best as Anna Clayton, Steven Mackintosh as Detective Superintendent Winter, Leilah de Meza as Daisy Clayton; Executive Producers: Gareth Neame, Gill Champion, Richard Fell, Stan Lee, Anne Mensah, Beverley Booker, Anna Ferguson; Creators: Neil Biswas, Stan Lee; 28 × 45 min.; Carnival Film & Television; POW! Entertainment; NBC Universal International Television; Sky One; Color.

Compulsive gambler Harry Clayton works as a detective inspector for London's Murder Squad. One fateful evening he meets the mysterious and beautiful Eve in a London casino. When he awakens after a night of sex Clayton finds a strange bracelet on his wrist, placed there by Eve. Thanks to the ancient Chinese bracelet on his wrist Clayton can now control luck to his own benefit. But the bracelet also has a dark side and has been used to kill people. Clayton discovers there are more bracelets identical to his own and the Wu Chi triad is intent on destroying them.

SEASON ONE

More Yang Than Yin (1:01); *Win Some, Lose Some* (1:02); *Evil Eye* (1:03); *A Higher Power* (1:04); *The Last Chance* (1:05); *A Twist of Fate* (1:06); *The Charm Offensive* (1:07); *My Brother's Keeper* (1:08); *The House Always Wins* (1:09); *Leap of Faith* (1:10).

SEASON TWO

Luck Be a Lady (2:01); *Playing With Fire* (2:02); *Double Bluff* (2:03); *The Trojan Horse* (2:04); *What Lies Beneath* (2:05); *The Point of No Return* (2:06); *Second Chance* (2:07); *The Fallen Angel* (2:08); *Lamb to the Slaughter* (2:09); *A Hero of Our Time* (2:10).

SEASON THREE

Facing Your Demons (3:01); *Run Rabbit*

Run (3:02); *The Zero Option* (3:03); *Missing Persons* (3:04); *The Sins of the Father* (3:05); *The Art of War* (3:06); *Blinded by the Light* (3:07); *End of Days* (3:08).

Steve Harrison [Short story character]
Author-Creator; Robert E. Howard; First appearance: "Fangs of Gold" a.k.a. "The People of the Serpent" *Strange Detective Stories* (February 1934).

Steve Harrison P.I. dabbles in cases with a supernatural or weird menace twist and confronts his enemy Erlik Khan, a descendant of Genghis Khan. Following Howard's untimely death his unpublished Steve Harrison stories were ignored for four decades until the first of five stories were published in 1976 in *The Second Book of Robert E. Howard*. The remaining four stories were published in *Skull Face* (1978), *Bran Mak Morn: A Play and Others* (1983) and *Two-Fisted Detective Stories* (1984).

Short stories: "Fangs of Gold" a.k.a. "the People of the Serpent" (February 1934); "The Tomb's Secret" a.k.a. "The Teeth of Doom" February 1934); "Names in the Black Book" (May 1934); "Graveyard Rats" (February 1936); "The House of Suspicion" (1976); "Lord of the Dead" (February 1978); "The Black Moon" (1983); "The Silver Heel" (May 1984); "The Voice of Death" (May 1984).

Storm Front (The Dresden Files Book #1)
Author: Jim Butcher; Publisher: New York: Penguin Roc, 2000.

In the first book in the series the reader is introduced to the main character. "My name is Harry Blackstone Copperfield Dresden. Conjure by it at your own risk. I'm a wizard. I work out of an office in midtown Chicago. As far as I know I'm the only practicing professional wizard in the country."

Dresden advertises in the Yellow Pages as a specialist in paranormal investigations and works as a consultant Chicago PD's Special Investigations Unit. In his first case he is contacted by Lieutenant Karrin Murphy, director of Special Investigations, to investigate a double murder involving black magic. Dresden tracks the killer to a dangerous black mage who now has Dresden in his sights.
See: **Fool Moon**

The Strange Case of the Alchemist's Daughter [Novel]
Author: Theodora Goss; First publication: New York: Saga Press, 2017.

Mary Jekyll, daughter of the late Dr. Jekyll is on the trail of her father's friend Edward Hyde following a series of grisly murders in London that are linked to him. Mary's prime motive is the reward money to alleviate her financial woes. But with the assistance of Sherlock Holmes and Watson she locates Hyde's feral daughter and a group of women who are all the product of a secret society of crazed scientists with a thirst for power. Now Beatrice Rappaccini, Catherine Moreau and Justine Frankenstein seek to better understand their origins and put an end to the killings.

The "Extraordinary Adventures of the Athena Club" continue in **European Travel For the Monstrous Gentlewoman**.

Strange Detective Mysteries [Comic book]
First publication: January 2015; Creators: Terry Pavlet, Sam Gafford; Story: Sam Gafford; Art: Rosario Battiloro; Publisher: caliber Comics.

Some of the greatest minds of the Victorian era are invited to New York City in August 1902. Bat Masterson, Arthur Conan Doyle, Nikola Tesla, Harry Houdini and H.G. Wells gather to investigate the mysterious death of Edgar Allan Poe. Decoding Poe's "murder diary" leads to more questions, the death of one of the invited guests, an encounter with "time agent" Ana and the potentially catastrophic ritual of the "Three-In-One."

Stranger Things (2016) [TV series]
Premiere: July 15, 2016; Main Cast: Winona Ryder as Joyce Byers; David Harbour as Police Chief Jim Hopper, Finn Wolfhard as Mike Wheeler, Millie Bobby Brown as Eleven, Gaten Matarazzo as Dustin Henderson, Caleb McLaughlin as Lucas Sinclair, Natalia Dyer as Nancy Wheeler, Charlie Heaton as Jonathan Byers, Cara Buono as Karen

Wheeler, Joe Keery as Steve Harrington, Noah Schnap as Will Byers, Sadie Sink as Max Mayfield. Dacre Montgomery as Billy Hargrove, Rob Morgan as Officer Powell, John Reynolds as Officer Callahan, Joe Chrest as Ted Wheeler, Matthew Modine as Dr. Martin Brenner, Priah Ferguson as Erica Sinclair, Executive Producers: Matt Duffer, Ross Duffer, Shawn Levy, Dan Cohen, Iain Paterson, Karl Gajdusek, Brian Wright, Cindy Holland, Matthew Thunell; Creators: Matt Duffer, Ross Duffer; 25 × 51 min.; 21 Labs Entertainment, Monkey Massacre, Netflix; Color.

In 1980s Hawkins, Indiana young Will Byers disappears. His mother and police chief Jim Hopper join the search for the boy. Meanwhile a girl escapes from the Hawkins National Laboratory where paranormal experiments on human subjects are being conducted for the United States Department of Energy. During the experiments the scientists have created a portal into a dimension known as the "Upside Down"—and Will Byers is trapped there.

SEASON ONE

Chapter One: The Vanishing of Will Byers (1:01); *Chapter Two: The Weirdo on Maple Street* (1:02); *Chapter Three: Holly Jolly* (1:03); *Chapter Four: The Body* (1:04); *Chapter Five: The Flea and the Acrobat* (1:05); *Chapter Six: The Monster* (1:06); *Chapter Seven: The Bathtub* (1:07); *Chapter Eight: The Upside Down* (1:08).

SEASON TWO

Chapter One: MADMAX (2:01); *Chapter Two: Trick or Treat, Freak* (2:02); *Chapter Three: The Pollywog* (2:03); *Chapter Four: Will the Wise* (2:04); *Chapter Five: Dig Dug* (2:05); *Chapter Six: The Spy* (2:06); *Chapter Seven: The Lost Sister* (2:07); *Chapter Eight: Chapter Two: (1:02); Chapter Three: (1:03); Chapter Four: (1:04); Chapter Five: (1:05); Chapter Six: (1:06); Chapter Seven: (1:07); Chapter Eight (1:08);* he *Mind Flayer* (2:08); *Chapter Nine: The Gate* (2:09).

SEASON THREE

Chapter One: Suzie, Do You Copy? (3:01); *Chapter Two: The Mall Rats* (3:02); *Chapter Three: The case of the Missing Lifeguard* (3:03); *Chapter Four: The Sauna Test* (3:04); *Chapter Five: The Source* (3:05); *Chapter Six: The Birthday* (3:06); *Chapter Seven: The Bite* (3:07); *Chapter Eight: The Battle of Starcourt* (3:08).

String City [Novel]

Author: Graham Edwards; First publication: Oxford UK: Solaris, 2019.

A nameless interdimensional detective can jump through realities as a stringwalker. When he is hired to investigate an explosion at a casino, he finds himself facing ancient Greek Titans, a spider god and a strange creature known as The Fool.

"A Study in Emerald" [Short story; Graphic Novel]

Author: Neil Gaiman; First publication: *Shadows Over Baker Street* (September 2003); Publisher: Del Rey Books.

In 1881 a detective who isn't named and Inspector Lestrade investigate the murder of inhuman Prince Franz Drago of Bohemia, the possessor of many limbs and green blood. He was visiting London as a guest of Queen Victoria, a Great Old One who defeated humans seven-hundred-years ago and now rules over them. The story merges the world of Sherlock Holmes with H.P. Lovecraft's Cthulhu Mythos.

Neil Gaiman's short story was adapted into a graphic novel, published by Dark Horse Books in June 2018 with art by Rafael Albuquerque.

Summer Knight (The Dresden Files Book #4)

Author: Jim Butcher; Publisher: New York: Roc, 2002.

Chicago wizard and paranormal investigator Harry Dresden is down on his luck. His girlfriend has turned half-vampire and left him, and his work has dried up. Enter the Winter Queen of Faerie with an offer to end has streak of bad luck and lift the supernatural hold of his faerie godmother. Dresden must find out who murdered the Summer Queen's right-hand man, the Summer Knight.

See: **Death Masks**

Supernatural (2005) [TV series]

Premiere: September 13, 2005; Main Cast: Jared Padalecki as Sam Winchester, Jensen Ackles as Dean Winchester, Misha Collins as Castiel/Lucifer/Jimmy Novak/Leviathan; Executive Producers: Philip Sgriccia, Robert Singer, Eric Kripke, McG, Jeremy Carver, Eugenie Ross-Leming, Brad Buckner, Adam Glass, Sera Gamble, Kim Manners, David Nutter; Creator: Eric Kripke; 44 min.; KEI Kripke Enterprises Scrap Metal & Entertainment; Warner Bros. Television; Wonderland Sound and Vision; Supernatural Films; The WB Television Network; The CW Network; Color.

Following the tragic death of their mother in a fire, two brothers, Sam and Dean Winchester track supernatural forces, ghosts, demons and their missing father as the travel across America in Dean's black 1967 Chevrolet Impala. When they eventually find their father, he tells Sam and Dean that their mother was killed by a demon and the only way to kill him is with a special gun created by Samuel Colt.

The brothers are essentially hunters of supernatural entities who become involved in detective work during investigations. On March 22, 2019, Jared Padalecki, Jensen Ackles and Misha Collins announced on Instagram that Season Fifteen would see the conclusion of the long-running show.

Supernatural (2005), starring Jensen Ackles as Dean Winchester (left) and Jared Padalecki as Sam Winchester (Warner Bros TV—CW Network).

SEASON ONE

Pilot (1:01); *Wendigo* (1:02); *Dead in the Water* (1:03); *Phantom Traveler* (1:04); *Bloody Mary* (1:05); *Skin* (1:06); *Hook Man* (1:07); *Bugs* (1:08); *Home* (1:09); *Asylum* (1:10); *Scarecrow* (1:11); *Faith* (1:12); *Route 666* (1:13); *Nightmare* (1:14); *The Benders* (1:15); *Shadow* (1:16); *Hell House* (1:17); *Something Wicked* (1:18); *Provenance* (1:19); *Dead Man's Blood* (1:20); *Salvation* (1:21); *Devil's Trap* (1:22).

SEASON TWO

In My Time of Dying (2:01); *Everybody Loves a Clown* (2:02); *Bloodlust* (2:03); *Children Shouldn't Play With Dead Things* (2:04); *Simon Said* (2:05); *No Exit* (2:06); *The Usual Suspects* (2:07); *Crossroads Blues* (2:08); *Croatoan* (2:09); *Hunted* (2:10); *Playthings* (2:11); *Nightshifter* (2:12); *Houses of the Holy* (2:13); *Born Under a Bad Sign* (2:14); *Tall Tales* (2:15); *Roadkill* (2:16); *Heart* (2:17); *Hollywood Babylon* (2:18); *Folsom Prison Blues* (2:19); *What Is and What Should Never Be* (2:20); *All Hell Breaks Loose: Part 1* (2:21); *All Hell Breaks Loose: Part 2* (2:22).

SEASON THREE

The Magnificent Seven (3:01); *The Kids Are Alright* (3:02); *Bad Day at Black Rock* (3:03); *Sin City* (3:04); *Bedtime Stories* (3:05); *Red Sky at Morning* (3:06); *Fresh Blood* (3:07); *A Very Supernatural Christmas* (3:08); *Malleus Maleficarum* (3:09); *Dream a Little Dream of Me* (3:10); *Mystery Spot* (3:11); *Jus in Bello* (3:12); *Ghostfacers* (3:13); *Long Distance Call* (3:14); *Time is on My Side* (3:15); *No Rest for the Wicked* (3:16).

Season Four

Lazarus Rising (4:01); *Are You There, God? It's Me. Dean Winchester* (4:02); *In the Beginning* (4:03); *Metamorphosis* (4:04); *Monster Movie* (4:05); *Yellow Fever* (4:06); *It's the Great Pumpkin, Sam Winchester* (4:07); *Wishful Thinking* (4:08); *I Know What You Did Last Summer* (4:09); *Heaven and Hell* (4:10); *Family Remains* (4:11); *Chris Angel is a Douchebag* (4:12); *After School Special* (4:13); *Sex and Violence* (4:14); *Death Takes a Holiday* (4:15); *On the Head of a Pin* (4:16); *It's a Terrible Life* (4:17); *The Monster at the End of This Book* (4:18); *Jump the Shark* (4:19); *The Rapture* (4:20); *When the Levee Breaks* (4:21); *Lucifer Rising* (4:22).

Season Five

Sympathy for the Devil (5:01); *Good God, Y'All!* (5:02); *Free to Be You and Me* (5:03); *The End* (5:04); *Fallen Idols* (5:05); *I Believe the Children Are Our Future* (5:06); *The Curious Case of Dean Winchester* (5:07); *Changing Channels* (5:08); *The Real Ghostbusters* (5:09); *Abandon All Hope ...* (5:10); *Sam Interrupted* (5:11); *Swap Meat* (5:12); *The Song Remains the Same* (5:13); *My Bloody Valentine* (5:14); *Dead Men Don't Wear Plaid* (5:15); *Dark Side of the Moon* (5:16); *99 Problems* (5:17); *Point of No Return* (5:18); *Hammer of the Gods* (5:19); *The Devil You Know* (5:20); *Two Minutes to Midnight* (5:21); *Swan Song* (5:22).

Season Six

Exile on Main St. (6:01); *Two and a Half Men* (6:02); *The Third Man* (6:03); *Weekend at Bobby's* (6:04); *Live Free or Twihard* (6:05); *You Can't Handle the Truth* (6:06); *Family Matters* (6:07); *All Dogs Go to Heaven* (6:08); *Clap Your Hands If You Believe ...* (6:09); *Caged Heat* (6:10); *Appointment in Samarra* (6:11); *Like a Virgin* (6:12); *Unforgiven* (6:13); *Mannequin 3: The Reckoning* (6:14); *The French Mistake* (6:15); *...And Then There Were None* (6:16); *My Heat Will Go On* (6:17); *Frontierland* (6:18); *Mommy Dearest* (6:19); *The Man Who Would Be King* (6:20); *Let It Bleed* (6:21); *The Man Who Knew Too Much* (6:22).

Season Seven

Meet the New Boss (7:01); *Hello, Cruel World* (7:02); *The Girl Next Door* (7:03); *Defending Your Life* (7:04); *Shut Up, Dr. Phil* (7:05); *Slash Fiction* (7:06); *The Mentalists* (7:07); *Season Seven, Time for a Wedding!* (7:08); *How to Win Friends and Influence Monsters* (7:09); *Death's Door* (7:10); *Adventures in Babysitting* (7:11); *Time After Time* (7:12); *The Slice Girls* (7:13); *Plucky Pennywhistle's Magical Menagerie* (7:14); *Repo Man* (7:15); *Out with the Old* (7:16); *The Born-Again Identity* (7:17); *Party on, Garth* (7:18); *Of Grave Importance* (7:19); *The Girl with the Dungeons and Dragons Tattoo* (7:20); *Reading is Fundamental* (7:21); *There Will Be Blood* (7:22); *The Survival of the Fittest* (7:23).

Season Eight

We Need to Talk About Kevin (8:01); *What's Up, Tiger Mommy?* (8:02); *Heartache* (8:03); *Bitten* (8:04); *Blood Brother* (8:05); *Southern Comfort* (8:06); *A Little Slice of Kevin* (8:07); *Hunter Heroici* (8:08); *Citizen Fang* (8:09); *Torn and Frayed* (8:10); *LARP and the Real Girl* (8:11); *As Time Goes By* (8:12); *Everybody Hates Hitler* (8:13); *Trial and Error* (8:14); *Man's Best Friend with Benefits* (8:15); *Remember the Titans* (8:16); *Goodbye Stranger* (8:17); *Freaks and Geeks* (8:18); *Taxi Driver* (8:19); *Pac-Man Fever* (8:20); *The Great Escapist* (8:21); *Clip Show* (8:22); *Sacrifice* (8:23).

Season Nine

I Think I'm Gonna Like It Here (9:01); *Devil May Care* (9:02); *I'm No Angel* (9:03); *Slumber Party* (9:04); *Dog Dean Afternoon* (9:05); *Heaven Can't Wait* (9:06); *Bad Boys* (9:07); *Rock and a Hard Place* (9:08); *Holy Terror* (9:09); *Road Trip* (9:10); *First Born* (9:11); *Sharp Teeth* (9:12); *The Purge* (9:13); *Captives* (9:14); *#THINMAN* (9:15); *Blade Runners* (9:16); *Mother's Little Helper* (9:17); *Meta Fiction* (9:18); *Alex Annie Alexis Ann* (9:19); *Bloodlines* (9:20); *King of the Damned* (9:21); *Stairway to Heaven* (9:22); *Do You Believe in Miracles?* (9:23).

Season Ten

Black (10:01); *Reichenbach* (10:02); *Soul Survivor* (10:03); *Paper Moon* (10:04); *Fan Fic-*

tion (10:05); *Ask Jeeves* (10:06); *Girls, Girls, Girls* (10:07); *Hibbing 911* (1:08); *The Things We Left Behind* (10:09); *The Hunter Games* (10:10); *There's No Place Like Home* (10:11); *About a Boy* (10:12); *Halt & Catch Fire* (10:13); *The Executioner's Song* (10:14); *The Things They Carried* (10:15); *Paint It Black* (10:16); *Inside Man* (10:17); *Book of the Damned* (10:18); *The Werther Project* (10:19); *Angel Heart* (10:20); *Dark Dynasty* (10:21); *The Prisoner* (10:22); *Brother's Keeper* (10:23).

Season Eleven

Out of the Darkness, Into the Fire (11:01); *Form and Void* (11:02); *The Bad Seed* (11:03); *Baby* (11:04); *Thin Lizzie* (11:05); *Our Little World* (11:06); *Plush* (11:07); *Just My Imagination* (1:08); *O Brother Where Art Thou?* (11:09); *The Devil in the Details* (11:10); *Into the Mystic* (11:11); *Don't You Forget About Me* (11:12); *Love Hurts* (11:13); *The Vessel* (11:14); *Beyond the Mat* (11:15); *Safe House* (11:16); *Red Meat* (11:17); *Hell's Angel* (11:18); *The Chitters* (11:19); *Don't Call Me Shurley* (11:20); *All in the Family* (11:21); *We Happy Few* (11:22); *Alpha and Omega* (11:23).

Season Twelve

Keep Calm and Carry On (12:01); *Mamma Mia* (12:02); *The Foundry* (12:03); *American Nightmare* (12:04); *The One You've Been Waiting For* (12:05); *Celebrating the Life of Asa Fox* (12:06); *Rock Never Dies* (12:07); *LOTUS* (12:08); *First Blood* (12:09); *Lily Sunder Has Some Regrets* (12:10); *Regarding Dean* (12:11); *Stuck in the Middle (With You)* (12:12); *Family Feud* (12:13); *The Raid* (12:14); *Somewhere Between Heaven and Hell* (12:15); *Ladies Drink Free* (12:16); *The British Invasion* (12:17); *The Memory Remains* (12:18); *The Future* (12:19); *Twigs & Twine & Tasha Banes* (12:20); *There's Something About Mary* (12:21); *Who We Are* (12:22); *All Along the Watchtower* (12:23).

Season Thirteen

Lost and Found (13:01); *The Rising Son* (13:02); *Patience* (13:03); *The Big Empty* (13:04); *Advanced Thanatology* (13:05); *Tombstone* (13:06); *War of the Worlds* (13:07); *The Scorpion and the Fog* (13:08); *The Bad Place* (13:09); *Wayward Sisters* (13:10); *Breakdown* (13:11); *Various & Sundry Villains* (13:12); *Devil's Bargain* (13:13); *Good Intentions* (13:14); *A Most Holy Man* (13:15); *Scoobynatural* (13:16); *The Thing* (13:17); *Bring 'em Back Alive* (13:18); *Funeralia* (13:19); *Unfinished Business* (13:20); *Beat the Devil* (13:21); *Exodus* (13:22); *Let the Good Times Roll* (13:23).

Season Fourteen

Stranger in a Strange Land (14:01); *Gods and Monsters* (14:02); *The Scar* (14:03); *Mint Condition* (14:04); *Nightmare Logic* (14:05); *Optimism* (14:06); *Unhuman Nature* (14:07); *Byzantium* (14:08); *The Spear* (14:09); *Nihilism* (14:10); (14:11); (14:12); *Lebanon* (14:13); (14:14); *Peace of Mind* (14:15); *Don't Go In the Woods* (14:16); *Game Night* (14:17); *Absence* (14:18); *Jack in the Box* (14:19); *Moriah* (14:20).

Season Fifteen

(15:01); (15:02); (15:03); (15:04); (15:05); (15:06); (15:07); (15:08); (15:09); (15:10); (15:11); (15:12); (15:13); (15:14); (15:15); (15:16); (15:17); (15:18); (15:19); (15:20).

Supernatural: The Anime Series (2011)
[Anime; Japan]

Premiere: January 12, 2011; Voice Cast: Hiroki Touchi as Dean Winchester, Yuya Uchida as Sam Winchester, Takashi Taniguchi as Bobby Singer, Takaya Hashi as John Winchester, Makoto Tsumara as Young Sam, Atsushi Abe as Young Dean, Mie Sonozaki as Jessica Moore, Seikko Tamura as Missouri Mosely; Executive Producer: Masao Maruyama; Creator: Eric Kripke; Directors: Shigeyuki Miya; Atsuko Ishizuka; 22 × 23 min.; Madhouse; Warner Bros.BS11 Digital; Color.

The Japanese anime is based on the first two seasons of the live action series.

Season One

The Alter Ego (1:01); *Roadkill* (1:02); *Home* (1:03); *Ghost on the Highway* (1:04); *Savage Blood* (1:05); *Till Death Do Us Part* (1:06); *Temptation of the Demon* (1:07); *Everlasting Love* (1:08); *The Spirit of Vegas* (1:09); *Moonlight* (1:10); *Nightmare* (1:11); *Darkness Rising* (1:12);

What Lives in the Lake (1:13); *Reunion* (1:14); *Devils Trap* (1:15); *In My Time of Dying* (1:16); *Rising Son* (1:17); *Crossroads* (1:18); *Loser* (1:19); *What Is and What Should Never Be* (1:20); *All Hell Breaks Loose: Part 1* (1:21); *All Hell Breaks Loose: Part 2* (1:22).

"The Swaying Vision" [Short story]

Author: Jessie Douglas Kerruish; First publication: *The Weekly Tale-Teller* (January 16, 1915).

"Chadwick bought the desirable semi-detached residences, Nos. 75 and 77, Herald Crescent, Willingborough, to fulfil the ideal of middle-class retirement; a house to live in and another to pay rates and taxes and the coal bill … and he found that the pair were the only ones to let in the Crescent…. On March 25 he, with his family consisting of Mrs. Chadwick and their two daughters, moved into No. 75. On the 26th he consorted with his next-door neighbor and learnt the worst. 'It was really nobody's affair,' the next-door neighbor protested. 'How could anybody warn you? Of course, you might,' he added, as the aggrieved Chadwick breathed threats relating to the ex-landlord of his new demesne and the house agent. 'Still, I must remind you it's a penal offence to kill people, even if they have landed you with one of the most notorious haunted houses in England.'"

Mr. Chadwick decides to contact old school friend Lester Stukeley who works for the Civil Service and shares his passion for psychic investigation. Chadwick describes "an utterly abominable smell … a sort of pale yellow-green, sticky stench."

Stukeley erects a pentacle of charred rowan wood as protection from possible harm.

"In the five points of the star he placed five crusts, each wrapped in a slip of linen, and between, in the five angles, five pinches of white powder. Bread and salt, with charcoal, are great protective influences,' he said, standing up. 'I'll guarantee that within this we will be safe from all molestation."

From the safety of the pentacle Chadwick and Stukeley notice a spreading shadow stream and above it an emerging figure.

"To each it appeared as though he was wearing spectacles unsuited to his eyes. The figure, naked and flaccid, was half-corpse, half-skeleton. In parts the bones protruded, but the head was untouched; a handsome young head, a face young behind its ashiness, hollow-cheeked and unshaven. As they looked it slowly rose in the air almost as high as the ceiling, then swept down again to the floor."

The following morning Stukeley interviews the neighbor Monsieur Duhamel who tells him of curiosities his father collected. Among the African witch-masks and mummy cases was a piece of wood from the raft of the *Medusa* that now formed part of the fireplace. In the back garden Stukeley kindles a fire with shavings and places the piece of wood on it, scratching a pentacle round the blaze.

"So, a collector of ghastly relics is to be blamed for it all! By Jove, one certainly never knows what the final reflex of one's actions may be!" Chadwick looked puzzled.

"But Stukeley, I do not understand. What was the Medusa? And the raft? I seem to recollect the name vaguely, but nothing about it." 'You might recollect it through Géricault's famous picture of it—a monument of ill-taste. The Medusa, Chadwick, was a French vessel, and she happened to be wrecked, decades and decades ago. The survivors made a raft, and on it knocked about the open sea until—it's a horrible tale, Chadwick, need I tell it all? Can't you piece it together? They were starving—think of the wood with the indelible stain on it—and the man with a lot of flesh hacked off him—that's what a relic of the Medusa's raft meant!'"

Sweet Silver Blues (Garrett P.I. #1) [Novel]

Author: Glen Cook; First publication: New York; Ace, 1987.

Private investigator Garrett searches for a missing heiress in Cantard mining country with the help of Morley Dotes, a renegade half-elf and three "grolls." In a land of predatory vampires, ill-tempered female gnomes, centaurs and unicorns Garrett P.I. must keep alert to remain alive.

Glen Cook's successful Garret P.I. series has resulted in fourteen books.

Book series: *Sweet Silver Blues* (1987); *Bitter Cold Hearts* (1988); *Gold Copper Tears* (1988); *Old Tin Sorrows* (1989); *Dread Brass Shadows* (1990); *Red Iron Nights* (1991); *Deadly Quicksilver Lies* (1994); *Petty Pewter Gods* (1995); *Faded Steel Heat* (1999); *Angry Lead Skies* (2002); *Whispering Nickel Idols* (2005); *Cruel Zinc Melodies* (2008); *Gilded Latten Bones* (2010); *Wicked Bronze Ambition* (2013).

Sweet, Sweet, Rachel (1971) [Telefilm]

Premiere: October 2, 1971; Main Cast: Stefanie Powers as Rachel Stanton, Alex Dreier as Dr. Lucas Darrow, Steve Ihnat as Dr. Simon Tyler, Chris Robinson as Carey Johnson, Brenda Scott as Nora Piper, Pat Hingle as Arthur Piper, Louise Latham as Lillian Piper; Producer: Stan Shpetner; Story: Anthony Lawrence; Director: Sutton Roley; 71 min.; American Broadcasting Company (ABC); Color.

Rachel Stanton hears voices telling her she's responsible for the death of her husband. She seeks help from Dr. Lucas Darrow, who has his own life changing experiences of Extra-Sensory-Perception, including telepathy. As Dr. Darrow investigates further, he shares Rachel's visions and feels mind control may be a factor.

This pilot was the basis for the series *The Sixth Sense* with Gary Collins replacing Alex Dreier.

Tactics (2004) [Anime; Manga; Japan]

Premiere: October 5, 2004; Voice Cast: Kouki Miyata as Kantarou Ichinomiya, Takahiro Sakurai as Haruka, Nana Mizuki as Suzu Edogawa, Tomoko Kawakami as Youko; Story: Kanechi Kanemaki; Director: Hiroshi Watanabe; 25 × 24 min.; Studio Deen; MediaNet; Studio Izena; TV Tokyo; Color.

In Taisho period Japan exorcist Kantarou Ichinomiya has befriended a supernatural being known as a Youkai that only he can see with his 6th sense. One of the Youkai is an ogre-eating Tengu that he names Haruka. Kantarou and Haruka join forces to tackle demonic hauntings along with shape-shifting kitsune demon Youko. Tagging along is schoolgirl, Suzu Edogawa who has a crush on Haruka.

SEASON ONE

The Black Tengu Awakens (1:01); *Yoshiwara's Mysterious Yearning* (1:02); *A Fairy Tale of the Mountain* (1:03); *Forbidden Pictures* (1:04); *Dancer in the Darkness* (1:05); *The 9.07 P.M. Streetcar Ghost* (1:06); *Alluring Call* (1:07); *She's a Fox* (1:08); *Yome Island Mystery Tale* (1:09); *The Spirit Wind's Words: Part 1* (1:10); *The Spirit Wind's Words: Part 2* (1:11); *Roses and Tengu* (1:12); *The Nightmare in the Sea of Trees* (1:13); *The Woman Who Loved Books* (1:14); *With the Summer's End Cicada Comes the Rain* (1:15); *Alas! The Lament of the Newlyweds* (1:16); *British Beauty* (1:17); *The Mystery Society* (1:18); *Maple-Colored Love* (1:19); *Daughter's Ballad, Oni's Racket* (1:20); *Gateway to Memory* (1:21); *Blue Eyes* (1:22); *Snow Scene of Glass* (1:23); *Hearts in the Distance* (1:24); *Strength that Cannot be Seen* (1:25).

[Manga] First publication: *Comic Avarus* (December 18, 2000); Story & Art: Sakura Kinoshita, Kazuko Higashiyama; Publisher: Mag Garden.

The inspiration for the anime TV series is ongoing at 15-volumes.

Tähdet ovat väärin (2010) [Film; Finland]

Premiere: October 28, 2010; Main Cast: Timo-Jussi Hamalainen as Komisario Palmu, Aleksi Kuutio as Etsiva Kokki; Producers: Petri Hiltunen, Toni Jerrman, Tapio Ranta-Aho; Story: Tapio Ranta-Aho, Hannu Blommila; Based on characters created by Mika Waltari and Robert E. Howard and the Cthulhu Mythos of H.P. Lovecraft; Director: Tapio Ranta-Aho; 63 min.; Espoon Science Fiction-ja Fantasiaseura; Color.

Police Inspector Palmu and assistant Kokki investigate the disappearance of three youngsters and discovers an evil cult and creature called Ghatanothea responsible.

The Tender Mercy of Roses [Novel]

Author: Anna Michaels; First publication: New York: Gallery Books, 2011.

When disgraced former detective Jo Beth Dawson discovers the body of twenty-six-year-old rodeo star Pany Jones in a field of roses her detective instincts surface again. The spirit of the murdered girl is also at work guiding her father Titus who seeks out Dawson to uncover the truth of his daughter's death.

Theodosia and the Serpents of Chaos
(The Theodosia Series Book 1) [Juvenile book]
Author: R.L. LaFevers; Illustrator: Yoko Tanaka; First publication: New York: Houghton Mifflin Books for Children, 2007.

Eleven-year-old Theodosia Throckmorton, the daughter of the Head Curator of London's Museum of Legends and Antiquities, has a special gift for detecting ancient, evil curses on artifacts. The latest arrival from Egypt where her mother works as an archaeologist is the black statue of Bastet the ancient fertility goddess in the form of a cat. Theodosia senses black magic attached to the cursed statue. Now she must find the source of the curse and remove it.

Books in the series: *Theodosia and the Serpents of Chaos* (2007); *Theodosia and the Staff of Osiris* (2008); *Theodosia and the Eyes of Horus* (2010); *Theodosia and the Last Pharaoh* (2011).

The 13 Ghosts of Scooby-Doo (1985) [Animated TV series]
Premiere: September 7, 1985; Voice Cast: Casey Kasem as Shaggy, Don Messick as Scooby-Doo, Scrappy-Doo, Heather North as Daphne, Vincent Price as Vincent Van Ghoul, Susan Blu as Flim Flam, Arte Johnson as Weerd, Howard Morris as Bogel; Executive Producers: William Hanna, Joseph Barbera; 13 × 25 min.; Hanna-Barbera Productions; Taft Broadcast; American Broadcasting Company (ABC); Color.

Scooby-Doo, Shaggy, Daphne and Scrappy-Doo crash land their Mystery Flying Machine aircraft in the Himalayas on route to Hawaii. Mischievous ghosts, Bogel and Weerd, have led them to the Temple where a chest containing 13 demonic ghosts can only be opened by the living. Before the ghosts were captured they placed a curse on the townspeople, turning them into werewolves. Shaggy and Scooby-Doo inadvertently set the evil ghosts free on the world. Now they must recapture them with the assistance of Vincent Van Ghoul.

This Scooby-Doo series steers away from the formula of criminals in spooky costumes to feature real ghosts and werewolves.

SEASON ONE

To All the Ghouls I've Loved Before (1:01); *Scoobra Kadoobra* (1:02); *Me and my Shadow Demon* (1:03); *Reflections in a Ghoulish Eye* (1:04); *That's Monstertainment* (1:05); *Ship of Ghouls* (1:06); *A Spooky Little Ghoul Like You* (1:07); *When You Witch Upon a Star* (1:08); *It's a Wonderful Scoob* (1:09); *Scooby in Kwackyland* (1:10); *Coast-to-Ghost* (1:11); *The Ghouliest Show on Earth* (1:12); *Horror-Scope Scoob* (1:13).

See: *Scooby Doo Where Are You!*

The Thirteenth Chair (1929) [Film]
Premiere: October 19, 1929; Main Cast: Conrad Nagel as Richard Crosby, Leila Hyams as Helen O'Neill, Margaret Wycherly as Madame Rosalie La Grange, Holmes Herbert as Sir Roscoe Crosby, Mary Forbes as Lady Crosby, Bela Lugosi as Inspector Delzante, John Davidson as Edward Wales, Charles Quartermaine as Dr. Philip Mason, Moon Carroll as Helen Trent, Clarence Geldert as Commissioner Grimshaw; Producer: Tod Browning; Writer: Elliott Clawson; Based on the play by Bayard Veiller; Director: Tod Browning; 71 min.; Metro-Goldwyn Mayer Corp.; Loew's, Inc.; b/w.

Irish medium Madame Rosalie la Grange is hired to stage a séance to uncover a killer in Calcutta, India. Suspects are invited to attend the séance in the hope the murderer will be revealed. But when another murder takes place Madame Rosalie and Inspector Delzante have two homicides to solve.

The second film adaptation of the stage play by Bayard Veiller includes Bela Lugosi as the Inspector, two years before Todd Browning directed him in *Dracula*. *The Thirteenth Chair* was also adapted as a silent film in 1919 and in 1937 under the direction of George B. Seitz.

Thomas Carnacki [Short story character]
Author-Creator: William Hope Hodgson; First appearance: *The Idler* (January 1910).

Occult detective Thomas Carnacki operates out of his home at 427 Cheyne Walk,

Chelsea. Carnacki invites four friends to dinner where they gather to hear his latest case. In his first published story "The Gateway of the Monster" a man called Anderson hires Carnacki to investigate a haunting at an old country house. The activity is centered on the Grey Room where the locked door slams in the dead of night and the bedclothes are thrown in a heap in a corner of the room.

"From Anderson I knew already that the room had a history extending back over a hundred and fifty years. Three people had been strangled in it—an ancestor of his and his wife and child."

Carnacki explores the room protected by his "Electric Pentacle" but realizes "the Grey Room was haunted by a monstrous hand." He discovers the pentagon shaped Luck Ring of the Anderson family under the skirting board. By wearing the ring Carnacki allows the Hand to enter the Pentacle and therefore trap it.

"The monster was chained, as surely as any beast would be, were chains riveted upon it"

Carnacki leaves the house and returns with an oxy-hydrogen jet and two cylinders containing gases. Erecting a small furnace in the center of the Electric Pentacle he destroys the Luck Ring and with it the trapped Hand. The Grey Room is haunted no more.

Thomas Carnacki has also appeared in many adaptations and stories by other authors including Alan Moore who features Carnacki in his *League of Extraordinary Gentlemen* graphic novel series as a member of the group led by Mina Murray in the early 20th century.

Short stories: "The Gateway of the Monster" (January 1910); "The House Among the Laurels" (February 1910); "The Whistling Room" (March 1910); "The Horse of the Invisible" (April 1910); "The Searcher of the End House" (June 1910); "The Thing Invisible" (1912); "The Haunted Jarvee" (1912); "The Hog" (1947).

Short story collection: *Carnacki the Ghost-Finder* (1913; Revised ed. 1947).

The Three Investigators and the Secret of Skeleton Island (2007)
[Film; Germany-South Africa]

Premiere: November 8, 2007; Main Cast: Chancellor Miller as Jupiter Jones. Nick Price as Pete Crenshaw, Cameron Monaghan as Bob Andrews, Naima Sebe as Chris, Nigel Whitney as Al Crenshaw, Akin Omotoso as Gamba, Fiona Ramsay as Miss Wilbur, Langley Kirkwood as Tom Farraday, James Faulkner as Bill; Executive Producer: Stuart Pollok; Screenplay: David Howard, Ronald Kruschak, Philip LaZebnik, Thomas Oliver Walendy; Original novel by Robert Arthur; Director: Florian Baxmeyer; 91 min.; Studio Hamburg International Pictures (SHIP); Medienfonds GP; Satire Entertainment; Industrial Development

Thomas Carnacki in *Carnacki: The Ghost Finder*. Cover illustrated by Frank Utpatel. Published by Mycroft and Moran, 1947.

Corporation of South Africa; Two Oceans Productions (TOP); Color.

After uncovering a case of art fraud, the Three Investigators are enjoying a well-deserved vacation on South Africa's Skeleton Island where Pete Crenshaw's father is working on a construction project. But their vacation becomes home to yet another investigation when they are hired by a young African girl to clear her father's name. This leads to a race to locate hidden treasure and a confrontation with the mythologic creature known as the Tokolosh.

The film disposes of most of the plot of Robert Arthur's original novel, changing location to South Africa. Despite a weak performance at the box-office a sequel *The Three Investigators and the Secret of Terror Castle* was released in 2009.

See: *The Secret of Skeleton Island*

The Three Investigators and the Secret of Terror Castle

(2009) [Film; Germany-South Africa]

Premiere: March 19, 2009; Main Cast: Chancellor Miller as Jupiter Jones. Nick Price as Pete Crenshaw, Cameron Monaghan as Bob Andrews, James Faulkner as Stephen Terrill/Victor Hugenay, Annette Kemp as Caroline, Jonathan Pienaar as Sheriff Hanson, Martin Le Maitre as Uncle Titus, Catherine Cooke as Aunt Mathilda, Ron Smerczak as Worthington, Axel Milberg as Julius; Executive Producer: Stuart Pollok; Screenplay: Philip LaZebnik, Aaron Mendelsohn; Original novel by Robert Arthur; Director: Florian Baxmeyer; 97 min.; Studio Hamburg International Pictures (SHIP); Medienfonds GP; Satire Entertainment; Industrial Development Corporation of South Africa; Two Oceans Productions (TOP); Color.

A video from Jupiter Jones' deceased parents surfaces at his surprise birthday party after a clown attempts to steal it. Jupiter's parents were investigating Steven Terrill when they died in an accident. The Three Investigators decide to follow up on clues in the tape that lead them to the mansion known as Terror Castle. Terrill is hiding something, and they intend to find out what it is. Meanwhile they meet a young girl with psychic gifts at the mansion who warns them of a curse and neverending bad luck.

This film bears little resemblance to the plot of the original novel by Robert Arthur apart from the names of the lead characters.

See: *The Secret of Terror Island*

Tokko (2006) [Anime; Manga; Japan]

Premiere: April 16, 2006; Voice Cast: Kana Veda as Kureha Suzuka, Orikasa Fumiko as Sakura Rokujo, Kenichi Suzumura as Ranmura Shindo; Producers: Daisuke Katagiri, Yoshihiro Iwasaki; Story: Mitsuhiro Yamada; Animation Directors: Kazuo Takigawa, Koji Watanabe; Director; Masashi Abe; 13 × 24 min.; AIC Spirits; Group TAC; Shochiku; Three Light; WOWOW; Color.

Ranmura Shindo works for the Special Mobile Investigation Force, Tokko, dedicated to keeping Japan safe from the undead, demons and general paranormal menace. Shindo has been traumatized by the brutal murder of his parents and his recurring nightmares include a half-naked woman with a sword. When he meets the woman in his dreams in real-life he joins her secret group to avenge his parent's murders.

Season One

Dawn: Awakening (1:01); *Dream: A Girl Appears* (1:02); *Bond: Moments Would Be Lost* (1:03); *Omen: Corpses in the Laboratory* (1:04); *Demon: A Father, All Alone* (1:05); *Sorrow: Who Kills My Brother* (1:06); *Love: A Telephone Call* (1:07); *Awake: Time to Say Goodbye* (1:08); *Dignity: We Were Born to Be* (1:09); *Waver: Never Mind* (1:10); *Prison: No Woman, No Cry* (1:11); *Indignation: If Not in Love* (1:12); *Dark: Remain Tender Together* (1:13).

[Manga] First publication: *Afternoon* (April 25, 2003); Story & Art: Tohru Fujisawa; Publisher: Kodansha.

The inspiration for the anime TV series. Three volumes were published. *Tokko: Devil's Awaken* (Vol.1–2) *Tokko: Phantom Hunter* (Vol. 3).

Tokyo Babylon (1992) [OVA; Manga; Japan]

Premiere: October 21, 1992; Voice Cast: Kappei Yamaguchi as Subaru Sumeragi, Miki

Itou as Hokotu Sumeragi, Takehito Koyasu as Seishirou Sakurazuka, Hiromi Tsuru as Kazami Asou, Koichi Yamadera as Yamagawa, Shuichi Ikeda as Shinji Nagumo, Ikuya Sawaki as President; Executive Producers: Megumi Sugiyama, Yumiko Masushima; Story: Tasuhiko Urahata, Hiroaki Jinno; Directors: Koichi Chigira, Kumiko Takahashi; 1 × 50 min.; 1 × 55 min.; Animate Film; MOVIC; SPE Visual Works; Color.

Onmyouji medium Subaru Sumeragi assists the police in investigations where his psychic powers are required. Assisting him is his twin sister Hokotu and friend Seishirou. A young woman has placed a curse on a construction worker who she believes killed her brother. Subaru must confront and exorcise the demons that apparently protect the man from dying.

The OVA was followed by the sequel *Tokyo Babylon 2*.

[Manga] First publication: Wings (1990); Story & Art: CLAMP; Publisher: Shinshokan.

The inspiration for the OVA series has been published in 7-volumes.

Torchwood (2006) [TV series; UK]

Premiere: October 22, 2006; Main Cast: John Barrowman as Captain Jack Harkness, Eve Myles as Gwen Cooper, Kai Owen as Rhys Williams, Gareth David-Lloyd as Ianto Jones, Burn Gorman as Owen Harper, Naoko Mori as Toshiko Sato, Mekhi Phifer as Rex Matheson, Alexa Havins as Esther Drummond, Bill Pullman as Oswald Jones; Executive Producers; Russell T. Davies, Julie Gardner, Jane Tranter, Bharat Nalluri; Creator: Russell T. Davies; 41 × 50 min.; BBC Wales; Canadian Broadcasting Corporation (CBC); BBC Worldwide; Color.

The Torchwood Institute founded by Queen Victoria acts as a secret organization dedicated to investigating the paranormal in all its many forms. Initially based in Cardiff, Wales the team comprises of former Police Constable Gwen Cooper now acting field agent, immortal rogue time agent and con-man Captain Jack Harkness, medical officer Dr. Owen Harper, support officer Ianto Jones and technical expert and computer specialist Toshiko Sato.

SEASON ONE

Everything Changes (1:01); *Day One* (1:02); *Ghost Machine* (1:03); *Cyberwoman* (1:04); *Small Worlds* (1:05); *Countrycide* (1:06); *Greeks Bearing Gifts* (1:07); *They Keep Killing Suzie* (1:08); *Random Shoes* (1:09); *Out of Time* (1:10); *Combat* (1:11); *Captain Jack Harness* (1:12); *End of Days* (1:13).

SEASON TWO

Kiss Kiss, Bang Bang (1:01); *Sleeper* (1:02); *To the Last Man* (1:03); *Meat* (1:04); *Adam* (1:05); *Reset* (1:06); *Dead Man Walking* (1:07); *A Day in the Death* (1:08); *Something Borrowed* (1:09); *From Out of the Rain* (1:10); *Adrift* (1:11); *Fragments* (1:12); *Exit Wounds* (1:13).

SEASON THREE

Children of the Earth: Day One (1:01); *Children of the Earth: Day Two* (1:02); *Children of the Earth: Day Three* (1:03); *Children of the Earth: Day Four* (1:04); *Children of the Earth: Day Five* (1:05).

Torchwood (2006), **starring Eve Myles as Gwen Cooper (BBC Worldwide).**

SEASON FOUR

Miracle Day: The New World (1:01); *Miracle Day: Rendition* (1:02); *Miracle Day: Dead of Night* (1:03); *Miracle Day: Escape to LA* (1:04); *Miracle Day: Miracle Day: The Categories of Life* (1:05); *Miracle Day: Miracle Day: he Middle Men* (1:06); *Miracle Day: Immortal Sins* (1:07); *Miracle Day: End of the Road* (1:08); *Miracle Day: The Gathering* (1:09); *Miracle Day: Miracle Day: The Blood Line* (1:10).

Touch Detective [Video game]

Release date: April 13, 2006; Developer: BeeWorks; Platforms: Nintendo DS, iOS; Publishers: Success Corporation (Japan); Atlus (U.S.); 505 Games (Europe).

The player controls young female detective Ozawa Rina/Mackenzie. Four mysteries require solving in the Japanese town of Osawari. If the young detective solves them, she will become a member of the Great Detective Society. The four mysteries are divided into episodes. In Episode One Manami/Penelope claims her dreams are being stolen. Episode Two sees Penelope go missing and all roads lead to the planetarium. Episode Three involves the life of an ice fairy being threatened with the closure of the ice-skating rink. Episode Four centers on a flea circus and a former performer looking for revenge on the fleas he blames for ruining his career.

Transylvania 6–5000 (1985) [Film]

Premiere: November 8, 1985; Main Cast: Jeff Goldblum as Jack Harrison, Ed Begley, Jr., as Gil Turner, Norman Fell as Mac Turner, Joseph Bologna as Dr. Malavaqua, Carol Kane as Lupi, Jeffrey Jones as Lepescu, John Byner as Radu, Geena Davis as Odette, Michael Richards as Fejos, Donald Gibb as Wolfman, Teresa Ganzel as Elizabeth Ellison, Rudy De Lucia as Lawrence Malbot, Inge Appelt as Madame Morovia, Bozidar Smiljanic as Inspector Percek; Executive Producers; Arnie Fishman, Paul Lichtman; Story/Director: Rudy De Luca; 93 min.; Balcor Film; Dow Chemical; New World Pictures; Color.

Tabloid reporters Jack Harrison and Gil Turner are told to prove Frankenstein lives by following a lead from a videotape allegedly showing two men running in fear from the monster in Transylvania. If they don't bring back a story, they'll both be fired. The two reporters find much more than Frankenstein's monster awaiting them in this comedy-horror film.

Trenchcoat Brigade [Comic book]

First publication: March 1999; 4-issue limited series; Writer: John Ney Reiber; Art: John Ridgway; Publisher: Vertigo/DC Comics.

Comprised of **John Constantine**, **Doctor Occult**, Mister E and Phantom Stranger, the four mystics reunite to save the world from the Russian god M'Nagalah.

The *Trenchcoat Brigade* first appear together as a group in *The Books of Magic* #1 (December 1990).

Trick (2000) [TV series; Japan]

Premiere: July 7, 2000; Main Cast: Yukie Nakama as Naoko Yamada, Hiroshi Abe as Professor Jiro Ueda, Katsuhisa Namase as Detective Kenzo Yabe, Kazuki Maehara as Detective Ishihara Tatsuya, Yoko Nogiwa as Satomi Yamada, Yoko Ohshima as Haru Ikeda, Abedin Mohammed as Jami-kun; Producers: Mitsuharu Makita, Akihiro Yamauchi; Story: Mitsuharu Makita, Makoto Hayashi; Directors: Hitoshi One, Yukihiko Tsutsumi, Hisashi Kimura; 31 × 60 min.; TV Asahi; Color.

Failing to follow in her father's footsteps as a great magician struggling illusionist Yamada Naoko accepts a financially rewarding challenge from cynical physics Professor Ueda to prove magic is real. First, she must uncover the truth behind a religious cult known as The Mother's Fountain. Naoko ultimately finds herself assisting Professor Ueda and the police working on cases exposing spiritualists, cult leaders and all manner of supernatural events. But Naoko discovers not all paranormal cases are fake when she contacts her dead father.

The successful comedy-mystery series has spawned many sequels including the one season television series *Trick 2* (2002) and *Trick 3* (2003) featuring the same lead actors and characters.

Season One

Toshi (1:01); *Kabenuke* (1:02); *Haha no shi* (1:03); *Murabito ga zenin kie ta* (1:04); *Mura ga kie ta ... kaiketsu-hen* (1:05); *Shunken ido satsujin no himitsu* (1:06); *Enkaku satsujin igai na torikku* (1:07); *Senrigan no otoko* (1:08); *Chichi o koroshita shinhan'nin* (1:09); *Shinhan'nin wa omaeda!!* (1:10).

Season Two

Six Graves Village: Part 1 (2:01); *Six Graves Village: Part 2* (2:02); *Six Graves: Part 3/The 100% Accurate Fortune Teller: Part 1* (2:03); *The 100% Accurate Fortune Teller: Part 2* (2:04); *The 100% Accurate Fortune Teller: Part 3* (2:05); *Psi-trailer: Part 1* (2:06); *Psi-trailer: Part 2* (2:07); *The Child Who Punishes the Guilty* (2:08); *The Child Who Punishes the Guilty: The Solution* (2:09); *Final Chapter: The Forest of Sorcery* (2:10); *Final Chapter: The Mystery of Witchcraft* (2:11).

Season Three

The Man Who Controls People with Spirits (3:01); *The Man Who Controls People by Suggestion-Solution* (3:02); *The Instantaneous Movement Mystery: Part 1* (3:03); *The Instantaneous Movement Mystery: Part 2* (3:04); *The Mystery of the Nursing Home Where Nobody Dies: Part 1* (3:05); *The Mystery of the Nursing Home Where Nobody Dies: Part 2* (3:06); *The Mystery Behind the Curse of the Old House* (3:07); *The Mystery of the Puns Which Bring Death-Solution* (3:08); *Final Chapter: A Woman Who Creates Things in Her Mind* (3:09); *The Truth About the Ability to Steal Spirits* (3:10).

Trick: The Movie (2002) [Film; Japan]

Premiere: November 9, 2002; Main Cast: Yukie Nakama as Naoko Yamada, Hiroshi Abe as Professor Jiro Ueda, Katsuhisa Namase as Detective Kenzo Yabe, Riko Narumbi as Young Naoko Yamada, Toshie Negeshi as Kikuhime, Kazuyuki Aijima as Sansboro hongo, Kazuki Maehara as Tasuya Ishihara, Yoko Nogiwa as Satomi Yamada, Yoko Ohshima as Haru Ikeda, Naoto Takenaka as Deity, Bengaru as Deity, Renji Ishibashi as Deity, Shinji Yamashita as Akio Kanzaki, Miyou Yoshimoto as Etsuko Minagawa; Producers: Mitsuharu Makita, Akihiro Yamauchi; Screenplay: Mitsuharu Makita; Director: Yukihiko Tsutsumi; 119 min.; Asahi Broadcasting Corporation (ABC); Asahi Shimbun; Nippon Shuppan Habai (Nippan) K.K.; Office Crescendo; Sponichi-SNS; Toho Company; Color.

Illusionist Naoko Yamada comes to the aid of superstitious villagers who believe a disaster strikes every 300 years. Posing as a goddess to comfort the villagers Naoko encounters multiple deities. It's time for Naoko to enlist the help of Professor Ueda and detective Yabe to uncover the reality behind the influx of self-imposed gods and the apparent paranormal events.

Followed by *Trick: The Movie 2* (2006), *Trick the Movie: Psychic Battle Royale* (2010) and *Trick the Movie: Last Stage* (2014) featuring the same lead players and director.

Turn Coat (The Dresden Files Book #11)

Author: Jim Butcher; Publisher: New York: Roc, 2009.

Paranormal investigator Harry Dresden protects the Warden Morgan against charges of treason by the Wizards of the White Council. There is a traitor at large within the Council and Dresden places himself in danger to uncover the culprit.

See: **Changes**

Twin Peaks (1990) [TV series]

Premiere: April 8, 1990: Main Cast: Kyle MacLachlan as Special Agent Dale Cooper, Michael Ontkean as Sheriff Harry S. Truman, Madchen Amick as Shelly Johnson, Dana Ashbrook as Bobby Briggs, Richard Beymer as Benjamin Horne, Lara Flynn Boyle as Donna Hayward, Sherilyn Fenn as Audrey Horne, Warren Frost as Dr. Will Hayward, Peggy Lipton as Norma Jennings, James Marshall as James Hurley, Everett McGill as Big Ed Hurley, Jack Nance as Pete Martell, Joan Chen as Jocelyn Packard, Piper Laurie as Catherine Martell/Mr. Tojamura, Michael Horse as Deputy Tommy "Hawk" Hill, Sheryl Lee as Maddy Ferguson/Laura Palmer, Ray Wise as Leland Palmer, Russ Tamblyn as Dr. Lawrence Jacoby; Executive Producers/Creators: David Lynch, Mark Frost; 1 × 94 min.; 29 × 47 min.; Lynch/Frost Productions; Propaganda Films; Spelling Entertainment; Twin Peaks Productions; American Broadcasting Company (ABC); Color.

FBI Special Agent Dale Cooper investigates the murder of homecoming queen Laura Palmer in the Pacific Northwest town of Twin Peaks. He soon discovers the town and its populace hold many secrets. Cooper is disturbed by a dream where a one-armed man claims to know Palmer's killer and a business-suited dwarf talks backward. These are followed by visions where a giant provides more clues. The world of the occult has entered Twin Peaks as Cooper's investigations become more complex leading to the Black Lodge.

SEASON ONE

Pilot (1:01); *Traces to Nowhere* (1:02); *Zen, or the Skill to Catch a Killer* (1:03); *Rest in Pain* (1:04); *The One-Armed Man* (1:05); *Cooper's Dreams* (1:06); *Realization Time* (1:07); *The Last Evening* (1:08).

SEASON TWO

May the Giant Be with You (1:01); *Coma* (1:02); *The Man Behind the Glass* (1:03); *Laura's Secret Diary* (1:04); *The Orchid's Curse* (1:05); *Demons* (1:06); *Lonely Souls* (1:07); *Drive with a Dead Girl* (1:08); *Arbitrary Law* (1:09); *Dispute Between Brothers* (1:10); *Masked Ball* (1:11); *The Black Widow* (1:12); *Checkmate* (1:13); *Double Play* (1:14); *Slaves and Masters* (1:15); *The Condemned Woman* (1:16); *Wounds and Scars* (1:17); *On the Wings of Love* (1:18); *Variations on Relations* (1:19); *The Path to the Black Lodge* (1:20); *Miss Twin Peaks* (1:21); *Beyond Life and Death* (1:22).

Twin Peaks: Fire Walk with Me (1992)
[Film]

Premiere: May 16, 1992; Main Cast: Sheryl Lee as Laura Palmer, Ray Wise as Leland Palmer, Kyle MacLachlan as Special Agent Dale Cooper, Madchen Amick as Shelly Johnson, Dana Ashbrook as Bobby Briggs, Peggy Lipton as Norma Jennings, James Marshall as James

Twin Peaks (1990), starring (left to right) Joan Chen as Jocelyn Packard, Michael Ontkean as Sheriff Harry S. Truman, Kyle MacLachlan as Special Agent Dale Cooper, and Piper Laurie as Catherine Martell (ABC Television Network).

Hurley, Phoebe Augustine as Ronette Pulaski, David Bowie as Special Agent Phillip Jeffries, Pamela Gidley as Teresa Banks, Heather Graham as Annie Blackburn, Miguel Ferrer as FBI Special Agent Albert Rosenfield, Chris Isaak as FBI Special Agent Chester Drummond, Kiefer Sutherland as FBI Special Agent Sam Stanley, David Lynch as Bureau Chief Gordon Cole, Moira Kelly as Donna Hayward, Michael J. Anderson as The Man from Another Place, Frank Silva As Killer BOB, Al Strobel as Phillip Michael Gerard/MIKE; Executive Producers: Mark Frost, David Lynch; Story: David Lynch, Robert Engels; Director: David Lynch; 134 min.; New Line Cinema; CIBY Pictures; Twin Peaks Productions; Color.

This prequel to the television series chronicles the final week leading to the murder of Laura Palmer. FBI Special Agent Dale Cooper experiences various spirits and is present in the dream of Laura Palmer as they enter the Black Lodge with the Man from Another Place. Demon possession plays a major part in the events of Palmer's final week.

Twin Peaks: The Return (2017) [TV series]
Premiere: May 21, 2017; Main Cast: Kyle MacLachlan as Dale Cooper/Dougie Jones, Michael Horse as Chief Tommy "Hawk" Hill, Chrysta Bell as FBI Agent Tammy Preston, Miguel Ferrer as FBI Agent Albert Rosenfield, David Lynch as FBI Deputy Director Gordon Cole, Robert Forster as Sheriff Frank Truman, Kimmy Robertston as Lucy Brennan, Naomi Watts as Janey-E Jones, Laura Dern as Diane Evans, Don Murray as Bushnell Mullins, Richard Beymer as Benjamin Horne, Sheryl Lee as Laura Palmer/Carrie Page, Peggy Lipton as Norma Jennings, James Marshall as James Hurley, Russ Tamblyn as Dr. Lawrence Jacoby, Sherilyn Fenn as Audrey Horne; Executive Producers: David Lynch, Mark Frost, Sabrina S. Sutherland; Creators: David Lynch, Mark Frost; Story/Teleplay: David Lynch, Mark Frost; Director: David Lynch; 18 × 60 min.; Showtime Networks, Rancho Rosa Partnership, Lynch/Frost Productions; Twin Peaks Productions; Color.

The timeline of the series has moved on twenty-five years with FBI Special Agent Dale Cooper assuming the form of Dougie Jones. Meanwhile his evil doppelganger is making plans.

Co-Creator-Director David Lynch has stated the series is a continuation of the original series and first two seasons.

Season Three

Part 1 (1:01); *Part 2* (1:02); *Part 3* (1:03); *Part 4* (1:04); *Part 5* (1:05); *Part 6* (1:06); *Part 7* (1:07); *Part 8* (1:08); *Part 9* (1:09); *Part 10* (1:10); *Part 11* (1:11); *Part 12* (1:12); *Part 13* (1:13); *Part 14* (1:14); *Part 15* (1:15); *Part 16* (1:16); *Part 17* (1:17); *Part 18* (1:18).

Ultraviolet (1998) [TV series; UK]
Premiere: September 15, 1998; Main Cast: Jack Davenport as Detective Sergeant Michael Colefield, Susannah Harker as Dr. Angela Marsh, Idris Elba As Vaughn Rice, Philip Quast as Father Pearse J. Harman, Colette Brown as Kirsty, Fiona Dolman as Frances, Thomas Lockyer as Jacob, Sean Cernow as Lestat; Executive Producer: Sophie Balhetchet; Story/Director: Joe Ahearne; 6 × 50 min.; World Productions; Channel 4 Television; Color.

While investigating the disappearance of his friend Jack the night before his wedding Detective Sergeant Michael Colefield uncovers a secret government organization involved in a war between humans and vampires.

Season One

Habeas Corpus (1:01); *In Nomine Patris* (1:02); *Sub Judice* (1:03); *Mea Culpe* (1:04); *Terra Incognita* (1:05); *Persona Non Gratis* (1:06).

Under the Lake [Novel]
Author: Stuart Woods; First publication: New York, NY: Simon & Schuster, 1987.

Intrigued by the history of Sutherland, North Georgia former investigative journalist John Howell finds his old investigative skills coming to good effect as he attempts to uncover the sinister truth of what lies beneath the town's lake. Visits from the spirit of a young girl begin to haunt him as his rustic cabin in the North Georgia mountains provides the backdrop for spectral images of the past. But other forces are at work trying to stop him from uncovering the truth.

Under the Skin (Ritual Crime Unit Book #1) [Novel]

Author: E. E. Richardson; First publication: Oxford, UK: Abaddon Books, 2013.

Fifty-four-year-old DCI Claire Pierce of the North Yorkshire Police heads the Ritual Crime Unit. She has been tracking unlicensed shapeshifters across Yorkshire for the last six months. But as she gets closer to the truth of the skinbinders who take on the form of the animal skins they have binded themselves to she is taken off the case. Now Claire Pierce must work off the record to search for the truth and in doing so discover something more terrible than she imagined.

Followed by *Disturbed Earth* (2015).

The Undying Monster (1942) [Film]

Premiere: November 27, 1942; Main Cast: James Ellison as Robert Curtis. Heather Angel as Helga Hammond. John Howard as Oliver Hammond, Bramwell Fletcher as Dr. Jeff Colbert. Heather Thatcher as Christy. Aubrey Mather as Inspector Craig, Halliwell Hobbes as Walton; Producer: Brian Foy; Screenplay: Lillie Hayward, Michel Jacoby; Based on the novel by Jessie Douglas Kerruish; Director: John Brahm; 63 min.; Twentieth Century–Fox; b/w.

Robert Curtis of Scotland Yard investigates why the Hammond family at Hammond Hall have been victims of a savage beast for generations. Curtis uncovers a centuries old Hammond family curse involving a werewolf.

The Undying Monster: A Taste of the Fifth Dimension [Novel]

Author: Jessie Douglas Kerruish; First publication: 1922; Publisher: London: Heath Cranton Ltd.

The family of Hammand of Dannow has been reduced to two surviving members, a brother and sister. In Dannow Old Manor Swanhild Hammand is growing anxious over her brother Oliver who is out late in bad weather. She goes searching for him with her Great Dane Alex and it is not long before Alex sniffs out a gruesome scene.

"One hind leg had been torn off, the whole body had been torn, twisted, and squeezed to an almost shapeless mass before being flung against the tree. Some diabolic force must have been needed to perform such an incredible atrocity. Alex, after snuffing mournfully at her dead kennel-friend, led on again, across the clearing to a curve in the line of trees, where the lightning struck ruin of a beech stood back, overshadowed by a large pine. At the pine's foot the light lit on black curls prone on the shuffled brown needles and cones. It was Oliver, sprawled over the roots with his head in a pool of blood."

Oliver still clinging to life, recovers his health back at the Manor and talks of a Monster attacking him. Supersensitive Miss Luna Bartendale, also referred to as the White Witch, is invited to the Manor to use her paranormal skills to investigate the cursed family history and the Monster that has haunted the Hammands dating back to the Crusades.

Luna hears of family rumors of a half-human, half-animal creature hidden in the Manor and Sir Magnus the Warlock who practiced the Black Arts in the Hidden Room. Luna states that the Monster may be a being from a Fifth Dimension, "beyond the supernatural." And the Monster "is the result of some incredible sin that is haunting down the sinner's line from age to age" through hereditary memory.

But there is still more investigating to do before the mystery can be solved.

The Unknown [Comic book]

Story: Mark Waid; Art: Minck Oosterveer; 4-issue mini-series; First publication: May 2009; Publisher: Boom! Studios.

World famous private investigator Catherine Allingham is dying from cancer and has been given six months to live. Haunted by a personal specter Allingham sets out to find the secrets of the after-life aided by night club bouncer James Doyle.

The Vampire Detective (2016) [TV series; South Korea]

Premiere: March 27, 2016; Main Cast: Lee Joon as Yoon San, Oh Jung-se as Yong Goo-Hyung, Lee Se-young as Han Gyeo-Wool, Lee Chung-ah as Yo-Na, Jo Bok-Rae as Kang Tae-Woo, Kim Yoon-Hye as Jung Yoo-Jin, Ahn Se-ha as Detective Park, Jei as Se-Ra, Han Soo-Yeon as Kim Yeon-Joo, Choi Gwi-Hwa as Jang Tae-Sik; Story: Yoo Young-Seon; Director: Kim Ga-Ram; 12 × 60 min.; OCN; Color.

When police detective Yoon San is betrayed and shot by his female partner in the line of duty, he starts his own private investigative agency with Yong Goo-Hyung. During a case investigating a mysterious blood bank in a night club Yoon San is mortally wounded. But his life is saved by a serum that turns into a vampire. Now he is determined to learn more about his own past as he continues to solve crimes.

SEASON ONE

The Night Life (1:01); *24 Hours* (1:02); *The Dragon Sleeps* (1:03); *Waiting in Darkness* (1:04); *The Actress Must Die* (1:05); *The Girl I Murdered* (1:06); *The Clients of the Night* (1:07); *Judgment of the Soul* (1:08); *Broadcasting of Death* (1:09); *Chain of Evil* (1:10); *Downfallen in the World* (1:11); *The Night Again* (1:12).

Vampire Holmes (2015) [Anime; Japan]

Premiere: April 3, 2015; Voice Cast: Yoshinobu Sena as Holmes, Nobunaga Shimazaki as Hudson, Ayahi Takagaki as Christina/Kira; Creator: Cucuri; 12 × 3 min.; Studio! Cucuri; Television Kanagawa; Color.

Private detective Holmes pays his assistant Hudson with as much tea as he can drink. Holmes is a mystery to Hudson because of his casual attitude. He claims he has no deductive reasoning, but he still manages to solve cases. The latest involves werewolf sightings in London. And Hudson is introduced to the talking demon cat Kira who claims to be black but is white. It all adds to Hudson's frequent outbursts of anger at the confusion surrounding him.

This light-hearted anime, adapted from a smartphone game app consists of three-minute episodes, with an emphasis on comedy.

SEASON ONE

Detective? His Name Is … (1:01); *The Unknown Case* (1:02); *The Ecology Holmes* (1:03); *The Clever Hawk Something Something* (1:04); *Walk With Me …* (1:05); *Pursuing the Difficult Case?!* (1:06); *Holmes Rising* (1:07); *Kira the Black Cat* (1:08); *What is Distorted?* (1:09); *A Long Walk* (1:10); *Even Just One Person* (1:11); *Holmes is a Great Detective?!* (1:12).

Vampire in Brooklyn (1995) [Film]

Premiere: October 7, 1995; Main Cast: Eddie Murphy as Maximillian/Preacher Pauly/Guido. Angela Bassett as Detective Rita Veder, Allen Payne as Detective Justice, Kadeem Hardison as Julius Jones, John Witherspoon as Silas Green, Zakes Mokae as Dr. Zeko, Joanna Cassidy as Captain Dewey; Executive Producers: Stuart M. Besser, Marianna Maddalena; Story: Eddie Murphy, Vernon Lynch, Charles Murphy; Screenplay: Charles Murphy, Michael Lucker, Christopher Parker; Director: Wes Craven; 100 min.; Eddie Murphy Productions; Paramount Pictures; Color.

Vampire Maximillian searches Brooklyn, New York to find a half-human, half-vampire mate to keep his line "alive." Detective Rita Veder investigates a spate of killings by the vampire and suffers nightmares. Unaware she is part-vampire and the target of Maximillian she falls for his charms, thus placing her human-half in mortal danger.

Vampire Prosecutor (2011) [TV series; South Korea]

Premiere: October 2, 2011; Main Cast: Jeong-hun Yeon as Min Tae-yon, Won-jong Lee as Detective Hwang Soon-bum, Young-Ah Lee as Yoo Jung-in, Joo-Young Kim as Choi Dong-man, Jae Hoon Park as La Jae-wook, Kyeong-yeong Lee as Jo Jung-hyun, Hyun-Sung Jang as Chief Jang Chui-oh, Ye Jin Kim as Soo Hee; Producer: Seung-Hoon Lee; Story: Jung-hoon Han, Eun-sun Kang; Directors: Byung-Soo Kim, Seon-dong Yu; 23 × 60 min.' CMG Chorok Stars; OCN; Color.

Min Tae-yon is a prosecutor with a secret life as a vampire who can solve crimes by smelling and tasting the blood of the victims.

Helping him in his detective work are novice prosecutor Yoo Jung-in, detective Hwan Soon-bum and intern Choi Dong-man.

SEASON ONE

Room with French Dolls (1:01); *Death Script* (1:02); *Pug's Memory Recall* (1:03); *Trauma* (1:04); *Real Game* (1:05); *Fight Club* (1:06); *Syndrome* (1:07); *Moon* (1:08); *Good Friends* (1:09); *Marry* (1:10); *The Final: Part 1* (1:11); *The Final: Part 2* (1:12).

SEASON TWO

The History of Violence (2:01); *Good Luck* (2:02); *What Ties of Friendship* (2:03); *Interview with the Vampire* (2:04); *Trap* (2:05); *Models* (2:06); *Stalker* (2:07); *Rude Min Tae-yeon* (2:08); *Cold Blood vs. Bad Blood* (2:09); *Birth of a Devil* (2:10); *Return of the Vampire* (2:11).

Van Helsing [Film; Video game]

Premiere: May 7, 2004; Main Cast: Hugh Jackman as Gabriel Van Helsing, Kate Beckinsale as Anna Valerious, Richard Roxburgh as Count Vladislaus Dracula, David Wenham as Carl, Shuler Hensey as Frankenstein's Monster, Samuel West as Dr. Victor Frankenstein, Robbie Coltrane as Mr. Hyde, Stephen H. Fisher as Dr. Jekyll, Elena Anaya as Aleera, Will Kemp as Velkan, Kevin J. O'Connor as Igor, Alun Armstrong as Cardinal Jinette, Silvia Colloca as Verona, Josie Maran as Marishka, Tom Fisher as Top Hat; Executive Producer: Sam Mercer; Story/Director: Stephen Sommars; 131 min.; Universal Pictures; The Sommars Company; Stillking Films; Color; b/w.

At the request of the Vatican Gabriel Van Helsing travels to Transylvania to track and destroy Count Dracula before he can restore life to thousands of his offspring. Helping him is Holy Order friar Carl and gypsy princess Anna Valerious.

2. [Video game] Release date: May 6, 2004; Voice Cast: Hugh Jackman as Gabriel Van Helsing, Richard Roxburgh as Count Vladislaus Dracula, Shuler Hensey as Frankenstein's Monster, Samuel West as Dr. Victor Frankenstein, Bob Joles as Hyde, Kat Cressida as Aleera, Will Kemp as Velkan/The Wolf Man, Kevin J. O'Connor as Igor, Alun Armstrong as Cardinal Jinette, Silvia Colloca as Verona, Josie Maran as Marishka, Many Steckelberg as Anna; Producer; William Oertel; Director: John Slowsky; Developer: Saffire Inc.; Platforms: PlayStation 2; Xbox; Perspective: 3rd-Person; Publisher: Sierra Entertainment.

The player is Van Helsing as they hunt down Count Dracula in Transylvania encountering Dr. Jekyll/Mr. Hyde, the Wolfman. Frankenstein's Monster, vampires and other creatures along the way.

Van Helsing: The London Assignment (2004) [Animated short]

Premiere: April 17, 2004; Voice Cast: Hugh Jackman as Gabriel Van Helsing, David Wenham as Friar Carl, Dwight Schultz as Dr. Henry Jekyll, Robbie Coltrane as Edward Hyde, Alun Armstrong as Cardinal Jinette, Tara Strong as Queen Victoria, Grey DeLisle as First Victim; Executive Producers: Stephen Sommars, Bob Ducsay; Story: Garfield Reeves-Stevens, Judith Reeves-Stevens; Director: Sharon Bridgeman; 30 min.; Universal cartoon Studios; Universal Home Video; Universal Pictures; Color.

In this prequel to the events in *Van Helsing* (2004) Gabriel Van Helsing and friar Carl investigate the mysterious deaths of young women in the streets of London that are linked to Dr. Jekyll and Mr. Hyde.

The Vanishing of Ethan Carter [Video game]

Release date: September 25, 2014; Voice Cast: Marty Allen as Paul Prospero, Jake Amigo as Ethan Carter, Kyle Harrington as Travis Carter, Steve Hirsh as Ed Carter, Dany Katiana as Chad Carter, Asley Laurence as Missy Carter, Michael Sinterniklaas as Dale Carter; Writers: Robert Auten, Tom Bissell; Directors: Adrian Chmielarz, Michael Csurics; Developer: The Astronauts; Platforms: PlayStation 4, Windows, Xbox One; Perspective: 1st-Person; Publisher: The Astronauts.

The player is occult detective Paul Prospero who possesses supernatural powers including the ability to view events of the past. A boy named Ethan Carter has been sending fan mail to Prospero, and it becomes obvious he has paranormal gifts. Now he is missing. Prospero travels to Red Creek Valley to track him down.

Vatican Miracle Examiner a.k.a. **Bachikan Kiseki Chosaken** [Novel; Manga; Anime; Japan]

[Novel] First publication: 2007; Author: Rin Fujiki; Illustrator: THORES Shibamoto; Publisher: Kadokawa Shoten.

This 13-volume series of illustrated novels features Italian priest Roberto Nicholas, an expert in ancient archives and cryptoanalysis. Joining him is Japanese priest and genius scientist Josef Kou Hiraga. They both work for the Assembly of the Saints at the Vatican. Their task to investigate the authenticity of alleged miracles worldwide.

[Manga] First publication: *Comic Kai* (January 24, 2012); Story: Eiji Kaneda; Publisher: Kadokawa Shoten.

This 2-volume manga was followed in August 2016 by a second manga serialized in *Monthly Comic Gene*.

[Anime] Premiere: July 7, 2017; Voice Cast: Junichi Suwabe as Roberto Nicholas, Nobuhiko Okamoto as Josef Kou Hiraga, Koji Yusa as Priest Julia, Masashi Ebara as Archbishop Saul, Hiroki Yasumoto as Bill Suskins, Soma Saito as Lauren Di Luca, Tsubasa Yonaga as Ryota Hiraga; Creator: Rin Fujiki; Story: Seishi Minakami, Takayo Ikami; Director: Yoshimoto Yonetani; 12 × 24 min.; J.C. Staff; WOWOW; Color.

Based on the novel and manga series.

SEASON ONE

Through God's Succor, My Eyes Are Opened (1:01); *The Endless Unease of Existence* (1:02); *Secrets of the Gods and the Beast of 666* (1:03); *Even So, I Still Believe in the Lord God* (1:04); *The Game of Angels and 'Demons* (1:05); *God Bestows Upon Us All His Revelations* (1:06); *Those Branded with a Curse* (1:07); *Only Through Death Can We Full Comprehend Rebirth into Eternal Life* (1:08); *The Decapitating Clown and the Tale of Solomon* (1:09); *The Ghosts of Past Appeared* (1:10); *The Gold of the Darkness; I am with the Lord* (1:11); *Sinfonia* (1:12).

The Veil [Comic book]

First publication: June 2009; 4-issue miniseries; Writer: El Torres; Art: Gabriel Hernandez; Publisher: IDW Publishing.

Private eye Chris Luna can pierce through the Veil between the living and the dead. But her detective work isn't paying the bills and she's forced to return to her hometown of Crooksville, Maine where ghosts are wandering the streets. Slug Man has ripped the Veil between realities allowing everyone to see beyond—but at a price to their sanity.

"A Victim of Higher Space" [Short story]

Author: Algernon Blackwood; First publication: *The Occult Review* (December 1914); Publisher: London: William Rider & Son Ltd.

Dr. Silence, psychic physician offers his services for free to those who cannot afford treatment. He is also part-time occult detective possessing the gift of clairvoyance. In his latest case the doctor's manservant Baker reports a frightening encounter with a gentleman in the hall of Dr. Silence's residence.

"He's so-so thin sir. I could hardly see 'im at all—at first…. He came in so funny, just like a cold wind."

Barker directs the middle-aged man "of very ordinary appearance" toward the green study, "calculated to induce calmness and repose of mind."

The man, named Racine Mudge, tells Silence of his experiences of Higher Space. "…accidentally, as the result of my years of experiment, I one day slipped bodily into the next world, the world of four dimensions, yet without knowing precisely how I got there, or how I could get back again. I discovered, that is, my ordinary three-dimensional body was but an expression—a projection—of my higher four-dimensional body!"

Adapting to his new situation was proving extremely difficult.

"It's seeing people and objects in their weird entirety, in their true and complete shapes, that is so distressing. It introduces me to a world of monsters. Horses, dogs, cats, all of which I loved, people, trees, children; all that I have considered beautiful in my life—everything from a human face to a cathedral—appear to me in a different shape and aspect to all I have known before."

Dr. Silence suggests a cure for Mr. Mudge who then disappears from his sight only to reappear in Bombay, India. Despite his unfortunate departure from the residence of Dr. Silence Mr. Mudge gradually learns to follow the instructions provided by Dr. Silence and block the entrances to the Higher Space. He can once more live in the three-dimensional world without the worry of disappearing into the 4th dimension.

This was the sixth and final Dr. John Silence story by Algernon Blackwood.

See: *John Silence: Physician Extraordinary*

Vidocq a.k.a. *Dark Portals: The Chronicles of Vidocq* (2001) [Film; France]

Premiere: September 19, 2001; Main Cast: Gerard Depardieu as Vidocq, Guillaume Canet as Etienne Boisset, Ines Sastre as Preah, Andre Dussollier as Lautrennes, Edith Scob as Sylvia, Moussa Maaskri as Nimier, Jean-Pierre Gos as Marine Lafitte, Andre Penvern as Veraldi; Executive Producer: Olivier Granier; Screenplay: Pitof, Jean-Christophe Grange; Based on the memoirs of Francois-Eugene Vidocq; Director: Pitof; 98 min.; RF2K; StudioCanal; TF1 Films Production; Canal+; CNC; Color.

In nineteenth-century Paris convict turned private investigator Francois-Eugene Vidocq dies a fiery death in a life-or-death struggle with his adversary the Alchemist who hides his identity behind a mirrored mask. Reporter Etienne Boisset takes up Vidocq's story in his biography. But after Boisset interviews people who knew Vidocq they die violent deaths. And all are connected to the Alchemist who has previously killed three politicians by lightning strikes.

Based on the real-life detective Vidocq, this is the first film made using digital technology. Shot in its entirety with a Sony HDCAM24PI high-definition digital camera.

Violet Rose (Comic book)

First publication: November 2007; Creator: Emma Davis; Story: Emma Davis, Cameron Cooke; Art: Brian Hess, Michael O'Sullivan, Elisa Falcone; Publisher: Bluewater Comics.

"Willoughby is a town known for the unexpected and Serling Middle School is Weirdness Central."

Violet Rose isn't an ordinary girl. Apart from speaking to her dead grandfather and her painted spirit friend Ciara she can talk to inanimate objects such as stuffed animals, statues, spoons and houses. They even help her solve mysteries. And Violet loves searching for clues and solving mysteries as a detective sleuth.

Visions a.k.a. *Visions of Death* (1972) [Telefilm]

Premiere: October 10, 1972; Main Cast: Monte Markham as Professor Mark Lowell, Barbara Anderson as Susan Schaeffer, Telly Savalas as Lt. Phil Keegan, Tim O'Connor as Bert Hayes, Lonny Chapman as Martin Binzech, Lou Antonio as Sgt. Ted Korel; Producer: Leonard Freeman; Teleplay: Paul Playdon; Director: Lee H. Katzin; 75 min.; CBS; Color.

Professor Lowell's clairvoyant powers are met with distrust and suspicion by the police when he informs them someone is about to plant a bomb.

The Void (2016) [Film]

Premiere: September 22, 2016; Main Cast: Aaron Poole as Daniel Carter, Kenneth Welsh as Dr. Richard Powell, Daniel Fathers as The Father, Kathleen Munroe as Allison Fraser, Ellen Wong as Kim, Mik Byskov as The Son, Art Hindle as Mitchell, Stephanie Belding as Beverly, James Millington as Ben, Evan Stern as James, Grace Munro as Maggie, Matthew Kennedy as Cliff Robertson, Trish Rainone as The Mother; Executive Producers: Todd Brown, Ross M. Dinerstein, Jeremy Gillespie, James Norrie, Jeremy Platt, David Watson; Story/Directors: Jeremy Gillespie, Steven Kostanski; 90 min.; 120dB Films; Cave Painting Pictures; JoBro Productions; XYZ Films; Screen Media Films; Color.

Deputy sheriff Daniel Carter and staff and patients at a run-down hospital find themselves under attack from mysterious hooded figures and abominable creatures.

Warehouse 13 (2009) [TV series]
Premiere: July 7, 2009; Main Cast: Eddie McClintock as Pete Lattimer, Joanne Kelly as Myka Bering, Saul Rubinek as Artie Nielsen, Allison Scagliotti as Claudia Donovan, Genelle Williams as Leena, Aaron Ashmore as Steve Jinks, CCH Pounder as Mrs. Irene Frederic, Jaime Murray as H.G. Wells, Simon Reynolds as Daniel Dickenson; Executive Producers: Jack Kenny, Mark Winemaker, David Simkins; Creators: Jane Espenson, D. Brent Mote; 1 × 87 min.; 63 × 43 min.; Universal Cable Productions; Syfy; Color.

U.S. Secret Service Agents Pete Lattimer and Myka Bering are re-assigned to a top-secret government facility in a remote area of South Dakota known as Warehouse 13. The facility is home to a centuries-old collection of supernatural objects. Lattimer and Bering must recover lost artifacts and investigate new ones that possess supernatural power.

Season One

Pilot (1:01); *Resonance* (1:02); *Magnetism* (1:03); *Claudia* (1:04); *Elements* (1:05); *Burnout* (1:06); *Implosion* (1:07); *Duped* (1:08); *Regrets* (1:09); *Breakdown* (1:10); *Nevermore* (1:11); *MacPherson* (1:12).

Season Two

Time Wil Tell (2:01); *Mild Mannered* (2:02); *Beyond Our Control* (2:03); *Age Before Beauty* (2:04); *13.1* (2:05); *Around the Bend* (2:06); *For the Team* (2:07); *Merge with Caution* (2:08); *Vendetta* (2:09); *Where and When* (2:10); *Buried* (2:11); *Reset* (2:12); *Secret Santa* (2:13).

Season Three

The New Guy (3:01); *Trials* (3:02); *Love Sick* (3:03); *Queen for a Day* (3:04); *3 ... 2 ... 1* (3:05); *Don't Hate the Player* (3:06); *Past Imperfect* (3:07); *The 40th Floor* (3:08); *Shadows* (3:09); *Insatiable* (3:10); *Emily Lake* (3:11); *Stand* (3:12); *The Greatest Gift* (3:13).

Season Four

A New Hope (4:01); *An Evil Within* (4:02); *Personal Effects* (4:03); *There's Always a Downside* (4:04); *No Pain No Gain* (4:05); *Fractures* (4:06); *Endless Wonder* (4:07); *Second Chance* (4:08); *The Ones You Love* (4:09); *We All Fall Down* (4:10); *The Living and the Dead* (4:11); *Parks and Rehabilitation* (4:12); *The Big Bang* (4:13); *The Sky's the Limit* (4:14); *Instinct* (4:15); *Runaway* (4:16); *What Matters Most* (4:17); *Lost and Found* (4:18); *All the Time in the World* (4:19); *The Truth Hurts* (4:20).

Season Five

Endless Terror (5:01); *Secret Services* (5:02); *A Faire to Remember* (5:03); *Savage Seduction* (5:04); *Cangku Shisi* (5:05); *Endless* (5:06).

Weird Detective [Comic book]
First publication: June 2016; Story: Fred Van Lente; Art: Guiu Vilanova; Publisher: Dark Horse Comics.

NYPD detective Sebastian Greene lives in a houseboat, can sense psychic impressions and communicates telepathically with his stray cat. But Sebastian Greene is an imposter whose body and mind have been taken over by an alien who left his dying world in psychic form. Now he is tracking a killer who leaves the empty skins of his victims.

Working with Greene is Sana Fayez who is spying on him for her boss who knows something isn't quite right with her detective partner from Canada.

The Werewolf's Tale [Novel; WW]
Author: Richard Jaccoma; First publication: New York: Ballantine Books, 1988.

Manhattan private detective Jimmy Underhill has returned from the Spanish Civil War to tackle cases involving vampirism, demons, witchcraft and the occult. His latest client, an attractive Jewish vampire leads to a female werewolf who transforms Underhill with one bite. Fighting the beast within, Underhill tracks the beasts hidden among the streets of New York. Nazis engaging in the occult to raise the undead and gather the forces of evil to empower the master beast at work in Europe.

Where Dead Soldiers Walk [Novel; WW]
Author: Lloyd Biggle, Jr.; First publication: New York: St. Martin's Press, 1994.

Private detective J. Pletcher investigates a series of murders in Napoleon Corners, Georgia that appear to involve monks, a witch, a grandfather who thinks he's a Confederate General and the ghosts of Union soldiers.

White Night (The Dresden Files Book #9)
Author: Jim Butcher; Publisher: New York: Roc, 2007.

Harry Dresden investigates the murders of an underclass of practitioners of magic who are incapable of becoming wizards. All clues lead to Dresden's half-brother Thomas, but a conspiracy is at work within the White Council of Wizards that threatens not only Dresden, but all those close to him.

See: ***Small Favor***

The Wicker Man (1973) [Film; UK]
Premiere: December 6, 1973; Main Cast: Edward Woodward as Sergeant Neil Howie, Christopher Lee as Lord Summerisle, Diane Cilento as Miss Rose, Britt Ekland as Willow MacGregor, Ingrid Pitt as Librarian, Lindsay Kemp as Alder MacGregor, Russell Waters as Harbor Master, Aubrey Morris as Old Gardner/Gravedigger, Irene Sunter as May Morrison, Walter Carr as School Master; Producer: Peter Snell; Screenplay: Anthony Shaffer; Director: Robin Hardy; 87 min.; British Lion Film Corporation; Color.

Sergeant Neil Howie of the West Highland Constabulary travels to Summerisle to investigate the disappearance of Rowan Morrison. But when he arrives her mother and the locals disavow any knowledge of her existence. Sgt. Howie finds himself surrounded by a community immersed in pagan beliefs that culminate in the ritual of the Wicker Man with Sgt. Howie taking center stage.

The Wicker Man (2006) [Film]
Premiere: September 1, 2006; Main Cast: Nicolas Cage as Edward Malus, Ellen Burstyn as Sister Summerisle, Kate Beahan as Sister Willow Woodward, Frances Conroy as Dr. T. H. Moss, Molly Parker as Sister Rose/Sister Thorn, Leelee Sobieski as Sister Honey, Diane Delano as Sister Beech, Mary Black as Sister Oak, Christine Willes as Sister Violet, Michael Wiseman as Officer Pete, Erika Shaye Gair as Rowan Woodward; Executive Producers: Danny Dimbort, George Furia, Josef Lautenschlager, Elisa Salinas, JoAnne Sellar, Trevor Short, Andreas Thiesmeyer; Screenplay: Neil LaBute; Based on the screenplay by Robin Hardy and Anthony Shaffer and the novel *Ritual* by David Pinner; Director: Neil LaBute; 102 min.; Alcon Entertainment; Brightlight Pictures; Emmett/Furla Films; Equity Pictures; Millennium Films; Nu Image; Redbus Pictures; Saturn Films; Warner Bros. Pictures; Color.

Uninspired remake of the British cult classic that shifts location from Scotland to Washington State. Some character names pay homage to Edward Woodward who appeared in the original movie.

The Wicker Man (1973), starring Edward Woodward as Sergeant Neil Howie and Barbara Ann Brown as Woman with Baby (British Lion).

Witch Hunter Robin (2002) [Anime; Japan]

Premiere: July 2, 2002; Voice Cast: Akeno Watanabe as Robin Sena, Takuma Takewaka as Amon, Hiro Yuuki as Michael Lee, Jin Yamanoi as Nagira, Masaaki Ohkura as Hattori, Michihiro Ikemizu as Takuma Zaizen, Hirotaki Nagai as Master/Yuri Kobari, Kaho Kouda as Miho Karasuma, Kyoko Hikami as Yurika Dojima; Producers: Atsushi Sugita, Kenichi Matsumura; Story: Toru Nozaki, Aya Yoshinaga, Hiroaki Kitajima, Shin Yoshida, Kenchi Araki; Director: Shukou Murase; 26 × 24 min.; Bandai Visual; Sunrise; Animax; TV Tokyo; Color.

15-year-old Robin Sena was born in Japan but raised a Roman Catholic in an Italian convent. She is the latest recruit for the Solomon Secret Action Group (STN-J), an organization that investigates and tracks anyone using the Craft for evil purposes. Robin was hired for her expertise in the Craft but comes into conflict with the STN-J policy of hunting and incarcerating anyone who is found to have witch genes in their ancestry.

Season One

Replacement (1:01); *Addicted to Power* (1:02); *Dancing in Darkness* (1:03); *Stubborn Aesthetics* (1:04); *Smells Like the Wandering Spirit* (1:05); *Raindrops* (1:06); *Simple-mind* (1:07); *Faith* (1:08);

Sign of the Craft (1:09); *Separate Lives* (1:10); *The Soul Cages* (1:11); *Precious Illusions* (1:12); *The Eyes of Truth* (1:13); *Loaded Guns* (1:14); *Time to Say Goodbye* (1:15); *Heal the Pain* (1:16); *Dilemma* (1:17); *In My Pocket* (1:18); *Missing* (1:19); *All I Really Oughta Know* (1:20); *No Way Out* (1:21); *Family Portrait* (1:22); *Sympathy for the Devil* (1:23); *Rent* (1:24); *Redemption Day* (1:25); *Time to Tell* (1:26).

Witchblade (Comic book; TV series)

[Comic book] First publication: November 1995; Creators: Michael Turner, Marc Silvestri, David Wohl, Bryan Haberlin; Publisher: Top Cow.

Kenneth Irons is seeking a worthy successor for the magical Witchblade among a group of shady business men. When Sara Pezzini of the NYPD interrupts the party, she comes under attack. Trying to save the life of her partner Sara is critically wounded herself. Because of her heroism the Witchblade restores Sara's life and transfer its power to her. She has become the latest "chosen one" in a long line of heroic females going back in time to the prehistoric era. The Witchblade is a living organism, the male offspring of the Darkness and the Angelus (the light) and requires a female host to bond with in order to maintain order in the world.

The Witchblade was first introduced in Top Cow's *Cyblade/Shi* #1 (January 1995).

[TV series] First broadcast: June 12, 2001; Main Cast: Yancy Butler as Detective Sara "Pez" Pezzini, David Chokachi as Detective Jake McCartey, Anthony Cistaro as Kenneth Irons, Will Yun Lee as Detective Danny Woo, Eric Etebari as Ian Nottingham, Lazar Rockwood as Lazar, John Hensley as Gabriel Bowman, Kathryn Winslow as Vicky Po, Nestor Serrano as Capt. Bruno Dante; Executive Producers: Ralph Hemecker, Dan Halsted, Marc Silvestri; Creators: Marc Silvestri, Michael Turner; 23 × 44 min.; Halsted Pictures, Top Cow Productions, Blade TV Productions, Mythic Films; Turner Television Network (TNT); Color.

"You're from a line going back through time and into the future. A part of a wave, a force, a warrior bloodline."

NYPD detective Sara "Pez" Pezzini fights crime using her natural skills and the magical arcane metal gauntlet known as the Witchblade.

Adapted from the comic book. A subsequent Japanese anime series changed the setting and the characters and ditched the police detective storyline.

Season One

Parallax (1:01); *Conundrum* (1:02); *Diplopia* (1:03); *Sacrifice* (1:04); *Legion* (1:05); *Maelstrom* (1:06); *Periculum* (1:07); *Thanatopsis* (1:08); *Apprehension* (1:09); *Convergence* (1:10); *Transcendence* (1:11).

Season Two

Emergence (2:01); *Destiny* (2:02); *Agape* (2:03); *Consectatio* (2:04); *Static* (2:05); *Nailed*

(2:06); *Lagrimas* (2:07); *Heirophant* (2:08); *Veritas* (2:09); *Parabolic* (2:10); *Palindrome* (2:11); *Ubique* (2:12).

The Wizard of Gore (1970 [Film])
Premiere: October 23, 1970; Main Cast: Ray Sagar as Montag the Magnificent, Judy Cler as Sherry Carson, Wayne Ratay as Jack, Phil Laurenson as Greg, Jim Rau as Steve, Don Alexander as Detective Kramer, John Elliot as Detective Harlan; Executive Producer: Fred M. Sandy; Screenplay: Allen Kahn; Director: Herschell Gordon Lewis; 95 min.; Mayflower Pictures; Color.

A television talk show host and her sportswriter boyfriend investigate the puzzling deaths connected to master illusionist Montag the Magnificent. In his stage act Montag dismembers female audience members in various gruesome manners only to have them return to their seats still alive and whole again. However, they are later discovered dead from their onstage tortures.

WolfCop (2014) [Film; Canada]
Premiere: June 6, 2014; Main Cast: Leo Fafard as Sheriff Lou Garou/WolfCop, Amy Matysio as Tina, Sarah Lind as Jessica, Corinne Conley as Mayor Bradley, Jesse Moss as Gang Leader, Jonathan Cherry as Willie Higgins, Aidan Devine as Chief; Executive Producers: Sean Buckley, J. Joly, Bill Marks, Brad Pelman, Brian Wideen; Screenplay/Director: Lowell Dean; 79 min.; The Coup Company; Echolands Creative Group; Color.

Low budget comedy-horror gorefest centered in the small town of Woodhaven. Alcoholic Sheriff Lou Garou encounters the occult on his beat and finds himself turning into a werewolf. As a werewolf cop he intends to put an end to reptilian shapeshifters looking to sacrifice him to enhance their magic.

The film spawned the sequel *Another WolfCop* (2017) with the same cast and director.

The World Beyond (1978) [Telefilm]
Premiere: January 21, 1978; Main Cast: Granville van Dusen as Paul Taylor, JoBeth Williams as Marian Faber, Bernard Hughes as Andy Borchard; Executive Producer: David Susskind; Creator-Writer: Art Wallace; Director: Noel Black; 50 min.; Time-Life Television Productions; Color.

Paul Taylor receives a command from the deceased Frank Faber to go to Logan's Island to protect his sister Marian from harm. On the island Taylor, Marian and boat captain Andy Borchard are threatened by a golem created by Faber out of mud and brought to life by magical incantations.

See: *The World of Darkness*

The World of Darkness (1977) [Telefilm]
Premiere: April 17, 1977; Main Cast: Granville van Dusen as Paul Taylor, Beatrice Straight as Joanna Sanford, Tovah Feldshuh as Clara Sanford, Gary Merrill as Dr. Thomas Madsen; Executive Producer: David Susskind; Creator-Writer: Art Wallace; Director: Jerry London; 50 min.; Time-Life Television Productions; Color.

A motorcycle accident gives sportswriter Paul Taylor an intimate knowledge of his own death. Aware of every moment during his two minutes and thirty-seven seconds of clinical death Taylor is revived on the operating table. But his life has been changed forever. He now has a connection to the dead who can reach his mind, forcing him to look for a person he's never met. Compelling him to protect that person from the world beyond.

This was the first of two failed pilots for a proposed series.

See: *The World Beyond*

Wynonna Earp [Comic book; TV series]
[Comic book] First publication: December 1996; Creator: Beau Smith; Publishers: Wildstorm/Image; IDW Publishing.

Wynonna Earp, great-great-granddaughter of legendary Old West lawman Wyatt Earp, is special agent for the U.S. Marshal Special Operations Unit, tackling supernatural threats.

[TV series] Premiere: April 2016; Main Cast: Melanie Scrofano as Wynonna Earp, Tim Rozon as Doc Holliday/Henry, Dominique Provost-Chalkley as Waverly Earp, Katherine

Barrell as Nicole Haught, Shamier Anderson as Agent Xavier Dolls, Varun Saranga as Agent Chetri, Greg Lawson as Sheriff Nedley, Michael Eklund as Bobo Del Rey; Executive Producers: Ted Adams. Brian Dennis, Rick Jacobs, David Ozer, Emily Andras, Todd Berger, Tom Cox, Jordy Randall; Based on the comic book by Beau Smith; 49 × 43 min.; Seven24 Films; IDW Entertainment; Syfy; Color.

In the cursed Ghost River Triangle Wynonna Earp battles supernatural entities with the aid of her 16-inch barrel Peacemaker revolver. As an agent of the secret Black Badge Division (BBD) she is joined by mutant lizard-man Deputy Marshal Xavier Dolls, the immortal Doc Holliday, Wynonna's half-sister Waverly whose father is an angel and Officer Nicole Haught who works alongside Black Badge.

Season One

Purgatory (1:01); *Keep the Home Fires Burning* (1:02); *Leavin' on Your Mind* (1:03); *The Blade* (1:04); *Diggin' Up Bones* (1:05); *Constant Cravings* (1:06); *Walking After Midnight* (1:07); *Two-Faced Jack* (1:08); *Bury Me with My Guns On* (1:09); *She Wouldn't Be Gone* (1:10); *Landslide* (1:11); *House of Memories* (1:12); *I Walk the Line* (1:13).

Season Two

Steel Bars and Stone Walls (1:01); *Shed Your Skin* (1:02); *Gonna Getcha Good* (1:03); *She Ain't Right* (1:04); *Let's Pretend We're Strangers* (1:05); *Whiskey Lullaby* (1:06); *Everybody Knows* (1:07); *No Future in the Past* (1:08); *Forever Mine Nevermind* (1:09); *I See a Darkness* (1:10); *Gone as a Girl Can Get* (1:11); *I Hope You Dance* (1:12).

Season Three

Blood Red and Going Down (1:01); *When You Call My Name* (1:02); *Colder Weather* (1:03); *No Cure for Crazy* (1:04); *Jolene* (1:05); *If We Make It Through December* (1:06); *I Fall To Pieces* (1:07); *Waiting Forever For You* (1:08); *Undo It* (1:09); *The Other Woman* (1:10); *Daddy Lessons* (1:11); *War Paint* (1:12).

Xenopath [*Bengal Station* Trilogy #2] [Novel]

Author: Eric Brown; First publication: Nottingham, UK: Solaris, 2009.

Jeff Vaughn is a telepath working for a detective agency on the spaceport Bengal Station. While investigating alien corpses on the colony world of Mallory Vaughn uncovers murder centered around the Sheering-Lassiter colonial organization.

See: ***Cosmopath***

The X-Files (1993) [TV series]

Premiere: September 10, 1993; Main Cast: Gillian Anderson as OSS Agent Dana Scully, David Duchovny as Special Agent Fox Mulder, Mitch Pileggi as Walter Skinner, William B. Davis as Smoking Man, Robert Patrick as John Doggett, Tom Braiwood as Melvin Frohike, Bruce Harwood as John Fitzgerald Byers, Dean Haglund as Richard "Ringo" Langly, Annabeth Gish as Monica Reyes; Executive Producers: Chris Carter, Frank Spotnitz; Creator: Chris Carter; 217 × 45 min.; Ten Thirteen Productions; 20th Century–Fox Television; X-F Productions; Fox Network; Color.

F.B.I. Agents Fox Mulder and Dana Scully investigate the paranormal and become involved in government conspiracies. Mulder's belief in extra-terrestrials and the supernatural is tempered with Scully's scientific skepticism.

The X-Files (1993), starring David Duchovny as Special Agent Fox Mulder and Gillian Anderson as Agent Dana Scully (20th Century–Fox Television).

Robert Patrick as John Doggett and Annabeth Gish as Monica Reyes took center stage after David Duchovny departed at the end of Season 7, and Gillian Anderson reduced her appearances. The show lasted nine seasons on its original run before returning for two final seasons with the original cast beginning January 24, 2016.

The series has spawned two feature films. *The X-Files* (2008) centers on an extraterrestrial virus and takes place between the events of Season Four and Season Five. ***The X-Files: I Want to Believe*** (2008) is a standalone story involving a psychic former priest.

Season One

Pilot (1:01); *Deep Throat* (1:02); *Squeeze* (1:03); *Conduit* (1:04); *The Jersey Devil* (1:05); *Shadows* (1:06); *Ghost in the Machine* (1:07); *Ice* (1:08); *Space* (1:09);*Fallen Angel* (1:10); *Eve* (1:11); *Fire* (1:12); *Beyond the Sea* (1:13); *Gender Bender* (1:14); *Lazarus* (1:15); *Young at Heart* (1:16); *E.B.E.* (1:17); *Miracle Man* (1:18); *Shapes* (1:19); *Darkness Falls* (1:20); *Tooms* (1:21); *Born Again* (1:22); *Roland* (1:23); *The Erlenmeyer Flask* (1:24).

Season Two

Little Green Men (2:01); *The Host* (2:02); *Blood* (2:03); *Sleepless* (2:04); *Duane Barry* (2:05); *Ascension* (2:06); *3* (2:07); *One Breath* (2:08); *Firewalker* (2:09); *Red Museum* (2:10); *Excelsis Dei* (2:11); *Aubrey* (2:12); *Irresistible* (2:13); *Die Hand Die Verletzt* (2:14); *Fresh Bones* (2:15); *Colony* (2:16); *End Game* (2:17); *Fearful Symmetry* (2:18); *Dod Calm* (2:19); *Humbug* (2:20); *The Calusari* (2:21); *F. Emasculata* (2:22); *Soft Light* (2:23); *Our Town* (2:24); *Anasazi* (2:25).

Season Three

The Blessing Way (3:01); *Paper Clip* (3:02); *D.P.O.* (3:03); *Clyde Bruckman's Final Repose* (3:04); *The List* (3:05); *2Shy* (3:06); *The Walk* (3:07); *Oubliette* (3:08); *Nisei* (3:09); *731* (3:10); *Revelations* (3:11); *War of the Coprohages* (3:12); *Syzygy* (3:13); *Grotesque* (3:14); *Piper Maru* (3:15); *Apocrypha* (3:16); *Pusher* (3:17); *Teso dos Bichos* (3:18); *Hell Money* (3:19); *Jose Chung's 'From Outer Space'* (3:20); *Avatar* (3:21); *Quagmire* (3:22); *Wetwired* (3:23); *Talitha Cumi* (3:24).

Season Four

Herrenvolk (4:01); *Home* (4:02); *Teliko* (4:03); *Unruhe* (4:04); *The Field Where I Died* (4:05); *Sanguinarium* (4:06); *Musings of a Cigarette Smoking Man* (4:07); *Tunguska* (4:08); *Terma* (4:09); *Paper Hearts* (4:10); *El Mundo Gira* (4:11); *Leonard Betts* (4:12); *Never Again* (4:13); *Memento Mori* (4:14); *Kaddish* (4:15); *Unrequited* (4:16); *Tempus Fugit* (4:17); *Max* (4:18); *Synchrony* (4:19); *Small Potatoes* (4:20); *Zero Sum* (4:21); *Elegy* (4:22); *Demons* (4:23); *Gethsemane* (4:24).

Season Five

Redux (5:01); *Redux II* (5:02); *Unusual Suspects* (5:03); *Detour* (5:04); *The Post-Modern Prometheus* (5:05); *Christmas Carol* (5:06); *Emily* (5:07); *Kitsunegari* (5:08); *Schizogeny* (5:09); *Chinga* (5:10); *Kill Switch* (5:11); *Bad Blood* (5:12); *Patient x* (5:13); *The Red and the Black* (5:14); *Travelers* (5:15); *Mind's Eye* (5:16); *All Souls* (5:17); *The Pine Bluff Variant* (5:18); *Folie a Deux* (5:19); *The End* (5:20).

Season Six

The Beginning (6:01); *Drive* (6:02); *Triangle* (6:03); *Dreamland* (6:04); *Dreamland II* (6:05); *How the Ghosts Stole Christmas* (6:06); *Terms of Endearment* (6:07); *The Rain King* (6:08); *S.R. 819* (6:09); *Tithonus* (6:10); *Two Fathers* (6:11); *One Son* (6:12); *Agua Mala* (6:13); *Monday* (6:14); *Arcadia* (6:15); *Alpha* (6:16); *Trevor* (6:17); *Milagro* (6:18); *The Unnatural* (6:19); *Three of a Kind* (6:20); *Field Trip* (6:21); *Biogenesis* (6:22).

Season Seven

The Sixth Extinction (7:01); *The Sixth Extinction II: Amor Fati* (7:02); *Hungry* (7:03); *Millennium* (7:04); *Rush* (7:05); *The Goldberg Variation* (7:06); *Orison* (7:07); *The Amazing Maleeni* (7:08); *Signs & Wonders* (7:09); *Sein und Zeit* (7:10); *Closure* (7:11); *X-Cops* (7:12); *First Person Shooter* (7:13); *Theef* (7:14); *En Ami* (7:15); *Chimera* (7:16); *All Things* (7:17); *Brand x* (7:18); *Hollywood A.D.* (7:19); *Fight Club* (7:20); *Je Souhaite* (7:21); *Requiem* (7:22).

Season Eight

Within (8:01); *Without* (8:02); *Patience* (8:03); *Roadrunners* (8:04); *Invocation* (8:05); *Redrum* (8:06); *Via Negativa* (8:07); *Surekill* (8:08); *Salvage* (8:09); *Badlaa* (8:10); *The Gift* (8:11); *Medusa* (8:12); *Per Manum* (8:13); *This Is Not Happening* (8:14); *Deadalive* (8:15); *Three Words* (8:16); *Empedocles* (8:17); *Vienen* (8:18); *Alone* (8:19); *Essence* (8:20); *Existence* (8:21).

Season Nine

Nothing Important Happened Today (9:01); *Nothing Important Happened Today II* (9:02); *Daemonicus* (9:03); *4-D* (9:04); *Lord of the Flies* (9:05); *Trust No 1* (9:06); *John Doe* (9:07); *Hellbound* (9:08); *Provenance* (9:09); *Providence* (9:10); *Audrey Pauley* (9:11); *Underneath* (9:12); *Improbable* (9:13); *Scary Monsters* (9:14); *Jump the Shark* (9:15); *William* (9:16); *Release* (9:17); *Sunshine Days* (9:18); *The Truth* (9:19).

Season Ten

My Struggle (10:01); *Founder's Mutation* (10:02); *Mulder & Scully Meet the Were-Monster* (10:03); *Home Again* (10:04); *Babylon* (10:05); *My Struggle II* (10:06).

Season Eleven

My Struggle III (11:01); *This* (11:02); *Plus One* (11:03); *The Lost Art of Forehead Sweat* (11:04); *Ghouli* (11:05); *Kitten* (11:06); *Rm9sbG93ZXJz* (11:07); *Familiar* (11:08); *Nothing Lasts Forever* (11:09); *My Struggle IV* (11:10).

The X-Files: I Want to Believe (2008) [Film]

Premiere: July 25, 2008; Main Cast: Gillian Anderson as Dr. Dana Scully, David Duchovny as Fox Mulder, Amanda Peet as FBI Agent Dakota Whitney, Billy Connolly as "Father" Joseph Fitzpatrick Crissman, Alvin 'Xzibit' Joiner as Special Agent Mosley Drummy, Mitch Pileggi as Assistant Director Walter Skinner, Callum Keith Rennie as Janke Dacyshyn, Adam Godley as Father Ybarra, Xantha Radley as Special Agent Monica Bannan, Fagin Woodcock as Franz Tomczeszyn, Nicki Aycox as Cheryl Cunningham, Alex Diakun as Gaunt Man; Executive Producer: Brent O'Connor; Story: Frank Spotnitz, Chris Carter; Director: Chris Carter; 104 min.; Ten Thirteen Productions; Crying Box Productions; Dune Entertainment III; Twentieth Century–Fox; Color.

Former F.B.I. agents Dana Scully and Fox Mulder are reunited for a case involving defrocked pedophile priest Joseph Crissman. He claims to have psychic visions of crimes related to the disappearance of several women in West Virginia including F.B.I. agent Monica Bannan.

Young Detective Dee: Rise of the Sea Dragon a.k.a. Di Renjie: Shen du long wang (2013) [Film; China]

Premiere: September 27, 2013; Main Cast: Mark Chao as Dee Renjie. Carina Lau as Wu Zetian, Sheng Chien as The Emperor, Angelababy as Yin Ruiji, Shaofeng Feng as Yuchi Zhenjin, Gengxin Lin as Shatou Zhong, Chen Kun as Doctor Wang Pu, Ian Kim as Yuan Zhen, Dong Hu as Huo Yi; Executive Producer: Zhongjun Wang; Story: Chia-Lu Chang, Kuo-Fu Chen, Hark Tsui; Director: Hark Tsui; 134 min.; Film Workshop; Huayi Brothers Media, Pixeltree studio; Color.

In his first case Dee Renjie of the Da Lisa police force investigates the kidnapping of courtesan Yin by a swamp monster. Helping him is his assistant Dr. Shatou Zhong and rival Detective Yuchi.

Followed by the sequel **Detective Dee: The Four Heavenly Kings** (2018).

Young Sherlock Holmes (1985) [Film]

Premiere: December 4, 1985; Main Cast: Nicholas Rowe as Sherlock Holmes, Alan Cox as John Watson, Sophie Ward as Elizabeth Hardy, Anthony Higgins as Professor Rathe, Susan Fleetwood as Mrs. Dribb, Freddie Jones as Chester Cragwitch, Nigel Stock as Rupert T. Waxflatter, Roger Ashton-Griffiths as Detective Sgt. Lestrade, Earl Rhodes as Dudley, Brian Oulton as Master Snelgrove, Patrick Newell as Bentley Bobster, Donald Eccles as the Reverend Duncan Nesbitt; Executive Producers: Kathleen Kennedy, Frank Marshall, Steven Spielberg; Screenplay: Chris Columbus; Based on characters created by Arthur Conan Doyle; Director: Barry Levinson; 109 min.; Amblin Entertainment; Industrial Light & Magic (ILM); Paramount Pictures; Color.

A teenage Sherlock Holmes along with his new friend John Watson and love interest Elizabeth Hardy investigate a series of deaths related to strange hallucinations experienced by the victims. The trio uncover a plot to murder former

Zero, Ghost Detective appearing in *Feature Comics* #62 (November 1942). Story by Toni Blum (as Noel Fowler). Art by Witner Williams (Quality Comics).

officers of the British Army by an Egyptian Osiris cult named Rame Tep. Meanwhile Holmes, Watson and Elizabeth experience their own vivid hallucinations after they stop a female sacrifice by the cult in an underground pyramid.

The young Sherlock is ultimately emotionally scarred by a tragedy that will affect his future life as the world's greatest detective.

Yu Yu Hakusho: Ghost Files (1992) [Anime; Japan]

Premiere: October 10, 1992; Voice Cast: Megumi Ogata as Kurama, Yuri Amano as Keito Yukimura, Mayum Tanaka as Koenma, Nobuyuki Hiyama as Hei, Nozomo Sasaki as Yuusuke Urameshi, Shigeru Chiba as Kazuma Kuwabara, Hisako Kyouda as Genkai, Katsumi Suzuki as Toguru Ani, Mayumi Tanaka as Loenma, Rokuro Naya as Sensui, Sanae Miyuki as Botan; Producers: Ken Hagino, Kyotaro Kimura, Kenji Shimizu, Koji Kaneda; Story: Hiroshi Hasimoto, Yukiyoshi Ohashi, Sukehiro Tomita, Katsuyuki Sumisawa, Shikichi Ohashi; Director: Noriyuki Abe; 112 × 30 min.; Studio Pierrot; Yomiko Advertising, Inc.; Fuji Television Network; Bandai Channel; Color.

14-year-old Yusuke Urameshi has a bad reputation at school. When he sacrifices his life saving a child from a speeding car he learns he died before his time. Botan, the messenger of death in female form offers Yusuke his life back, but first he must meet Koenma, the young son of the leader of the Spirit World. He gives Yusuke a golden egg and tells him he must emit enough good energy to allow the spirit beast to emerge from the egg and return him to his body. He succeeds in his task and is restored to life along with his new vocation as a Spirit Detective.

Various spin-offs include two feature length animated films and three OAV's.

[Manga] First publication: Weekly Shonen Jump (December 3, 1990); Story & Art: Yohihiro Togashi; Publisher: Shueisha.

The manga that inspired the anime TV series differs slightly in that Yusuke goes under the title of "Underworld Detective." Between 1990 and 1994 the manga ran to 19-volumes.

Zero Ghost Detective (Comic book character)

First appearance: *Feature Comics* #32 (May 1940); Story: Toni Blum; Art: Dan Zolnerowich (as Arthur Hamon Doyle); Publisher: Quality Comics.

"Master of occult phenomena, Zero seeks to unravel the conspiracies schemed by grim specters who emerge from their restless graves to avenge their eternal fate."

In #62 (November 1942) actress Diana Markham visits Zero at his home to tell him her former fiancé has been trying to kill her. And he's been dead for five years! That night as Miss Markham appears on stage a falling stage prop almost kills her. Meanwhile backstage Zero notices "an unearthly character." The following night Zero dresses as Miss Markham to lure the ghost but his attempt only places her life in greater danger. Zero finally defeats the ghosts with his 'disintegrator beam' as he rescues Miss Markham from her late fiancé.

Detective Zero's five-page comic book mysteries extended to 22 issues between May 1940 and October 1943.

Appendix: Listing by Medium

Animated Film
Justice League Dark

Animated Short
The Facts in the Case of Mister Hollow
Van Helsing: The London Assignment

Animated Television Series
Archibald the Koala
Clue Club
Goober and the Ghost Chasers
The Funky Phantom
Gravity Falls
Invader Zim
Justice League Action
Martin Mystery
Mona the Vampire
Scooby-Doo, Where Are You?
The 13 Ghosts of Scooby-Doo

Animated Web Series
Constantine: City of Demons

Anime
Black Butler
Black Butler: Book of the Atlantic
Black Butler: Book of Circus
Black Butler: Book of Murder
Chrono Crusade
Darker Than Black
Death Note
Descendants of Darkness
Detective Conan
Devil May Cry
Dusk Maiden of Amnesia
Ga-Rei: Zero
Ghost Hunt
Ghost Sweeper Mikami
Hellsing
Muhyo & Roji: Bureau of Special Investigations
Mythical Detective Loki Ragnarok
Nightwalker: The Midnight Detective
Neuro: Supernatural Detective
Occult Academy
Phantom Quest Corp
Psychic Detective Yakumo
Psychic Squad
Silent Mobius
Supernatural: The Anime Series
Tactics
Tokko
Tokyo Babylon
Vampire Holmes
Vatican Miracle Examiner
Witch Hunter Robin
Yu Yu Hakusho: Ghost Files

Audio Drama
All-Consuming Fire
Sapphire & Steel

Book Series
Anita Blake: Vampire Hunter

Comic Book (WD titles)
The Amazing Screw-On Head
The Baker Street Peculiars
Batman: Damned
B.R.P.D.: 1946
Caballistics Inc.
Creature Cops Special Varmint Unit
Criminal Macabre
Darkness Visible
Dylan Dog
Fiction Squad
Gotham by Midnight
Hoax Hunters
iZombie
Jim Butcher's The Dresden Files
Joe Golem: Occult Detective
Justice Inc.
Lady Mechanika
The Lurkers
Mistry, P.I.
Nightstalkers
O.C.T.: Occult Crimes Taskforce
The Occult Files of Dr. Spektor
Poe
Rivers of London: Detective Stories
R.I.P.D.
Rotten

Sir Edward Grey Witchfinder: In the Service of Angels
Spectacle
Strange Detective Mysteries
The Unknown
The Veil
Violet Rose
Weird Detective
Witchblade

Comic Book (Titles featuring WD stories)

Blue Bolt
Jumbo Comics
Look-In
Rangers Comics
The Sandman
Thrilling Comics
2000 A.D.

Comic Book Character

Ambrose Bierce
Ampney Crucis
Anita Blake: Vampire Hunter
Bix Barton
The Dead Boy Detectives
Detective Chimp
Dr. Desmond Drew
Doctor Thirteen
Doctor Occult
Dr. Spektor
Drew Murdoch
Elongated Man
The Ghost, Master Magician
Harry Absalom
Hellboy
John Constantine
Martian Manhunter
Plastic Man
Question
Sapphire & Steel
Sergeant Spook
The Spectre
The Trenchcoat Brigade
Zero, Ghost Detective

Film

Alone in the Dark
Angel Heart
Aversion
Black Magic
Bless the Child
The Borderlands
Bright
Buffy the Vampire Slayer
Carry On Screaming
The Cat Creeps
Chandu the Magician
Charlie Chan's Secret
Charlie Chan at Treasure Island
The Conjuring
Constantine
Curandero
Curse of the Demon
Dark Intruder
Dark Tower
Dead Men Tell
Dead of the Nite
Deliver Us From Evil
Detective Dee: The Four Heavenly Kings
Detective Dee: Mystery of the Phantom Flame
Devil
The Devil Rides Out
Don't Knock Twice
Double Vision
Dracula
Dylan Dog: Dead of Night
Dylan Dog: Il trillo del diavolo
The Exorcist III
Eyes of Laura Mars
Fallen
The First Power
1408
From Hell
Ghostbusters
Ghosts of Mars
God Told Me To
The Harrowing
Hellbound
Hellraiser: Judgment
The House that Dripped Blood
The Hound of the Baskervilles
The Howling
In the Electric Mist
In the Mouth of Madness
Invisible Avenger
Last Shift
The Leopard Man
Let Us Prey
Lord of Illusions
Mark of the Vampire
Moon of the Wolf
The Mothman Prophecies
The Nun
Occult Detective Club: The Doll Cemetery
Odd Thomas
Out of the Shadows
Pokemon Detective Pikachu
The Reaping
Regression
The Return of Doctor X
The Ring
Ringu
R.I.P.D.: Rest in Peace Department
Ritual of Evil
Route 666
Satan Returns
The Scarlet Claw
The Shadow
Sherlock Holmes
Sleepy Hollow
Tähdet ovat väärin
The Thirteenth Chair
The Three Investigators and the Secret of Skeleton Island
The Three Investigators and the Secret of Terror Castle
Transylvania 6–5000
Trick: The Movie
Twin Peaks: Fire Walk with Me
The Undying Monster
Vampire in Brooklyn
Van Helsing

Vidocq
The Void
The Wicker Man
The Wizard of Gore
WolfCop
The X-Files: I Want to Believe
Young Detective Dee: Rise of the Sea Dragon
Young Sherlock Holmes

Film Serial

The Master Mystery
The Return of Chandu

Graphic Novel

Guinea PIG: Pet Shop Private Eye series
Hope.... For the Future
The Incredible Adventures of Dog Mendonça and PizzaBoy
Scoop, Vol. 1: Breaking News
A Study in Emerald

Juvenile Book

The Amazing Ghost Detectives
Baylor's Guide to Dreadful Dreams
Baylor's Guide to the Other Side
The Clockwork Scarab
The Dead Kid Detective Agency
The Diviners
Ghost Detectives: The Lost Bride
Ghost Detectives: The Missing Dancer
Gilda Joyce: The Bones of the Holy
Gilda Joyce: The Dead Drop
Gilda Joyce: The Ghost Sonata

Gilda Joyce: The Ladies of the Lake
Gilda Joyce: Psychic Investigator
Jackaby
The Mystery of the Blazing Cliffs
The Mystery of the Coughing Dragon
The Mystery of the Cranky Collector
The Mystery of the Dancing Devil
The Mystery of the Green Ghost
The Mystery of the Invisible Dog
The Mystery of the Magic Circle
The Mystery of Monster Mountain
The Mystery of the Scar-Faced Beggar
The Mystery of the Singing Serpent
The Mystery of the Sinister Scarecrow
The Mystery of the Vanishing Treasure
The Mystery of the Wandering Caveman
The Mystery of the Whispering Mummy
The Rivers of London
The Screaming Staircase
The Secret of the Haunted Mirror
The Secret of Skeleton Island
The Secret of Terror Castle
Skullduggery Pleasant
The Spiritglass Charade
Theodosia and the Serpents of Chaos

Manga

Angel Cop
Black Butler

Blood Alone
Chrono Crusade
Death Note
Descendants of Darkness
Detective Conan
Dusk Maiden of Amnesia
Ga-rei
Ghost Hunt
Ghost Sweeper Mikami Gokuraku Daisakusen!!
Ghost Talker's Daydream
Hellsing
Kindaichi Case Files
Muhyo & Roji: Bureau of Special Investigations
Neuro: Supernatural Detective
Psychic Detective Yakumo
Tactics
Tokko
Tokyo Babylon
Vatican Miracle Examiner
Yu Yu Hakusho: Ghost Files
Zettai Karen Children

Novel

Abby Cooper, Psychic Eye
All-Consuming Fire
An American Weredeer in Michigan
Anno Dracula
Anonymous Rex: A Detective Story
Aunt Dimity's Death
The Beetle: A Mystery
Black Alibi
Black House
Black Magic Woman
Blood Rites
Bookburners
The Burrowers Beneath
The Case of the Man Who Died Laughing: From the Files of Vish Puri, Most Private Investigator
The Cat Who Talked to Ghosts
Celestial Dogs

Changes
Cold Days
Cosmopath
The Dain Curse
The Dark Side of the Cross
Dead Beat
The Dead Detective
The Dead Letter
Death Masks
Death Warmed Over: Dan Shamble, Zombie P.I.
The Devil Rides Out
Dracula
18 Seconds
European Travel For the Monstrous Gentlewoman
Eye of the Daemon
The Eyre Affair
Falling Angel
Firewalk
Fool Moon
Ghost Detective
Ghost Hunt
Ghost of a Chance
Ghost Story
Grave Peril
Grey Shapes
Greywalker
Hex-Rated
Holy Ghost
The Humbug Murders: An Ebenezer Scrooge Mystery
The Hypnotist
I Was a Teenage Weredeer
The Idylls of the Queen
In the Electric Mist With the Confederate Dead
The Invisible Detective
Joe Golem and the Drowning City
A Kiss Before the Apocalypse
Laced: A Regan Reilly Mystery
London Falling
Mark of the Demon
Necropath
Pall in the Family
Proven Guilty
The Psychic Detective
Psychic Detective Yakumo
Romeo Spikes
Sherlock Holmes: The Breath of God
Sherlock Holmes and the Servants of Hell
Skin Game
Small Favor
Snake Agent
Something From the Nightside
Spell Blind
Stalin's Ghost
Storm Front
The Strange Case of the Alchemist's Daughter
String City
Summer Night
Sweet Silver Blues
The Tender Mercy of Roses
Turn Coat
Under the Lake
Under the Skin
The Undying Monster: A Taste of the Fifth Dimension
Vatican Miracle Examiner
The Werewolf's Tale
Where Dead Soldiers Walk
White Night
Xenopath

Novella

"Ancient Sorceries"
"The Camp of the Dog"
"Foreign Devils"
"The Inmost Light"
"Loot of the Vampire"
"The Nemesis of Fire"
"A Psychical Invasion"
"Secret Worship"

Original Video Animation (OVA)

Angel Cop
Ghost Talker's Daydream

Pulp Fiction Title

The Avenger
The Ghost, Super-Detective
The Ghost Detective
The Green Ghost
The Shadow

Pulp Fiction Character

Ascott Keane
The Avenger
The Cobra
Doctor Dale
Doctor Martinus
Jeffery Wren
Jimmy Holm and the Secret Twelve
John Thunstone
Judge Pursuivant
Jules de Grandin
The Shadow

Radio Drama

The Avenger
Ectoplasm
The Shadow

RPG Game

The Dresden Files Roleplaying Game

Short Story

"The Adventure of the Sussex Vampire"
"Aylmer Vance and the Vampire"
"The Call of Cthulhu"
"The Dead Hand"
"The Detective's Album: The Phantom Hearse"
"The Ghost of the Grate"
"The Horror at Red Hook"
"The Last Illusion"
"The Leather Funnel"
"Letter to Sura"
"The Mystery the Djara Singh: A Spiritual Detective Story"

"The Mark of the Beast"
"The Specter of the Yellow Quarter"
"A Study in Emerald"
The Swaying Vision
"A Victim of Higher Space"

Short Story Character

Andrew Latter
Diana Marburg
Dr. Edward Carstairs M.D.
Dr. Ivan Brodsky
Dr. Martin Hesselius
Dr. Miles Pennoyer
Dr. John Richard Taverner
Flaxman Low
Francis Chard
Harry Escott
Lord Darcy
Lord Syfret
Lucius Leffing
Moris Klaw
Neils Orsen
Professor Arnold Rhymer M.D.
Professor Nathan Enderby
Semi Dual
Sheila Crera
Simon Ark
Simon Iff
Solange Fontaine
Steve Harrison
Thomas Carnacki

Short Story Anthology

John Silence: Physician Extraordinary
Shadows Over Baker Street

Stage Play–Theater

Dracula
Falling Angel

Telefilm

Baffled
Border Patrol
The Case of the Whitechapel Vampire
Cast A Deadly Spell
Curse of the Black Widow
Dark Intruder
The Dead Don't Die
The Eyes of Charles Sand
Fear No Evil
Gargoyles
Moon of the Wolf
Nick Knight
The Night Stalker
The Night Strangler
The Norliss Tapes
The Possessed
Ritual of Evil
Satan's School for Girls
Spectre
Sweet, Sweet Rachel
Visions
The World Beyond
The World of Darkness

Television Series (featuring WD episodes or themes)

Alphas
Angel
Bishaash
Blood Ties
Brimstone
Buffy the Vampire Slayer
The Case-Book of Sherlock Holmes
The Champions
Cheo Yong: The Paranormal Detective
Constantine
Continuum
The Dain Curse
Death Note
Death Valley
Detective Anna
Dirk Gently's Holistic Detective Agency
The Dresden Files
Eureka
Father Dowling Mysteries
Forever Knight
Fringe
From Dusk Till Dawn: The Series
The Gates
The Ghost Busters
Ghosted
Gotham
Grimm
Haven
Houdini and Doyle
iZombie
Jonathan Creek
Kolchak: The Night Stalker
Legends of Tomorrow
The Lost Room
Lucifer
Manifest
Medium
Millennium
Moonlight
Murdoch Mysteries
Past Life
Penny Dreadful
Poltergeist: The Legacy
Pushing Daisies
PSI Factor: Chronicles of the Paranormal
Psych
Psychic Detective Yakumo
Raines
Randall and Hopkirk (Deceased)
The Rivals of Sherlock Holmes
Sapphire & Steel
Saving Grace
Shadow Chasers
The Sixth Sense
Sleepy Hollow
Special Unit 2
Stan Against Evil
Stan Lee's Lucky Man
Stranger Things
Supernatural
Torchwood
Trick
Twin Peaks
Twin Peaks: The Return

The Vampire Detective
Vampire Prosecutor
Warehouse 13
Witchblade
Wynonna Earp
The X-Files

Video Game

Adam Wolfe
Again
Alone in the Dark
Alone in the Dark 2
Alone in the Dark 3
Alone in the Dark: Illumination
Alone in the Dark: The New Nightmare
Bureau 13: Stalking the Night Fantastic
Call of Cthulhu: Dark Corners of the Earth
Cognition: An Erica Reed Thriller
Dark Parables
Darkness Within: In Pursuit of Loath Nolder
Dark Tales: Edgar Allan Poe's
The Darkside Detective
The Dead Case
Deadly Premonition
Detective Pikachu
Discworld Noir
D4: Dark Dreams Don't Die
Ghost Trick: Phantom Detective
The Interactive Adventures of Dog Mendonça and Pizzaboy
Murdered: Soul Suspect
Nocturne
Parascientific Escape: Gear Detective
Psychic Detective
Sherlock Holmes: The Awakened
Silent Mobius: Case: Titanic
Touch Detective
Van Helsing
The Vanishing of Ethan Carter

Bibliography

Books and Periodicals

Clements, Jonathan, and Helen McCarthy. *The Anime Encyclopedia: A Century of Japanese Animation.* Berkeley, CA: Stone Bridge, 2015.

Crawford, Hubert H. *Crawford's Encyclopedia of Comic Books.* Middle Village, N.Y.: Jonathan David, 1978.

De Camp, Lyon Sprague. *Lovecraft: A Biography.* Garden City, N.Y.: Doubleday, 1975.

Dunning, John. *Tune in Yesterday.* Englewood Cliffs, N.J.: Prentice-Hall, 1976.

Gerani, Gary, with Paul H. Schulman. *Fantastic Television.* Godalming, Surrey, UK: LSP Books, 1977.

Lewis, John E., and Penny Stempel. *Cult TV.* London: Pavilion Books, 1993.

Marill, Alvin H. *Movies Made for Television: The Telefeature and the Mini-Series 1964–1979.* Westport, CT: Arlington House, 1980.

Peithman, Stephen, ed. *The Annotated Tales of Edgar Allan Poe.* New York: Avenel Books, 1986.

Steinberg, S.H., ed. *Cassell's Encyclopedia of World Literature, Vol. 1: Histories and General Articles.* New York: William Morrow, 1973.

Steranko, James, *The Steranko History of Comics, Volume 1.* Reading, PA: Supergraphics, 1970.

Steranko, James, *The Steranko History of Comics, Volume 2.* Reading, PA: Supergraphics, 1972.

Internet Sources

Amazon https://www.amazon.com
Anime News Network https://www.animenewsnetwork.com
Barnes & Noble https://www.barnesandnoble.com
Comic Vine https://comicvine.com
Crime, Mystery & Gangster Fiction Magazine Index www.philsp.com
Crunchyroll https://crunchyroll.com
Dailymotion https://www.dailymotion.com
Digital Comic Museum https://digitalcomicmuseum.com
Goodreads https://www.goodreads.com
Grand Comics Database (GCD) https://www.comics.org
Heritage Auctions https://www.ha.com
Hoopla https://www.hoopladigital.com
Internet Archive https://archive.org
Internet Movie Database https://imdb.com
The Internet Speculative Fiction Database www.isfdb.org
LibraryThing https://www.librarything.com
MobyGames https://www.mobygames.com
Occult Detectives/Ghost Hunters in Fact and Fiction https://brombonesbooks.com/occult-detectives-ghost-hunters-in-fact-and-fiction/
Penn Libraries digital.library.upenn.edu
Project Gutenberg www.gutenberg.org
Simon & Schuster www.simonandschuster.com
Smithsonian https://www.smithsonianmag.com
ThePulp.Net https://thepulpnet.com/pulpsuperfan
TV Tropes https://tvtropes.org
Wikipedia https://www.wikipedia.org
The Works of G.T. Fleming-Roberts www.mysteryfile.com
WorldCat https://www.worldcat.org
YouTube https://youtube.com

Index

Numbers in ***bold italics*** indicate pages with photographs.
Characters are listed alphabetically by title (e.g., Dr. Detective) or first name.

Abby Cooper, Psychic Eye 11, 189
Accidental Detective 3
Ackles, Jensen ***160***
Adam Wolfe 11, 192
"The Adventure of the Sussex Vampire" 11–12, 190
Again 12, 192
Alfred Hitchcock and the Three Investigators 120–124, 144
All-Consuming Fire 12, 189
Allison DuBois 9, 112–113
Alone in the Dark 12–13, 192
Alone in the Dark: Illumination 13, 192
Alone in the Dark: The New Nightmare 13, 192
Alone in the Dark 2 13, 192
Alone in the Dark 3 13, 192
Alphas 13–14, 191
amateur detective 3, 7–8, 121
The Amazing Ghost Detectives 14, 189
The Amazing Screw-On Head 14, 187
Ambrose Bierce 14, 188
An American Weredeer in Michigan 15, 189
Ampney Crucis 14–15, 188
"Ancient Sorceries" 95–96, 190
Anderson, Gillian ***181***, 182–183
Andrew Latter 15, 191
Angel 15–16, 29, ***30***, 191
Angel Cop 16–17, 189
Angel Heart 17, 66, 188
Anita Blake: Vampire Hunter 17, 187–188
Anno Dracula 17, 189
Anonymous Rex: A Detective Story 17–18, 189
Arcana 18
Archibald the Koala 18, 187
Arquette, Patricia 113
The Artful Detective 118, ***119***, 191
Ascott Keane 9, 18, ***19***, 190
Athenodorus 17
Atwill, Lionel ***109***
Aunt Dimity's Death 19–20, 189
The Avenger (I) 9, ***20***, 21, 190
The Avenger (II) 21, 190
Aversion 21, 188
Aylmer Vance 8, 21–22, 190
"Aylmer Vance and the Vampire" 21–22, 190

Baffled 22, 191
Bailey, Bernard ***155***
The Baker Street Peculiars 22, 187
Bastedo, Alexander ***34***

Batman: Damned 22, 187
Baylor's Guide to Dreadful Dreams 22–23, 189
Baylor's Guide to the Other Side 23, 189
"A Beautiful Vampire" 106
The Beetle: A Mystery 23, 189
Begbie, Harold 15
Bishaash 23, 191
Bix Barton 23, 188
Black Alibi 24, 104, 189
Black arts 93, 102, 172
Black Butler 24, 187, 189
Black Butler: Book of Circus 25, 187
Black Butler: Book of Murder 25, 187
Black Butler: Book of the Atlantic 24–25, 187
Black House 25, 189
Black Magic 25–26, 188
Black magic 19, 33, 41, 66, 106, 131, 138, 157, 164
Black Magic Woman 26, 117, 189
Blackwood, Algernon 8, 95, 175–176
Bless the Child 26, 188
Blood Alone 26, 189
Blood Rites 26, 189
Blood Ties 26–27, 191
Blue Bolt 145, 188
Blum, Toni ***184***
Border Patrol 27, 191
The Borderlands 27–28, 188
Boreanaz, David 15, 29, ***30***
Bourbon Street Shadows 91
Brett Kingsford ***42***
Bright 28, 188
Bright Falls Mysteries 15, 88
Brimstone 28, 191
Brimstone, James 85–86
Brimstone Files 85–85
Brown, Barbara Ann ***178***
Bruce, Nigel ***87***, 142
Brundage, Margaret ***54***, ***105***
Buffy the Vampire Slayer 28–29, ***30***, 188, 191
Bureau 13: Stalking the Night Fantastic 30, 154, 192
The Burrowers Beneath 30, 189
Butcher, Jim 26, 35, 38, 45, 48, 60, 68, 76, 80, 93, 131, 151, 153, 157–158, 169, 178

C. Auguste Dupin 7, 43
Caballistics Inc. 30–31, 82, 187
Cal McDonald 40–41
"The Call of Cthulhu" 9, 31, 190

Call of Cthulhu: Dark Corners of the Earth 31, 192
"Camp of the Dog" 97–98, 190
Carnacki the Ghost-Finder ***165***
Carry on Screaming 31, ***32***, 188
Carter, Chris 2, 101, 113–114, 181–183
The Case-Book of Sherlock Holmes 12, 33, 191
The Case of the Man Who Died Laughing: From the Files of Vish Puri, Most Private Investigator 32, 189
"The Case of the Thing That Whimpered" 123
The Case of the Whitechapel Vampire 32–33, 191
Cast a Deadly Spell 33, 191
The Cat Creeps 33, 188
The Cat Who Talked to Dogs 33, 189
Catholic church 5, 28, 43
Celestial Dogs 34, 189
The Champions 34, 191
Chandu the Magician 34, ***35***, 188
Changes 35, 190
Charles B. Ethredge 104–105
Charlie Chan at Treasure Island 35–36, 188
Charlie Chan's Secret ***36***, 188
Charlotte "Chuck" Charles ***136***
Chen, Joan 169, 183
Cheo-Yong: The Paranormal Detective 36–37, 191
Cherry, Sam 93
Christie, Agatha 54, 56
Chrono Crusade 37, 187, 189
clairvoyance 7, 21, 45, 47, 71, 95, 175–176
The Clockwork Scarab 37, 189
Clue Club 37, 187
The Cobra 38, 190
Cognition: An Eric Reed Mystery 38, 192
Cold Days 38, 190
Collins, Wilkie 7
Conan Doyle, Arthur 8, 11–12, 25, 33, 86–87, 99, 102, 118, 142, 148, 157, 183
The Conjuring 38–39, 188
Constable George Crabtree ***119***
Constantine 39, 188, 191
Constantine: City of Demons 39, 187
Continuum 39–40, 191
Corbett, Harry H. ***32***
Cosmopath 40, 190
Creature Cops Special Varmint Unit 40, 187
Criminal Macabre 40–41, 187
Curandero 41, 188

Index

Curse of the Black Widow 41, 191
Curse of the Demon **41**, 42, 188
Curtis, Dan 41, 124–125

D4: Dark Dream's Don't Die 53, 192
The Dain Curse 42, 190–191
Dark Intruder **42**, 43, 188, 191
Dark Parables 43, 192
The Dark Side of the Cross 43, 190
Dark Tales: Edgar Allan Poe's 43, 192
Dark Tower 43–44, 188
Darker Than Black 44, 187
Darkness Visible 44
Darkness Within: In Pursuit of Loath Nolder 44, 192
The Darkside Detective 45, 192
Davidson, Hugh **54**
Dead Beat 45, 190
The Dead Boy Detectives 45, 188
The Dead Case 45, 192
The Dead Detective 45, 190
The Dead Don't Die 45, 191
"The Dead Hand" 45–46, 190
The Dead Kid Detective Agency 46, 189
The Dead Letter 46–47, 190
Dead Men Tell 47, 188
Dead of the Nite 47, 188
Deadly Premonition 47–48, 192
Dean Winchester **159**
Death Masks 48, 190
Death Note 48–49, 187, 189, 191
Death Valley 49, 191
Death Warmed Over: Dan Shamble, Zombie P.I. 49, 190
Deliver Us from Evil 49, 188
demon hunter 14, 52
demons 3, 6, 12, 15–16, 27, 29, 39, 44, 60, 68, 73, 82, 86, 94, 97, 99–100, 102, 131, 140, 159, 166–167, 177
Depp, Johnny **152**
Descendants of Darkness 49–50, 187, 189
Detective Anna 50, 191
Detective Chimp 9, 50, 188
Detective Conan 50–51, 187, 189
Detective Dee: Mystery of the Phantom Flame 51, 188
Detective Dee: The Four Heavenly Kings 51, 188
Detective Lieutenant Peters 104–105
Detective Michaela Stone **108**
Detective Pikachu 51, 129, 192
Detective William Murdoch **119**
"The Detective's Album: The Phantom Hearse" 51–52, 190
Devil 52, 188
The Devil 17, 28, 31, 52, 67, 90, 97, 99, 120, 139, 145
Devil May Cry 52, 187
The Devil Rides Out 52–53, 188, 190
Dewhurst, Henry 123
Diana Marburg 45–46, 191
Dime Detective Magazine 92, 93
Dirk Gently's Holistic Detective Agency 53, 191
Discworld Noir 53, 192
The Diviners 53–54, 189

Doctor Dale 54, 190
Dr. Desmond Drew 54, **55**, 188
Dr. Edward Carstairs M.D. 54–55, 191
Dr. Ivan Brodsky 56, 191
Dr. John Richard Taverner 56, 191
Dr. Julia Ogden **119**
Dr. Martin Hesselius 56–57, 191
Doctor Martinus 57, 190
Dr. Miles Pennoyer 57, 191
Doctor Occult 57–58, 188
"Doctor Satan" 9, 18, **19**
Dr. Spektor 9, **126**, 188
Doctor Thirteen 58, 188
Dr. Watson 12, 32, **87**, 99, 142–143, 148–149
Doctor Who 12, 68–69
Don't Knock Twice 58, 188
Double Vision 58, 188
Douglas, Angela **32**
Downey, Robert, Jr. **148**
Dracula 1, 58, **59**, 60, 188, 190–191
The Dresden Files 60, 191
The Dresden Files Role-Playing Game 60, 190
Drew Murdoch 60, **61**, 62, 188
Drury, William 6
DuBois, Allison 9, 112–113
Duchovny, David **181**, 182–183
Dusk Maiden of Amnesia 52, 187, 189
Dylan Dog 62, 187
Dylan Dog: Dead of Night 62, 188
Dylan Dog: Il trillo del diavolo 62–63, 188

Ectoplasm 63
Edward Carnby 12–13
18 Seconds 63, 190
Elongated Man 63, 188
Emily Hartwood 12–13
Ernst, Paul 9, 18–19, 20, 99
Escott, Harry 7, 82–83, 191
Eureka 63–64
European Travel for the Monstrous Gentlewoman 64, 190
Exorcist 37, 44, 64, 72, 76, 94, 117, 131, 163
The Exorcist III 64–65, 188
Eye of the Daemon 65, 190
The Eyes of Charles Sand 65, 191
"The Eyes of Doom" 147–148
Eyes of Laura Mars 65, 188
The Eyre Affair 65, 190

The Facts in the Case of Mister Hollow 65–66, 187
Fairytale Detective 43
Fallen 66, 188
Falling Angel 66, 190–191
Father Dowling Mysteries 66–67, 191
FBI Special Agent Dale Cooper 170, **171**, 172
FBI Special Agent Fox Mulder **181**
Fear No Evil 67, 191
Feature Comics 183, **184**
Fiction Squad 68, 187
Fielding, Fenella **32**
Firewall 68, 190

The First Power 68, 188
Flaxman Low 8, 68, 191
Fleming-Roberts G.T. 92–93
Fool Moon 68, 190
"Foreign Devils" 69–70, 190
Forever Knight 70, 191
1408 70, 188
Fowler, Noel **184**
Francis Chard 70, 191
Friel, Anna **135**
Fringe 70–71, 191
From Dusk Till Dawn: The Series 71, 191
From Hell 71, 188
The Funky Phantom 71–72, 187

Ga-Rei 72, 189
Ga-Rei: Zero 72, 187
Gaiman, Neil 45, 107, 147, 158
Gargoyles 72, 191
The Gates 72–73, 191
"The Gateway of the Monster" 165
Gellar, Sarah Michelle 29, **30**
The Ghost Busters 73, 191
Ghost Detective 73–74, 190
Ghost Detectives: The Lost Bride 74, 189
Ghost Detectives: The Missing Dancer 74, 189
Ghost Hunt 74, 187, 189–190
The Ghost, Master Magician 74–75, 188
Ghost of a Chance 75, 190
"The Ghost of the Grate" 75–76, 190
Ghost Story 76, 190
The Ghost, Super-Detective **76**, 190
Ghost Sweeper Mikami 76–77, 187
Ghost Sweeper Mikami Gokuraka Daisakusen!! 77, 189
Ghost Talker's Daydream 77, 189–190
Ghost Trick: Phantom Detective 77, 192
Ghostbusters 2, 73, 188
Ghosted 77–78, 191
Ghosts of Mars 78, 188
Gibson, Walter 21, 45–46
Gilda Joyce: Psychic Investigator 79, 189
Gilda Joyce: The Bones of the Holy 78, 189
Gilda Joyce: The Dead Drop 78, 189
Gilda Joyce: The Ghost Sonata 78, 189
Gilda Joyce: The Ladies of the Lake 78–79, 189
Glanvill, Reverend Joseph 6
God Told Me To 79, 188
Goober and the Ghost Chasers 79, 187
Gotham 79–80, 191
Gotham by Midnight 80, 187
Gothic 7, 79
Grandenetti, Jerry 54, 55
Grave Peril 80, 190
Gravity Falls 80, 187
The Green Ghost 75, 76, 190
The Green Ghost Detective 75, **76**, 190

Grey Shapes 80, 190
Greywalker 81, 190
Grimm 81–82, 191
Guinea PIG: Pet Shop Private Eye 82, 189
Gwen Cooper **167**

Hammett, Dashiel 42
Hampshire, Susan **22**
The Harrowing 82, 188
Harry Absalom 30–31, 82, 188
Harry Dresden 26, 35, 38, 45, 48, 60, 68, 76, 80, 93, 151, 153, 158, 169, 178
Harry Escott 7, 82–83, 191
Haunting 3, 6, 8, 75, 78, 163, 165, 172
Haven 83–84, 191
Hellbound 84, 188
Hellboy 84–85, 188
Hellboy: The Science of Evil 85, 192
Hellraiser: Judgment 85, 188
Hellsing 85, 187, 189
Help for the Haunted 85
Hermetic Order of the Golden Dawn 8, 149
Hex-Rated 85–86, 190
Hoax Hunters 86, 187
Holy Ghost: a Virgil Flowers Novel 86, 190
Hope…for the Future 86, 189
"The Horror at Red Hook" 8–9, 86, 190
"Horror on the Links" 8
Houdini, Harry 8, 86–87, 111, 157, 191
Houdini and Doyle 86–87, 191
The Hound of the Baskervilles **87**, 188
The House That Dripped Blood 87–88, 188
Howard, Robert E. 8, 157, 163
The Howling 88, 188
The Humbug Murders: An Ebenezer Scrooge Mystery 88, 190
The Hypnotist 88, 190

I Was a Teenage Weredeer 88, 190
Ichabod Crane **152**
The Idylls of the Queen 89, 190
In the Electric Mist 89, 188
In the Electric Mist with the Confederate Dead 89, 190
In the Mouth of Madness 89, 188
The Incredible Adventures of Dog Mendonça and PizzaBoy 89, 189
"The Inmost Light" 89–90, 190
Inspector George Brackenreid **119**
Inspector Neumann **109**
The Interactive Adventures of Dog Mendonça and Pizzaboy 90, 192
Invader Zim 90, 187
investigative reporter 2–3, 9, 88, 101, 117, 125, 135
Invisible Avenger 91, 188
The Invisible Detective 91, 190
iZombie 91–92, 187, 191

Jack Helman Files 92
Jack the Ripper 17, 24, 101
Jackaby 92, 189
Jeffery Wren 92, **93**, 190

Jim Butcher's The Dresden Files 93, 187
Jimmy Holm and the Secret Twelve 93–94, 190
Joe Golem and the Drowning City: An Illustrated Novel 94, 190
Joe Golem: Occult Detective 94, 187
John Constantine 22, 39, **94**, 95, 100, 103, 168, 188
John Raymond Legrasse 9, 31
John Silence: Physician Extraordinary 95–98, 191
John Thunstone 98, 190
Jonathan Creek 98–99, 191
Judge Pursuivant 99, 190
Jules de Grandin 8, 99, 190
Jumbo Comics 60, **61**, 62, 188
Justice Inc. 99, 187
Justice League Action 100, 187
Justice League Dark 100, 187

Katrina Van Tassel **152**
Kindaichi Case Files 100–101, 189
King, Stephen 25, 69, 83
A Kiss Before the Apocalypse 101, 190
Kolchak, the Night Stalker 1–2, 9, 101–102, 124, 191

Laced: A Regan Reilly Mystery 102, 190
Lady Mechanika 102, 187
"The Last Illusion" 102, 190
Last Shift 102, 188
Laurie, Piper 169, **170**
League of Extraordinary Gentlemen 165
"The Leather Funnel" 102–103, 190
Legends of Tomorrow 103, 191
The Leopard Man 104, 188
Let Us Prey 104, 188
"Letter to Sura" 5, 190
Lincoln, Abraham 14, 78
London Falling 104, 190
Look-In 141, 188
"Loot of the Vampire" 104, **105**, 190
Lord Ciel Phantomhive 24–25
Lord Darcy 105, 191
Lord Henry Blackwood **148**
Lord of Illusions 105–106, 188
Lord Syfret 106, 191
The Lost Room 106, 191
Love Is the Law 106
Love Trap 41
Lovecraft, H.P. 1–2, 8–9, 12, 30–31, 33, 44, 86, 147, 158, 163, 193
Lucifer 106–107, 191
Lucius Leffing 107–108, 191
Lugosi, Bela **35**, **59**, 109, 138, 164
The Lurkers 108, 187

Machen, Arthur 8, 89–90
Manifest **108**, 191
MacLachlan, Kyle 169, **170**, 171
"The Mark of the Beast" 108–109, 191
Mark of the Demon 109, 190
Mark of the Vampire **109**, 110, 188
Marsh, Marguerite **111**
Martian Manhunter 110, 188

Martin Mystery 110, 187
The Master Mystery **111**, 112, 189
McClusky, Thorp 104, *105*
McGavin, Darren 1, 101, 124
Medium 112–113, 191
"Medium Dead" **93**
mediums 6, 8, 11, 22–23, 26, 36, 44, 74, 77, 94, 112, 118, 134, 149, 164, 167
Meek, Donald **109**
Mercer, Marilyn 54, **55**
The Methods of Moris Klaw **116**
Millennium 113–114, 191
Mr. John Bell 8
Mistry P.I. 114, 187
Mona Vampire 114, 187
Moon of the Wolf 114–115, 188
Moonlight 115, 191
More Fun Comics **155**
Moris Klaw 8, 115, **116**, 191
Morris and Chastain Supernatural Investigations 115, 117
The Mothman Prophecies 117, 188
Muhyo & Raji: Bureau of Special Investigations 117, 187, 189
"Murder in an Omnibus" 15
Murdered: Soul Suspect 117, 192
Murdoch Mysteries 118, **119**, 191
My Partner the Ghost 136
Myles, Eve **168**
"The Mysteries of the Greek Room" **116**
The Mystery of the Blazing Cliffs 119, 189
The Mystery of the Coughing Dragon 120, 189
The Mystery of the Cranky Collector 120, 189
The Mystery of the Dancing Devil 120, 189
The Mystery of the Djara Singh: A Spiritual Detective Story 120, 190
The Mystery of the Green Ghost 121, 189
The Mystery of the Invisible Dog 121, 189
The Mystery of the Magic Circle 121, 189
The Mystery of the Monster Mountain 121, 189
The Mystery of the Scar-Faced Beggar 121, 189
The Mystery of the Singing Serpent 121, 189
The Mystery of the Sinister Scarecrow 121–122, 189
The Mystery of the Vanishing Treasure 122, 189
The Mystery of the Wandering Caveman 122, 189
The Mystery of the Whispering Mummy 122, 189
Mythical Detective Loki Ragnarok 122, 187

Napoli, Vincent 19
Necropath 122–123, 190
Neils Orsen 123, 191
Nemesis Agent Sharron Macready **34**

"The Nemesis of Fire" 96, 190
Neuro: Supernatural Detective 123, 187, 189
Nick Knight 123–124
Nielsen, Leslie **42**
Night of the Demon **41**
The Night Stalker 1–2, 9, 101, 124–125, 191
The Night Strangler 1, 105, 124, 191
Nightstalkers 124, 187
Nightwalker: The Midnight Detective 124–125, 187
Nimoy, Leonard **22**, 70
Nocturne 125, 192
The Norliss Tapes 125,
The Nun 125, 188

O'Brien, Fitz-James 7
Occult Academy 125–126, 187
occult detective 3, 8–9, 14, 19, 22, 39, 55–56, 58. 68. 89–90, 94–95, 99–100, 102–103, 106–107, 126, 149–150, 164–165, 174–175
Occult Detective Club: The Doll Cemetery 126, 188
The Occult Files of Dr. Spektor **126**, 187
O.C.T.: Occult Crimes Taskforce 126–127, 187
Odd Thomas 127, 188
Oland, Warner 36
Ontkean, Michael 169, **170**
OSS Agent Dana Scully **181**
Out of the Shadows 127, 188

Padalecki, Jared **160**
Pall in the Family 127, 190
Parascientific Escape: Gear Detective 127–128, 192
Past Life 128, 191
Penny Dreadful 128–129, 191
Phantom Quest Corp 129, 187
Plastic Man 129, 188
Pliny the Younger 5, 7
Poe 129, 187
Poe, Edgar Allan 7, 28, 43, 129, 157, 187, 192–193
Pokemon Detective Pikachu 129, 188
Poltergeist: The Legacy 129–130, 191
The Possessed 130–131, 191
"A Pot of Tulips" 7
Price, Frank **1**, 2, 65
Professor Arnold Rhymer, M.D. 131, 191
Professor Nathan Enderby 131, 191
Proven Guilty 131, 190
PSI Factor: Chronicles of the Paranormal 131–132, 191
Psych 132–133, 191
Psychic Detective 133–134, 192
The Psychic Detective 134, 190
Psychic Detective Yakumo 134, 187, 189–191
psychic investigator 21, 78–79, 92, 107, 145, 151
Psychic Squad 134–135, 187
"Psychical Invasion" 95, 190
Purgatory 5, 27
Pushing Daisies **135**, 191

Queen Victoria 17, 24–25, 150, 158, 167, 174
Quentin Locke **111**
Question 135–136, 188
Question II 136, 188
Quinn, Seabury 8, 99

Raines 136, 191
Randall and Hopkirk (Deceased) (I) 136–137, 191
Randall and Hopkirk (Deceased) (II) 137, 191
Rangers Comics 54, **55**, 188
Rathbone, Basil **87**, 142
The Reaping 137, 188
Regression 137–138, 188
The Return of Chandu 138, 189
The Return of Doctor X 138, 188
Rex the Wonder Dog 9, 50
Ricci, Christina **152**
The Ring 138, 188
Ringu 139, 188
R.I.P.D. 139, 187
R.I.P.D.: Rest in Peace Department 139, 188
Ritual of Evil 139, 188, 191
The Rivals of Sherlock Holmes 139–140, 191
Rivers of London: Detective Stories 140, 187, 189
Rohmer, Sax 115–116
Romeo Spikes 140, 190
Rotten 140, 187
Route 666 140, 188
Roxburgh, Melissa **108**
Rozen, George **146**
Ryan, Matt 39, **94**, 100, 103

Sam Winchester **159**
The Sandman 45, 188
Santos, Jesse 126
Sapphire & Steel 141, 187–188, 191
Satan Returns 141, 188
Satanic cult 26, 41, 52–53, 97, 102, 138
Satan's School for Girls 141–142, 191
Saving Grace 142, 191
The Scarlet Claw 142–143, 188
Scooby-Doo, Where Are You? 143, 187
Scoop, Vol. 1: Breaking News 143–144, 189
Scott H.W 20
The Screaming Staircase 144, 189
The Secret Files of Dr. Drew 54, 55
The Secret of Skeleton Island 144, 189
The Secret of Terror Castle 144, 189
The Secret of the Haunted Mirror 144–145, 189
"Secret Worship" 97, 190
Semi Dual 145, 191
Sergeant Neil Howie **179**
Sergeant Spook 145, 188
The Shadow 145, **146**, 147, 188, 190
Shadow Chasers 147, 191
The Shadow Detective Monthly **146**
"The Shadow Over Innsmouth" 31
Shadows Over Baker Street 147, 191
Shapeshifter 88, 172, 180

Sheila Crerar 8, 147–148, 191
Sheriff Harry S. Truman **170**
Sherlock Holmes 8, 11–12, 22–23, 32–33, 37, 63, 67, **87**, 104, 139, 142–143, 147, 149, 155–158, 183–184, 188–192
Sherlock Holmes (film) **148**, 188
Sherlock Holmes and the Servants of Hell 148, 190
Sherlock Holmes: The Awakened 148–149, 192
Sherlock Holmes: The Breath of God 149, 190
Silent Mobius 149–150, 187
Silent Mobius: Case: Titanic 150, 192
Simon Ark 150, 191
Simon Iff 150, 191
Sir Edward Grey Witchfinder: In the Service of Angels 150, 188
The Sixth Sense 150–151, 191
Skin Game 151, 190
Skullduggery Pleasant 151, 189
Sleepy Hollow 151, **152**, 188, 191
Small Favor 152–153, 190
Smith, Clark Ashton 8
Snake Agent 153, 190
Society for Psychical Research 6–8
Solange Fontaine 153, 191
Something from the Nightside 153, 190
Sorcerer 39, 94, 98, 105
Special Unit 2 153–154, 191
Spectacle 154, 188
Specter 79, 172, 185
"The Specter of the Yellow Quarter" 154, 191
Spectre (film) 154–155, 191
The Spectre **155**, 188
Spell Bind 155, 190
The Spiritglass Charade 155–156, 189
spiritualism 6, 8, 45, 118
Stalin's Ghost 156, 190
Stan Against Evil 156, 191
Stan Lee's Lucky Man 156–157, 191
Steve Harrison 157, 191
Stoker, Bram 37, 58, 60, 87, 155
Storm Front 157, 190
"The Strange Case of Dr. Arthur Carmichael" 54, 56
"The Strange Case of the Absent Floor" 54, **55**
The Strange Case of the Alchemist's Daughter 157, 190
Strange Detective Mysteries 157, 188
Stranger Things 157–158, 191
String City 158, 190
Strong, Mark **148**
"A Study in Emerald" 158, 189, 191
suicide 12, 16, 33, 35, 39, 51–52, 58, 74, 106, 123, 125–126, 134, 140, 142, 154
Summer Night 158, 190
Supernatural **159**, 160–161, 191
Supernatural: The Anime Series 161–162, 187
"The Swaying Vision" 162, 191
Swedenborg, Emanuel 6
Sweet Silver Blues 162–163, 190
Sweet, Sweet Rachel 163, 191

Tactics 163, 187, 189
Tähdet ovat väärin 163,188
telepathy 7, 21, 34, 40, 75, 91, 97, 110, 122, 131, 141, 145, 163, 177, 181
teleportation 58, 110, 131
The Tender Mercy of Roses 163–164, 190
Theodosia and the Serpents of Chaos 164, 189
The 13 Ghosts of Scooby-Doo 164, 187
The Thirteenth Chair 164, 188
Thomas Carnacki 164, **165**, 191
Thomas F. Malone 8–9, 86
The Three Investigators and the Secret of Skeleton Island 165–166, 188
The Three Investigators and the Secret of Terror Castle 166, 188
Thrilling Comics 74–75, 188
Tokko 166, 187, 189
Tokyo Babylon 166–167, 187, 189
Torchwood **167**, 168, 191
Touch Detective 168, 192
Tourneur, Jacques 41–42, 104
Transylvania 6-5000 168, 188
The Trenchcoat Brigade 58, 168, 188
Trick 168–169, 191
Trick: The Movie 169, 188
Turn Coat 169, 190
Twin Peaks 169, **170**, 191
Twin Peaks: Fire Walk with Me 170–171, 188
Twin Peaks: The Return 171, 191
2000 A.D. 14–15, 30–31, 82, 86, 188

Under the Lake 171–172, 190
Under the Skin 172, 190
The Undying Monster 172, 188
The Undying Monster: A Taste of the Fifth Dimension 172, 190
The Unknown 172, 188
Utpatel, Frank **165**

The Vampire Detective 172–173, 192
Vampire Holmes 173, 187
vampire hunter 17, 20, 26, 58, 85, 87, 124, 187–188
Vampire in Brooklyn 173, 188
Vampire Prosecutor 173–174, 192
Van Helsing 174, 188, 192
Van Helsing: The London Assignment 174, 187
The Vanishing of Ethan Carter 174–175, 192
Van Sloan, Edward **59**
Vatican 13, 27–28, 125, 174–175
Vatican Miracle Examiner 175, 187, 189, 190
The Veil 175, 188
"A Victim of Higher Space" 175–176, 191
Vidocq 176, 189
Vidocq, Eugene Francois 7, 176
"Village of the Dead" 150
Violet Rose 176, 188
Visions 176, 191
The Void 176, 189
voodoo 13, 17, 31, 34, 45, 66, 92, 101

Warehouse 13 177, 192
The Washington Herald **116**
Weird Detective 177, 188
Weird Tales 8–9, 18, 19, 31, **54**, 56, 86, 98–99, 104, **105**
Wellman, Manly Wade 98–99, 131
Werewolf 9, 53, 88, 90, 97–99, 101, 118, 124, 128, 172–173, 177, 180

The Werewolf's Tale 177, 190
Wheatley, Dennis 52, 123
Where Dead Soldier's Walk 177–178, 190
White Night 178, 190
Whitechapel 17, 32–33, 71
The Wicker Man (I) **178**, 189
The Wicker Man (II) 178, 189
Williams, Kenneth **32**
Williams, Witner **184**
Witch Hunter Robin 179, 187
Witchblade 179–180, 188, 192
witchcraft 6, 121, 131, 177
Wizard 11, 26, 31, 38, 48, 51, 60, 75, 93, 100, 155, 157–158, 169, 178
The Wizard of Gore 180, 189
Wolfcop 180, 189
Woodward, Edward **178**
The World Beyond 180, 191
The World of Darkness 180, 191
Wynonna Earp 180–181, 192

The X-Files 2, 9, 114, **181**, 182–183, 189, 192
The X-Files: I Want to Believe 182–183, 189
Xenopath 123, 181, 190

Young Detective Dee: Rise of the Sea Dragon 183, 189
Young Sherlock Holmes 183–184, 189
Yu-Yu Hakusho: Ghost Files 185, 187, 189

Zero, Ghost Detective **184**, 185, 188
Zettai Karen Children 134–135, 189

www.ingramcontent.com/pod-product-compliance
Lightning Source LLC
Chambersburg PA
CBHW060344010526
44117CB00017B/2955